Y0-BDW-847

Common Ground at the Nexus of Information Literacy and Scholarly Communication

Edited by

Stephanie Davis-Kahl
Merinda Kaye Hensley

ZA
3075
.C734
2013

Association of College and Research Libraries
A Division of the American Library Association
Chicago 2013

The paper used in this publication meets the minimum requirements of American National Standard for Information Sciences–Permanence of Paper for Printed Library Materials, ANSI Z39.48-1992. ∞

Library of Congress Cataloging-in-Publication Data

Common ground at the nexus of information literacy and scholarly communication / Stephanie Davis-Kahl and Merinda Kaye Hensley, editors.
    pages cm
  Includes bibliographical references and index.
  ISBN 978-0-8389-8621-9
  1. Information literacy--Study and teaching (Higher) 2. Communication in learning and scholarship. 3. Academic libraries--Relations with faculty and curriculum. 4. Libraries and publishing. 5. Scholarly publishing. 6. Open access publishing. 7. Libraries and colleges--United States--Case studies. I. Davis-Kahl, Stephanie, editor of compilation. II. Hensley, Merinda Kaye, editor of compilation.
  ZA3075.C67 2013
  028.7071'1--dc23
                              2012051812

Chapter 2 is a reprint of the following article: Willinsky, John and Juan Pablo Alpern. "The academic ethic of open access to research and scholarship," in *Ethics and Education*, vol 6, #3, October 2011. This article is reprinted with permission and by license from the journal publisher, Taylor & Francis.

This chapter does not appear in the Open Access Edition of *Common Ground at the Nexus of Information Literacy and Scholarly Communication* (Davis-Kahl and Hensley, Editors), Open Access Edition. Chicago, IL: ACRL Press, 2013.

Copyright ©2013 by The Association of College & Research Libraries, a division of the American Library Association.

All rights reserved except those which may be granted by Sections 107 and 108 of the Copyright Revision Act of 1976.

Printed in the United States of America.

17 16 15 14 13   5 4 3 2 1

Cover art by Lisa Peltekian

Table of Contents

Closing the Gap between Information Literacy and Scholarly Communication

Joyce L. Ogburn
University of Utah

Two cornerstone programs of the academic library are poised to bring new life to each other as librarians look to close the gap between information literacy and scholarly communication. It has been easy for these two library-based programs, designed and created along different paths and for different purposes and audiences, each with highly specialized skills and knowledge, to develop without intersecting. Now, however, the connections are starting to be explored by librarians, as demonstrated in the essays in this volume.

The time is right to make these connections. The early part of the twenty-first century has been characterized as both the Information Age and the Digital Age, its economy as both the creative economy and the knowledge economy. Whatever label one prefers, clearly creativity has become highly valued for its economic, educational, personal, and communal benefits. It is encouraged by an expanding array of tools readily available to everyone, not just the privileged, as are the channels and venues for sharing creative outpourings. Moreover, the lines between the acts of creation and use are now quite blurry and permeable. Use can be a form of creation, creation can be an act of destruction and remaking, and rapid and open sharing and transformative use of information can lead to amazing new works and insights. Moreover, design thinking is employed as a catalyst for innovation within and across disciplines; the network economy is energized by social media that connects people, regardless of location, and that both encourages existing and potential new relationships; the marketplace of ideas is a valued component of the public sphere, as well as the commercial sector; and many academic institutions are employing interdisciplinary approaches to research, teaching, performance, and practice.

Perhaps more troubling, present-day practices and interpretations regarding intellectual property are tipping copyright law's delicate balance toward authors and producers. Due to restrictive licensing terms, increases in the length of copyright protection, and the problem of orphan works, much of the knowledge of the twentieth century is difficult for researchers and students to access and simultaneously use legally and technologically. Fortunately, many libraries and such entities as *Wikipedia,* the Internet Archive, HathiTrust, and the Digital Public Library of America are working to make readily available the vast knowledge encapsulated in books and other media and in the heads of experts. In the process these organizations are exposing and preserving the world's best thinking and ideas.

The current burst of creativity is producing an abundance of new information. Although the natural world has always been replete with information, what is new is that humans are generating, discovering, gathering, analyzing, translating, and repurposing an enormous amount of information at great speed. Indeed, often those who aspire to be contributors and those who plan to be utilizers of information are the same people—and it seems the more information we find, the more new information we make.

In addition to its bounty, the current information environment is increasingly global in its extent and confounding in its contradictions and complexity. Each of us consumers/creators is swimming in a fast-flowing stream of information in various stages of formulation and codification while confronting shifting educational and social expectations, increasing ethical dilemmas, and legal quicksand. We must think critically about the expectations, obligations, rights, values, privileges, and standards of evidence and quality in this environment and must assess each of these against our individual motivations and assumptions. The creative age, with all of its fine attributes and troublesome faults, presents enormous opportunities to (re)generate, (re)use, and (re)distribute work to make a better world.

Librarians, researchers, teachers, and students alike must learn to cope with this dynamic environment. Let's begin with the librarians.

Academic libraries are being reinvented as their institutions' knowledge commons that encompasses much of the information world's variation and permutations. Librarians are embracing their roles in the entire cycle of knowledge creation, dissemination, access, use, and preservation. They are plunging headfirst into the generation of knowledge by developing many new printed and online works; becoming formal publishers, in some cases by assuming responsibility for the university press; launching services and partnerships that underpin other kinds of publishing and dissemination of locally produced scholarly content; and partnering in creating, managing, and preserving various forms of digital scholarship. Today's librarians are seeking to become deeply immersed in the creative processes on their campuses.

As for faculty, they have been generating new research, inventions, and cultural products for some time, largely through traditional means and practices. They may not be aware of all the possibilities available to them and how these possibilities compare with the limitations (and strengths) of traditional approaches. Faculty are often unaware of the impact their individual decisions on where and how to publish their work can have on a larger system of scholarly exchange. They may desire to experiment with new approaches but may not know how to get started. The reinvented library has become a natural place for advice, exploration, and implementation of the new ideas.

Students now face expectations to perform more research, utilize more tools and technology, embed media in their work, create posters and graphic material, assemble attractive portfolios, and publish while still engaged in their studies. These expectations have precipitated a need for higher-order skills equal to the task of higher-level research and problem solving. Beyond academic expectations, students are choosing to create more media and share, swap, and reuse each other's work and that of others. They are exercising their creative impulses through informal social channels as well as formal educational and scholarly outlets. As new forms of information and exchange gain prominence, it is essential for students to understand why these forms are useful and how to use them to good effect. Students are also expected to prepare to be informed global citizens who are ready to participate in or lead the processes of policy formation and decision making that will shape the future. This will require great facility with producing and evaluating information and knowledge of many kinds and from many origins.

Much of student learning now occurs apart from the formal classroom and faculty oversight, thus presenting librarians with enormous opportunities to influence the student experience. Beyond the services and attributes traditionally associated with libraries, librarians are accelerating student success by designing flexible, high-quality, and diverse physical environments that encourage learning and social interaction; making available sophisticated technology and software for creative expression, learning, and leisure; offering internships and other experiential learning opportunities; collaborating with and hosting companion services such as academic advising and writing centers; and providing access to food and everyday supplies to keep students on task without leaving the library. Much like the developing service model for faculty, the library is an amalgam of services tailored to new definitions of student success.

Library instruction programs that impart skills for navigating and evaluating the convoluted information environment have long been essential to the library's integration with student learning. One of the critical approaches to engaging the faculty has been to increase awareness about the system enveloping the creation and sharing of knowledge and to promote changes. These two traditionally separate efforts can come together by arming individual librarians or teams with knowledge of both information literacy and scholarly communication. To do so requires learning how to teach students and faculty to be informed and able authors—and users—who understand the array of choices that confront them. It requires adding knowledge of copyright law and other intellectual property issues—complicated to understand, convey, and apply under the most straightforward of circumstances— to the current repertoire of literacies. It requires expecting librarians to provide guidance to their users in engaging with the myriad aspects of information and scholarship at different stages and roles in their life and work. It also requires teaching the user how to assemble the right resources and assimilate the right knowledge at the right time. Each requirement on its own constitutes a formidable challenge; dealing with all of them will require a herculean effort, but librarians are up to the task.

Ironically, the sweeping changes in scholarship, heightened librarian aspirations, and the integration of disparate library programs may be returning academia to its roots in the Republic of Letters. The desire of the early humanists was "to bring new public worlds into existence" (Grafton 2009, 1) through their conversations and letter writing. The inspirations and insights of their scholarly life were achieved through their material, social, and intellectual networks that interwove the creation, teaching, collecting, organizing, discussing, sharing, and publishing of knowledge. The attempt to unite information literacy with scholarly communication—designed to foster a comprehensive and inclusive system—reflects back to these earlier times.

Ultimately, librarians are committed to promoting the exchange of ideas and increasing understanding in the world. In so doing they celebrate the discovery and propagation of high-quality, imaginative, life-affirming, and life-changing knowledge. This book won't provide all the answers to the challenges and possibilities I have posed, but it is a strong beginning in the journey to expose and exploit the intersections between the creative impulse and the need to access and use information wisely. As you read these informative chapters, I hope that you will be inspired by the tremendous and exciting prospects that lie ahead for all of us.

Reference

Grafton, Anthon. 2009. *Worlds Made by Words: Scholarship and Community in the Modern West*. Cambridge, MA: Harvard University Press.

Introduction and Acknowledgements

Stephanie Davis-Kahl and Merinda Kaye Hensley
Editors

The library world, on the whole, is a small place; in the Midwest it seems even smaller. A mutual interest in working with undergraduates on the publishing, dissemination, and preservation of original student research brought our paths together and shaped the beginning of our collaboration. It all began with our colleague, Sarah L. Shreeves, and an idea to examine library support for formal undergraduate research programs. We proposed an Institute for Museum and Library Services (IMLS) National Leadership Grant, and while it was unfunded, we forged ahead with our idea and shared our work as an ACRL panel presentation, "Completing the Research Cycle: The Role of Libraries in the Publication and Dissemination of Undergraduate Student Research" (Davis-Kahl, Hensley, and Shreeves 2011). We recently completed a survey of library deans and directors across the country, examining library support for undergraduate research programs. Through the process of planning the panel, writing the grant application, and developing our current study, we quickly saw that even though we work at much different institutions, we share the same goal: to bring scholarly communication issues into mainstream information literacy instruction.

This volume aims to connect key concepts and strategies from scholarly communication and information literacy in order to help other librarians see new opportunities within these two broad and vital areas of librarianship. Our aim is to set the stage for librarians to engage new ideas and to forge partnerships with others in their organizations to enrich both information literacy and scholarly communication programs. Our hope is that the conversation continues—in our literature, on blogs, during conferences—and that this is the start of something new and exciting for our profession. We've learned through this process that librarians in both areas bring a deep sense of responsibility, thoughtfulness and passion to their work, and we are confident that future efforts to collaborate are full of possibility.

The chapters within represent the diversity of our profession and the creativity in approaching core scholarly communication topics such as open access, copyright, authors' rights, the social and economic factors of publishing, and scholarly publishing through the lens of information literacy. When we sent out the call for proposals, we were hopeful that our colleagues in the profession would have stories to tell, and our expectations were exceeded.

We are thrilled that Joyce Ogburn agreed to write the foreword for this volume. Her phrase "Lifelong learning requires lifelong access" (2011) resonated with us throughout the planning process. Joyce sets the stage for us by recognizing that librarians are deeply embedded in the generation of knowledge, calling on librarians to incorporate the vast changes in publishing into our pedagogical teaching strategies.

We begin our discussion with Catherine Palmer and Julia Gelfand comparing the histories of information literacy and scholarly communication, remembering where we came from in order to set forth on a new path. That path, Palmer and Gelfand argue, is a close examination of ALA's *Core Values of Librarianship* (ALA 2004) that will interweave two high-impact library initiatives.

John Willinsky and Juan Alperin graciously agreed to re-print their article, originally published in *Ethics and Education*. They argue that digital publishing formats provide an opportunity to explore the ethical dimensions of increased access to knowledge. We were unable to secure rights to include their article in the Open Access edition of our book, however, the authors have deposited the post-print (2011) in the Graduate School of Education Open Archive.

Kim Duckett and Scott Warren challenge the reader to go beyond the Association of College and Research Libraries' *Information Literacy Competency Standards* introduce a sociocultural and economic framework of scholarly communication when teaching undergraduate students.

Gail Clement and Stephanie Brenenson share their curriculum, *Theft of the Mind*, originally constructed as a freshman seminar, examining plagiarism and copyright education through a series of scenarios that illustrate the complexities facing students as consumers and creators of information. The course proactively teaches students about the legal and ethical use of information.

Isaac Gilman discusses the origins of a digital publishing course and how it evolved into successful collaboration between the library and a department to offer a minor within the university's curriculum.

Cheryl E. Ball, a professor of English, contributes a lively piece on her work with undergraduates and a semester-long metadata-harvesting project, connecting her professional work editing the rhetoric journal *Kairos* with her teaching.

Merinda Kaye Hensley shares her work with a multidisciplinary program in helping students bring together different elements of research—archival, ethnographic, and historical—to not only effectively research but also present and share their results with their peers and the public.

Margeaux Johnson and Matthew Daley describe their work with the Sparky Awards, detailing how media offers abundant opportunity for discussions of copyright, fair use, and the "remix culture."

Margeaux Johnson, Amy Buhler, and Sara Gonzalez discuss how they interweave scholarly communication topics, especially open access, into the content and assignments of a for-credit undergraduate course in the sciences.

Bethany Nowviskie and Eric Johnson, in an interview with co-editor Stephanie Davis-Kahl, detail their work at the UVA Scholar's Lab and how the scope of what they do enacts the connections between infrastructure, creation of scholarship, and the ethos of openness.

Alex Hodges explores the increasingly important area of supporting international students in their understanding of scholarly communication topics and information literacy, using teaching opportunities and orientation sessions to aid in students' academic and personal development.

Marianne A. Buehler and Anne E. Zald focus their chapter on enlightening graduate students with a critical view into the world of scholarly publishing in order to prepare them for working alongside faculty in their current and future roles as scholars. We would like to extend our gracious thanks to Marianne and Anne, who agreed to let us use a phrase from their chapter as the title of this volume.

Abigail Goben shares her experiences as an embedded librarian in a professional school, working with faculty and students to develop and assess a curriculum that explicitly requires students to become familiar with and adept in evidence-based dentistry through mastery of information literacy concepts, awareness of access to scholarship, and an understanding of academic publishing.

Christine Fruin tackles the inherent challenges of collaborating with extension faculty and researchers through outreach and education around scholarly communication issues, using a survey to assess their needs around topics of copyright, open access, repositories, and more.

Jennifer Duncan, Susanne Clement, and Betty Rozum provide insight into educating faculty and administration about copyright issues for their own research and teaching, discussing the work of a cross-campus committee charged to develop copyright education for a large campus.

Nick Shockey, in an interview with co-editor Stephanie Davis-Kahl, discusses the strengths and knowledge librarians need to enact change on their campuses and provides a view into the Right to Research Coalition and its work on open access advocacy.

In the final chapter, Joy Kirchner and Kara J. Malenfant tell the story of how the Association for College and Research Libraries'

Scholarly Communication Roadshow was conceived and developed for librarians to gain an understanding of the complexities of the scholarly communication landscape.

Acknowledgements

We have many people to thank for their time, help, and encouragement. First, to the ACRL Publications Advisory Board, which gave us positive and invaluable feedback in the beginning, and to Kathryn Deiss, ACRL Content Strategist, whose unflagging support and insightful advice helped us navigate the publication process with ease. We would also like to extend our thanks and appreciation to ACRL for allowing us to publish the book open access simultaneously with the print and e-book editions.

To our authors, a thousand thanks. It is your diligent work that made this book possible. We are impressed with your ideas and your creativity. We are also appreciative of your willingness to accept our editorial comments with grace. Our teamwork has resulted in what we feel is a strong volume that will be useful and valuable to others in our profession.

We would like to thank our colleagues participating in the Association of College and Research Libraries Scholarly Communication/Information Literacy White Paper Task Force. The depth of our conversations pushed us to think more expansively about what it means to bring information literacy and scholarly communication into the same conversation.

We'd also like to thank our colleagues at Illinois Wesleyan University and the University of Illinois at Urbana-Champaign, especially Rick Lindquist, Technology Trainer at Illinois Wesleyan University, for his technical support, and Lisa M. Peltekian, currently a senior at Illinois Wesleyan University, for our gorgeous book cover design. We are very grateful to our University Librarians, Karen Schmidt, PhD, and Paula Kaufman, PhD, for their fierce support and commitment in furthering library-related research. The authors also wish to acknowledge the Research and Publication Committee of the University of Illinois at Urbana-Champaign Library, which provided financial support toward the completion of this project.

Immeasurable thanks to Emma Clausen, our fearless and dedicated graduate assistant, who read and copyedited each and every chapter, and to Seth Robbins, who graciously edited the interview chapters.

As with most projects in life, it is our families that make ventures like this possible.

Stephanie would like to thank her lovely and amazing husband, Chad, and her funny and sweet kid, Xavier, for their encouragement along the way and for generally making her life beautiful, messy, and fun. To my mom and dad, thank you for everything, every day, always. To Merinda, who has been a fantastic colleague and friend in this endeavor, and who has expanded my thinking on this and many other topics in our profession—I'm lucky to have you in my corner.

Merinda's family forgave her when she had to work instead of play, remembered to bring her food, and made her laugh when she needed it the most. Thank you, Shawn and Dahlia, for being the light in my life. To my parents, whose encouragement has never wavered, thank you. And to Stephanie, my librarian kindred spirit, life is so much better with your smile—professionally and personally.

We hope you enjoy, learn from, and are inspired by this book.

References

ALA (American Library Association). 2004. *Core Values of Librarianship.* (Chicago: ALA Council, June 29), http://www.ala.org/offices/oif/statementspols/corevaluesstatement/corevalues.

Davis-Kahl, Stephanie, Merinda Kaye Hensley, and Sarah L. Shreeves. 2011. "Completing the Research Cycle: The Role of Libraries in the Publication and Dissemination of Undergraduate Student Research." Panel presentation at the ACRL Conference 2011, Philadelphia, PA, March 30.

Ogburn, Joyce L. 2011. "Lifelong Learning Requires Lifelong Access: Reflections on the ACRL Plan for Excellence." *College and Research Libraries News* 72, no. 9 (October): 514–515. http://crln.acrl.org/content/72/9/514.full.

Willinsky, J. & Alperin, J. P. (2011). The academic ethics of open access to research and scholarship, Ethics and Education, 6(3) [post-print: http://opendev.stanford.edu/sites/default/files/Wilinsky_Alperin_0.pdf]

CHAPTER 1

Weaving Scholarly Communication and Information Literacy

[Strategies for Incorporating Both Threads in Academic Library Outreach]

Julia Gelfand
University of California, Irvine

Catherine Palmer
University of California, Irvine

Introduction

In this chapter, we examine the alignments and disconnects between information literacy and scholarly communication. Our goal is to identify a common theoretical framework that academic librarians can use to design and provide outreach and education activities incorporating both themes for students and faculty. In looking at ways to weave scholarly communication and information literacy into academic library outreach, it is useful to review how each of these programmatic areas emerged as responses by academic libraries to trends and issues in the larger arena of higher education. Both information literacy and scholarly communication offer a conceptual framework in which to think about the scholarly materials provided by academic libraries to foster the creation of new knowledge. Both emerged as topics of universal professional concern in response to transformations in postsecondary education, information production, technology, and publishing. Both emphasize subject strengths, interdisciplinary links, evaluation of content, and incorporation of technology, and both attempt to respond to new information formats and information needs. Professional conversations about each area have matured and evolved over time, and yet, until very recently, the two conversations have taken place in separate and seemingly disconnected venues. We argue that, by using the American Library Association (ALA 2004) *Core Values of Librari-*

anship as a framework, librarians can bring the conversations about information literacy and scholarly communication together to enhance and strengthen their respective impacts by providing a common loom on which to weave a rich, enlightening, and valuable tapestry.

This chapter will first attempt debunk the myth the academic library focuses on either collection building to support scholarly communication *or* user-centered instruction to fulfill information literacy missions. We will discuss the background and identify current issues within both realms—information literacy and scholarly communication—including values, goals, and objectives that they hold in common. We will then examine the history and present state of both areas within academic libraries in the United States, identifying key documents and milestones. Finally, we will review and analyze current conversations taking place in the literature and in our professional organizations in order to gain perspective and provide guidance on how librarians can build stronger alliances between information literacy and scholarly communication. The alignments, parallels, and relationships suggest more common elements than the differences that may have defined earlier library organizations. We conclude with an interpretation of how information literacy and scholarly communication can be effectively connected using the *Core Values*.

Collection Development and Management: Background and Current Issues

Several years after Anthony Cummings's (1992) seminal work, *University Libraries and Scholarly Communication*, defined scholarly communication, the advent of mainstream electronic publishing transformed library collection development practices. During the late 1990s, collection development librarians moved beyond selecting and deselecting or withdrawal of materials and into the realm of actively managing collections.

Today, librarians have adopted the ACRL's (2003) definition of scholarly communication as:

> the system through which research and other scholarly writings are created, evaluated for quality, disseminated to the scholarly community, and preserved for future use. The system includes both formal means of communication, such as publication in peer-reviewed journals, and information channels, such as electronic listservs. (para. 1)

The original focus of scholarly communication centered on the unsustainable economic practice of "buying back"—through library journal subscriptions—scholarly content from commercial publishers and scholarly or professional societies that were publishing faculty research output. The now-famous graph (Figure 1.1) indicating sharp price increases over time illustrates the negative impact on libraries' budgets as they attempted to cover the escalating costs of library and institutional subscriptions. This does not take into account adding new resources that are always on the horizon but instead emphasizes a steady state.

Figure 1.1

Monograph and Serial Expenditures in ARL Libraries, 1986–2004 (includes electronic resources from 1999–2000 onward) (Used with permission.)

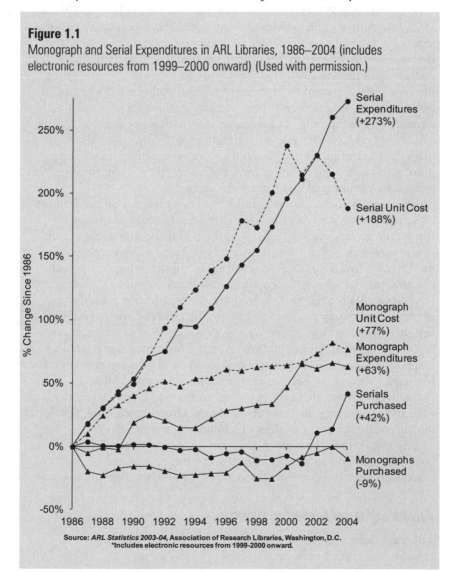

Source: *ARL Statistics 2003-04,* Association of Research Libraries, Washington, D.C.
*Includes electronic resources from 1999-2000 onward.

While sustainability issues related to journals were clearly the focus of scholarly communication initiatives, the scholarly monograph also faced its own set of challenges. Publishers and book vendors in the mid-1990s began to experience a decline in sales of scholarly monographs to libraries as changing methods of scholarship altered the ways that libraries acquired books. The traditional acquisition model of purchasing individual book titles began to compete with alternative options, including annual subscription models and the purchase of subject packages assembled by publishers and aggregators. Licensing and format access restrictions have challenged libraries' ability to share e-content through traditional services such as resource sharing or interlibrary loan. Due to flattening materials budgets and the assumption of ever-higher costs of materials, more availability of content, and the increasing tendency toward research specialization, libraries have departed from their traditional collection development policy of acquiring materials "just in case" and began to develop alternative "just in time" practices, such as patron- or demand-driven acquisitions. University presses are increasingly concerned about their sales figures and profit margins and are more selective in accepting manuscripts, making it harder for scholars to publish and forcing them to look to commercial and trade publishers.

Opinion pieces, editorials, and letters to university administrators and publishers have been plentiful, sharing different viewpoints on the perceived crisis in scholarly publishing and the untenable nature of the current scholarly journal subscription and monograph pricing model (see Owens 2012). As a response to this growing concern, the conversation of scholarly communication has evolved to include a call for sustainable pricing and alternatives to the traditional publishing models of scholarly and commercial publishers. The current conversation also encourages the awareness of the cycle of creation, transformation, dissemination, and preservation of knowledge related to teaching, research, and scholarly endeavors. It argues for new roles for libraries, so that they become not just repositories and buyers' clubs, but active participants in the endeavor of making information available and supporting the generation of new efforts to educate, develop, and advocate for best practices in scholarly communication.

As one of these best practices, most academic research libraries have created ways to inform faculty and students about best practices associated with the core content areas of scholarly communication.

Authors' Rights and Intellectual Property

The legal right of authors, composers, translators, illustrators, editors, and all contributors to the scholarly product to retain or confirm the right to distribute one's work broadly is at the core of scholarly communication. Even if the work has been published, oftentimes an addendum can be secured so that the work can be deposited within a disciplinary or institutional repository, capitalizing on the potential to reach a greater readership as well as to ensure perpetual access, regardless of where the content was originally published.

Copyright and Fair Use

According to the US Copyright Office (2012), this form of intellectual property law "protects original works of authorship including literary, dramatic, musical, and artistic works, such as poetry, novels, movies, songs, computer software, and architecture. Copyright does not protect facts, ideas, systems, or methods of operation, although it may protect the way these things are expressed." Copyright and fair use have enormous consequences in teaching and research because of the limits and rights bestowed on copying, distribution, and access. The Copyright Law of the United States (17 U.S.C.; see US Copyright Office 2011) governs the making of reproductions of copyrighted material and makes users liable for any infringement. Most institutions of higher education adhere to this statute, relying on educational exemptions provided to libraries and the fair use provisions of the copyright law and obtaining the permission of the copyright holder when required. The Copyright Act of 1976 (17 U.S.C §107) contains a fair use doctrine, known as the "Four Factors Test," to evaluate and determine if something falls under an allowed fair use.

Dan Lee, Director of the Office of Copyright Management and Scholarly Communication at the University of Arizona, summarizes the approach that many libraries have adopted:

> The primary issue is to promote access to the scholarly literature, and that is done on various levels... On the copyright side, it's making sure we don't overstep our bounds, but in making sure we don't broadly define those bounds or have tight controls... The access we want would allow the scholars on campus to have the publications reach the communities they want to reach. (Everett-Haynes 2008)

The advent of digitization, which provides a means both to produce and to distribute content and can be used to convert analog content to digital, necessitates new understanding of these limits and rights. As distance education becomes more common and widely available, both faculty and students need to be educated on their legal rights and responsibilities related to the distribution, access, and use of e-content. For example, alternatives to traditional copyright such as Creative Commons licensing[1] allow creators to communicate which rights they retain and which rights they waive for the benefit of readers, researchers, or other creators.

Open Access (OA)

Open access (OA) is defined as a mode of publication or distribution of research results that limits or removes payments, fees, licensing, or other barriers to readers' access to research reports, journal articles, conference proceedings, books, or any other type of scholarly literature or research product. Although many of the best-known discussions of OA focus on scientific, medical, and technology research, open access publishing occurs in all subject areas. OA publishing requires nontraditional business models to pay the costs of publishing because the usual modes of payment, such as subscriptions, are eliminated or minimized. Some publications offset costs by requiring the authors to pay publication charges after the manuscript has been peer-reviewed and accepted for publication; others use a membership model (e.g., BioMed Central, PeerJ). There are different "flavors" of OA that define ways that it can be achieved while still reducing or eliminating costs associated with accessing the publication. For example, publishers sometimes build endowments or ask for financial support from the communities that most benefit from their work. Universities, research centers, and libraries have occasionally subsidize researchers to enable them to participate in open access opportunities. Many traditional publishers are joining the effort to make OA a choice with some of their journals. There are a number of social and political initiatives that promote OA, such as the Alliance for Taxpayer Access, Students for Free Culture, the Right to Research Coalition, and the Scholarly Publishing and Academic Resources Coalition (SPARC) developed by the Association of Research Libraries (ARL).[2]

Management of Research Data

Libraries have been instrumental in helping scientists and scholars honor the recent mandates from federal funding agencies that require research data to have a management plan so that it can be found, curated, shared, potentially reused, and archived. New toolkits and resources have become available to support e-science and other disciplines, making a broader statement of support for e-research. Again, libraries and librarians are centrally positioned in these efforts. Examples of this emphasis are seen in the recent rollout and adoption of the Data Management Plan Tool issued by the California Digital Library to provide instructions and guidance about articulating a data management plan and the Purdue Data Curation Profiles Toolkit launched by Purdue University to create communities of scholars, librarians, and archivists who are exploring ways to manage research data.[3]

New Publishing Opportunities and Options

Scholarly output has experienced many changes in recent years. Technology drove many of these changes; however, new product lines and experiences by readers, students, and scholars point to different expectations that have transformed creative output. The journal has experienced fundamental changes, but the scholarly monograph has been challenged as well. Electronic books, or e-books, are becoming part of the mainstream and present many choices in the publishing process. Print versus online is one choice, but compatibility with different distribution channels, migrating technologies and devices, and shifts in readership trends create an ever-changing landscape. The availability of online publishing and digital services has pushed libraries to take on new roles previously assumed only by publishers. In this new environment, more libraries are exploring and engaged in publishing services and finding opportunities to provide greater discoverability to and curatorial support for unique content in their own collections. University archives and special collections units have been instrumental in actively digitizing collections and creating finding aids to increase access to users both locally and globally. Libraries have also provided the momentum in establishing institutional repositories in which members of the academic community can place their scholarly output and intellectual property so it can be more widely shared and discovered by search engines such as Google. Educating the academic community about these issues has been enlightening for faculty and librarians, and growing awareness of scholarly communication issues has influenced the services and collection management practices in libraries.

Reporting a series of interviews in the article "Whither Science Publishing?" science journalist Bob Grant (2012) concludes:

> To keep up with the blistering pace of scientific and technological advances, publishers are getting creative. In recent years, new concepts such as post-publication peer review, all scientist editorial teams, lifetime publishing privilege fees, and funder-supported open access have entered the publishing consciousness. (para. 3)

The publishers, researchers, and information scientists who participated in these interviews concur that the current publishing system is broken and badly in need of repair, that peer review is imperfect and needs to remedy its cumbersome processes and time-consuming delays, that open access is the wave of the future but still in need of refinement, and that hybrid publishing that merges subscription models with open access may be a good alternative. These new directions are already having an impact on the practices of researchers, librarians, and readers and will continue to do so in the future.

Let us turn our attention from this brief overview of the background and current issues in scholarly communication to those in information literacy.

Information Literacy: Background and Current Issues

Like scholarly communication, information literacy emerged in response to developments in the academic and information environment as a way for librarians to focus their individual and institutional instructional efforts and establish legitimacy in the curriculum of higher education beyond the library. Just as the increase in available materials caused collection librarians and bibliographers to change collection management practices, it also drove the need for information literacy and instruction librarians to teach students how to find, use, and evaluate those materials. As higher education became more accessible, students entered the academy with more diverse educational backgrounds and with varying levels of skills and familiarity with the methods of scholarly research. And finally, as the curriculum expanded to meet different needs, instruction methods shifted from lecture to inquiry-based instruction with increased emphasis on the pursuit of individual research interests. The debates around the purpose, outcome, and placement of library instruction—whether is it most effective as a separate course or as an integrated component of a subject or discipline—began early and continue to the present (Salony 1995).

The modern library instruction movement emerged in the 1960s in response to research that documented the tendency of students then, as now, to be uncritical in their use of information (Grassian and Kaplowitz 2009). Even before the advent of electronic publishing, information in print formats was increasing exponentially during this decade. Research interests of faculty became more specialized, which resulted in an increasing number of specialized publications written for smaller and more focused communities of scholars. The curriculum of higher education diversified and expanded to include both specialized researchers and more focused, pragmatic programs intended to teach vocational skills. As more information became available, students needed guidance in learning the skills necessary to locate, evaluate, and use it.

The professional literature of information literacy reveals that the debates around the placement, methods, goals, and objectives of library instruction in academic libraries continued and intensified in the thirty-year period from 1960 to 1989 (Grassian and Kaplowitz 2009, 14). In 1989, the chair of the ALA Presidential Committee on Information Literacy, Patricia Breivik, reconceptualized the intended outcome of library instruction as "information literacy," and the committee developed the core definition we use today: "To be information literate, a person must be able to recognize when information is needed and have the ability to locate, evaluate, and use effectively the needed information" (ALA 1989, para. 3).

It is also evident from the literature that the range of activities in information literacy instruction is very broad. Articles and conference presentations that focus on providing information literacy instruction to discrete sets of students in specific disciplines and in defined educational contexts are numerous and common. Much of the information literacy literature is directed toward the librarian practitioner and offers useful solutions to common instructional challenges. Most librarians familiar with information literacy will agree that the literature reflects both a broad range of institutional environments and a wide variety of programs designed to teach students information literacy skills and concepts. They would probably also agree, upon reflection, that the ACRL (2000) *Information Literacy Competency Standards for Higher Education*, while imperfect, provide a common set of learning outcome expectations that span different environments and provide some commonality regardless of the educational context.

Recently, inspired and informed by the literature of teaching and learning, many professionals have started to build a more solid theoretical foundation of praxis that moves beyond the *Information Literacy Competency Standards* (Accardi, Drabinsky, & Kumbier 2010; Elmborg 2006; Simmons 2005; Jacobs and Berg 2011; Townsend, Brunetti, and Hofer 2011). Examining and applying learning principles espoused in critical literacy, threshold concepts, appreciative inquiry, and problem-posing education will allow academic librarians to use a common core set of values, identified in the *Core Values of Librarianship*, to design outreach programs that will reach both students (the traditional audience for information literacy instruction) and faculty (the traditional audience for scholarly communication).

Another feature of the professional conversation around information literacy is the way in which it addresses scholarly communication, either explicitly or implicitly. Part of the debate about the placement of information literacy attempts to answer the question of whether it is a defined subject content area of its own or whether it is most effectively addressed as an understanding of the research methods of a discipline (Badke 2008). Regardless of where it is placed in the curriculum, we suggest that information-literate members of the academy should understand how knowledge is created, evaluated, shared, and preserved within a discipline. If we define scholarly communication as the ways in which subject knowledge is created (research methodology), evaluated (peer review), shared (through scholarly journal articles, monographs, conference proceedings, and research reports), and preserved (repositories writ large), then it is clear that an information-literate individual is one who understands both the issues *and* processes of scholarly communication.

While giving a high-level summary of the content and focus of the information literacy literature, it is worthwhile to consider the differences that we observed between the professional literature of information literacy and that of scholarly communication. These differences serve to illustrate the ways in which professional conversations about each area have taken place in separate and seemingly disconnected venues.

Scholarly Communication: Audience and Changing Realities

Scholarly communication, as central as it is to the mission of most academic libraries, is sometimes perceived as distant from the daily processes and procedures that members of the library staff engage in with typical users. Instead, it often appears to be centralized as a relatively new rollout of practices and services directed by library leaders and management teams that have close relationships with campus leadership, such as the provost, academic deans, directors of the university press (if there is one), university counsel, deans or vice chancellors of research, faculty who serve as editors of prestigious journals, and the like. Special programming has increasingly widened to include presentations to broader audiences that now typically attract more graduate students, who are considered an important target as they are the next generation of scholars and are currently engaged in research and creative enterprises and being exposed to current best practices while working under advisors and mentors. As bibliographers and subject liaison librarians strive to develop closer relationships with faculty and students, it is clear that librarians need to be increasingly comfortable with and well-versed in the options in each of the topical areas of scholarly communication.

As thematic emphases in scholarly communication mature, one now sees entire books dedicated to open access, copyright issues in libraries, institutional repositories, and data management plans. In addition to books exploring these topics, rich conference papers and proceedings provide insight through the use of case studies and local approaches that can be revised and replicated. Most academic libraries today devote portions of their websites to sharing information on how they promote and manage scholarly communication. In addition, there are many specialized scholarly communication workshops, webinars, seminars, and conferences held by nearly every local and national professional library association that offer professional development opportunities. Scholars and students are increasingly relying upon blogs, Twitter feeds, and preprint servers to capture scholarly conversations and commentary. This application of social media, often called "altmetrics," uses methods of crowdsourcing peer review to determine impact, learn about new applications, and solicit and use feedback and assessment on the scholarly information provided. The next generation of bibliographic management software, such as Mendeley and Zotero, described as reference managers, are free and Web-based and help users manage not just what they write, but what they read, discover, and retrieve from information seeking and conducting literature reviews.

Scholarship, learning, and publishing trends all have an international, if not global, reach. It follows that the scholarly communication and open access movement is not limited to a North American audience. The international history now extends over a decade, with the Budapest Open Access Initiative arising from an Open Society Institute meeting in 2001 that envisioned accelerating progress by making scholarship freely available on the Internet (BOAI 2012a). Today over 635 organizations are signatories, and nearly six thousand individuals have shown their support (BOAI 2012b). The Berlin Declaration on Open Access to Knowledge in the Sciences and Humanities was signed in 2003 and today has more than 300 institutional signatories (Max Planck Society 2012). Each year since 2003, the Berlin Conference convenes to discuss and strategize around issues of open access and publishing.

Open Access Week, during the month of October, is an opportunity for the academic and research community to learn about the potential benefits of open access and to inspire wider participation in helping to make open access a new norm in scholarship and research. Another public advocacy group is the Right to Research Coalition, which encourages students, scholars, professionals and librarians to promote open access as a method to democratize and share research.[4]

Indeed, publishing today is a worldwide enterprise with publishers and agents seeking and competing for the best manuscripts and submissions. Responding to the increasing need to develop consistency across the global publishing industry, the National Institute of Standards Organization (NISO) issues standards that inform the publishing industry and increasingly influence the work of libraries. According to its mission statement, "NISO fosters the development and maintenance of standards that facilitate the creation, persistent management, and effective interchange of information so that it can be trusted for use in research and learning" (NISO 2012). NISO's work explicitly addresses scholarly communication themes; examples of these contributions include the issuing of SERU: Shared Electronic Resource Understanding, which codifies best practices for the sale of e-resources without licenses;[5] the standardization of the digital object identifier (DOI) standard, which has been extended more recently to data by the DataCite community; and the more current engagement with the Open Archives Initiative in the ResourceSync Project to synchronize Web-scale data repositories allowing replication of content and metadata between repositories in close to real time.[6] These examples of the NISO standards offer parallel structure to the *ACRL Information Literacy Competency Standards* and suggest that the publishing industry and librarians share concerns regarding technical issues and infrastructure in the realm of scholarly publishing. Finally, the works of Jingfeng Xia (2008) and Bruce and Katina Strauch (2002) are representative of the many lucid examples in the literature for how academic library communities around the globe have responded to scholarly communication.

Professional Resources and Programming (Toolkits, Standards, or Something Else?)

The American Library Association (ALA), the Association of Research Libraries (ARL), the Association of Academic and Research Libraries (ACRL)and other specialized librarian groups and professional societies have formed committees that are dedicated to educating members about scholarly communication. Rather than developing unique scholarly communication standards that parallel the *Information Literacy Competency Standards*, the ACRL (2009), the ARL (2010), and SPARC (2012) have each produced resources in the form of toolkits that assist the library community in promoting an understanding of scholarly communication principles. There have also been successful ACRL roadshows and regional meetings of academic librarians, publishers, and vendors that have addressed different aspects of the toolkits. Programming that resonates with users builds confidence in best practices and ensures that they are exposed to legitimate options subscribed to by their peers in a specific discipline. The best-practices approach suggests what lessons have been learned and points to new directions that are likely to evolve. Trends of publishing on the Web, self-publishing, new forms of grey literature, and more multiformat and multimedia integration complement the already diverse range of scholarly publishing. These new products will continue to use peer review and allow for the role of citation metrics, impact factors, and other measures to define value.

For those working in information literacy, ACRL supports programs in the areas of professional development, assessment, and instructional development. Spearheading many of these programs is the ACRL Institute for Information Literacy (IIL). IIL is charged with preparing librarians to become effective teachers in information literacy programs; supporting librarians, other educators, and administrators in taking leadership roles in the development of information literacy programs; and forging new partnerships within the educational community to work towards information literacy curriculum development (ACRL 2012, para. 20–23). In addition to the IIL, conferences such as LOEX in the United States, WILU in Canada, and LILAC in the United Kingdom focus on practical topics of interest to teaching librarians and provide opportunities to create information literacy communities of practice. With the emphasis on teaching the ability to evaluate information, some aspects of scholarly communication, such as those related to establishing authority, are addressed in these arenas, but scholarly communication rarely emerges as a stand-alone topic.

Although scholarly communication toolkits emphasize practicality in outreach and demonstrate an understanding of the need to reach diverse audiences with a clear educational message, we found it interesting and revealing that we could not find any explicit reference to information literacy in discussions of scholarly communication. The differences in the audiences, purposes, intent, and content found between the literatures of information literacy and scholarly communication are illustrative of the administrative and professional disconnects between these two fundamental areas of academic librarianship. Where can we find common ground between the two?

Information Literacy: Understanding the Context of the Standards

Although the ACRL *Information Literacy Competency Standards for Higher Education,* which followed the 1989 final report of the ALA Presidential Committee on Information Literacy, focus almost exclusively on describing the skills, knowledge, and abilities of an information-literate individual, it is useful to point out that the committee's final report presents the need for information literacy in a much larger context. An understanding of information literacy is introduced as follows:

> How our country deals with the realities of the Information Age will have enormous impact on our democratic way of life and on our nation's ability to compete internationally. Within America's information society, there also exists the potential of addressing many long-

> standing social and economic inequities. To reap such benefits, people—as individuals and as a nation—must be information literate. (ALA 1989, para.3)

The report also states:

> Information is expanding at an unprecedented rate, and enormously rapid strides are being made in the technology for storing, organizing, and accessing the ever growing tidal wave of information. The combined effect of these factors is an increasingly fragmented information base—large components of which are only available to people with money and/or acceptable institutional affiliations. (ALA 1989, para. 1)

By expanding our focus beyond the definition of information literacy to the broader, more inclusive context of the whole report, the document begins to offer a foundation for outreach efforts by academic librarians that includes and implicitly connects both information literacy and scholarly communication.

Other, more recent documents build upon the idea of access to information as a foundation of a democratic society, a key tenet of both information literacy and scholarly communication. In his proclamation which designated October 2009 as National Information Literacy Awareness Month, President Barack Obama declared:

> An informed and educated citizenry is essential to the functioning of our modern democratic society, and I encourage educational and community institutions across the country to help Americans find and evaluate the information they seek, in all its forms. (Obama 2009, para. 4)

The Alexandria Proclamation on Information Literacy and Lifelong Learning jointly adopted by representatives from UNESCO, IFLA, and the National Forum on Information Literacy states:

> Information Literacy lies at the core of lifelong learning. It empowers people in all walks of life to seek, evaluate, use and create information effectively to achieve their personal, social, occupational and educational goals. It is a basic human right in a digital world and promotes social inclusion of all nations. (NFIL 2005, para. 2)

These and other statements provide a vision that can inspire and inform our efforts to eliminate the disconnect and strengthen the alignment between scholarly communication and information literacy.

Broadening the Information Literacy Focus beyond Undergraduate Education

Another feature of the professional conversations about information literacy is its focus on the undergraduate as the target population for instruction. There is some mention of information literacy needs of professional populations (engineering, business, and medicine are common examples), but for the most part, the programs and practices described are directed toward undergraduates. This is not surprising in view of the placement of information literacy within the library organizational structure and its integration into the curriculum of the academy. It stands in contrast to the corpus of scholarly communication literature, which focuses on the information needs of faculty and graduate students.

However, there is evidence that undergraduates are not the only students who can benefit from a better understanding of information literacy, an understanding that incorporates core scholarly communication concepts. *Researchers of Tomorrow* is the United Kingdom's largest study to date on the research behavior of Generation Y doctoral students (born between 1982 and 1994). The study, commissioned in 2009 by the Joint Information Systems Committee (JISC) and the British Library, involved 17,000 doctoral students from 70 universities over three years (Education for Change 2012, 5). The research findings revealed:

- Doctoral students are increasingly reliant on secondary research resources (e.g. journal articles, books), moving away from primary materials (e.g. primary archival material and large datasets).
- Access to relevant resources is a major constraint for doctoral students' progress. Authentication access and license limitations to subscription-based resources, such as e-journals, are particularly problematic.
- Open access and copyright appear to be a source of confusion for Generation Y doctoral students, rather than encouraging innovation and collaborative research.
- This generation of doctoral students operates in an environment where their research behavior does not use the full potential of innovative technology.
- Doctoral students are insufficiently trained or informed to be able to fully embrace the latest opportunities in the digital information environment. (JISC 2012a)

Although the students surveyed for the report were affiliated with British institutions, it is likely that the results of a survey of American graduate students would parallel the findings of the British survey in many important aspects. It is particularly revealing to note that the students surveyed demonstrate:

> a continuing lack of understanding about the nature of open access. Generation Y students felt that putting their own work out openly will bring them no positive benefits, and may even have a negative impact. Equally, doctoral students' understanding of the intellectual property and copyright environment appears to be a source of confusion, rather than an enabler of innovation. (JISC 2012b, para. 7)

Open access and intellectual property rights are key to addressing many of today's scholarly communication challenges, yet graduate students, the researchers and faculty of tomorrow, don't understand how these issues affect them. This lack of understanding, while distressing in the short term, presents a golden opportunity to expand the focus of information literacy from its traditional undergraduate audience to align more closely with scholarly communication efforts to educate graduate students on how to protect their own intellectual work at the same time as they make it available to others in order to facilitate innovation and the advancement of research.

Using the Core Values to Connect Information Literacy and Scholarly Communication

The comprehensive nature of the current *ACRL Information Literacy Competency Standards (IL Standards)* is laudable, and after twelve years of using them in the library classroom, we can learn from our experience in future revisions and new efforts. The experience of using scholarly communication toolkits has proven that they are a viable method to implement training and influence librarian, publisher, and faculty behavior. The literature on content standard development offers guidance on how to develop standards and toolkits that will help us focus on the big ideas and core concepts of information literacy and scholarly communication (Townsend, Brunetti, and Hofer 2011). The fact that librarians have embraced, used, applied, assessed, and critiqued the *IL Standards* attests to their practical application. Scholarly communication toolkits serve a purpose similar to the *IL Standards* in that they provide guidelines for action and a core curriculum and suggest important content that needs to be shared and acted upon in order for the desired outcomes to be achieved. Just as information literacy standards guided the development of content for library instruction programs and scholarly communication toolkits guided the development of resources for collection development and management activities and advocacy efforts, professional resources that incorporate the best practices of both information literacy and scholarly communication are needed to guide the development of education and outreach programs.

The ALA's *Core Values of Librarianship* states:

> The foundation of modern librarianship rests on an essential set of core values that define, inform, and guide our professional practice. These values reflect the history and ongoing development of the profession and have been advanced, expanded, and refined by numerous policy statements of the American Library Association. Among these are:
>
> • Access
> • Confidentiality/Privacy
> • Democracy
> • Diversity
> • Education and Lifelong Learning
> • Intellectual Freedom
> • Preservation
> • The Public Good
> • Professionalism
> • Service
> • Social Responsibility (ALA 2004)

A close examination of the *Core Values of Librarianship* provides a vision that more closely aligns the big ideas and core concepts of information literacy and scholarly communication. In working to support this alignment, we can use the *Core Values* as a foundation and framework to guide the development of robust professional resources that will begin to bridge the disconnect between the scholarly communication toolkits and the *Information Literacy Competency Standards*.

Examining the Standards through the Lens of Core Values

Jacobs and Berg's (2011) article, "Reconnecting Information Literacy Policy with the Core Values of Librarianship," which inspired and informed our thinking on the alignments between information literacy and scholarly communication, provides an excellent critique of the limiting nature of defining information literacy instruction as an activity by which librarians deposit knowledge about the location, evaluation, and use of information into students. Instead, the authors encourage incorporating a problem-posing approach to teaching information literacy. In this model, the librarian actively encourages students to consider and question the social, economic, political, and cultural aspects of information creation, distribution, retention, and ownership as part of the information literacy curriculum. This approach clearly supports the idea that concepts of scholarly communication, such as open access versus paid subscriptions, the role of the library in knowledge creation and dissemination, and issues of copyright and intellectual property are essential components of information literacy (Jacobs and Berg 2011, 390).

We strongly advocate that future revisions of the ACRL *Information Literacy Competency Standards* incorporate a basic understanding of scholarly communication principles and include explicit statements that an information-literate individual understands:

- the basic concepts, issues, and methods of scholarly communication
- the fact that methods of scholarly communication differ between disciplines
- the methods of scholarly communication within his or her field of study or area of expertise

By using the phrase "information-literate individual" instead of "information-literate student," we can also imply that an understanding of these concepts is important to all members of society and broaden the audience for information literacy education beyond undergraduates.

Applying the Core Values

Although it is unrealistic in this chapter to provide a comprehensive analysis of the possible ways that the *Core Values of Librarianship* can be used to align information literacy and scholarly communication, this is a good time to provide examples of how this process might work and some of the challenges librarians might encounter. First, let us look closely at the idea of access as a core value of librarianship and consider how this value is expressed in information literacy and in scholarly communication.

ACRL (2000) Information Literacy Competency Standard Two states, "The information literate student accesses needed information effectively and efficiently." In this case, *access* refers to the method or process of finding the needed information. On the other hand, *access* in scholarly communication typically refers to the availability of information and includes such issues as perpetual access, barriers to access, and open access. The ALA *Core Values* statement on access reads,

"All information resources that are provided directly or indirectly by the library, regardless of technology, format, or methods of delivery, should be readily, equally, and equitably accessible to all library users" (ALA 2004, para. 5). In this instance, it is clear that the *Core Values* statement relates more closely to the scholarly communication concept of access than it does to the information literacy application. Although librarians support the idea that "All information resources ... should be readily, equally, and equitably accessible to all library users," some findings suggest that faculty attitudes towards archiving publications, peer review, and open access may not reflect this lofty ideal. As King and Harley (2006) conclude in one study of University of California Berkeley faculty attitudes toward scholarly communication issues, "approaches that try to 'move' faculty and deeply embedded value systems directly toward new forms of archival, 'final' publication are destined largely to failure in the short-term" (2). The King et al. study attempts to more fully explore the academic value system by associating different levels of access within a discipline and holistically within the universe of scholarly publication and communication and finds that the complexity and interconnectedness of peer review, e-publishing, economic and cost issues, open access, electronic communication, data storage, data management needs, and archival specifications contribute to a lack of understanding among faculty and authors of critical decision-making elements in promoting scholarly communication principles more widely. Today, half a decade later, the comfort level among faculty with e-publishing is greater, and the publishing milieu is more mature. The faculty concerns expressed in this study, although still factors, are no longer the barriers they were just a few years ago. Any conversation addressing an alignment between the information literacy implications, understanding, and applications of access and those of scholarly communication will need to acknowledge and address the differing perspectives of several populations, including undergraduates, graduate students, librarians, and faculty.

Next, the broad and overarching value of education and lifelong learning is another example of a natural connection between information literacy and scholarly communication. The *Core Values* state:

> ALA promotes the creation, maintenance, and enhancement of a learning society, encouraging its members to work with educators, government officials, and organizations in coalitions to initiate and support comprehensive efforts to ensure that school, public, academic, and special libraries in every community cooperate to provide lifelong learning services to all. (ALA 2004, para. 9)

Although lifelong learning is not mentioned in the *Information Literacy Competency Standards,* the introduction to the standards proclaims:

> Information literacy forms the basis for lifelong learning. It is common to all disciplines, to all learning environments, and to all levels of education. It enables learners to master content and extend their investigations, become more self-directed, and assume greater control over their own learning. (ACRL 2000, para. 2)

Recent discussions of the ACRL Scholarly Communication Committee explored issues of lifelong learning. Following the discussion of how librarians could "encourage the use of a committee discussion group to draw the connection between the earlier efforts to develop information literacy as a core expertise for librarians with emerging work regarding scholarly communication" (Ogburn 2011, para. 3). At the ACRL Scholarly Communications Discussion Group meeting at ALA Annual 2011, Joyce Ogburn, the past president of ACRL, raised the following questions:

- How can information literacy programs help students learn about the whole cycle of scholarly communication?
- Scholarly communication librarians are frequently teachers; what can they learn from the information literacy experts?
- What lessons can be learned and ideas exchanged by librarians incorporating information literacy and scholarly communication into their work? (Ogburn 2011, para. 5)

Her conclusions led her to coin the phrase "Lifelong learning requires lifelong access." She expands on her ideas by stating, "In other words, creating critical thinkers and expectations of continuous learning requires highly credible resources to be available, easily found and recognized for their quality among the abundance of information propagated so freely on the Web" (Ogburn 2011, para. 7).

In the introduction to *Transforming Research Libraries for the Global Knowledge Society,* Barbara Dewey (2010) argues that librarians need to take a lead role in what she terms "creation literacy," which she defines as "the ability to create and disseminate new knowledge in meaningful ways in our global networked society" (5). She goes on to state that "creation literacy goes beyond information literacy in that it focuses on research output and its impact beyond the process of find appropriate resources and solving problems of a given

•

project or task" (5). While we might argue with both the terminology (the phrase "creation literacy" might be more likely to bring up the idea of creationism than is intended) and the characterization of information literacy as focused simply on process and "solving problems of a given project or task," the creation and dissemination of new knowledge is a powerful role for libraries, one that academic librarians need to understand in order to undertake the work of achieving this goal.

As these two recent examples illustrate, the role of libraries in fostering a learning society is central to the alignment of information literacy and scholarly communication. This can be used as a guiding principle as the profession develops strategies for information literacy, collection management, and subject liaison librarians to take a larger role in promoting awareness of scholarly communication issues. As we noted earlier, a distributed model will give scholarly communication more traction than depending on a single administrator, copyright officer, or "evangelist" for the cause to spread the scholarly communication message. Extending the focus beyond economic issues to include societal and cultural impacts on scholarship and academic publishing has the potential to create programmatic synergies across library and publishing organizations that are valued by all librarians and stakeholders with investments in research and learning.

Conclusion

Now is an opportune time for academic librarians at all levels to undertake an effort to more closely align scholarly communication and information literacy. As of summer 2012, a formal review of the ACRL *Information Literacy Competency Standards* is underway. The 2011 ACRL Plan for Excellence identifies both student learning and scholarly communication as strategic directions. These efforts will, as we share Joyce Ogburn's confidence, bridge "student learning and the research and scholarly environment" by extending a call "for librarians to transform student learning, pedagogy and instructional practices through creative and innovative collaborations and to accelerate the transition to a more open system of scholarship" (Ogburn 2011, 514). As this speculative and preliminary attempt to use the ALA *Core Values* to take information literacy and scholarly communication out of their silos and weave them more seamlessly into the collective consciousness of academic librarians indicates, the resulting conversations will introduce many issues that both sides care passionately about, and will undoubtedly serve as the foundation for action plans to address the identified disconnect.

Notes

1. For more information, see the Creative Commons website at http://www.creativecommons.org.
2. For more information, see the websites of these organizations: Alliance for Taxpayer Access, http://www.taxpayeraccess.org; Students for Free Culture, http://freeculture.org; Right to Research Coalition, http://www.righttoresearch.org; Scholarly Publishing and Academic Resources Coalition, http://www.arl.org/sparc.
3. For more information, see the websites for these planning tools: Data Management Plan Tool, https://dmp.cdlib.org; Data Curation Profiles Toolkit, http://datacurationprofiles.org.
4. For more information, see the Right to Research Coalition website at http://www.righttoresearch.org.
5. For more information, see NISO's SERU webpage at http://www.niso.org/committees/seru.
6. For more information, see NISO's ResourceSync webpage at http://www.niso.org/workrooms/resourcesync.

References

Accardi, Maria T., Emily Drabinski, and Alana Kumbier, eds. 2010. *Critical Library Instruction: Theories and Methods*. Duluth, MN: Library Juice Press.

ACRL (Association of College and Research Libraries). 2000. *Information Literacy Competency Standards for Higher Education*. Chicago: ACRL, January 18. http://www.ala.org/acrl/standards/informationliteracycompetency.

———. 2003. "Principles and Strategies for the Reform of Scholarly Communication 1." ACRL. June 24. http://www.ala.org/acrl/publications/whitepapers/principlesstrategies.

———. 2009. "Scholarly Communication Toolkit." Last revised January. http://scholcomm.acrl.ala.org.

———. 2011. "ACRL Plan for Excellence." April. http://www.ala.org/acrl/aboutacrl/strategicplan/stratplan.

———. 2012. "ACRL History." Accessed November 28. http://www.ala.org/acrl/aboutacrl/history/history.

ALA (American Library Association). 1989. "Presidential Committee on Information Literacy: Final Report." American Library Association. January 10. http://www.ala.org/acrl/publications/whitepapers/presidential.

———. 2004. *Core Values of Librarianship*. (Chicago: ALA Council, June 29).

http://www.ala.org/offices/oif/statementspols/corevaluesstatement/corevalues.

ARL (Association of Research Libraries). 2010. "Know Your Copy Rights." Last modified June 21. http://www.knowyourcopyrights.org.

Badke, William. 2008. "A Rationale for Information Literacy as a Credit-Bearing Discipline." *Journal of Information Literacy* 2, no. 1: 1–22.

BOAI (Budapest Open Access Initiative). 2012a. "Frequently Asked Questions." Last revised September 14. http://www.earlham.edu/~peters/fos/boaifaq.htm.

———. 2012b. "View Signatures." Accessed November 28. http://www.opensocietyfoundations.org/openaccess/list_signatures.

Cummings, Anthony M. 1992. *University Libraries and Scholarly Communication: A Study Prepared for the Andrew W. Mellon Foundation.* Washington DC: Association of Research Libraries.

Dewey, Barbara I. 2010. "Transforming Research Libraries: An Introduction." In *Transforming Research Libraries for the Global Knowledge Society*, edited by Barbara I. Dewey. Chandos Information Professional Series. Oxford: Chandos Publishing.

Education for Change. 2012. *Researchers of Tomorrow: The Research Behaviour of Generation Y Doctoral Students.* London: British Library and HEFCE, June 28. http://www.jisc.ac.uk/publications/reports/2012/researchers-of-tomorrow.

Elmborg, James. 2006. "Critical Information Literacy: Implications for Instructional Practice." *The Journal of Academic Librarianship* 32, no. 2 (March): 192–199.

Everett-Haynes, La Monica. 2008. "UA Opens New Copyright Office." *UA News,* October 24. http://uanews.org/node/22186.

Grant, Bob. 2012. "Whither Science Publishing?" *The Scientist* 26, no. 8 (August 1), http://www.the-scientist.com/?articles.view/articleNo/32378/title/Whither-Science-Publishing-.

Grassian, Esther S., and Joan R. Kaplowitz. 2009. *Information Literacy Instruction: Theory and Practice*, 2nd ed. New York: Neal-Schuman.

Jacobs, Heidi L. M., and Selinda Berg. 2011. "Reconnecting Information Literacy Policy with the Core Values of Librarianship." *Library Trends* 60, no. 2 (Fall): 383–394.

JISC (Joint Information Systems Committee). 2012a. *Researchers of Tomorrow* report webpage. June 28. http://www.jisc.ac.uk/publications/reports/2012/researchers-of-tomorrow.

———. 2012b. "The Results Are In: Major Study into the Behavioural Habits of the 'Generation Y' PhD Students Released by JISC and the British Library" (news release). June 28. http://www.jisc.ac.uk/news/stories/2012/06/generationy.aspx.

King, C. Judd, Diane Harley, Sarah Earl-Novell, Jennifer Arter, Shannon Lawrence, and Irene Perciali. 2006. *Scholarly Communication: Academic Values and Sustainable Models.* Berkeley, CA: Center for

Higher Education. http://cshe.berkeley.edu/publications/docs/scholar-lycomm_report.pdf.

Max Planck Society. 2012. "Berlin Declaration." Accessed November 28. http://oa.mpg.de/berlin-prozess/berliner-erklarung.

NFIL (National Forum on Information Literacy). 2005. "Beacons of the Information Society: The Alexandria Proclamation on Information Literacy and Lifelong Learning." International Federation of Library Associations and Institutions. November 9. http://archive.ifla.org/III/wsis/BeaconInfSoc.html.

NISO (National Information Standards Organization). 2012. "NISO Mission Statement." Accessed October 17. http://www.niso.org/about.

Obama, Barack. 2009. "Presidential Proclamation National Information Literacy Awareness Month. " October 1. http://www.whitehouse.gov/the_press_office/Presidential-Proclamation-National-Information-Literacy-Awareness-Month.

Ogburn, Joyce L. 2011. "Lifelong Learning Requires Lifelong Access: Reflections on the ACRL Plan for Excellence." *College & Research Libraries News* 72, no. 9 (October): 514–515. http://crln.acrl.org/content/72/9/514.full.

Owens, Simon. 2012. "Is the Academic Publishing Industry on the Verge of Disruption?" *US News and World Report.* July 23. http://www.usnews.com/news/articles/2012/07/23/is-the-academic-publishing-industry-on-the-verge-of-disruption.

Salony, Mary F. 1995. "The History of Bibliographic Instruction: Changing Trends from Books to the Electronic World." *The Reference Librarian* 24, no. 51–52: 31–51.

Simmons, Michelle Holschuh. 2005. "Librarians as Disciplinary Discourse Mediators: Using Genre Theory to Move toward Critical Information Literacy." *portal: Libraries and the Academy* 5, no. 3 (July): 297–311.

SPARC (Scholarly Publishing and Academic Resources Coalition). 2012. "Resources." Accessed November 28. http://www.arl.org/sparc/resources/index.shtml.

Strauch, Katina, and Bruce Strauch, eds. 2002. *Scholarly Publishing: Books, Journals, Publishers, and Libraries in the Twentieth Century.* New York: Wiley.

Townsend, Lori, Korey Brunetti, and Amy R. Hofer. 2011. "Threshold Concepts and Information Literacy." *portal: Libraries and the Academy* 11, no. 3 (July): 853–869.

US Copyright Office. 2011. *Copyright Law of the United States and Related Laws Contained in Title 17 of the United States Code.* Circular 92. Washington DC: US Copyright Office, December. http://www.copyright.gov/title17/circ92.pdf.

US Copyright Office. 2012. "What Does Copyright Protect?" Last modified June 4. http://www.copyright.gov/help/faq/faq-protect.html.

Xia, Jingfeng, ed. 2008. *Scholarly Communication in China, Hong Kong, Japan, Korea and Taiwan.* Oxford: Chandos.

CHAPTER 2

The Academic Ethics of Open Access to Research and Scholarship

Reprinted (with permission) from
Ethics and Education, 6:3, 217–223

John Willinsky
School of Education, Stanford University, Stanford, USA

Juan Pablo Alperin
School of Education, Stanford University, Stanford, USA

In this article, we present the case for regarding the principles by which scholarly publications are disseminated and shared as a matter of academic ethics. The ethics of access have to do with recognizing people's right to know what is known, as well as the value to humanity of having one of its best forms of arriving at knowledge as widely shared as possible. The level of access is often reduced by the financial interests of publishers in a market in which there is little sense of a rational order, given huge discrepancies in prices for similar products. At the same time, there are risks to limiting researchers' access to scholarly resources, both for the quality of the knowledge that is not entirely open to review and for the production of new knowledge that it might inspire. Then, there are issues of access beyond the academy for professional practice and out of human interest, for both of which undue limitations raise what are, for us, more than academic ethical questions.

In introducing a recent collection of essays, *Creating the Ethical Academy*, Tricia Bentham Gallant, the Academic Integrity Coordinator for the University of California, San Diego, and Lester F. Goodchild, professor of Higher Education at Santa Clara University, place the ethical focus squarely on the misconduct of students, admission officers, and faculty members. They ask, in light of the repeated media coverage of cheating, bending, and fudging of the rules of academic conduct, 'are we heading down a road of inevitable corruption? Or is there an alternative way forward?' (Gallant and Goodchild 2010, 3).

Attending to those who break the rules is a common enough approach to academic ethics. This approach carries with it, however, the implication that, if and when such misconduct is eliminated, ethical questions would politely disappear from view. We raise this point because our contribution to this special issue of *Ethics and Education* 'in search of the ethical university takes a somewhat different approach to finding an alternative way forward for the ethical academy.

We are treating the ethical domain as a realm of positive action—in which, for example, one goes out of one's way to help someone—rather than an arena of moral failings, as suggested by exam cheating and research fudging. We believe that with the coming of the digital era, the university faces an unprecedented ethical opportunity to act in a positive fashion by reaching out to help others. We wish to present the ethical case for going out of one's way to ensure that one's research and scholarship has been made as widely available as possible to other scholars around the world, as well as to interested members of the public. With this approach, we are following, in effect, the identification by Gallant and Drinan (2010, 215), a political science professor at the University of San Diego, of the university's 'ethical center—which is, after all, the infrastructure and base for the pursuit and transmission of knowledge'. As this ethical center moves into the twenty-first century, the new digital publishing medium affords higher education a whole new range of opportunities for sharing what is discovered and learned within these institutions. The literature on the contribution and value of 'open access' (OA), as it is widely known, to scholarly research continues to grow dramatically during the first decade of the twenty-first century (Bailey 2010). We recognize that there is a host of related ethical issues associated with openness and the academic integrity of research and scholarship.[1] However, the ethics of access to the published literature takes on a particularly timely, if not urgent, quality amid the relatively rapid transition from the print culture to digital publishing for scholarly journals (and soon, perhaps, scholarly books). While other ethical dilemmas, such as cheating and fudging, have a timeless quality to them, there is something of a limited-time opportunity for ethical action when publishing models are changing and in this unsettled period are radically split between tendencies toward increasingly restrictive (for reasons of profit) and open (for a wider sharing) practices. There are even some very recent signs of some crossover, with publishers looking to advance profits through OA, with the financial consequences providing their own potential damper on the circulation of knowledge.

Thus, there is a need to consider the wide, if sometimes confusing, range of initiatives underway to direct this new publishing medium toward a more ethical and responsible approach to the basic human right to know and to knowledge. To ensure that the momentum gained around greater access over the last decade is not lost, we review the ethical dimensions of OA in scholarly communication. Much within the current academic culture of publish-and-perish-the-thought-of-doing-anything- more-with-the-work militates against the extra effort that is still required to ensure that the work done by scholars and researchers is distributed as widely and fairly (in terms of costs to readers) as possible. Once there was a time when having a study published in a scholarly journal was the only way to make the work public in a timely and responsible (peer-reviewed) way. Publishing it in a highly reputed journal further guaranteed that the work was more widely circulated, as such journals had more subscribers. There was no more to do than that, except perhaps respond to those pre-printed postcards, typically from Eastern Europe, requesting an 'off-print' of your paper, which they had somehow caught wind of.

That is no longer the case. As libraries struggle to afford even their current subscriptions, the new means of achieving almost universal online access presents itself. We, as scholars, face new responsibilities for thinking about how widely our work circulates, which does not preclude publishing in the prestigious journals, but which does call for a more ethical approach to the sharing of our work.

During the first decade of this century, there has been an active debate about OA within the scholarly publishing field. It has typically involved advocates calling for transparency, fairness, and accountability on one side, while opponents of OA express concerns over unproven economic models and the threats posed to the quality and sustainability of peer-reviewed scholarly publishing if the money is not there, on the other (Davis 2009). OA advocates hold that people do not only have an ethical right to this knowledge, but that the wider circulation achieved by OA is better for the quality and utilization (as well as the public support) of this knowledge. The advocates have been ragtag group of researchers, scholar publishers, and a few well-financed OA publishers, such as BioMed Central (for profit and now owned by Springer) and PLoS (non-profit foundation funded). The opponents of OA are the corporate and society publishers, operating through organizations such as the International Organization of Science, Technical and Medical Publishers, where concern has been expressed that 'achieving widespread sustainability for OA journals will not be particularly quick or easy' given that the two leaders in OA publishing, BioMed Central and PLoS, were not 'even close to profitability,' while fear abounded that OA would 'have a serious impact on journal subscriptions' (Ware 2006, 4). In this way, some publishers have turned OA into an ethical dilemma: *Do efforts to make research and scholarship more widely available to the public, educators, and scholars justify placing publisher and society revenues at risk?*

We think that the answer is an emphatic yes, especially given the lack of evidence of such a risk at this point. The economic viability of the various OA models may not be assured in this time of transition, with bookstores closing and the record industry in a tailspin. However, the Directory of Open Access Journals (DOAJ; http:// www.doaj.org/) operated by the University of Lund Library lists well over 6000 OA peer-reviewed journals. This includes large commercial publishers such as BioMed Central, thousands of small journals, and everything in between. The Public Knowledge Project (http://pkp.sfu.ca) is tracking over 8000 OA journals using its open source software (Open Journal Systems), the majority of which are not in DOAJ. It is difficult to tell what percentage of journals are OA, as the commonly used total of 25,000 journals (Harnad et al. 2004) is clearly itself only a portion of the journals currently being published.

Still, it can be said that a good number of journals are making a go of it with OA. A study of the journals using the free open source software developed by the Public Knowledge Project (with which we work) found that the scholar–publisher dominates these titles, with an average per article cost under US$200 (Edgar and Willinsky 2010). In addition, the majority of large commercial publishers now provide an OA choice within their subscription journals. That is, authors can purchase OA, in effect, for their individual article through a substantial 'article processing fee,' in the area of $3000, paid for by the author's research account or institution. A number of major corporate publishers, such as the Nature Group and Wiley, have recently announced new journals that will be OA, on this article-processing fee basis.[2] This could well signal a shift in publishing models. If publishers move their economic model from high-priced subscription journals to high-priced article-processing fees that may well put new pressures on research budgets and, for those without generous funding, university budgets. This commercialization of OA will need to be evaluated in comparison to non-commercial approaches, including those pursued by the vast majority of OA journals, which do not charge article-processing fees.

A second channel to OA that also appears to be proving itself economically is the author self-archiving route. Somewhat more than 60% of all publishers (including the publisher of this journal) allow authors to deposit their pre-prints and/or post-prints in OA archives or on their websites (SHERPA/RoMEO 2011). In the case of one of the oldest pre-print repositories known as arXiv.org, the time from deposit to citation has decreased as the repository approaches 100% of the publications in high energy particle physics and astrophysics (Swan 2007). Providing pre-prints (post peer-review) ensures a rapid turnaround between research and uptake, without sacrificing quality. There are now over 1800 OA repositories in which to deposit their pre- or post-prints (ROARMAP 2011). According to one estimate, the time needed to self-archive is less than 10 min per paper and, assuming that any one of the co-authors can perform the work, even a prolific scholar would need to invest no more than 40 min per year on self-archiving time (Carr and Harnad 2005). The few keystrokes and time cannot, by any standard, be considered onerous and the institutional repository alternative provides an answer to those who are concerned about the quality of OA journals.

The willingness of commercial publishers to adopt OA policies for their authors demonstrates that the publishing industry itself accepts the ethical imperative of OA. They are not taking any chances with this perceived risk, and are allowing that it may yet play a role in their long-term sustainability if not profitability. We would be remiss in overlooking some of the potential effects of researchers making their work available as soon as it has been accepted through an institutional or central repository. When looking at the entire research cycle, the time between finishing the research and it being used is one of the only aspects of the cycle that can easily be improved. For their part, publishers have yet to report a decline in subscription revenue that can be attributed to author archiving, although they have observed a drop in visits to their websites, which they blame on OA (Ware 2006, 4). As a result of these various efforts, somewhat more than 20% of the literature published in 2009 has been made available on an OA basis through authors archiving their work or publishing in OA journals (Björk et al. 2009). It all adds up to a certain viability for OA, and reduces the ethical dilemma posed by publishers who hold that OA places publisher revenues at risk and thus undermines the very publishing process.

The other side of this ethical question concerns the demonstrable value of OA. Is it having any impact on the readership and utilization of the work that is being made freely available? The evidence gathered to date indicates that this is the case. Work that has made OA is attracting more readers than similar materials that have not been made OA; what can also be said is that OA materials are also being cited more often, according to the majority of studies that Hitchcock (2011) surveys on this phenomenon. This vanity and career-advancing aspect of OA may even seem to compromise the ethical element of more widely circulating this knowledge. Professorial vanity poses an ethical risk, as noted by Cahn (2010), former provost of the Graduate Center, CUNY, in introducing the 25th anniversary edition of his *Saints and Scamps: Ethics in Academia*. However, this OA advantage in citations and readership is also part of the transition, with early adopters rewarded, while others play catch-up, at which point the vanity advantage disappears.

Where the large publishers have joined in on the efforts to provide OA out of an ethical concern for access in the world's poorest nations, as with bio-medical (the HINARI program), agricultural (the AGORA program), and environmental research (the OPARE program), the impact has been considerable. For example, 2.5 million PDFs have been downloaded by non-research institutions in developing countries alone (medical schools, teaching hospitals, and government offices) between 2003 and 2006 through the World Health Organization's Health Inter-Network Access to Research Initiative (HINARI 2006). However, this only points to the ethical gap faced by developing countries that are not poor enough to qualify for these programs, such as India, as well as the disciplines and areas of knowledge that are not covered by these programs (Aronson 2004).

Now some have also argued against OA by pointing out that some sensitive research material could pose a risk to the public. Controversial cases, such as the alleged link between MMR vaccines and autism, have been used as examples (Wakefield et al. 1998). We would argue that limiting access on the basis of financial resources is not an ethical but rather an expedient way to protect public interest. The public, in turn, benefits from being able to judge the evidence for themselves by reading both the original Wakefield et al. (1998) article and the evidence of fraud (Deer 2011). However, we are willing to concede that those who seriously believe that their research would cause harm if released to the public are exempt from any moral obligation to distribute their work widely. However, it is worth noting that the US and UK governments have recognized that access to health research sponsored by the National Health Institute and the Department of Health/National Institute for Health Research, respectively, should be made publicly available to health personnel and patients (NIH 2011; DH/NIHR 2011). However, the same principle applies to other fields, even if not all have such direct implications for physical well-being. As a further endorsement of the OA approach to sharing knowledge, just under 200 funding agencies and institutions (including departments and some entire universities) have passed policies calling for the deposit of at least the final draft of published work in OA archives (ROARMAP 2011).

Be that as it may, it would be unfair to characterize this as an issue of the wealthy needing to provide access to the poor, not least because much of the research that goes behind pay barriers originates in lower income countries. In the North American context, the rising costs of subscriptions are placing limits on what even the wealthiest libraries can afford (ARL 2006; K4All 2011), and students have begun to claim a right to OA research (Right to Research Coalition 2011), as too have taxpayers and patient advocacy groups (Alliance for Taxpayer Access

2011). The voices of librarians, students, patients, and scholars on the issue are a sufficient indication that there is a demand for greater access.

The university has long been regarded as a center of knowledge creation, one that has often been held to strict ethical standards. In addition, certainly when it comes to the best ways of engaging in scholarly publishing, we can accept that there will be a debate as to where the balance lies in terms of how to organize, finance, and structure this increased access to knowledge. What we cannot do is ignore the ethical dimensions of this issue. We must come to a shared understanding of what our obligations are in undertaking this research and scholarship. As we found in recent work on academic ethics, even those who are taking the lead in defining the scope of ethical matters in higher education have yet to consider the moral good to be realized by taking advantage of new technologies to increase access to research and scholarship. Our hope is that as we might move forward 'in search of the ethical university,' so that the ways and means by which we distribute what we have learned, as a matter of public trust and public good, might become more public and widely available. It seems like the right thing to do.

Notes

1. Wellen (2004, 14) calls OA advocates to task for failing to recognize that the commercialization of research itself (for example, by pharmaceuticals) is 'almost certainly a greater long-run threat to openness than today's publication system'.
2. For Nature Group, see http://www.nature.com/srep/marketing/index.html; for Wiley, see http://www.wileyopenaccess.com/view/index.html.

References

Alliance for Taxpayer Access. 2011. http://www.taxpayeraccess.org/ (accessed November 24, 2011).

ARL. 2006. *Monograph and serial expenditures in ARL libraries, 1986–2006.* http://www.arl.org/bm~doc/monser06.pdf (accessed March 23, 2011).

Aronson, B. 2004. "Improving online access to medical information for low-income countries." *The New England Journal of Medicine* 350, no. 10: 966–8. http://www.ncbi.nlm.nih.gov/pubmed/14999107 (accessed March 23, 2011).

Bailey Jr, C. 2010. *Transforming scholarly publishing through open access: A bibliography.* Houston, TX: Digital Scholarship. http://digital-scholarship.org/tsp/transforming.htm

Björk, B-C, P. Welling, M. Laakso, P. Majlender, T. Hedlund, and G. Gudnasson. 2009. "Open access to the scientific journal literature: Situation." *PLoS ONE* 23, no. 6: e11273. doi:10.1371/journal.pone.0011273 (accessed March 23, 2011).

Cahn, S.M. 2010. *Saints and scamps: Ethics in academia.* Plymouth, UK: Rowman & Littlefield Publishers.

Carr, L. and Harnad, S. 2005. *Keystroke economy: A study of the time and effort involved in self-archiving.* Technical report, ECS, University of Southampton. http://eprints.ecs.soton.ac.uk/10688/ (accessed March 23, 2011).

Davis, P.M. 2009. "How the media frames open access." *Info* 12, no. 1. doi:10.3998/3336451.0012.101 (accessed March 23, 2011).

Deer, B. 2011. "How the case against the MMR vaccine was fixed." *British Medical Journal* 342: c5347.

DH/NIHR. 2011. *DH/NIHR funded research and UK PubMed Central.* http://www.nihr.ac.uk/research/Pages/Research_Open_Access_Policy_Statement.aspx (accessed March 23, 2011).

Edgar, B.D. and J. Willinsky. 2010. "A survey of the scholarly journals using open journal systems." *Scholarly and Research Communication* 1, no. 2. http://journals.sfu.ca/src/index.php/src/article/view/24/41 (accessed March 23, 2011).

Eysenbach, G. 2006. "Citation advantage of open access articles." *PLoS Biol* 4, no. 5: e157.

Gallant, T.B., and L.F. Goodchild. 2010. "Introduction." In *Creating an ethical academy: A systems approach to understanding misconduct and empowering change,* ed. T.B. Gallant, 3–12. New York, NY: Routledge.

Gallant, T.B., and P. Drinan. 2010. "The future of the ethical academy: Preliminary thoughts and suggestions." In *Creating an ethical academy: A systems approach to understanding misconduct and empowering change,* ed. T.B. Gallant, 215–8. New York, NY: Routledge.

Harnad, S., T. Brody, F. Vallieres, L. Carr, S. Hitchcock, Y. Gingras, C. Oppenheim, C. Hajjem, and E. Hilf. 2004. "The access/impact problem and the green and gold roads to open access: An update." *Serials Review* 34: 36–40.

HINARI. 2006. "Who is using HINARI." *Bulletin of the World Health Organization* 84, no. 9: 685–764. September 6. http://www.who.int/bulletin/volumes/84/9/hinari_0906/en/index.html (accessed March 23, 2011).

Hitchcock, S. 2011. "The effect of open access and downloads ('hits') on citation impact: A bibliography of studies." Unpublished annotated bibliography. http://opcit.eprints.org/oacitation-biblio.html (accessed March 23, 2011).

K4All. 2011. "Press release—Librarians are angry and they're not going to take it anymore," February 2. http://www.k4all.ca/news/2011/02/press-release-librarians-are-angry-and-theyre-not-going-take-it-anymore (accessed March 23, 2011).

NIH. 2011. NIH public access policy details. http://publicaccess.nih.gov/policy.htm (accessed November 24, 2011)

Right to Research Coalition. 2011. http://www.righttoresearch.org (accessed November 24, 2011)

ROARMAP. 2011. Registry of open access repository material archiving policies. http://roarmap.eprints.org/ (accessed March 23, 2011).

SHERPA/RoMEO. 2011. Statistics on publishers' copyright policies and self-archiving. http://www.sherpa.ac.uk/romeo/statistics.php (accessed March 23, 2011).

Swan, A. 2007. "Open access and the progress of science: The power to transform research communication may be at each scientist's fingertips." *American Scientist*. http:// www.americanscientist.org/issues/pub/open-access-and-the-progress-of-science (accessed March 23, 2011).

Wakefield, A.J., S.H. Murch, A. Anthony, J. Linnell, D.M. Casson, M. Malik, M. Berelowitz, et al. 1998. "Ileal-lymphoid-nodular hyperplasia, non-specific colitis, and pervasive developmental disorder in children." *Lancet* 351, no. 9103: 637–41.

Ware, M. 2006. *Scientific publishing in transition: An overview of current developments*. Bristol: Mark Ware Consulting.

Wellen, R. 2004. "Taking on commercial scholarly journals: Reflections on the open access movement." *Journal of Academic Ethics* 2, no. 1: 101–18.

CHAPTER 3

Exploring the Intersections of Information Literacy and Scholarly Communication

[Two Frames of Reference for Undergraduate Instruction]

Kim Duckett
North Carolina State University

Scott Warren
Syracuse University

> *You can know the name of a bird in all the languages of the world, but when you're finished, you'll know absolutely nothing whatever about the bird... So let's look at the bird and see what it's doing—that's what counts. I learned very early the difference between knowing the name of something and knowing something.*
>
> —Richard Feynman, (2010)

> *Unfortunately, students are too often asked to use the tools of a discipline without being able to adopt its culture. To learn to use tools as practitioners use them, a student, like an apprentice, must enter into that community and its culture.*
>
> —John Seely Brown, Alan Collins, and Paul Duguid (1989, 33)

Introduction

When librarians, regardless of their professional role, hear the phrase "scholarly communication," they likely think of topics such as peer review, the journal "crisis," open access, impact factors, licensing, copyright, authors' rights, and institutional repositories. On the surface, these topics might seem far removed from what librarians think of as tenets of information literacy instruction, especially when they are working with undergraduates. Many librarians consider the one-shot instruction session as too brief to successfully engage students about the ins and outs of open access. They may regard undergraduates as the wrong audience for a discussion about the journal pricing crisis, the cost of procuring and producing information for academic consumption, and the troubling need to reduce or cancel campus subscriptions. Yet all of the scholarly communication phenomena listed above radiate from a more basic and central core that is highly relevant to the undergraduate experience in higher education: *how scholars communicate,* how they create, share, vet, discover, process, and access new knowledge. This is the basis of scholarly communication. The issues in librarianship commonly associated with that highly charged term deal with the practices and tools that support the communication processes of researchers. These are the same processes that students are asked to participate in when they must find scholarly literature and use it in their assignments in ways perceived as valuable and appropriate to the academic community.

If librarians are to help students become information literate within an academic context—one in which they must find, understand, and use scholarly sources—teaching students about how scholars communicate seems like a pretty fundamental undertaking and one that must be approached carefully. Perhaps not every topic associated with scholarly communication is relevant, but many of the central issues can be used in powerful and transformative ways within information literacy instruction. Librarians who teach undergraduates just need the right frames of reference and a common understanding of the "languages" that attach and derive from those frames of reference. Indeed, they are likely already to be using a few scholarly communication tactics and issues without labeling them as such. Often, however, librarians could go deeper—perhaps much deeper—in exploring scholarly communication issues with students in order to provide greater context for how to search and how to find by exploring "Why is it this way?"

In a recent publication, we outlined a suite of instructional strategies to incorporate scholarly communication and economic topics systematically into a one-shot library workshop (Warren and Duckett 2010). These strategies have been developed, tested, and refined through seven years of experience providing a seventy-five minute session equally divided between hands-on practice with using disciplinary databases and Google Scholar and a rich discussion of peer review, journal pricing, a research library's collections budget, open access, and more.[1]

Based on this experience, we developed a strong conviction that teaching students about scholarly communication has an *essential* place within library instruction. The students' and instructors' reception to learning about these scholarly communication topics has been so overwhelmingly positive that this work has infiltrated instruction for other contexts, including a freshman composition program and a three-credit undergraduate honors seminar at the school where this instruction model originated (North Carolina State University). Parts of this instruction model have also been used with audiences as disparate as engineering and textiles management undergraduates and education and communication graduate students. Moreover, these ideas have been presented to other librarians at conferences as diverse as ASEE (American Society for Engineering Education), LOEX (Library Orientation Exchange), ACRL (Association of College and Research Libraries), and the Charleston Conference to positive response, so we believe we are onto something.

In this chapter we will explore the essential role of scholarly communication in information literacy instruction within higher education, especially as it pertains to undergraduate students, and provide two frames of reference that can be used for thinking about the information imparted. The first of these is a sociocultural perspective that focuses on exposing the dynamics at play in the creation of scholarship. The second is an economic perspective that brings the business side of scholarly information into instruction to shed light on today's complex information landscape. Obviously these two perspectives cannot be wholly divorced from each other, and though they can be used separately, they have natural intersections as well. We will share examples of instructional contexts and strategies for which these two perspectives make sense in information literacy instruction.

Academic Information Literacy and Scholarly Communication

In higher education, library instruction is often focused on supporting students in understanding how to find, evaluate, access, and use scholarly information. In other words, the focus is on developing what Elmborg (2006) calls "academic information ... the ability to read, interpret, and produce information valued in academia"(196). From the very beginning of their academic careers, students are initiated into these practices through their course readings and research assignments. Many students are required to find and use peer-reviewed, scholarly articles written for the academic community. They are expected to write and cite like historians, sociologists, or physicists—practices that are very far removed from how they communicate in their daily lives. Of course, academic information literacy does not represent the full spectrum of what it means to be information literate, but within higher education, a great deal of attention has been devoted to it as it seems to remain a perpetual challenge for students. None of the new search tools or improved interfaces ever quite removes the barrier.

Placing boundaries around what we are describing as information literacy in the context of this article is important. Since the early 1990s, researchers have focused on literacy from a variety of disciplinary perspectives and now believe that there are many "literacies." These literacies span domains such as information literacy, digital literacy, media literacy, and visual and spatial literacy, among others, but many researchers also emphasize that literacies are given meaning within specific social groups. Many proponents of the new literacies argue that literacy is to a great extent a sociocultural rather than simply a mental or psychological phenomenon (i.e., developing a literacy is part of participating in a social or cultural group rather than something that simply transpires within an individual; see, for example, Gee 2010). Accordingly, we can view becoming academically information literate as a process of enculturation into academic and disciplinary practices, which is in line with many of the objectives of higher education.

Teaching students about the sociocultural dynamics at play in scholarship also finds support from a situative learning perspective and the concept of communities of practice, both of which hold that all learning is intimately tied to cultural and social contexts. Hence, we learn concepts and skills, not simply by doing, but specifically by doing in a way that is consistent with how the doing is done by real practitioners (in this case, faculty members). As Brown, Collins, and Duguid (1989) described in their seminal article, "Situated Cognition and the Culture of Learning," concepts are tools that are progressively learned through authentic activity. Chemical concepts cannot be truly learned by studying formulas in a textbook; they must be experienced through chemical manipulation as chemists use them in their practice. We learn the intricacies of language through its use in real social contexts rather than by studying grammar. Furthermore, they argue that learning is inevitably tied to enculturation because concepts and core skills—which they label tools—cannot be divorced from the communities of practice in which they function and have meaning. As they explain, "Because tools and the way they are used reflect the particular accumulated insights of communities, it is not possible to use a tool appropriately without understanding the community or culture in which it is used" (33).

In the context of academic writing and research, peer review (a core concept and value), journals, articles, and databases or indexes (all core tools), plus the more recent addition of repositories, should be brought into play in activities that help students better understand how the academic community produces and shares knowledge. It can be argued that the frequent requirement for students to use scholarly literature is instructors' shorthand for "Don't use Google, use the library." It may be an effort to steer students towards what instructors perceive as higher quality information. At other times, this require-ment represents an intentional desire to have students grapple with how disciplinary researchers communicate and have them emerge with an understanding that knowledge in the academy is being produced as the result of many conversations and discussions and often is not in a settled state such as textbooks present. In either case, the "peer-reviewed" requirement can leave students bewildered. As Brown, Col-lins, and Duguid (1989) warn, "Unfortunately, students are too often asked to use the tools of a discipline without being able to adopt its culture. To learn to use tools as practitioners use them, a student, like an apprentice, must enter into that community and its culture" (33). In the case of academic information literacy, without situating concepts, values, and tools within their academic cultural context, they too often remain arbitrary and disjointed for students. This is certainly the situa-tion many librarians confront when trying to gauge why students have such difficulty in transferring practical searching and discovery skills across resources, much less understanding how a library works in a holistic way.

True enculturation takes time, but if students must find, read, understand, and use peer-reviewed literature in a rhetorical style mim-icking scholars, they deserve to have these concepts, tools, and values explained to them in order to facilitate the process of becoming more academically information literate and hence better students.[2] Librar-ians are well-positioned to provide the bigger picture of how academic information is created, vetted, distributed, stored, and accessed. In aca-demia we *are* usually the most knowledgeable experts on these topics and often the only ones who see the larger context. If the disciplinary information taught by faculty is the trees, the structures that delimit how that information is shared are the forest. This bigger picture of scholarly communication can be brought down into language students can understand and into contexts that help them make sense of the requirements imposed on their assignments.

The ACRL's (2000) *Information Literacy Competency Standards for Higher Education* provide an oft-cited common framework for de-signing, implementing, and assessing instruction sessions and programs in higher education librarianship. Scholarly communication issues are right there among the standards, though the term is never used explicitly. Standard 5 describes that "the information literate student understands many of the economic, legal, and social issues surround-ing the use of information and accesses and uses information ethically and legally." The performance indicators focus attention on a range of issues important in scholarly communication—privacy, copyright, plagiarism, intellectual property, correct use of citation, and the ability to identify and discuss "issues related to free vs. fee-based access to information" (5.1–5.3). But in practice, how often do librarians bring scholarly communication topics into the library instruction classroom or even use that term in relation to their work? While the phrase "scholarly communication" may not resonate with students, citation, intellectual property, and plagiarism often do and may be incorporated into library instruction. Meanwhile, there are other "economic, legal, and social issues surrounding the use of information" that are less commonly woven into the lesson plan.

Bringing scholarly communication into library instruction means teaching students about information—what it is, how it comes to be, and the forces at play in scholarly publication. We believe that providing students with such context goes hand-in-hand with teaching the discovery, evaluation, and use of information for academic purposes. Over the past decade, librarians such as Elmborg (2006), Pawley (2003), Swanson (2004), and others (Accardi, Drabinsky, and Kumbier 2010) have collectively brought a critical approach to information literacy similar to that which has also penetrated literacy studies and education in general. At the heart of this movement is the belief that helping students become more information literate inevitably means teaching students about the social, economic, and political forces at work in the creation, evaluation, and interpretation of information. Such an emphasis is important in order to help students see information as more than simply an object out there to be discovered (Pawley 2003), which is too often the common perspective of librarians and library users alike. Information is created within social contexts and can be valued differently by various groups or individuals, including the student herself. Getting students to understand that they may actually develop a critical perspective on whatever field they are studying, and that doing so is often the mark of becoming a scholar, is a general challenge within higher education. Providing this social, political, and economic context to information literacy means telling students the "back stories" of information (Chung and Duckett 2009) in addition to teaching them to use search tools such as library catalogs, article databases, repositories, and Google Scholar.

Proponents of critical information literacy argue that standards such as the ACRL's (2000) *Information Literacy Competency Standards* may lead to an excessive focus on teaching skills related to finding, accessing, and evaluating information at the expense of teaching students about how information is intimately tied to the social contexts in which it is created and used. The ACRL standards may be useful in outlining the research process, but to echo Swanson

(2004), "Before we train students to use search tools, before we send them to books, periodicals, or Web sites, we need to teach them *about* information. What is it? How is it created? Where is it stored?" (259). Frequently in the library instruction setting in higher education, teaching about information is teaching about scholarly information and, therefore, about scholarly communication. "How" is important, but cannot be everything. "Why" has a place as well.

Two Frames of Reference

Becoming literate in the world of academia is no small feat, and too often an assumption is made that it just happens, as if by osmosis. Academic information functions in ways foreign to outsiders. The peer-review system, publication practices, and disciplinary rhetorical styles are complicated parts of academic culture that reveal subtle and not-so-subtle values and structural templates not only for understanding, but also for engaging with the world.

Understanding the social world of academic communication, discourse, and publication practices goes hand-in-hand with students developing the skills to discover, evaluate, and use scholarly information in their academic research projects. Thus academic information literacy sits on the bedrock of scholarly communication—it is completely based on how scholars create, share, and vet new knowledge, as well as their specific rhetorical and citation traditions. It requires knowledge and skill in how to discover and access scholarly information using a variety of search tools, or how to successfully engage with a library, itself a complex culture with its own internal norms and literacies. Teaching students about these social dynamics gives them greater context for understanding why instructors ask them to use peer-reviewed sources and how scholarly information comes to be. We call this social focus the *sociocultural frame of reference* for scaffolding library instruction. And again, at its heart is scholarly communication.

Additionally, as part of information literacy instruction, librarians strive to help students understand why they should use the library's article databases, indexes, journals, catalog or journal locator, repository (if one exists), and other tools. Herein lies perhaps the most powerful reason to bring scholarly communication into information literacy instruction: to expose the business side of libraries and thereby emphasize how the library's resources *relate to* and *complement* the *free* search tools students use every day—Google and *Wikipedia*. It can help them understand the value of the information available through their library and why they must often go through the hassle of using the library's website instead of Google to find what they need for their assignments. It also exposes how the for-free and for-fee parts of the Web are becoming more porous, but are certainly not yet homologous. This is exactly why sometimes one can see a message to buy an article from a publisher when using Google Scholar and not when going to the same journal via the library. More importantly, such instruction teaches students why this phenomenon occurs and what to do about it. Using this *economic frame of reference* (as simple as saying "Things cost money") can have powerful implications for teaching students the distinction between *discovery* of information (proof of publication) and *access* to information (how you get your hands on what you need). Indeed, arriving at an understanding of that simple dichotomy between discovery and access is a threshold concept for all of the work we have done in incorporating scholarly communication into information literacy.

Instructional Strategies in Practice

The Sociocultural Frame

Librarians often use the scholarly versus popular versus trade trichotomy in order to illustrate the key differences between these publication formats. Through such instruction, students may learn that peer-reviewed articles:
- are written by expert researchers
- are intended for a scholarly audience (faculty, graduate students)
- detail original research or build on other researchers' findings
- have been peer-reviewed
- contain disciplinary jargon
- provide references

These descriptions are used to help students view the scholarly article as something different from what they know from their more everyday conception of articles built from the use of magazines and newspapers. They are also used to help students distinguish a scholarly article from a popular article when they find one online.

The features highlighted in the typical scholarly/popular/trade trichotomy barely scratch the surface of scholarly communication. They touch only on rhetorical and structural issues inherent in a specific end product of scholarship—the author, audience, purpose, and writing features. Talking to students about the peer-review process, how it happens, and its role in research takes the student deeper. It begins to bring to light the person or persons involved in the process behind the end product: what each of their roles may be and why those roles exist, are valued, and came to be. The question here is how often the process is actually explained in sufficient detail to make real comprehension take place. Some instructors, forgetting what it is like to be a novice, may assume students already understand the process. They might assume the students learned about peer review in previous courses. Librarians might assume instructors have described the process to their students. In our experience, however, it is not uncommon to talk with upper-level students who need to find peer-reviewed articles, yet have no clear idea what the term *peer review* actually means; they are often unsure or simply cannot describe it accurately.

As a result, at North Carolina State University (NCSU), librarians created a short video, "*Peer Review in Five Minutes*," which highlights the importance of peer review in the vetting of new knowledge and describes how the process takes place (NSCU Libraries 2009). It begins by framing the issue in relation to how knowing about peer review affects one as a student. It asks, "Have you gotten the peer-reviewed article assignment yet? If not, you will at some point in college. Why do profs ask you to find these articles? What's the big deal with peer review? What is peer review anyway? And why is it so important?" The video outlines how researchers share their ideas from inception to publication and describes how peer review can happen not only as part of the journal submission process, but also when researchers are sharing their work through conference papers and presentations. It touches on the competitiveness of publication and the high rejection rates for top-level journals. It mentions that researchers often have to make changes or improve the article based on feedback from the peer reviewers. These issues are brought up in order to enhance students' understanding that not all articles are created equal and that researchers undergo a lot of rigorous processes behind the scenes in order to get their work into highly coveted journals. (This insight is especially important for students who are strongly considering graduate school and an academic career.)

At NCSU, this video is incorporated into the standard instruction session for freshman writing courses immediately following a breakdown of the scholarly/popular/trade distinction. It is incorporated into the libraries' information literacy tutorial and elsewhere on the library website. It is also available via YouTube and is currently used by librarians, writing instructors, and other educators across the United States and beyond.[3]

With upper-level students, murkier terrain has been explored to highlight the social dynamics at play in the publication process. Part of a professional writing course for junior- and senior-level science majors begins by asking students what they know about the importance of journal articles in scientific research based on their previous encounters with them at college. Students will often highlight that the journal article is a way for the scientists to package their research to share with others. Several students commonly volunteer that journals help with peer review, which ensures that the research quality is high. Experience bears out that upper-level students are interested in acquiring a deeper understanding of journal publishing. Instruction then reinforces that it is important for scientists to publish in the "right" journal through (1) the scope of readership, (2) exposure of his or her findings, (3) gaining tenure, (4) securing grants, and (5) general prestige for professional accomplishment. These sociocultural aspects of publication shed light on what researchers actually do and what they care about. Many of these students are considering careers as researchers or work with campus faculty in labs, so bringing this back story into instruction illuminates the "Why is it this way?" behind the articles. These issues also highlight why journal articles are treated with such special consideration in academia (especially in the STEM disciplines) and provide an important foundation for understanding the economic dynamics of publication, explored below.

The Economic Frame

As mentioned earlier, in a recent publication we outlined a suite of instructional strategies to incorporate scholarly communication topics systematically into a one-shot library workshop in order to expose the business side of libraries (Warren and Duckett 2010). The setting for this instruction is a seventy-five minute library workshop for a professional writing course at NCSU called English (ENG) 333: Communication for Science and Research. The course is a requirement for several science majors as well as a popular elective. Each semester librarians work with four to six sections of twenty-two students. The library session is equally split between a rich discussion of scholarly communication topics and teaching search strategies and techniques for using disciplinary databases and Google Scholar. Again and again while teaching this course, we have been struck by the deep engagement of these students during the library workshop. The session begins by laying down the sociocultural foundation for understanding journal articles and their prominence in scholarly communication among scientists. Then it moves into building an understanding of the business side of academic information—that journal publishers sell subscriptions to their products, and that is why you can sometimes *find*, but not *access*, scholarly articles via Google Search. From there the following points are systematically covered:

- In every field of research there are top-tier, middle-tier, and lower-tier journals that vary in how competitive it is to get published in them—just as colleges vary in how competitive they are in admissions.

- Many journals cost money (though not all do), usually much more than individuals can afford to pay.
- Journals in the science, medical, and technology fields typically cost more than journals in the social sciences and humanities, but no researcher, regardless of the field, can personally buy all the information she would ever need to use.
- Libraries act as gateways to information and sophisticated search tools like article databases (most of which cost a lot of money) for their campus communities.

The librarian then leads the students through a game-like exercise in which they guess the cost of a high-price journal such as *Brain Research* or *Tetrahedron*. When a range of guesses have been put forward, the librarian tallies up the number of students who vote for each suggested price. She prompts the students to justify their votes before revealing the current subscription price for the journal, to students' shock and sometimes outrage. Then a simple breakdown of the library's collection budget is presented, and students are asked to grapple with complex questions such as why a journal publisher can commonly charge four-figure and sometimes even five-figure prices per year for a journal and why a library is willing to pay that price—and why some journals are so much more expensive than others. The facts that journals get the bulk of most libraries' collection spending and that the aggregate figure spent *annually* is in the millions (at least for research libraries) never cease to amaze. It is not uncommon for students to express pride that their library buys so much for them and to acknowledge that they should take greater advantage of everything available to them.

Having laid a foundation for understanding the business side of information with this simple exercise, the discussion moves on to how search technologies are shaped by these economic dynamics. Using the metaphor of the Deep or Invisible Web, the librarian explores the distinctions between Google (open Web), library subscription-based resources (primarily "Deep"), and Google Scholar (where the open Web and "deeper" Web converge). These distinctions help students understand why Google cannot always provide access to scholarly articles, why you need a library to have access to portions of JSTOR or to any of Academic Search Premier, and why you sometimes see a message to buy an article when using Google Scholar. It also affords the opportunity to discuss broader—and generally troubling to students—societal implications for the cost of information through questions such as:

- What happens when you are no longer affiliated with the university?
- How can the costs of information affect access to publications at institutions without as much money as ours? How about researchers not affiliated with a university and its resources?

- How might these economic factors impact research at universities in developing countries?

Highlighting the economic forces at work in scholarly publication often allows the librarian to bring the students back around to the sociocultural aspects, thereby tying both perspectives together. She can discuss the open access movement and highlight how researchers are standing up for change. Current events impacting scholarly communication can be used to emphasize the issues at stake. For example, in spring and summer 2012 the following events provided invaluable opportunities for teaching scholarly communication in ways undergraduates could appreciate:

- the Cost of Knowledge website (http://thecostofknowledge. com), where researchers took a stand against Elsevier by publicly declaring their personal boycott of publishing, peer-reviewing, and serving on the publisher's editorial boards
- the public petition to have the Obama Administration implement policies to "require free access over the Internet to scientific journal articles arising from taxpayer-funded research" (John W. 2012)
- the debate over the Research Works Act as well as Stop Online Piracy Act (SOPA) and PROTECT IP Act (Preventing Real Online Threats to Economic Creativity and Theft of Intellectual Property Act, or PIPA), the latter of which had been publicly brought to students' attention by *Wikipedia*'s and Google's educational efforts

The second half of the seventy-five minute session is dedicated to navigating the library's website, exploring search strategies for using disciplinary databases, and exposing students to the advanced search features and setting configurations in Google Scholar. Having built a foundation for "Why it is this way," the librarian now shows how to use search tools to the students' advantage, tailoring the presentation and activities to the course assignment.

Going beyond this, more advanced relevant economic concepts such as inelastic markets and fungible commodities could be introduced to advanced students in a seminar setting and have occasionally been discussed. Librarians at NCSU have also begun to leverage the economic frame of reference, albeit in a more limited way, at the other end of the spectrum when introducing the library to freshmen through ENG 101: Academic Writing and Research, the central course in the Freshman Writing Program. Instruction sessions incorporate information about the library's collection budget as well as the costs of scholarly journals (using the sticker shock of *Brain Research's* $23,000+ price tag) to help students understand as early as possible how the library (any library, really) plays a fundamental business role in access to information and to present the library's online collection in relation to Google or the free Web. A core message is, "Scholarly information is generally expensive, and the library has to buy much of it for you. Now we will teach you to use the library's website to access it, or at least that portion of it that you cannot otherwise reach via the free Web."

The Scholarly Communication–Information Literacy Dichotomy

Having shared both the sociocultural frame of reference and the economic frame of reference and noted how they could all come together, it may be worth exploring the limits of overlap between scholarly communication and information literacy and determining what is out of scope—or is it? Indeed, while we have argued all along that there is overlap, we do not believe that every concern that occupies the scholarly communication world in fact is highly relevant to undergraduate instruction or, if shared in such a setting, would successfully impact pedagogy and lead to improved learning outcomes. For instance, we have definitely never broached topics in the classroom such as the h-index or other trends in bibliometrics, data preservation, open peer review, etc., that certainly pertain to scholarly communication. So what makes sense and what doesn't?

It may be instructive to first to look at how some other librarians view this dichotomy. A poster presented at the 2011 ACRL Conference by Catherine Palmer, Head of Education and Outreach, and Julia Gelfand, Applied Sciences & Engineering Librarian, both from the University of California, Irvine, is highly useful (Palmer and Gelfand 2011). The poster uses a Venn diagram model to look at what topics belong squarely to information literacy, what topics belong to scholarly communication, and which overlap. For instance, on the scholarly communication side of the diagram, one sees topics such as tenure, authors' rights, and accreditation. Within the information literacy circle, we see topics such as plagiarism, citation, attribution, lifelong learning, etc. The overlap includes resource sharing, economic benefit, open access, and knowledge generation. Though what is placed inside or outside the shared overlap is debatable, we believe that Palmer and Gelfand are essentially correct in constructing the relationship between these two spheres of academic librarianship as a Venn diagram. Our contention is that set boundaries are not rigidly fixed, however. As the students engaged become more advanced (honors students, seniors intending to go to graduate school, graduate students, or those in graduate seminars, for instance), the pool of "nonapplicable" scholarly communication topics should shrink. But for regular undergraduate sessions, topics like authors' rights, accreditation, data storage plans, and the preservation functions of repositories are indeed a stretch. We would be hard-pressed to claim they have a primary place in instruction. The things we should focus on, such as understanding why going through the library as a portal is so important, why one might see messages to buy articles when using Google Scholar, and why repositories and open access journals represent a portion of knowledge but that such openness is still a minority position, are topics we have mostly already mentioned and developed instructional strategies around. If time and student interest permit exploration beyond that, it is good and welcome, but not as crucial.

What Palmer and Gelfand's Venn diagram image of scholarly communication and information literacy elegantly illustrates is that scholarly communication, when more deeply explored, is a subtle field itself and has passed well beyond its early stage of just being about a journal crisis or the high prices of bundled Big Deal packages. Let us be emphatic here: scholarly communication is *not* simply about libraries having larger budgets and journals being expensive (though students do need to understand that first to understand anything else that follows). Rather it could be said to be the exploration and perhaps embracement of a series of positions relating to "rights" that pertain to information. Those rights can and generally are legally defined in contracts, but can be disputed, and what libraries do vis-à-vis online resources might be better understood as paying for rights, which allows a select campus population certain *uses* of information, not the information itself. *Access* is perhaps the fundamental use, but there are others, too.

That crucial distinction is one that has not really been explored in any meaningful way within the classes we worked with. However, we believe that the emphasis on rights is at the heart of contemporary scholarly communication and perhaps could serve as a template for encouraging librarians engaged in information literacy to become more knowledgeable about scholarly communication. Earlier we summarized some of the theoretical underpinnings of information literacy pedagogy, but there are legal, political, and economic theories that contribute to, delineate positions on, and generally inform scholarly communication as well. If a librarian who teaches considers himself a neophyte in the world of scholarly communication, reading three seminal books can rather quickly provide a comprehensive and often startlingly illuminating basis of understanding:

1. *The Access Principle* by John Willinsky (2009)
2. *Understanding Knowledge as a Commons* by Charlotte Hess and Elinor Ostrom (2011)
3. *The Wealth of Networks* by Yochai Benkler (2007)

The first argues strongly for open access for scholarly material.

The second and third describe economic, political, and legal perspectives that encourage or hinder the creation of knowledge and why it might be socially beneficial if knowledge were construed as a common good rather than a privately held and sold commodity, as well as what impact the online world has on this. Hess is a librarian, but Willinsky has a long career as an education professor studying the intersections of technology and literacy; the recently deceased Ostrom was a political scientist who won the Nobel Prize for Economics for her work on commonly held goods, and Benkler is a noted legal scholar. Therefore, their frames of reference may seem quite far removed from libraries in general, yet what they have to say does in fact resonate in the more workaday world of procuring, providing, and teaching about information in libraries. Regardless of whether one agrees or disagrees with any of their conclusions (and the above explanation is a gross oversimplification of complex ideas), exploring scholarly communication at this level is probably not appropriate for younger undergraduate students in library instruction sessions due to their lack of context, but makes sense for librarians.

The reference to disagreements within some of the legal, political, and economic discussions taking place (mostly outside the library sphere too!) brings us to another fundamental distinction between scholarly communication and information literacy. Information literacy is grounded in the present tense; even what we do in exploring ideas and not just focusing on skills is still intended to grant students a deeper contextual understanding of the library and scholarly communication world as it *presently* works so that they become more proficient at their academic tasks in the here and now. Students, after all, have rather imminent deadlines for writing and are rarely looking too far ahead.

On the other hand, the professional practice of scholarly communication and much of the deeper theoretical writing, such as the three works mentioned earlier, is generally *future*-oriented. That is, it is intended to bring about a transformation of the manner in which scholars communicate, not just explain how it happens in the present day. It often embodies an advocacy orientation, is not neutral in assumption of values, and strongly critiques market-based solutions to dissemination of academic information. In fact, for some proponents of open access, scholarly communication actually assumes a singularly teleological interpretation, which means they believe that a particular outcome *must* result, often because of changes in technology. Usually this translates to everything freely available to all online— "Information *wants* to be free." The future of scholarly communication is predetermined in such a worldview. Another, perhaps simpler analogy might be that information literacy is like a descriptive dictionary, while scholarly communication is a prescriptive one.

Regardless, by reaching this analogy, have we entered a philosophical realm too removed from the initial, practical concern for
instruction that we should never lose sight of: improving student understanding and use of the library *today* in order to facilitate academic
performance? We certainly note these deeper distinctions for the sake
of librarians rather than students. If librarians bring scholarly communication into the classroom, then being aware of the implications
of that act and thinking hard about the cultural differences between
scholarly communication and information literacy as both have historically been practiced becomes necessary for the self-aware instructor. And yet, even given that caveat lector about a dive off the cliff into
esoteric concerns in the classroom, we cannot forget that ideas have
power and thus perhaps not so much of contemporary scholarly communication lies outside of the concerns of information literacy after
all.

What all this points to is that scholarly communication itself,
as practiced within libraries, is a literacy as well, one defined, as
mentioned earlier, by its proponents and practitioners. Once enough
vocabulary and pertinent rhetorical narratives are mastered, any
librarian can become part of that community. However, scholarly communication is a bit trickier to define as a community because there are
multiple parties who have competing, or at least nonparallel, goals.
While we have mostly discussed librarians and researchers, there are
publishers, funders, vendors, etc. that also have ideas about scholarly
communication and how it should play out. For a librarian deciding
to include scholarly communication in the classroom, an important
question is whether it is necessary to adopt the advocacy voice. Or
is describing the situation enough? Should arguments from multiple
perspectives be shared? This ethical quandary harkens back to what
the librarian is trying to achieve—instruction that improves contemporary student performance by providing contextual understanding
of today's academic information ecosystem or exploring, and possibly
championing, certain desired transitional or perhaps even transformative changes in how that ecosystem functions. Can both be handled at
once? At the very least, a librarian should be aware of whether she is
making polemical assertions in a classroom as opposed to just raising
issues. It may be a fine line, but without a doubt, that threshold does
exist. Therefore, we might ask: Does it make sense to pursue these
topics along advocacy lines, especially with those students destined for
graduate studies?

Perhaps it does if we remember that the kernel of these complex
discussions is premised on certain quite simple concepts that almost
anyone can relate to (even though disagreement prevails regarding
how they should play out, or what the best outcomes might be): shar-

ing, ownership, use (and reuse), credit for creation, payment, career advancement, sustainability, etc.

Conclusion

Thus while not every topic associated with scholarly communication may be equally relevant to information literacy, many of the central issues can be used in powerful and transformative ways within instruction. In the introduction to this chapter, we described how teaching students about scholarly communication is fundamental to helping them become academically information literate and stated that with the right frames of reference and language librarians can find natural intersections between scholarly communication and information literacy. By then introducing the sociocultural and economic frames of reference, we provided two mutually reinforcing lenses that allow librarians to appropriately and effectively filter scholarly communication issues into information literacy instruction. We also provided working examples of how these frames of reference improve learning by giving students the necessary concepts they need rather than just how-to skills and how they can easily be implemented in the one-shot instructional setting. We also argued that, like any other literacy, information literacy requires not just a grammar that says what order to put the words in, but a deeper conceptual understanding of the world that the words are expressing.

The limits of how scholarly communication and information literacy overlap and some broader questions that arise from pairing these two seemingly disparate areas of practice were also explored. While a dichotomy exists, we believe there is value in instruction librarians reflecting on scholarly communication and the broader conversations taking place around it to see how readily they can adapt those topics into their own pedagogy. They may discover innovative means for doing so that we have not yet identified or even considered.

Finally, remember that right there among the ACRL *Information Literacy Competency Standards* is Standard 5, which says that "the information literate student understands many of the economic, legal, and social issues surrounding the use of information and accesses and uses information ethically and legally" (ACRL 2000). Given that standard, is it so far-fetched in the advanced undergraduate classroom to discuss ideas of information as a commonly held good or explore the legal ramifications of rights to information? Why not ask students to consider these questions of political economy as they apply to information consumed in the classroom and produced on the campus? Why not teach students that the modern library is engaged in a challenging real-time experiment about rights rather than the simple procurement of stuff—and that the outcome is far from predetermined? All of these are merely extensions of the simpler topics (peer review, finding scholarly articles, etc.) that they are already tasked with learning. Trust the student to rise to the challenge.

Perhaps the surest way to gauge whether scholarly communication makes a difference to library instructional sessions is to just ask students. For instance, following the library workshop in ENG 333, the instructor engages students with discussion board questions within the course learning management site. The following sample of student comments sheds light on their level of engagement and how they think about what they learned and provides ample proof that students are indeed willing to confront salient hot-button issues in scholarly communication.

- "How is it possible that much of the research published in these journals was published by taxpayers' money through federal grants yet publishers make it almost impossible for those same taxpayers to have access to the research they helped fund?"
- "With today's ability to rapidly and efficiently share information electronically through e-mail, websites, etc. and with companies like Google having the infrastructure necessary to, if they so please, set up a secure, all-encompassing location to publish science on the web, I don't see how scientific journals are going to survive without changing the way they do business." (both NCSU ENG 333 students, spring 2012)

Questioning is surely the beginning of knowledge, and this level of understanding can best be achieved by merging and meshing information literacy and scholarly communication. Librarians not only can, but should, build on the best theory and practice that each sphere has produced and use the results to the fullest advantage of the student learner.

Notes

1. Warren originally began teaching this workshop in 2002. He left North Carolina State University in 2008 for a collections position at the Syracuse University Library. From 2004 to the present, Duckett has been teaching the workshop. From 2004 to 2008, the authors always team-taught the instruction sessions.
2. The core assumption here, an axiom for instruction librarians, is that information literacy can improve learning outcomes.
3. "Peer Review in Five Minutes" (NCSU Libraries 2009) and other "big picture" videos can be accessed at the NCSU Libraries You-Tube channel: http://www.youtube.com/user/libncsu/videos.

References

Accardi, Maria T., Emily Drabinski, and Alana Kumbier, eds. 2010. *Critical Library Instruction: Theories and Methods*. Duluth, MN: Library Juice Press.

ACRL (Association of College and Research Libraries). 2000. *Information Literacy Competency Standards for Higher Education.* Chicago: ACRL, January 18. http://www.ala.org/acrl/standards/informationliteracycompetency.

Benkler, Yochai. 2007. *The Wealth of Networks: How Social Production Transforms Markets and Freedom.* New Haven, CT: Yale University Press.

Brown, John Seely, Alan Collins, and Paul Duguid. 1989. "Situated Cognition and the Culture of Learning." *Educational Researcher* 18, no. 1 (January–February): 32–42.

Chung, Hyun-Duck, and Kim Duckett. 2009. "Narrating the Back Story through E-Learning Resources in Libraries." *In the Library with the Lead Pipe* (blog). January 28. http://www.inthelibrarywiththeleadpipe.org/2009/narrating-the-back-story-through-e-learning-resources-in-libraries.

Elmborg, James. 2006. "Critical Information Literacy: Implications for Instructional Practice." *The Journal of Academic Librarianship* 32, no. 2 (March): 192–199.

Feynman, Richard. 2010. "R. P. Feynman on the Difference between Knowing the Name of Something and Knowing Something." YouTube video, 1:58. Posted March 15. *Have a Bit website.* http://www.haveabit.com/feynman/2.

Gee, James Paul. 2010. "A Situated-Sociocultural Approach to Literacies." In *The New Literacies: Multiple Perspectives on Research and Practice*, edited by Elizabeth A. Baker, 165–193. New York: Guildford Press.

Hess, Charlotte, and Elinor Ostrom. 2011. *Understanding Knowledge as a Commons: From Theory to Practice.* Cambridge, MA: MIT.

John W. 2012. "Require Free Access over the Internet to Scientific Journal Articles Arising from Taxpayer-Funded Research." Online petition. Created May 13, 2012. https://petitions.whitehouse.gov/petition/ require-free-access-over-internet-scientific-journal-articles-arising-taxpayer-funded-research/wDX82FLQ.

NCSU (North Carolina State University) Libraries. 2009. "Peer Review in Five Minutes." YouTube video, 5:07. Last modified January. http://www. lib.ncsu.edu/tutorials/pr.

Palmer, Cathy, and Julia Gelfand. 2011. "Information Literacy and Scholarly Communication Alignments and Disconnects: What Can We Learn?" Poster presented at the 2011 ACRL Annual Conference, Philadel-phia, PA, April. http://lgdata.s3-website-us-east-1.amazonaws.com/ docs/108/215883/2011ACRLposter.pdf.

Pawley, Christine. 2003. "Information Literacy: A Contradictory Coupling." *Library Quarterly* 73, no. 4 (October): 422–452.

Swanson, Troy. 2004. "A Radical Step: Implementing a Critical Information Literacy Model." *portal: Libraries and the Academy* 4, no. 2 (April): 259–273.

Warren, Scott, and Kim Duckett. 2010. "Why Does Google Scholar Sometimes Ask for Money? Engaging Science Students in Scholarly Communica-tion and the Economics of Information." *Journal of Library Adminis-tration* 50, no. 4: 349–372.

Willinsky, John. 2009. *The Access Principle: The Case for Open Access to Research and Scholarship.* Cambridge, MA: MIT Press.

CHAPTER 4

Theft of the Mind

[An Innovative Approach to Plagiarism and Copyright Education]

Gail Clement
Texas A&M University

Stephanie Brenenson
Florida International University

Introduction: Theft of the Mind as a Model Curriculum

This chapter presents an innovative approach to plagiarism and copyright education that invites students to explore these challenging topics in a thought-provoking, nonthreatening, and effective manner. The *Theft of the Mind* curriculum is designed to engage learners in the issues of intellectual honesty and integrity "as something that matters to them personally" rather than as matters of compliance or punishment (Brown et al. 2010, 40). The substance of *Theft of the Mind* integrates core information handling competencies from information literacy and scholarly communication but situates each lesson in popular culture or familiar media. The authors prefer the term *information handling* to describe the relationship between student and source material because it is "role-agnostic": it applies equally to students who are handling sources created by others and to students handling the works they produce themselves for eventual use by others. However, for reasons of style and text economy, the somewhat synonymous terms *source use* and *source misuse* are used interchangeably with *information handling* in this chapter. The use of movies and songs, current literature, YouTube videos, news, advertisements, etc. generates interest and demonstrates relevance of the subject matter to real life[1] while also providing a safe space in which students can consider intimidating subjects without feeling defensive (Price 2002).

At the heart of *Theft of the Mind* is a comprehensive set of learning outcomes that ask students to contemplate their roles, responsibilities, and choices as they create and disseminate projects and papers throughout the course of their academic careers.[2] The integration of principles from both information literacy and scholarly communication provides a framework for students to see themselves both as users of other people's work and as creators of new works of potential use to others. The reliance on carefully selected case studies drawn from popular culture and familiar media illuminates the range of real-life questions, predicaments, and conflicts that surround the legal and ethical use of information and culture in the twenty-first century. As students work through each case study or scenario, they explore the various stages within the creative cycle, from assignment or inspiration to completed work of scholarship or culture. In doing so, students consider the choices that authors and creators make in handling source materials (both others' and their own) and what consequences those choices have. In this way, students gain an understanding that the oft-maligned forms of "mind theft"—plagiarism and piracy—are but endpoints on a continuum between source use and misuse. Students come to see that many real-life information handling choices in the Digital Age do not quite line up at either end of the scale. Rather, the authorship choices so familiar to NetGen students—mimicking, satirizing, sampling, blending, mashing up, remixing, and transforming—fall somewhere along the continuum.

The *Theft of the Mind* curriculum was originally conceived as a progressive series of learning experiences that students would complete as part of their university education at both the undergraduate and graduate levels. To that end, a comprehensive set of student learning outcomes was developed based on information literacy and scholarly communication principles. These outcomes were then mapped to student audience level (see Appendix 4.1). Sample lesson plans were also developed to demonstrate the use of popular culture and familiar media as case studies for student exploration and analysis. (For a sample lesson plan, see Appendix 4.2).

In early 2011, the first opportunity to implement the *Theft of the Mind* curriculum arose at Texas A&M University in the form of a credit-bearing, semester-long seminar for incoming freshmen. The proposed course, "Theft of the Mind: Tales of Piracy and Plagiarism from History to Hollywood," was approved by the Associate Provost for Undergraduate Studies and added to the group of carefully selected offerings for the First Year Seminar program in the fall of 2011. After quickly enrolling its maximum of twenty freshmen, the course proceeded according to plan. This first implementation of *Theft of the Mind* provided an opportunity to test the curriculum design and to gain feedback for improving it.

The ultimate aim of this chapter is to describe the rationale and processes for developing the model curriculum for *Theft of the Mind* and then implementing appropriate elements of it within the context of a freshman seminar at Texas A&M. The materials presented in this chapter are intended as a starting point for discourse and deliberation about transforming plagiarism and copyright education on our campuses into a more meaningful, relevant, and enjoyable element of the college experience. The authors have shared the learning outcomes and some sample lessons for this curriculum in the hopes that readers will implement, adapt, assess, and further enhance the materials in their own settings, sharing alike their own results and insights.

Background: The Case for a New Approach to Plagiarism and Copyright Education

The phrase "Theft of the Mind" is a translation of the ancient Hebrew expression *gneivas da'as,* a term historically used to describe a form of stealing through deception (Fountain and Fitzgerald 2008). Rabbi Jeremy Wieder (2012), when speaking on the topic of cheating at Yeshiva University, translated the phrase as "attempting, through creating a false impression, to ingratiate one's self with someone else, presumably in the hope of gaining some favor or some future benefit" (para. 3). In applying the concept at an institution of higher learning, Rabbi Wieder explained that *gneivas da'as* can be simply explained to mean "when we take work that is not ours and we submit it in our name" (para. 14). The authors of this chapter have interpreted this explanation to embody and apply to both plagiarism and copyright infringement. In the former case, the student may gain something (a good grade, respect, additional opportunities) for something she did not create. In the latter, she may gain rewards (monetary, social) for sharing something that is not hers.

Central to the *Theft of the Mind* approach is the principle that this form of stealing is egregious as much for what it takes from the community as for what it takes from the owner. Any gain a "mind thief" achieves through his act of deception (be it monetary, reputational, or strategic) comes at a heavy price for the thief and his community—lost trust and a fractured sense of fairness. It is for this reason that the phrase *Theft of the Mind* was chosen as the name for a university-level plagiarism and copyright education program. *Theft of the Mind* reflects the special expectations placed on students as they take their place in the academy (and, by extension, in society). They are expected to make reasoned and responsible choices in all aspects of their information handling practices. The *Theft of the Mind* approach reflects the view that intellectual honesty and integrity are cornerstone principles of higher education, underpinning the entire teaching, learning, and scholarly enterprise. In the words of one American research university, the exploration and discovery of ideas, the exchange of findings, and the dissemination of knowledge are pursuits that must be based on a foundation of mutual trust and respect, enveloped in "an atmosphere of confidence and fairness" (University of North Carolina Chapel Hill 2012, para. 2).

Theft of the Mind is innovative because it departs from the generally moralistic, compliance-based forms of plagiarism and copyright education found on many campuses today. Such programs commonly take the form of prevention campaigns that teach students to follow the rules or face serious consequences. Stern messages and rigorously enforced honor codes may be augmented with technological prevention measures (for instance, wide-scale use of plagiarism-detection software or file-sharing monitors). In combination, these compliance-based approaches can be effective in notifying a large percentage of the student population about the consequences they face should they violate the code. But these approaches may not actually *reach* the students and elicit their understanding, as pointed out by college English professor Amy Robillard (2008). In "Situating Plagiarism as a Form of Authorship," she admonishes, "Lectures to students—especially first year students—likely become increasingly draconian, and students likely become increasingly immune to the warnings and threats" (27).

That is not to say that compliance with the law and with standards of ethical conduct is not critical for institutions of higher education today. Indeed, there are now a variety of requirements for integrity and copyright instruction that campuses must fulfill. Legal mandates for campus copyright instruction now come from the Higher Education Opportunity Act of 2008;[3] the Technology, Education, and Copyright Harmonization Act of 2002;[4] and the Digital Millennium Copyright Act of 1998.[5] Additionally, some regional accreditation bodies have added information ethics and law in their instructional framework (Saunders 2007). Additional impetus for training on information ethics and law is also now coming from federal funding agencies such as the National Science Foundation (2009), which requires that grant recipients "provide appropriate training and oversight in the responsible and ethical conduct of research to undergraduate students, graduate students, and postdoctoral researchers participating in the proposed research project."

An element of such agency-required training includes "Publication Practices and Responsible Authorship" and "Data Management"—two categories likely to include issues of copyright and proper attribution of research materials (TAMU 2012a).

But campus reliance solely on compliance-based training is not enough to help students develop the necessary information handling skills to succeed in the increasingly complex society of the twenty-first

century. In the words of Chris Anson (2008), writing in "We Never
Wanted to Be Cops," "A 'solution' to plagiarism that focuses primarily on policy, detection, and punishment does nothing to advance
our presumed mission, which is education" (140). Indeed, educators
concerned with providing a meaningful education that "empowers
individuals and prepares them to deal with complexity, diversity, and
change" (AAC&U 2012b, para. 1) may find that compliance-based
plagiarism and copyright training are antithetical to the core principles
of modern education. Such training demands mindless conformity to
black-and-white rules rather than spurring critical thinking to address
problems in myriad shades of gray. What's more, campus educators
may see that compliance-based programs shortchange learners by presenting the complex issues of intellectual honesty and integrity in an
overly simplistic, black-and-white manner. With regard to plagiarism,
for example, teaching students that they have to cite any source they
use unless it is common knowledge ignores the fact that what knowledge is considered common is highly subjective, varying considerably
from one discipline or context to the next. With regard to copyright,
compliance-based instruction that advises students to always ask the
owner's permission before copying and reusing source materials in a
paper gives short shrift to legitimate rights and opportunities to share
content through fair use, Creative Commons licensing, and leveraging
of the public domain.

Educators need look only as far as the campus library, where
instructional programs are being developed through the offices of information literacy and scholarly communications. By drawing together
core principles from both of these areas of academic librarianship,
today's educators can build a framework for engaging students in a
deeper understanding of, and appreciation for, intellectual honesty and
integrity. *Theft of the Mind* offers one such model for how that framework can be implemented.

Methods: Developing the Curriculum

The impetus to develop an innovative model curriculum for plagiarism
and copyright education was born out of a perceived lack of standards
in this essential area of student learning. As described below, the first
two steps in the curriculum development process (Step 1: Assessing the
Need; Step 2: Developing Student Learning Outcomes) were initiated
well before there was any expectation concerning implementation.
However, when the opportunity to design and deliver a freshman seminar arose, a third step (Step 3: From Outcomes to Lessons) was needed
to transform the learning outcomes and approaches into a course syllabus and corresponding lesson plans.

Step 1: Assessing the Need

Drawing on extensive experience in responding to student questions about plagiarism and copyright, the authors began the development of the *Theft of the Mind* curriculum with an analysis of need. Learners' needs were grouped into three primary categories:

1. What constitutes use and misuse, and who decides?
2. What are my information handling choices?
3. What are the costs and consequences of misuse?

The first category embodies student needs for clear definitions of plagiarism and copyright infringement as standards of source misuse, for clear explanations of how these standards are established and by whom, and for a clear understanding of the purpose that each standard serves. Student questions under this category typically include, "What exactly is plagiarism or copyright?" "Why should I care about these issues?" "How do I know if my use or handling of information is OK or not OK?" An important aspect of *Theft of the Mind* is that these questions are addressed not only for the benefit of information users, but also for the benefit of information producers. In doing so, this curriculum covers many aspects of copyright law that might be overlooked in compliance-based instruction, such as the right of copyright owners to transfer their rights to others (e.g., publishers) and the right of owners to reserve some but not all of their copyright rights to allow wider sharing of their works. Other more basic outcomes for plagiarism and copyright education, such as the definition of *intellectual property, common knowledge,* and *public domain,* are also located under this first category.

The second category of student need addresses what information handling choices are OK or not OK. Student questions under this category can essentially be summarized as, "How can I get my desired task done while avoiding plagiarism or infringement?" This category is where the authors place outcomes relating to the "how to" and "which style" aspects of citation. It is also where they place outcomes relating to users' rights under copyright law (e.g., exercising exemptions in the law such as fair use and leveraging public domain materials) and outcomes relating to the effect that contracts, licenses, and institutional policies may have on information handling choices. Finally, outcomes relating to authors' choices in managing their own copyrighted works also fall within this category.

The third category of student need most closely aligns with compliance-based education. The most common student concern under this category is "What happens to me if I plagiarize or infringe?" But the authors also place under this category a few outcomes that cover the costs of plagiarism, infringement, or transferring away one's copyright as borne by the community and by society. This additional aspect of the cost and consequences question distinguishes *Theft of the Mind* from many other instructional approaches.

Step 2: Developing Student Learning Outcomes

Outcomes from Information Literacy

From information literacy comes the recognition that plagiarism and copyright are equally critical concepts for students of higher education to understand, that these concepts are interrelated and sometimes overlapping, and that both fit within the larger context of social issues surrounding information use. These principles are embodied within Standard 5 of the *Information Literacy Competency Standards for Higher Education* developed by the Association of College and Research Libraries and endorsed by other higher education groups (ACRL 2000).

The plagiarism- and copyrighted-related outcomes derived from ACRL Standard 5 (and presented in Table 4.1) provide much of the framework needed for *Theft of the Mind*. Indicator 1, Outcome d, under Standard 5 ("Demonstrates an understanding of intellectual property, copyright, and fair use of copyrighted material") is sufficiently broad to encompass all of the copyright-related outcomes needed, as well the few trademark and patent outcomes included in the curriculum. This outcome is so expansive, in fact, that the authors estimated that a semester-long, three-credit course would be needed to fulfill its

Table 4.1
Learning Outcomes from the ACRL (2000) *Information Literacy Standards for Higher Education*, Standard 5, Incorporated into *Theft of the Mind*

Standard 5: The information literate student understands many of the economic, legal, and social issues surrounding the use of information and accesses and uses information ethically and legally.	
Demonstrates an understanding of intellectual property, copyright, and fair use of copyrighted material	Indicator 1, Outcome d
Legally obtains, stores, and disseminates text, data, images, or sounds	Indicator 2, Outcome e
Demonstrates an understanding of what constitutes plagiarism and does not represent work attributable to others as his/her own	Indicator 2, Outcome f
Selects an appropriate documentation style and uses it consistently to cite sources	Indicator 3, Outcome a
Posts permission granted notices, as needed, for copyrighted material	Indicator 3, Outcome b

scope. For this reason, the authors segmented Indicator 1, Outcome d, into numerous related mini-outcomes that could be fulfilled in individual sessions such as the typical one-hour class meeting, a one-shot session of course-related instruction, or a stand-alone workshop. These are the delivery formats most common among academic librarians.

ACRL Indicator 2, Outcome e ("Legally obtains, stores, and disseminates text, data, images, or sounds"), for Standard 5 is scoped to include "legal" forms of information handling, which could include not only copyright, trademarks, and patents but also materials governed by contract or license. This is therefore a particularly important outcome because so much content used and produced in academia is subject to publishers' licensing terms and conditions. Students need to understand that any rights they may have had under copyright law (including fair use) could be eclipsed by restrictions stated in the license.

Two plagiarism-related outcomes under ACRL Standard 5 needed for *Theft of the Mind* are Indicator 2, Outcome f ("Demonstrates an understanding of what constitutes plagiarism and does not represent work attributable to others as his/her own"), and Indicator 3, Outcome a ("Selects an appropriate documentation style and uses it consistently to cite sources"). Somewhat related to these in terms of learning objectives is the last outcome under Standard 5: Indicator 3, Outcome b, which covers the need to acknowledge the copyright status of reprinted work ("Posts permission granted notices, as needed, for copyrighted material").

In sum, the ACRL *Information Literacy Competency Standards for Higher Education* provide a solid framework for teaching students about the information handling choices they may make as they incorporate source materials in their papers and projects. Additionally, Standard 5, Indicator 1, Outcome d, is broad enough to also cover some choices that student authors make as they prepare to disseminate their works for use by others. Yet in their present form, the ACRL standards alone do not fully support students' roles and responsibilities as authors of scholarly works. Considering the highly active and prolific nature of the today's student researchers and creators, this gap seems like a significant oversight. It is therefore important to also draw on the principles of scholarly communication to fulfill the objectives of *Theft of the Mind*.

Outcomes from Scholarly Communication

According to the ACRL (2003), scholarly communication is "the system through which research and other scholarly writings are created, evaluated for quality, disseminated to the scholarly community, and preserved for future use. The system includes both formal means of communication, such as publication in peer-reviewed journals, and information channels, such as electronic listservs" (para. 1). While many academic libraries have established scholarly communication programs, most of the instruction in these programs has been aimed at faculty, research associates, and graduate students.[6] This unfortunate circumstance means that no student learning outcomes have been formally established in support of scholarly communication principles. The situation is beginning to change, as librarians recognize the importance of reaching this audience not only as experienced producers of digital media to satisfy course assignments, but also as researchers and published authors in their own right. Opining on this very issue in her column, "Engaging Undergraduates in Scholarly Communication," Stephanie Davis-Kahl (2012) writes:

> Undergraduate student awareness of, and engagement with, issues such as open access, public access, creator rights, and the economics of publishing should become part of our mission and vision of undergraduate education so students can become effective advocates for access to their own work, or for access to research that can aid them in becoming informed and critical researchers, consumers, and citizens. (212)

In her column, Davis-Kahl indicates that the information literacy standards are now under review, giving hope that scholarly communication principles may be incorporated into a future revision. For the present, however, the authors chose to draw on the ACRL (2003)

Table 4.2

Learning Outcomes Derived from Principles Supported in "Principles and Strategies for the Reform of Scholarly Communication" (ACRL 2003) and Incorporated into *Theft of the Mind*

Scholarly Communication Defined	Principles Supported
"Scholarly communication is the system through which research and other scholarly writings are created, evaluated for quality, disseminated to the scholarly community, and preserved for future use. The system includes… formal means of communication, such as publication in peer-reviewed journals."	• the broadest possible access to published research and other scholarly writings • increased control by scholars and the academy over the system of scholarly publishing • open access to scholarship • extension of public domain information • fair use of copyrighted information for educational and research purposes

white paper "Principles and Strategies for the Reform of Scholarly Communication" for the scholarly communication–related outcomes developed for *Theft of the Mind*. Table 4.2 represents the principles deemed relevant for student scholars.

The complete list of student learning outcomes for *Theft of the Mind*, representing both information literacy and scholarly communication principles, is presented in Appendix 4.1. It will be apparent that these outcomes reflect a range of cognitive levels within Bloom's Taxonomy.[7] This circumstance reflects the authors' expectation that achieving the higher-order cognitive objectives—Application, Analysis, Synthesis, and Evaluation—is essential to internalizing course goals, even at the freshman level. For example, the lower-level outcome "Explain what is meant by 'common knowledge' in the context of citing sources" is necessary so that students will understand that there is an exception to the directive to cite anything that they themselves did not create. This outcome may be fulfilled simply by reciting a generic definition of *common knowledge* as found on a university plagiarism site or on the pages of *Wikipedia*: "Common knowledge is knowledge that is known by everyone or nearly everyone, usually with reference to the community in which the term is used" (*Wikipedia* 2012). Yet the related outcome "Explain why the definition of common knowledge might change from one context to the next" is also essential to fill out the incomplete picture left by the lower-level outcome that established that common knowledge is community-based. The higher-level outcome requires that students think of each course they take, or each discipline they study, as a separate community, each with its own expectations and standards of what needs to be cited. Students can thus come to appreciate that they cannot be complacent in their plagiarism education after completing that initial tutorial in freshman English or reading and accepting the university's honor code during freshman orientation. Rather, they need to sustain an ongoing effort to learn the multiplicity of citation guidelines and style manuals used in each discipline in order to meet professors' expectations and perform well in each course.

Finally, as noted in the key to Appendix 4.1, the authors emphasize that the outcomes devised for *Theft of the Mind* may be applied and adjusted for any level of campus constituent: undergraduate, graduate, and even faculty. The Student Level indicator in the last column of Appendix 4.1 represents only a general recommendation as to when an outcome is best introduced, or reintroduced and refreshed. Some outcomes are recommended for introduction at a particular level in order to satisfy the various mandates and standards for plagiarism and copyright education discussed earlier in this chapter. Others are recommended for a later point of introduction, when students encounter more sophisticated assignments requiring information handling practices that could put them at legal risk: significant use of licensed source materials, inclusion of existing works into a project or paper, or distributing their works via Web-based open access publishing.

The Orphaned Outcome

Finally, it is important to recognize the one important student learning outcome that did not find representation in either set of library principles. This outcome is essential to NetGen learners who have been copying, remixing, and transforming existing works since early adolescence. For *Theft of the Mind*, this outcome is written as follows: "Explain why the concepts of 'original authorship' and 'uniquely new creation' are changing in the 21st century due to technological innovations, and that laws and standards may lag behind what is possible with technology."

This outcome was not originally considered when the model curriculum was developed, but the need for it quickly arose during the freshman seminar version of *Theft of the Mind* at Texas A&M. Students in this course continually challenged the presumption that an idea, or even a published work, is a unique asset belonging to one person exclusively. In analyzing the movie *The Social Network*, for example, students pondered the likely possibility that, on a campus where social networking apps were a wildly popular part of everyday life, unassociated students at Harvard could have conceived of different online Facebook sites "at pretty much the same time" (Ferguson 2011). In watching the documentary "Everything Is a Remix: Part 3" (Ferguson 2011), students realized that the phenomenon of "multiple discovery," a term introduced in the film to explain similar innovations that arise from different sources at the same time, was not limited to the past (e.g., in the case of Newton's and Leibniz's contemporaneous discovery of calculus, or Bell's and Gray's simultaneous patent applications for the telephone) but occurs continually in their own familiar world of YouTube videos, top forties songs, and smartphone apps.

In essence, the NetGen freshmen at Texas A&M intuitively arrived at the same point as a whole school of scholars working in the field of plagiarism education. Exemplified by Rebecca Moore Howard (1995) in her article, "Plagiarisms, Authorships, and the Academic Death Penalty," these scholars have been challenging the modern notion of "normative autonomous, individual author" (791) for over a decade. Howard's artfully articulated questions about the very meaning of authorship and the possibilities that any work is entirely original are reflected in her "Proposed Policy on Plagiarism," which opens with this statement: "It is perhaps never the case that a writer composes 'original' material, free of any influence. It might be more accurate to think of creativity, of fresh combinations made from existing sources, or fresh implications for existing materials" (789).

Affording today's students the opportunity to explore the meaning of authorship and creativity in the context of plagiarism and copyright validates their authentic experiences, eliciting their confidence and trust in the educational system. But just as importantly, it also equips them to function more effectively in a society in which laws and policy lag behind digital technology and the Internet. It may have been a fortuitous coincidence that the *Theft of the Mind* seminar first ran in fall 2011, as news feeds and comedy shows were paying increasing attention to the recently introduced Stop Online Piracy Act (SOPA) and the PROTECT IP Act (Preventing Real Online Threats to Economic Creativity and Theft of Intellectual Property Act, or PIPA). But there was no more effective teaching tool than seeing daily headlines threatening "Under SOPA, 'Justin Bieber Would Be In Jail'" (Rapoza 2012) to underscore the importance of the lessons students were engaged in as part of *Theft of the Mind*.

Step 3: From Outcomes to Lessons

Transforming learning outcomes into effective and engaging learning experiences is more art than science, and there is no one formula for success. The various factors to consider in designing each lesson include number of sessions with the students, duration of the sessions, amount of homework time available, facilities and resources available, and individual characteristics of the enrolled students (age group, level of study, major discipline selected). In the case of the freshman seminar *Theft of the Mind* at Texas A&M, lessons had to fit within the course parameters: thirteen weekly fifty-minute class meetings and thirteen weekly homework assignments of no more than three hours' duration. Moreover, an additional factor governing lesson design was the requirement that high-impact learning practices be incorporated into all First Year Seminars at Texas A&M. According to the university's Associate Provost for Undergraduate Studies, "High-impact pedagogical practices deepen learning and foster student engagement and thus lead to better outcomes. High-impact practices have been shown to go beyond grade point averages or even degree attainment in increasing undergraduate student success" (TAMU 2012b, para. 1). In the context of freshman seminars, high-impact learning involves, among other things, "critical inquiry … information literacy, collaborative learning, and other skills that develop students' intellectual and practical competencies" (AAC&U 2012a).[8]

The topics of plagiarism and copyright are natural candidates for high-impact learning. They represent both practical concerns and philosophical considerations that have direct relevance to student life. They implicitly encompass many areas of gray, requiring students to wrestle with opposing viewpoints and critically evaluate multiple possibilities. And because plagiarism and copyright exist, in part, to protect creative and commercially valuable media, these topics lend themselves to a rich variety of newsworthy and media-driven examples to pique student interest. Examples of lessons integrating high-impact learning practices into *Theft of the Mind* follow.

Sample Lesson 1

The lesson "Fair Use or Foul?" was devised to guide students through the critical-thinking process necessary to determine whether a given use of copyrighted material could qualify as a fair use. In this lesson, students analyzed a real-life case of alleged copyright infringement and determined whether the defendant's use met the standards of fair use based on a Four Factors evaluation. (See Appendix 4.2 for the corresponding lesson plan.) The infringer in question was a presidential candidate running in the primaries for the 2012 election; the infringing use was a political ad he produced using ABC News footage from the 1980 Olympics. In the ad, the candidate touts his record as a champion and hero by juxtaposing his own likeness against images of the "Miracle on Ice"—the US hockey team scoring its final upset goal over Russia. After learning about fair use and the Four Factors Test in class, students completed a homework assignment to view the political ad for themselves, read a newspaper article about the alleged infringement, and then perform a fair use analysis of the TV ad using a popular Four Factors evaluation tool (the Fair Use Checklist produced by Columbia University Libraries [2008]). The following class session was dedicated to a presentation of the students' fair use findings and a discussion and debate about the case.

This lesson elicited a high level of engagement and an impressive degree of critical thinking from the students. The results of the student's individual fair use evaluations are shown in bar graph form in Figure 4.1. This data shows that the majority of students determined the use was not fair because the politician was using the Olympics footage for personal gain when he had the funds necessary to license the video from ABC. But opposing views on this case made for a very dynamic, interesting and insightful discussion. For example, analysis of the first factor (purpose of the use) centered on the notions of "profit" and "societal good." Students who opposed a fair use finding for the politician believed that the candidate could profit from the Olympics footage by improving his image as a hero and fighter against an "axis of evil" (the former Soviet Union). They further reasoned that the reputational gain achieved from the ad could also translate into monetary profit through improved fundraising and even a hefty executive salary should the candidate's election bid go his way. Those students who argued in favor of fair use for this political ad asserted that running for, and serving as, president of the United States is a public service and that any political ad in aid of a candidate's election serves the public good. With regard to the third fair use factor (amount of the work used and its substantiality), the fair use proponents pointed to the relatively short duration of the clip used. The fair use opponents, however, emphasized that the brief clip captured the moment of victory, thereby representing the heart of the work. Finally, with regard to the fourth fair use factor (effect on the market), the fair use opponents felt that the politician had surely raised enough funds to pay fees to license the clip from ABC. The fair use proponents felt the candidate should not have to pay to use the footage.

Figure 4.1

Graph showing the results of a fair use analysis performed by students in the freshman seminar *Theft of the Mind at Texas* A&M in fall 2011. Fourteen students analyzed a real-life case of alleged copyright infringement and then evaluated the defendant's claim of fair use using the Four Factors Test required by US copyright law.

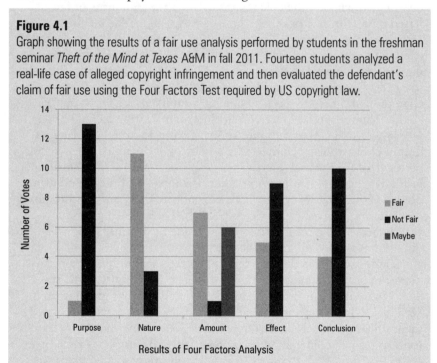

The points and counterpoints made by the students in the in-class discussion of "Fair Use or Foul?" closely resembled the kind of debates that commonly surround fair use cases. In this way, the intrinsic uncertainties surrounding fair use in real life were made real to the students, exposing them to the complexities involved in applying copyright law to everyday decision making. Additionally, students reflected on the fact that their individual political leanings could have affected their views on the fairness of the candidate's use of copyrighted material in his TV ad. This insight led to some speculation about whether the judges who rule on fair use cases in federal court can be completely objective in their decision making.

Sample Lesson 2

High-impact learning in the *Theft of the Mind* seminar was also observed during a culminating activity that took place after the copyright and plagiarism modules were concluded. In this lesson, students critiqued a popular academic integrity video tutorial—"The Dr. Dhil Show"—that contains several factual mistakes concerning the definition of plagiarism (Mezzocchi 2004). By identifying several of these errors in the video tutorial and validating their findings with other members of the class, students reinforced their newly acquired understanding of source misappropriation. They also came to recognize that not all sources of plagiarism education are accurate and complete, regardless of how popular they are on the Internet.

Because it closely parodies a familiar TV talk show, the plagiarism video is appealing to students for its humor and irony. In the video, Tania—an attractive college student with a "plagiarism problem"—is lured onto the talk show and forced to face up to her best friend, Jim, who claims his life has been ruined because of all the things Tania "took from him and made her own." The video cuts to flashback scenes depicting a series of Tania's "thefts": an essay written by Jim but copied and turned in under Tania's name, Tania's removal of several mechanical parts from Jim's car without permission, and Tania's "borrowing" of Jim's original story about cutting his face while shaving (while Jim laments that the story couldn't possibly be hers because girls don't shave!). Students were asked to reflect on each act of alleged plagiarism shown in the video and identify which ones are actual examples of source misappropriation. Most of the students in *Theft of the Mind* completed this part of the assignment perfectly.

The final component of the "The Dr. Dhil Show" assignment was more challenging, testing whether students could distinguish between an act of plagiarism and an act of copyright infringement. The students were asked to identify any and all forms of "mind theft" that occurred in the concluding scene of the Dr. Dhil video. In this scene, best friends Tania and Jim had reconciled their differences and had shared a pledge to fight the scourge of plagiarism together. They sealed their vow with the performance of a jointly created song called "Cite the Source" from their newly recorded CD *Plagiaristic Contemplation*. As Tania and Jim break into the chorus, a third friend objects to the performance as blatant plagiarism because it uses the tune of the popular song "We Are the World." Jim and Tanya quickly remedy their error by citing the source of the tune.

Only a couple of the freshmen students recognized that Jim and Tanya had infringed the copyright in the tune for "We Are the World" and that citing the source of the song would not be sufficient. Yet because they did successfully meet the challenge, they were most eager to share their understanding and insight with their fellow students. They provided a highly effective explanation of Jim and Tania's act of "mind theft," and even suggested that perhaps the class perform a Four Factors evaluation to see if they did not really need permission to adapt and perform someone else's song for their own purpose. The experience of leading the classroom discussion around "Dr. Dhil" was as impactful for the students who achieved the outcome as for the rest of the students, who improved their own understanding by learning from their peers.

Assessment of the Curriculum

As a First Year Seminar at Texas A&M University in fall 2011, "Theft of the Mind: Tales of Piracy and Plagiarism from History to Hollywood" proved to be an enjoyable, meaningful, and positive learning experience that academic administrators have recognized as having impact on student success. Evidence that students fulfilled the learning objectives for the course comes from the students' individual performances, with 95 percent passing the class. The majority of students (90 percent) achieved a final grade of B or higher. The final grade represented ten individual homework assignments, nine in-class activities, and a group project requiring a minimum of twelve hours of effort per student.

Additionally, an end-of-semester evaluation administered by the Provost's office indicated that the majority of students in the course expressed satisfaction with their course experience and felt they benefited from high-impact learning practices by improving critical thinking, dialoguing across differences, and working collaboratively on their group projects. Most students named specific activities of particular interest and benefit in their evaluations of the course, including these:

- using the Fair Use Checklist to perform Four Factor evaluations on real-life cases
- playing different roles in a "You Be the Judge"–style scenario involving a fictionalized case of plagiarism and copyright infringement on campus
- evaluating whether the trademark on Hormel's canned meat product was violated in advertisements for computer spam-pro-

tection programs and in scenes from *Muppet Treasure Island*
featuring the hairy porcine muppet named Spam
- deciding whether Facebook founder Mark Zuckerberg infringed the copyright of the Winklevoss twins, as depicted in
the movie *The Social Network*

Another qualitative indicator of success for the freshman seminar was the number of learning outcomes fulfilled by the students by
semester's end. The course design initially included only a subset of the
outcomes listed in Appendix 4.1 because of the experimental nature of
the course and uncertainties about student ability and degree of prior
knowledge. To the instructor's surprise, however, the students exceeded
expectations for engagement, curiosity, and self-directed learning. They
asked questions and spurred debate in class and shared links of case
studies and examples on the online course site. Most came early to
class to chat informally, and a dedicated few lingered after each class
session to continue discussion. Since the class ended, students have
remained in contact, asking for information about becoming a student
member of the Honor Council and asking for a reference for a summer
honors scholars program. This evidence about freshman acceptance of
the *Theft of the Mind* curriculum has prompted the authors to mark
more of the student learning outcomes as suitable for introduction at
the lower-division undergraduate level.

Moving beyond implementation as a freshman-year seminar,
evidence that the *Theft of the Mind* curriculum has promise for
more advanced students comes from numerous sessions developed
for honors undergraduates as well as graduate students. Examples
of implementations at these levels include sessions on authors' rights
and publishing choices delivered in a weekly seminar for the summer
scholars undergraduate program, for a graduate-level chemistry ethics course, and at a monthly seminar for veterinary science graduate
students. Regularly scheduled clinics on fair use, Creative Commons
licensing, and negotiating with publishers have become well-attended
offerings for students writing their theses and dissertations (as well as
their faculty advisors). What's more, the curriculum for *Theft of the
Mind* is also being adapted for other settings on campus. The United
States Electronic Thesis and Dissertation Association (USETDA) has
approved elements of the curriculum for adoption in its continuing
education certificate program Copyright Essentials for ETD Professionals. Several dozen graduate school professionals and administrators have recently completed the basic course, reflecting the fact that
a new approach to plagiarism and copyright education has benefit
not only for librarians and the students they serve, but also for other
campus professionals who are integrally involved in student writing
and publishing.

Conclusion

Theft of the Mind was designed to teach students that making good choices in information handling is important not only for their own success and well-being, but for the progress and health of their communities and for society as a whole. By affording students the opportunity to explore, discuss, and gain some comfort level with the complexities of authorship, attribution, and copyright in the Digital Age, it is hoped that they will ultimately leave campus better prepared to enter the workforce and contribute to society as effective consumers of, and contributors to, the body of human knowledge and culture.

Initial successes of the *Theft of the Mind* curriculum make evident that the subjects of plagiarism and copyright can be highly engaging and interesting to NetGen learners—young adults who have grown up in an era of information superabundance, saturated in media and adept at interacting with it in new and transformative ways. By drawing on core principles from both information literacy and scholarly communication, the *Theft of the Mind* approach invites students to more deeply understand their roles, responsibilities, *and* opportunities as both users and creators of information. Teaching with situations familiar to and preferred by the students transforms potentially intimidating or unpleasant subject matter into something far more engaging, interesting, and relevant. In this way, students gain genuine confidence and comfort in navigating the complexity of legal and ethical issues they will encounter on campus and beyond. These important competencies will help them fully participate as digital citizens within the fast-changing cultural, legal, and ethical contours of the twenty-first century.

Theft of the Mind Student Learning Outcomes

Key
Not all learning outcomes on this master list are intended for use at all levels or in all contexts.
The Student Learning Outcomes in column one have been sorted according to the Student Need category, but otherwise reflect no particular order.
The Student Need column refers to the three questions students want to answer, as outlined in the section Step 1: Assessing the Need in this chapter: 1. What constitutes use and misuse, and who decides? 2. What are my information handling choices? 3. What are the costs and consequences of misuse?
The Student Role column reflects whether the outcome is designed for the student as a user of source materials produced by others; or as an author of source materials to be used by others. This distinction is discussed in the introduction to the chapter.
The column Map to ACRL IL Std. 5 refers to the outcomes included in Standard Five, as discussed in the section Outcomes from Information Literacy in this chapter.
The column Map to ACRL SC Principles column refers to the statement "Principles and Strategies for the Reform of Scholarly Communication" (ACRL 2003), as discussed in the section Outcomes from Scholarly Communication in this chapter.
The Student Level column reflects a general recommendation as to when the outcome is best introduced (or reintroduced and refreshed), but certainly will vary according to instructional goals and student needs.
U = lower-division undergraduate; G = upper-division undergraduate or graduate student

Student Learning Outcome	Student Need	Student Role	Map to ACRL IL Std. 5	Map to ACRL SC Principles	Student Level
Explain the meaning and purpose of copyrights, patents, and trademarks.	use and misuse defined	user author	Indicator 1, Outcome d		U
Given examples of each, distinguish between a fact of nature, an original idea, and a protectable expression or invention.	use and misuse defined	user author	Indicator 1, Outcome d		U
Summarize the university's definition of plagiarism, as posted at <url>.	use and misuse defined	user author	Indicator 2, Outcome f		U
Identify one statement in the university's definition of plagiarism that you do not fully understand, and name at least one office/unit on campus that can clarify what you don't understand.	use and misuse defined	user	Indicator 2, Outcome f		U
Explain what is meant by "common knowledge" in the context of citing sources.	use and misuse defined	user	Indicator 2, Outcome f		U
Explain why the definition of common knowledge might change from one class to the next.	use and misuse defined	user	Indicator 2, Outcome f		U
Summarize the university's copyright policy, as posted at <url>.	use and misuse defined	user author	Indicator 1, Outcome d Indicator 2, Outcome e		U, G
List the "bundle of rights" that copyright owners have to control the use of their works.	use and misuse defined	user author	Indicator 1, Outcome d	Open access to scholarship	U, G

Student Learning Outcome	Student Need	Student Role	Map to ACRL IL Std. 5	Map to ACRL SC Principles	Student Level
List three categories of expression that are in the public domain and why they are not protected by copyright.	use and misuse defined	user author	Indicator 1, Outcome d Indicator 2, Outcome e	Extension of public domain information	U
List the forms of intellectual property that are eligible for federal legal protection in the United States.	use and misuse defined	user author	Indicator 1, Outcome d		U, G
Give examples of forms of expression that are not eligible for copyright protection but may be protected by trademark.	use and misuse defined	user	Indicator 1, Outcome d		U, G
Give examples of useful articles that are not eligible for copyright protection but may be protected by a patent.	use and misuse defined	user	Indicator 1, Outcome d		U, G
Identify a credible source on campus for guidance on plagiarism avoidance.	use and misuse defined	user	Indicator 2, Outcome f		U, G
Identify a credible source on campus for guidance on infringement avoidance.	use and misuse defined	user	Indicator 2, Outcome e		U, G
Explain why the concepts of "original authorship" and "uniquely new creation" are changing in the 21st century due to technological innovations, and that laws and standards may lag behind what is possible with technology.	use and misuse defined	user	Orphaned Outcome! (See the section The Orphaned Outcome in the chapter for discussion.)		U, G
Demonstrate how to cite a source used in a paper or project, following an assigned style guide.	info-handling choices	user	Indicator 3, Outcome a		U

Student Learning Outcome	Student Need	Student Role	Map to ACRL IL Std. 5	Map to ACRL SC Principles	Student Level
Demonstrate how to acknowledge an idea or story contributed by someone else and used in a student paper or project.	info-handling choices	user	Indicator 3, Outcome a		U
When provided a webpage, determine whether the source is copyrighted or not.	info-handling choices	user	Indicator 1, Outcome d		U
When obtaining an electronic resource from the library, from a Web service, or from a computer/phone app, determine whether it is subject to licensing terms and conditions.	info-handling choices	user	Indicator 2, Outcome e	Broadest possible access to published research and other scholarly writings	U, G
Give an example illustrating when a student must ask permission to include a copyrighted work in his assignment.	info-handling choices	user	Indicator 1, Outcome d		U, G
Give two examples of fair use of copyrighted works and explain why they are fair.	info-handling choices	user	Indicator 1, Outcome d	Fair use of copyrighted information for educational and research purposes	U, G
Explain why a source that is free of copyright restrictions still needs to be cited if used in a paper or project.	info-handling choices	user	Indicator 1, Outcome d		U, G

Student Learning Outcome	Student Need	Student Role	Map to ACRL IL Std. 5	Map to ACRL SC Principles	Student Level
Given a sample student paper that incorporates copyrighted material used with permission, insert a proper permission-granted notice in the appropriate spot in the document.	info-handling choices	user	Indicator 2, Outcome b		U, G
Given a sample student paper that incorporates copyrighted material distributed with a Creative Commons license, insert a proper attribution for the included material.	info-handling choices	user	Indicator 3, Outcome b		U, G
Using the Fair Use Checklist, perform a Four Factor analysis to determine if using a copyrighted work meets the standard for the fair use exemption.	info-handling choices	user	Indicator 1, Outcome d	Fair use of copyrighted information for educational and research purposes	U, G
Articulate the reason why citing a source excerpted at length in a student paper is not enough to fulfill legal requirements.	info-handling choices	user	Indicator 1, Outcome d Indicator 3, Outcome b	Fair use of copyrighted information for educational and research purposes	U, G
List two benefits of registering a copyrighted work with the US Copyright Office.	info-handling choices	author	Indicator 1, Outcome d		G
Explain how an author/creator gets her work protected by copyright.	info-handling choices	author	Indicator 1, Outcome d		U, G
Determine copyright ownership for a student project developed collaboratively.	info-handling choices	author	Indicator 1, Outcome d		G

Student Learning Outcome	Student Need	Student Role	Map to ACRL IL Std. 5	Map to ACRL SC Principles	Student Level
Describe an example where a university policy controls how a student must distribute his copyrighted work.	info-handling choices	author	Indicator 2, Outcome e	Broadest possible access to published research and other scholarly writings Increased control by scholars and the academy over the system of scholarly publishing	U, G
Demonstrate how to affix a copyright notice to a textual work	info-handling choices	author	Indicator 1, Outcome d		U, G
Demonstrate how to affix a Creative Commons license to a textual work.	info-handling choices	author		Open access to scholarship	G
List the types of content licenses available through Creative Commons and what uses are allowed under each license.	info-handling choices	author		Open access to scholarship	G
Describe what an open access journal is and what the benefits are to users of these publications.	info-handling choices	user author	Indicator 1, Outcome b	Open access to scholarship	U, G
Describe the benefits of publishing an article in an open access journal.	info-handling choices	user author		Broadest possible access to published research and other scholarly writings	G

Student Learning Outcome	Student Need	Student Role	Map to ACRL IL Std. 5	Map to ACRL SC Principles	Student Level
List two sanctions a student may face if found to have plagiarized.	costs and consequences	user	Indicator 2, Outcome f		U, G
List two legal consequences a student may face if found to have infringed copyright.	costs and consequences	user	Indicator 1, Outcome d		U
Articulate the cost borne by a community from an act of plagiarism.	costs and consequences	user	Indicator 2, Outcome f		U
Articulate the cost borne by society from an act of copyright infringement.	costs and consequences	user	Indicator 1, Outcome d		U
Articulate the cost borne by society from an act of transferring copyright to a publisher.	costs and consequences	author	Indicator 1, Outcome d	Broadest possible access to published research and other scholarly writings	G

APPENDIX 4.2

Theft of the Mind Sample Lesson Plan

 **TEXAS A&M** UNIVERSITY **Lesson Plan**

Course Information	*Theft of the Mind: tales of piracy and plagiarism from headlines to Hollywood* UGST 181-517. Fall 2011
Lesson name	Fair use or Foul?: Was Pawlenty's Use of Olympic Footage an Infringement
Lesson delivered date(s):	

Description of Lesson:

Students individually analyze a real-life case of alleged copyright infringement where the defendant claims his use was Fair. Based on news reports of the case and a screening of the actual commercial containing the allegedly infringing material, students perform a four factors analysis and decide if they believe the use is fair.

They compare their findings with classmates and defend their positions in class.

Student Learning Outcome(s) Addressed in this Lesson

- List two examples of Fair Use of copyrighted works and why they are Fair.
- Gain practice using a Four Factor analysis to determine if using a copyrighted work meets the standard for the Fair Use exemption

Resources Needed

Article "ABC Sports says Pawlenty violated copyright with 'Miracle on Ice' footage" *Iowa Caucuses website*, Online, URL: abc-sports-says-pawlenty-violated-copyright-with-miracle-on-ice-footage

Video (approx. 30 seconds) "TV Ad: The American Comeback," Online, URL: http://youtu.be/a5q1RmQQEso

Fair Use Checklist from Columbia Copyright Advisory Office, Online, URL: http://copyright.columbia.edu/copyright/files/2009/10/fairusechecklist.pdf. [NOTE: handed out in class under Fair Use's provision for making multiple —download additional copies yourself if needed]

In-Class Activity/ies	Out of Class Activity/ies
• Turn in completed Fair Use Checklist • Screen video in class • Project Fair Use Checklist on screen and review each factor together. Allocate approx. 30 minutes to cover each factor and allow students to discuss and debate • Project bar graph showing results of evaluations. Question to class: why do you think the results are mixed?	• Read assigned article • Watch assigned video • Perform Four factors evaluation using Fair Use Checklist. Fill in relevant boxes on form and write findings (Fair | Infringement) at the top of the form • E-mail results of Fair use evaluation to professor by deadline

Take-home messages to offer at conclusion of class

- Fair use can be risky—the only findings that matter are the judge's ruling
- Options to avoid risk?
- Ask permission.
- Use material that does not present copyright issues
  — Material you make yourself
  — Material already licensed for your use
  — Material that is in the public domain

Assessment Method

- Timely completion and submission of e-mail reporting results of Fair Use evaluation
- Timely completion and submission of Fair Use Checklist at beginning of class
- Participation in in-class review and discussion of Four Factors evaluation

Notes on Improving this Lesson for next time

For in-class review and discussion of four factors analysis, use clickers in order to

- Anonymize each student's findings
- Also ask students to key in their political affiliation or leanings

Ask class if they think a Fair Use evaluation could be influenced by bias on the part of the judge?

Notes

1. For more information, see Springer and Yelinek 2011 and Ariew and Runyan 2006.
2. The learning outcomes developed for *Theft of the Mind*, along with a sample lesson plan, are provided at the end of the chapter in Appendices 4.1 and 4.2, respectively. The authors encourage readers to adapt, expand on, and assess the curriculum in their own campus settings, with the hope that any resulting materials will be shared alike.
3. Pub. L. No. 110-315, 122 Stat. 3078.
4. Pub. L. No. 107-273, 116 Stat. 1758.
5. Pub. L. No. 105-304, 112 Stat. 2860; for more information about legal mandates for campus copyright instruction, see Gilliland and Clement 2012.
6. For more information, see Newman, Bleic, and Armstrong 2007.
7. For more information about Bloom's Taxonomy, see UNC Charlotte 2012.
8. For more on high-impact practices in higher education at Texas A&M, see TAMU 2012b; for more information about research into high-impact practices, see AAC&U 2012a.

References

AAC&U (Association of American Colleges and Universities). 2012a. "High-Impact Educational Practices: A Brief Overview." Excerpt from Kuh 2008. Accessed November 30. http://www.aacu.org/leap/hip.cfm.

———. 2012b. "What Is a 21st Century Liberal Education?" Accessed November 30. http://www.aacu.org/leap/What_is_liberal_education.cfm.

ACRL (Association of College and Research Libraries). 2000. *Information Literacy Competency Standards for Higher Education.* Chicago: ACRL, January 18. http://www.ala.org/acrl/standards/informationliteracycompetency.

———. 2003. "Principles and Strategies for the Reform of Scholarly Communication 1." ACRL. June 24. http://www.ala.org/acrl/publications/whitepapers/principlesstrategies.

Anson, Chris M. 2008. "We Never Wanted to be Cops: Plagiarism, Institutional Paranoia, and Shared Responsibility." In Howard and Robillard 2008, 140–157.

Ariew, Susan, and Heather Runyan. 2006. "Using Scenarios to Teach Undergraduates about Copyright, Fair Use, and Plagiarism." Presentation at the 34th Annual LOEX Conference. College Park, MD, May 4–6,

2006. http://www.emich.edu/public/loex/handouts/slides2006.html.

Brown, Malcolm, Mark Auslander, Kelly Gredone, David Green, Bruce Hull, and Walt Jacobs. 2010. "A Dialogue for Engagement." *EDUCAUSE Review* 45, no. 5 (September/October): 38–56. http://www.educause. edu/ero/article/dialogue-engagement.

Columbia University Libraries. 2008. "Fair Use Checklist." Most recent revision May 14. http://copyright.columbia.edu/copyright/files/2009/10/ fairusechecklist.pdf.

Davis-Kahl, Stephanie. 2012. "Engaging Undergraduates in Scholarly Communication: Outreach, Education and Advocacy." *College & Research Libraries News* 73, no. 4 (April): 212–222. http://crln.acrl.org/content/73/4/212.full.

Ferguson, Kirby. 2011. "Everything Is a Remix: Part 3: The Elements of Creativity." Vimeo video. http://www.everythingisaremix.info/watch-the-series.

Fountain, T. Kenny, and Lauren Fitzgerald. 2008. "'Thou Shalt Not Plagiarize'? Appealing to Textual Authority and Community at Religiously Affiliated and Secular Colleges." In Howard and Robillard 2008, 101-123.

Gilliland, Anne, and Gail Clement. 2012. "Copyright Education Approaches for Our Campus Constituencies." Panel presentation at 2012 CIP Biennial Symposium: Adventures in Copyright. Baltimore, University of Maryland University College, Center for Intellectual Property, June 6–8, 2012.

Howard, Rebecca Moore. 1995. "Plagiarisms, Authorships, and the Academic Death Penalty." *College English* 57, no. 7 (November): 788–806.

Howard, Rebecca Moore, and Amy E. Robillard, eds. 2008. *Pluralizing Plagiarism: Identities, Context, Pedagogies.* Portsmouth, NH: Boyton/ Cook.

Kuh, George D. 2008. *High-Impact Educational Practices: What They Are, Who Has Access to Them, and Why They Matter.* Washington, DC: Association of American Colleges and Universities.

Mezzocchi, Jared. 2004. "Dr. Dhil Show" [Plagiarism]. Online video. Directed by Jared Mezzocchi and Brian Merry. Fairfield University Media Center. http://www.staff.fairfield.edu/sevans/qtl/dr_dhil.qtl.

National Science Foundation. 2009. "Responsible Conduct of Research." 74 Fed. Reg. 42126 (August 20). http://www.gpo.gov/fdsys/pkg/FR-2009-08-20/html/E9-19930.htm.

Newman, Kathleen A., Deborah D. Blecic, and Kimberly L. Armstrong. 2007. "Executive Summary." In *Scholarly Communication Education Initiative: SPEC Kit 299,* 11–17. Association of Research Libraries. http://publications.arl.org/Scholarly-Communication-SPEC-Kit-299.

Price, Margaret. 2002. "Beyond 'Gotcha!': Situating Plagiarism in Policy and Pedagogy." *College Composition and Communication* 54, no. 1 (September): 88–115.

Rapoza, Kenneth. 2012. "Under SOPA, 'Justin Bieber Would Be In Jail.'" *Forbes*. January 20. http://www.forbes.com/sites/kenrapoza/2012/01/20/under-sopa-justin-beiber-would-be-in-jail.

Robillard, Amy E. 2008. "Situating Plagiarism as a Form of Authorship." In Howard and Robillard 2008, 27–42.

Saunders, Laura. 2007. "Regional Accreditation Organizations' Treatment of Information Literacy: Definitions, Collaboration, and Assessment." *Journal of Academic Librarianship* 33, no. 3 (May): 317–326.

Springer, Amy, and Kathryn Yelinek. 2011. "Teaching with the Situation: Jersey Shore as a Popular Culture Example in Information Literacy Classes." *College & Research Libraries News* 72, no. 2 (February 12): 78–80, 85, 118.

TAMU (Texas A&M University). 2012a. "CITI [Collaborative Institutional Training Initiative] Course in the Responsible Conduct of Research." Accessed June 29 (requires Texas A&M login). http://rcb.tamu.edu/more/otherprograms/rcr/responsibleconduct.

———. 2012b. "High Impact Practices in Undergraduate Education." Undergraduate Studies. Accessed June 29, 2012. http://us.tamu.edu/for-faculty/high-impact-practices-in-undergraduate-education.

UNC (University of North Carolina) Chapel Hill Graduate School. 2012. "Academic Integrity and Ethics." Accessed June 28. http://gradschool.unc.edu/publications/ethics.html#intro.

UNC (University of North Carolina) Charlotte. 2012. "Bloom's Taxonomy of Educational Objectives." Center for Teaching & Learning. Accessed June 30, 2012. http://teaching.uncc.edu/articles-books/best-practice-articles/goals-objectives/blooms-taxonomy-educational-objectives.

Wieder, Jeremy. 2002. "A Rosh Yeshiva's Response to Cheating." *The Commentator* 67, no. 4 (November 10). http://commie.droryikra.com/v67i4/oped/cheating.html.

Wikipedia. 2012. "Common Knowledge." Last modified November 27. http://en.wikipedia.org/wiki/Common_knowledge.

CHAPTER 5

Scholarly Communication for Credit

[Integrating Publishing Education into Undergraduate Curriculum]

Isaac Gilman
Pacific University

Introduction

As academic libraries place increased emphasis on educating students and faculty about issues related to scholarly publishing, it has become clear that workshops, events, and even course-integrated instruction are often not enough to fully engage students and faculty. To be most effective, scholarly communication education should be integrated into the formal academic life—and mission—of an institution and must offer tangible benefits to students and faculty. For most institutions (especially those with an emphasis on liberal arts), the core mission centers around the teaching and learning experience: in other words, the classroom and the curriculum. In order for scholarly communication to be recognized as anything more than an optional adjunct to this mission, it must become a regular part of the curriculum. A practical way to accomplish this is by strategically developing credit-bearing courses and programs that simultaneously support the goals of the academic departments and educate students about scholarly communication issues. At Pacific University, library faculty developed a course on scholarly journal publishing for undergraduates and collaborated with academic faculty to create a new academic minor in editing and publishing.

Publishing Practices in Undergraduate Coursework

Integrating information about the scholarly publishing process into academic coursework is already recognized as a vital component in preparing undergraduates to be more effective researchers, to be more successful in graduate work, and to be contributing scholars within their respective disciplines. In a study of undergraduate science students, Tenopir et al. (2003) noted that educating students about the mechanics of publishing, particularly peer review, can help students grasp the importance of using peer reviewed articles to inform their own research. Tang and Gan (2005) emphasize that familiarity with the nature of scientific literature and the peer review process (in this case, for grants) is also vital preparation for graduate research activities, and the authors created a course for senior undergraduates to focus on these topics. For similar reasons, Guildford (2001) successfully used practical exercises to teach undergraduate engineering students about author guidelines and the peer review process.

While attention is certainly paid to educating students about the mechanics of preparing manuscripts for publication and participating in the peer review process, there are fewer examples of courses dedicated to providing students with a more comprehensive picture of scholarly publishing. One of the strongest case studies presented in the literature is provided by Jones et al. (2006), who developed a course on scientific publishing for undergraduate neuroscience majors. As the authors note, "The processes of peer reviewing, editing, and publishing, [are] largely invisible to students," and the course was designed to educate students about *all* aspects of publishing, "from the practical issues to the philosophical challenges" (A60). The specific topics addressed in their curriculum allow students to engage in the complex issues of the formal scholarly communication system: editing methods, ethics in scientific communication, open access publishing, impact factor and h-index, the role of undergraduate journals, the role of English in global science, scientific misconduct/peer review, scientific lay publishing, alternative media, and website design (A61). During the course, students also have the opportunity to review and edit manuscripts that have been submitted to the school's undergraduate journal, *IMPULSE*.

In the discussion of their motivation for this course, Jones et al. (2006) make a connection between the growing emphasis on undergraduate research and the need for students to be educated about the means through which research is formally shared (i.e., publishing). Indeed, if undergraduate colleges and universities want to devote resources to building a robust infrastructure for undergraduate research and scholarship, it is only logical that such a program should require students to engage with the issues and practices that directly affect the ability of their future work to have the greatest impact possible. Furthermore, Davis-Kahl (2012) observes, "Undergraduates … have an important role to play as future graduate students, scholars, and as citizens" (212). Educating students not only about peer review and manuscript preparation, but also about the importance, opportunities, and challenges of the scholarly communication system will best prepare them for these roles.

Pacific University and Scholarly Communication

Pacific University (Forest Grove, Oregon) is a prime example of an institution with a growing emphasis on undergraduate research and scholarship. Pacific University, founded in 1849, is a small private university with a strong tradition of both liberal arts education and graduate professional education in health care and teaching. Within the past four years, the university has created both a Research Office (headed by a Vice Provost for Research) and a Director of Undergraduate Research position (held by a full-time faculty member). While faculty members within the undergraduate College of Arts and Sciences are supportive of this growth in undergraduate research activities, many also feel strongly that the primary emphasis of the institution should remain on teaching.

Accordingly, as the Pacific University Library has developed its scholarly communication program, it has been a goal of the library to explicitly connect its services and initiatives (e.g., journal publishing) both to the scholarly and research aspirations of the university and to its traditional teaching and learning mission. Connecting scholarly communication services and content directly to undergraduate curriculum not only provides an expanded opportunity for education and advocacy, but also increases the likelihood that undergraduate faculty will view the content and issues as worthy of time and discussion.

The most direct and meaningful way to integrate any topic into the curriculum is to develop a new course devoted to that topic. The subject of scholarly journal publishing was selected because it could be directly connected to the library's services and because it offered a context in which issues relevant to scholarly communication could be discussed. The course content also provides useful knowledge for students who are interested either in publishing careers or in graduate education that will require engagement with the scholarly publishing environment.

Shortly after the scholarly publishing course—Introduction to Scholarly Journal Publishing—was first offered within the college, library faculty began to investigate additional ways that the library's publishing services (and now, the publishing course) could further support the teaching and learning mission of the college. Discussions with English department faculty led to the collaborative development of an academic minor in editing and publishing, a multidisciplinary program that includes courses from English, media arts, art, and business. The mix of required coursework has strong ties to the traditional liberal arts (e.g., an English course on major writers and their contemporaneous publishing practices) and to practical skills (e.g., copyediting and web design). One of the courses included in the minor is the library's scholarly publishing course.

As the following discussion will demonstrate, both the minor in editing and publishing and the journal publishing course have served to embed scholarly communication into the undergraduate curriculum, to provide new roles for the library in supporting undergraduate learning, and to give students opportunities to gain knowledge and skills that will serve them in future academic or professional careers.

Minor: Editing and Publishing

Although the university library's publishing program is a relatively recent development, there is a strong publishing culture at Pacific University, both within an on-campus center (the Berglund Center for Internet Studies) and in academic departments. One of the most notable examples is within the department of English, which publishes a professional literary magazine, *Silk Road*. The magazine is edited by English faculty, but is largely staffed by graduate and undergraduate students, who manage most aspects of the publication. Undergraduates working on the magazine are enrolled in a one-credit, semester-long course, Literary Magazine Production. Many students who have been involved with the magazine have gone on to graduate programs in publishing or to employment in the publishing field.

Apart from the literary magazine production course—and now the scholarly journal course, which will be discussed shortly—there has not been a formal mechanism in place at Pacific University to provide interested students with additional education related to careers in editing and publishing. The library's promotion across campus of its publishing services and publishing course led to discussions with English department faculty as to how the two units could collaborate to coordinate editing and publishing resources (e.g., academic advising, career guidance, and coursework) for undergraduate students. Library and English department faculty developed an internal grant proposal, which resulted in the creation of the Editing and Publishing Center, a virtual home for the collaboration.[1] The purpose of the center is to connect students with existing opportunities at Pacific University (e.g., internships in the library, Berglund Center, or University Relations; the literary and scholarly publishing courses; etc.) and to cultivate expanded options for education and skill building (e.g., courses and external internships).

A shared vision of the faculty involved in the Editing and Publishing Center project was the creation of a formal academic program that would offer students recognition for coursework and internships related to editing and publishing. No similar program existed in the region, though we were able to identify limited instances across the country: for example, at California State University, Chico, and Florida State

University. However, many programs that were identified are certificate programs or are for graduate or professional students only. After evaluating potential comparable programs, the following rationale for the creation of a minor in editing and publishing was identified:

- Specialized education and experience are necessary for students who may be interested in careers in editing and publishing.
- Students who have no career interest in editing and publishing, but who may pursue graduate or academic careers, will benefit from knowledge of the publishing process and industry.
- Coursework in writing, editing, and publishing will reinforce effective communication skills and will support the growing undergraduate research program.
- Editing and publishing knowledge and skills will be a practical complement to many academic majors, from business to English literature and beyond.
- The minor program will build on existing strengths of Pacific University and distinguish us from peer institutions that lack similar offerings.
- Student retention will be positively impacted by offering coursework, experiential learning, and mentoring relationships in connection to a career (for interested students).
- The "applied arts" nature of the program will be attractive to prospective students and parents who may have concerns about the employment prospects of traditional liberal arts graduates.

During development of the academic minor proposal, discussions frequently touched upon the concept of "applied arts," which is simultaneously seen as a positive and a negative by various stakeholders on campus. Some faculty are understandably protective of the traditional liberal arts curriculum and are wary of diluting the strength of that model through the addition of programs that are "professional" in nature. At the same time, however, Pacific University already provides opportunities for students to experience the liberal arts curriculum while also preparing for professional careers, primarily in education and the health professions. To address concerns about adding another program (even a minor) with a focus on professional preparation, in the minor program proposal, we presented the minor as an opportunity to educate professionals who would also possess the knowledge and skills inherent in a liberal arts program:

> The Minor in Editing and Publishing will build on this strength by educating editing/publishing professionals within the context of a curricular experience that fosters critical thinking, creativity, adaptability and understanding of diverse perspectives. Students in a wide variety of disciplines, with either a creative or a scholarly focus, will

> benefit from participation in the minor, and will be pre-
> pared for either graduate study or professional success.

Although the stated curricular objectives of the minor are largely
skill-based (see Table 5.1), a new course was also proposed as part
of the curriculum that tied the minor more explicitly to the liberal
arts emphasis of the English department (the sponsoring department
for the minor). The course, Literature and Publishing: Special Topics,
examines a major author within the context of his or her contemporaneous publishing practices. For example, a section of the course that
focuses on Emile Zola or Charles Dickens might examine serial publication and its impact on nineteenth-century fiction and novels.

Table 5.1

Minor in Editing and Publishing—Program Objectives

The primary objective of the Minor in Editing and Publishing is to educate students about the theories and practices of editing and publishing. Upon completion of the minor, students should be able to:

- Understand and articulate the publication process, from initial manuscript submission to final publication, for both monographic and serial publications.

- Distinguish between, and describe the relative benefits of, different publishing models (in terms of both format and economics).

- Understand the legal relationships between author, publisher and reader in order to protect their own intellectual property rights as authors and to respect others' rights.

- Understand the process for selecting, editing and preparing manuscripts for publication.

- Distinguish between, and perform, developmental editing, substantive editing, copyediting and proofreading.

- Demonstrate competence in utilization of relevant technology: editorial management platforms, design software and web editing software.

- Articulate a marketing strategy appropriate to different types of publications.

Minor Curriculum

Though new courses are included in the course of study, the minor is
largely a formal coordination of courses that already existed within
the College of Arts and Sciences. Courses from the departments of
art, business, English, and media arts are all included (see Table 5.2),
providing students with multidisciplinary elective options. While some

students may not be interested in business courses, including electives like Marketing or Advertising and Promotion makes it easier for business majors to complete the minor and gives other students the option of learning business practices that are vital for the publishing industry.

Table 5.2
Minor in Editing and Publishing—Curriculum

Required Courses		
ENGW-203*	Professional Writing and Editing	4.00 credits
MEDA-122	Introduction to Digital Media	2.00 credits
MEDA-363	Publication Editing & Design	4.00 credits
ENGW-475*	Editing Practicum	2.00 credits
Required Elective Students must take at least one of the following courses. NOTE: Some courses have pre-requisites.		
MEDA-364	Introduction to Scholarly Journal Publishing	2.00 credits
ENGW-300*	Book Editing, Design and Production	2.00 credits
ENGW-466	Literary Magazine Production	2.00 credits
Elective Courses Students must take at least 8 credits from the following courses. NOTE: Some courses have pre-requisites.		
ARTST-239	The Artist Book I	4.00 credits
ARTST-339	The Artist Book II	4.00 credits
BA-309	Marketing	4.00 credits
BA-410	Marketing Research	4.00 credits
BA-440	Advertising and Promotion	4.00 credits
ENGL-431*	Literature & Publishing: Special Topics	4.00 credits
ENGW-300*	Book Editing, Design, and Production	2.00 credits
ENGW-466	Literary Magazine Production	2.00 credits
MEDA-150	Pacific Index (Student Newspaper)	1.00 credits
MEDA-265	Web Design	4.00 credits
MEDA 364	Introduction to Scholarly Journal Publishing	2.00 credits
MEDA-450	Pacific Index-Management	2.00 credits

Two of the most significant new additions are the courses related to book publishing and the practicum requirement. Book editing and production have many characteristics that are unique (in comparison to serial publishing), and adding appropriate coursework to address this type of publication is key to providing a comprehensive publishing education. Furthermore, the structure of the minor allows students to informally select a "track" and focus on the type of publishing that interests them the most: book, literary magazine, or scholarly journal. In addition, the practicum requirement ensures that students receive hands-on experience and possess more than a theoretical knowledge of publishing practices. Beyond the general hour requirement for the practicum, students will be able to select a setting that is of the greatest interest to them, whether that is a literary magazine, a graphic novel publisher, a university press, or a commercial publisher.

Next Steps

The College of Arts and Sciences faculty approved the Minor in Editing and Publishing in the spring of 2012, and students are able to begin applying credits toward the minor requirement in the fall of 2012. It is important to note that not every new course approved as part of the minor will be available in the 2012–2013 academic year; taking in account existing faculty teaching loads and the need to hire additional adjunct faculty, the book publishing courses will likely not roll out until the 2013–2014 academic year.

A key component of growing the minor is the development of relationships with potential practicum sites for students. The Portland metropolitan area is home to a number of small publishing houses, as well as larger companies like Dark Horse Comics, so there are ample opportunities for student interested in literary fiction. The most challenging area to provide students with local experience is within scholarly publishing. Certainly, the Pacific University Library's own publishing program is one opportunity, but we are also trying to establish connections with the few university presses in the area, in both Washington and Oregon. For students who are willing and able to undertake practica at sites across the country, there are obviously more options.

Course: Introduction to Scholarly Journal Publishing

Though not a practicum site, one scholarly publishing–related option close to home is the library's scholarly journal publishing course. An initial impetus for developing the course was to provide a mechanism to train student editors and reviewers to work with the undergraduate journal founded by faculty from Pacific University and from Central Washington University and published by the university library. Dependent on student availability and interest, the course may also be used in the future to train students to work in support of the library's other publications. This model, of providing undergraduates opportunities to work on both student and scholarly publications (which is not to say that student journals are not capable of being as scholarly as those in which faculty publish), has been applied successfully at other institutions: the *Xchanges* journal project at New Mexico Tech (Boles and Newmark 2011), *Young Scholars in Writing* at the University of Missouri–Kansas City, Illinois Wesleyan University's work with its *Undergraduate Economic Review* and economics capstone students (Davis-Kahl 2012), and the opportunities for students with the Southeast Missouri State University Press.

While cultivating student editorial support for local journals was an initial motivating factor, a journal publishing course was also seen as an ideal opportunity to provide students with an intensive introduction to the issues surrounding scholarly journal publishing in general (as in Jones et al. 2006). By creating a course that focused more generally on the practices and challenges of scholarly journal publishing (rather than connecting it solely to the undergraduate journal), we believed the content would be more applicable and useful to a broader range of students. In addition, we also anticipated the potential for the course to serve as a powerful advocacy tool, giving students the opportunity to actively interrogate scholarly communication issues, such as open access and author rights, within the context of a credit-bearing course, rather than a one-time workshop (which may be easily forgotten or missed).

At Pacific University, the library is currently unable to offer credit courses under its own designation. Because of this, in order to propose a credit-bearing course in the College of Arts and Sciences, library faculty must identify a department that is willing to "adopt" the course and approve it as part of the departmental curriculum. In this case, the media arts department agreed to receive the course proposal for a course on scholarly journal publishing; the curriculum committee and arts and sciences faculty subsequently approved the course.

Course Description and Objectives

The catalog description and objectives of the course, as proposed, were:

> Scholarly publishing is a vital industry, providing a venue for sharing the results of research, study and creative activities. This course will explore the process through which scholarly writing is solicited, reviewed, accepted

and prepared for publication, both in a traditional print environment and in the growing online environment. A variety of issues related to scholarly communications including economics, open access publishing models and citation metrics will be discussed. Students will have the opportunity to participate in mock editorial/review processes and to hear from a variety of guest speakers actively involved with scholarly journals.

The goal of this course is to prepare students to be actively engaged as authors, reviewers and editors in the scholarly publication process. For students who are considering graduate work and/or further careers as academics or researchers, understanding of scholarly communications will be a tremendous asset. This course will also provide students interested in the publishing industry with an overview of the opportunities that exist within journal publishing.

Upon completion of this course, students should be able to:

- Understand and articulate the publication process, from initial manuscript submission to final publication.
- Identify the process/resources necessary to establish a new publication.
- Distinguish between, and describe the relative benefits of, different publishing models.
- Understand the legal relationships between author, publisher and reader in order to protect their own intellectual property rights as authors and to respect others' rights.
- Understand the process for selecting, editing and proofreading manuscripts for publication.
- Organize the review process for a scholarly publication.
- Demonstrate competence in utilization of an online editorial management/publishing platform.

The course was designed as a two-week winter term course; at Pacific University, these courses are held during January for a varying number of weeks, dependent on the credits. As a two-credit course, the publishing class meets ten times over the two weeks, for three hours each session. The compressed time period limits the scope of assignments that can be given, but also provides students the opportunity to focus intensely on one course for that period of time.

Course Curriculum

The topics covered in the course were developed by examining the syllabi of similar courses (e.g., the content described in Jones et al. 2006) and by identifying areas that would be informative and useful for all potential students, whether they are pursuing publishing as career, will be engaging with publishing as a graduate student, or are simply taking the course out of general interest in the topic.

Because of the compressed course schedule, it was important to design the curriculum in ways that would (a) allow opportunity for information to be shared with students, (b) integrate active learning to avoid lecture burnout, and (c) provide assignments that would be meaningful but still reasonable to complete in the time allotted. In addition, guest speakers were incorporated into the syllabus to give students a chance to interact with people who are actively working in scholarly publishing, both within and outside the university. The course calendar is shown in Table 5.3.

Table 5.3
Scholarly Journal Publishing—Course Calendar (January 2012)

Date	Topics/Assignments
January 9	Course Introduction Introduction to Scholarly Publishing Overview of Debate Topics *Activity*: Group Prep for Debates
January 10	Publishing Models: Traditional/Open Access (OA)/Hybrid Editorial Workflow EdiKit® Demo
January 11	Writing for Publication *Guest*: John Medeiros Journal of Manual & Manipulative Therapy (JMMT)
January 12	Starting a New Online Journal *Guest*: Hanna Neuschwander (Democracy & Education) *Assignment DUE*: Scholarly Publishing Debate
January 13	Peer Review *Activity*: Peer Review
January 16	NO CLASS - MLK DAY *Assignment DUE*: Topics in SP Paper
January 17	Ethics in Scholarly Publishing Copyright/Author Rights/CTAs *Activity*: Copyright Transfer Agreements (CTAs) Exploration

Table 5.3
Scholarly Journal Publishing—Course Calendar (January 2012)

January 18	Journal Evaluations *Activity*: Journal Site Mock-Up *Assignment DUE*: Peer Review
January 19	Copyediting *Activity*: Copyediting Workshop *Guest*: Jill Kelly
January 20	*Guest*: Marina Kukso (PLoS) [Webcast] Citation Metrics/Impact Factor Indexing (ISSN, DOI, databases, etc.) *Assignment DUE*: Revised Paper (by midnight) Course Evaluations
January 23	*Assignment DUE*: New Journal Proposal *Assignment DUE*: TSP Presentations

Course assignments (see Table 5.4) were developed to help students connect with philosophical and practical issues related to scholarly journal publishing while simultaneously giving them the opportunity to gain hands-on experience as authors, reviewers, and editors/publishers. The culminating assignments of the course are the presentation of a research paper and the submission of a proposal for a new scholarly journal. Throughout the course, the paper is treated as a scholarly manuscript and is submitted for peer review by classmates; the journal proposal requires students to think about how they would address the issues raised during the course if they were to start a new publication.

Table 5.4
Scholarly Journal Publishing—Assignment Descriptions (January 2012)

Topics in Scholarly Publishing Paper/Presentation

5–7 pages on an issue of relevance to the scholarly publishing industry. Possible topics include (but are not limited to): Open access publishing, open peer review, citation metrics/impact factor, economics of publishing, transition from print to online publication, journal pricing, or review of a publishing-related technology (e.g. Open Journal Systems). If selecting a topic not on this list, please review it with the instructor prior to starting work. Papers must include citations to relevant literature. At least 3 sources must be peer reviewed, and a minimum of 5 total sources are required. Papers must use either Chicago, MLA, or APA formatting.

Papers will be submitted twice: an initial submission and then a revised submission which will incorporate changes based on your classmates' peer review of your paper. Papers will be evaluated on the quality of writing and rhetorical organization, the presence of critical analysis/thought and the use of appropriate references/literature to support the ideas presented. Paper topics will be presented to the class; visual aids (slides, live web demos, etc.) are encouraged for the presentations. Presentations should be at least 10 minutes in length (not including time for questions).

Scholarly Publishing Debates

The scholarly publishing debates will cover three common areas of disagreement within the scholarly community: the merits of open access publishing, copyright ownership of journal articles, and the efficacy of the peer review system. Students will be assigned to one of two teams for one of the debate topics. Each team member will be expected to contribute to an in-class debate on his/her assigned topic. Teams will be expected to prepare a 5 minute opening statement, as well as be able to rebut their opponent's arguments and answer questions raised by the instructor.

Topic A: Open Access Publishing

- Pro OA team: "Open access is beneficial and necessary to the process of scholarly communication."
- Con OA team: "Open access is not beneficial or necessary to the process of scholarly communication."

Topic B: Copyright Ownership

- Author team: "Authors should retain the copyright for their articles."
- Publisher team: "It is necessary and beneficial for authors to transfer copyright ownership to publishers."

Topic C: Peer Review

- Status Quo team: "The current system of peer review works well and is necessary for maintaining the quality of scholarly publishing."
- Change team: "The current system of peer review is broken and should be replaced with alternate forms of review."

New Journal Proposal

Students must research and compile a proposal for a new scholarly journal in an area of interest to them. The proposals must establish the need for the publication, discuss the proposed publishing model, and provide an estimated budget of the costs of starting (and sustaining) the publication. Students will also design a homepage for their journal (a mock-up, not an active site). Final submission of the assignment should include a) the completed proposal template, b) a completed ISSN application form, and c) an image file of the journal homepage design.

| **Table 5.4 (Continued)** |
| Scholarly Journal Publishing—Assignment Descriptions (January 2012) |
| **Peer Review** |
| Students are required to perform a review of their classmates' Topics in Scholarly Publishing papers. Reviews must be completed according to the provided template, and will be simulated "double blind" reviews coordinated through the Berkeley Electronic Press editorial workflow system. (True double blind reviews are not possible due to the structure of the course). |
| **Journal Evaluation** |
| Select a journal in your discipline (if you are undeclared, pick an academic area of interest to you) that interests you or from which you have previously read an article. You may evaluate a print journal, an online journal or a journal that is published both in print and online. Complete the following survey about the journal you have selected; provide as much detail as possible in your responses to open-ended questions: Journal Evaluation Survey. |

To the extent possible, the course was designed to engage students in self-directed learning and discovery. For example, rather than hearing a lecture that describes both sides of certain issues related to publishing, students are assigned to research and debate those issues. This gives them a stake in understanding different sides of an issue and also allows the students to educate each other through participating in and observing the debates. Similarly, the research paper encourages students to independently investigate (to the extent possible in five to seven pages) a relevant publishing topic, while the journal proposal requires them to creatively apply information from the lectures, assigned readings, and in-class activities.

Outcomes

Student evaluations of the course have been largely positive in both years that it has been offered (see Table 5.5), even though the majority of students enrolled in the course have not been actively interested in publishing or scholarly communication. Most students who have taken the course have done so either for the upper-division credit or because it was recommended by an advisor. However, a small (but growing) number of students have also been attracted to the class because of the creation of the minor in editing and publishing.

The general consensus of students who provided comments in their course evaluations has been that they learned a lot about publishing that they had not known. Not surprisingly, students also indicated that the information provided through the course would likely be most useful for someone who was interested in publishing or in starting a

Table 5.5
Student Course Evaluations, 2011–2012

Evaluation Item	January 2011 (1 = extremely poor, 7 = excellent)	January 2012 (1 = extremely poor, 7 = excellent)
Provide an overall rating of the course	n = 5 μ = 6.4 Med = 6	n = 10 μ = 5.6 Med = 6
Rate the likelihood that you would recommend this course to another student.	n = 5 μ = 6.2 Med = 6	n = 10 μ = 5.7 Med = 6
Rate your increase in skills/ understanding as a result of taking this course.	n = 5 μ = 6.4 Med = 6	n = 10 μ = 6.3 Med = 6.5

journal. But the comments that best illustrate the intended value of the course were those that indicate the unique role that the course fills: "I learned a lot from this course I didn't know and probably wouldn't have had the chance to learn" and "Each [of the guest speakers] offered awesome information that I don't think I would have ever encountered." Whether these students go on to become researchers, authors, publishers, or simply citizens, they are now more informed about the ways in which scholarly knowledge is shared and disseminated and the ways in which that process can be improved. The debate assignment has been particularly useful as means of encouraging critical thinking about issues relevant to scholarly publishing; although students are provided with broad and polarized positions to debate, they have brought careful and nuanced arguments to the table.

Next Steps

The course itself evolved from its first to second year and will likely continue to change. An initial objective of the course, to have students "demonstrate competence in utilization of an online editorial management/publishing platform," has proved unrealistic given the time frame of the course, though students do still experience Berkeley Electronic Press's EdiKit platform as part of the research paper and peer review assignments. And while more activities (e.g., a copyediting workshop) have been added to the course since the first year, student feedback indicates that they would like to see a further reduction in the amount of content delivered via lecture, and this will be a focus for future iterations of the course. We'll also be seeking further collaboration with Pacific University's undergraduate research journal. Currently, students in the class participate in the peer review of a manuscript that has been submitted to the journal, but there will likely be other opportunities to assist with editorial tasks and marketing activities as the journal grows. As the university library's broader publishing services program expands and activities related to the minor in editing and publishing also expand, there will also be opportunities to integrate more "live" examples and projects into the course syllabus, allowing students to contribute to active journals.

Conclusion

Regardless of whether institutions like Pacific University have placed increased emphasis on research and scholarship, whether by students or faculty, the core of the undergraduate experience will always remain in the "classroom" (in the many forms that it now takes). Given this, the best opportunity to engage students in critical thinking and discussion about scholarly communication issues is within the context of an academic course or program. This is not a new revelation for librarians; we already question the efficacy of the one-shot instruction session or workshop when it comes to information literacy, and engagement with scholarly communication is no different. To be most effective, it should not be an optional activity or in-class intrusion, but an academic exercise that provides students with an incentive (i.e., credit) for engagement. For lack of a better term, discussion of scholarly communication should be "mainstreamed,"[2] not segregated. Incorporating it into a credit-bearing course and into an academic major, minor, or concentration is one of the best ways to accomplish this. Not only are students introduced to ideas that affect their lives (think textbook pricing and public access to health research), but it is accomplished within a context where they also gain valuable skills and knowledge that will benefit them in their future academic or professional careers.

This approach not only benefits students, it also strengthens the library's position as an institutional leader. Library leadership and involvement in developing courses and academic programs can help others at an institution to think about the library in new ways and can provide a strong example of the library's commitment to student learning and success. That commitment has always existed, but at a time when libraries are being called upon to demonstrate their value to the educational process (Oakleaf 2010), helping to shape that process at its core (the classroom) is an invaluable marker. And, of course, being able to connect the library's scholarly communication activities to the educational process helps demonstrate relevance and value in that area to faculty and others who may be less engaged with open access policies or institutional repositories.

With that being said, the specific path followed at Pacific University may not be the best means at other institutions of mainstreaming scholarly communication and connecting it to the undergraduate curriculum. Much depends on the culture of the individual institution and the opportunities that are present. But the opportunities, in some form, do exist to connect students with scholarly communication. For example, working as advisors, or even publishers, for undergraduate literary magazines or newspapers would provide an opening to discuss the economics of publishing and open access. Coteaching a course with a history or sociology professor on intellectual property in the Digital Age would be the perfect opportunity to engage students around author rights, alternative content licensing, and the relationship between copyright and course-pack pricing—or simply encouraging or working with faculty to make the experience of authorship a requirement for students in their courses, following the model of Jones et al. (2011). Whatever the method, though, the strategy should remain the same: integrate the issues of scholarly communication into the teaching and learning activities of the institution in a format and context that are familiar and meaningful to students.

Notes

1. See the Editing and Publishing Center at http://www.pacificu.edu/library/epc.
2. For a discussion of "mainstreaming" scholarly communication within the work of academic libraries, see: Malenfant, K.J. (2010). Leading change in the system of scholarly communication: A case study of engaging liaison librarians for outreach to faculty. *College & Research Libraries*, 71: 63-76.

References

Boles, Jacoby, and Julianne Newmark. 2011. "Xchanges Journal: Web Journal as the Writing Classroom." *Kairos* 16, no. 1 (Fall). http://kairos.technorhetoric.net/16.1/praxis/boles.

Davis-Kahl, Stephanie. 2012. "Engaging Undergraduates in Scholarly Communication." *College & Research Libraries News* 73, no. 4 (April): 212–222.

Guildford, William H. 2001. "Teaching Peer Review and the Process of Scientific Writing." *Advances in Physiology Education* 25, no. 3 (September): 167–175.

Jones, Leslie Sargent, Laura Allen, Kim Cronise, Natasha Juneja, Rebecca Kohn, Katherine McClellan, Ashley Miller, Azka Nazir, Andy Patel,

Sarah M. Sweitzer, Erin Vickery, Anna Walton, and Robert Young. 2011. "Incorporating Scientific Publishing into an Undergraduate Neuroscience Course: A Case Study Using IMPULSE." *Journal of Undergraduate Neuroscience Education* 9, no. 2: A84–A91.

Jones, Leslie Sargeant, L. Codi Black, Lauren Bright, Catherine Meekins, Vivek Thakur, and Cade Warren. 2006. "An Undergraduate Course on Publishing in Neuroscience." *Journal of Undergraduate Neuroscience Education* 4, no. 2: A60–A67.

Oakleaf, Megan. 2010. *Value of Academic Libraries: A Comprehensive Research Review and Report*. Chicago: Association of College and Research Libraries, September. http://www.ala.org/acrl/sites/ala.org.acrl/files/content/issues/value/val_report.pdf.

Tang, Bor Luen, and Yunn Hwen Gan. 2005. "Preparing the Senior or Graduating Student for Graduate Research." *Biochemistry and Molecular Biology Education* 33, no. 4 (July): 277–280.

Tenopir, Carol, Richard Pollard, Peiling Wange, Dan Greene, Elizabeth Kline, Julia Krummen, and Rachel Kirk. 2003. "Undergraduate Science Students and Electronic Scholarly Journals." *Proceedings of the American Society for Information Science and Technology* 40, no. 1 (October): 291–297. doi:10.1002/meet.1450400136.

CHAPTER 6

"Pirates of Metadata"

[Or, The True Adventures of How One Journal Editor and
Fifteen Undergraduate Publishing Majors Survived a
Harrowing Metadata-Mining Project]

Cheryl E. Ball
Illinois State University

Introduction

In this chapter, I discuss the use of metadata in digital publishing as both a necessary means for creating accessible and sustainable scholarship and a method of promoting information literacy in students. To make this point, I argue that information literacy extends beyond technical competence and into a critical understanding of the contexts and ecologies in which information is created and used. That is, while understanding metadata, as a concept, is a functional part of information literacy, understanding the role metadata plays in information communication, such as scholarly publishing, requires far more rhetorical and critical understanding, which enhances information literacy practices. The study that showcases this practice centers on a digital publishing class during which I asked undergraduates to mine metadata from an open access scholarly journal that publishes exclusively hypertextual and multimedia scholarship.

Setting the Scene: The Precarious Scholarly Landscape of the World Wide Web

The Internet was built for scholarly communication, and the Web made its distribution that much friendlier. While the military and the sciences had been using the Internet for decades, the Web's arrival in 1994 allowed aficionados in the digital humanities to take better advantage of this technological and scholarly infrastructure. Within a year of the Web's debut, online journals proliferated (Hitchcock,

Carr, and Hall 1996), and a group of graduate students from around the United States decided to start their own scholarly journal in the interdisciplinary areas of rhetoric, technology, and pedagogy—a field then known as "computers and composition," populated primarily by college writing instructors who also happened to be techies. The journal is now called *Kairos: A Journal of Rhetoric, Technology, and Pedagogy*. The field of computers and composition (sometimes more recently known as digital writing studies or digital rhetoric) research-es how writing functions and is taught in networked digital writing environments. This research overlaps with information literacy. As digital rhetorician Stuart Selber (2004) aptly explained in his book, *Multiliteracies for a Digital Age*, computer literacy programs often overemphasize technical skills to the disservice of students (and teachers) who need to engage in higher-level literacy practices. It is generally agreed in digital writing that although information literacy practices necessarily include functional, practical computing skills (e.g., one needs to know how to use a word processing program in order to write in it), these lower-level skills should be incorporated only into teaching and learning practices that frame learning within contextually driven spaces that focus on higher-level rhetorical and critical-literacy practices. Thus, the approach to information literacy practices that I espouse in this chapter is akin to what the Associa-tion of College and Research Libraries (ACRL 2000) states as the goal of information literacy (versus information technology) in reporting on the differences between these two terms: "Information literacy's focus [is] on content, communication, analysis, information searching, and evaluation; whereas information technology 'flu-ency' focuses on a deep understanding of technology and graduated, increasingly skilled use of it" (para. 5). In the next section, I describe how the journal I edit, *Kairos*, served as an experiment in informa-tion literacy learning for students in an undergraduate publishing class.

Rising Action: Everything Seems under Control until ... Metadata!

It won't be news to librarians, information literacy specialists, and digital communication scholars that 1996 was a time filled with both promise and peril for any new publication starting on the Web. *Kairos*'s editorial staff knew that and planned well, filling a niche in scholarly publishing that was made for the Web: hypertextual and (as Web-based design technologies matured) media-rich scholarship. In the spirit of the academic discipline that the journal calls home—one in which writing is composed and taught as a collaborative process between multiple authors in networked computing environments—

Kairos has always peer-reviewed submissions collaboratively and has always been an open access journal, making itself freely available to anyone with Internet access.[1] It is the longest-running journal of its kind in the world.

From the first issue in January 1996, the editors had the foresight in planning for the future of the journal to find in-kind server space, plan editorial collaboration via e-mail distribution lists, create sustainable information architecture for the journal's twice-a-year publication, distribute the workload through co-editors who work virtually with each other, and commit to being an independent publishing venue so that the mission and vision of this experimental journal could remain strong. However, what the original staff didn't know was how crucial metadata would be to finding information on the Web in five, ten, or (as of the writing of this chapter) seventeen years later—or what kinds of metadata would be important to capture the history and exponentially growing future of scholarly multimedia, or how expensive the process of creating metadata after the fact could be, a particular problem for an independent journal with a no-money-in/no-money-out business model.

In 2008, there was a brief lull in the action when the editors began implementing a small metadata schema in every newly accepted webtext (*Kairos*'s term for scholarly multimedia articles). Using a version of Dublin Core, the editorial staff began copying, pasting, and tweaking a dozen or so lines of metadata into the header of every HTML page the journal would publish, starting with the Fall 2008 issue. Keeping in mind that all webtexts are built with a series of linked, interactive webpages, media files, and file directories, the process of pasting, tweaking, and also copyediting and proofreading the metadata for *every* HTML page in an issue is no small undertaking. As an example, the Summer 2012 issue of *Kairos* had 128 HTML pages across fifteen folders and subfolders, and the metadata had to be pasted into and changed to match the unique data (such as URI) of each page, never mind all of the other editorial production work that the staff completes to ensure the highest quality scholarship possible.

In addition, this metadata work is done manually, which isn't at all surprising given the editorial workflow the journal has always used. In fact, every step in the publishing process—from soliciting and reviewing submissions, to copyediting and design-editing webtexts, to publishing an issue—has been performed manually by staff members for the entirety of the journal's history. This means staff members employ functional information literacies such as downloading zip files or folders using a free secure file transfer protocol (SFTP) program,[2] copyediting those files in an HTML editor, uploading those files to another virtual server using SFTP, and e-mailing the staff distribution list to indicate that the text is ready for the next stage of copyediting. Those functional, technical skills support the rhetorical and critical information literacies they practice as editorial and disciplinary specialists in digital media composition, technical communication, user experience design, and so on. Of course, the problem is that it's not 1996 anymore, and *information literacy* no longer refers simply to functional skills but also incorporates the higher-level rhetorical and critical skills. The journal's own communicative practices needed to adapt.

In early 2010, the senior editors knew that the journal's workflow needed to change to keep up with the proliferation of submissions as well as the technologies and technical standards required of Web-based scholarship. We needed a system that would help us automate and sustain this otherwise functional process, a system that would be technologically well beyond our current practice of relying on one editor's personal e-mail archives and "Type-A" approach to publication timelines (myself, as editor) and another editor's extensive server knowledge (Douglas Eyman, senior editor of *Kairos*). This system should also allow us to set up a workflow that didn't rely on our institutional memories so that new editors could step into these roles without problems. But there were no editorial management systems on the market (either open-source or commercial) that, out of the box, could handle the kind of multimedia content *Kairos* publishes. And with no budget, we couldn't afford to buy a commercial system and request tweaks, nor could we implement an open-source system and pay a programmer to make changes suitable for us. So, we applied for a National Endowment for the Humanities (NEH) Digital Humanities Start-Up Grant, which would allow us to pay a programmer to build multimedia-specific plug-ins for the open-source software Open Journal Systems (OJS).

OJS has been around since 2001 and is distributed for free by the Public Knowledge Project (PKP).[3] *Kairos* chose OJS as the foundation for its editorial-system grant because PKP's founder, John Willinsky, is extremely dedicated to open access scholarship and to making OJS open-source, including opening its codebase to programmers, which was an important requirement for completing the grant project on time and on budget. In addition, with OJS we wouldn't have to maintain our own system; we would just have to build plug-ins that work with the existing system and offer those plug-ins back to the open-source community for others to make use of and improve. We were lucky to get the NEH grant on the first try, and the *Kairos*-OJS plug-ins should be available to the public by the fall of 2012. But, in our excitement at getting the grant, we'd forgotten one thing.

The Climax: The Specter of Metadata Returns!

OJS runs on a database, and in order for that database to work, it needed data that we didn't have. We had only a very limited set of Dublin Core metadata for two years of the journal's then fourteen years of publication, and that data was not easily extracted from the code in which it was embedded. So the first order of business was to create a metadata schema that would capture the data *we* wanted to capture within OJS, which uses a limited variation of Dublin Core. Doug Eyman, myself, and Kathie Gossett, *Kairos*'s associate editor, spent three months creating a crosswalk comparing Dublin Core, OJS, and *Kairos*'s unique metadata needs specific to its multimedia content. (Unfortunately, space precludes me from detailing the outcomes of that process in this chapter.)

In the process of discussing schemata, we realized we wanted to capture data not only at the webtext (or article) level, but also at the level of the media element, such as a path-specific URI that identifies where a media element falls within the architecture of a specific webtext (e.g., /images/header.gif). With this goal in mind, we ended up with twenty-nine fields to capture at the webtext and media element levels, including Title, Creator, Keyword, Description, Designer, Status, Genre, FileType, and others. We could use a metadata field such as Title to refer not only to the title of a webtext but also to the title of an HTML page, since each page in a webtext functions as a discrete, nonlinear unit in our publications. In addition, a metadata field such as Description could stand in for a webtext's abstract but also, at the media element level, as the alt text for an image used in the webtext. This level of granularity would allow us to provide more comprehensive and more finely tuned research opportunities for readers and potential authors, eventually allowing us to tag every media element in a webtext so that it would be independently searchable and remixable and could be cited appropriately. This granularity would also allow us to better describe and preserve, if only through metadata, some of the webtext components that become technologically obsolete with age. A good example is *Kairos*'s most-cited webtext, "a bookling monument" by Anne Wysocki. It's a Shockwave piece from 2002, designed in Macromedia Director (when, alas, there was such a program), that only occasionally still runs, depending on whether browser companies decide to keep the Shockwave browser plug-in up-to-date. For several years in the late 2000s, the piece was completely inaccessible, but people still cite it because it is one of the most cutting-edge and unusually designed pieces in the journal's history. Metadata would help us preserve the import of the Shockwave piece for archival and research purposes, even if the medium—or, more specifically, file format—in which the piece is delivered becomes inaccessible again in the future.

We were so wrapped up in what data we wanted to collect in our redesigned version of OJS, however, that we forgot we would need to collect data for all of our back issues as well. To populate the impending OJS database, we would need to *create* metadata for what was, on early counts, over 500 webtexts and 25,000 media elements that the journal had already published. Worse, having already spoken with several supercomputing experts on data mining, we knew there was no way to do this algorithmically with our multimedia content. (In fact, those experts are only now, two years later, starting a project where this work *might* be possible.) At the time, not a few tears were shed during the confrontation with this massive metadata-mining challenge, which we knew could be completed only with human labor and a ton of perseverance. But how? The journal staff consists of around twenty-five PhD students and tenure-track scholars who volunteer a few hours a week (and sometimes much more) on top of their high teaching loads (the average is four classes per semester) to put out two or three issues a year. The additional workload would have been an undue burden for them, and the documentation I would have had to prepare to make this project work at twenty-five different sites (since the staff is distributed) would have been an undue burden for me. And if I took this project on myself, what could I learn from it? Better yet, I realized, my students could learn from mining metadata from scholarly, open access multimedia?

Yes, I would have a captive audience of fifteen undergraduates in my digital publishing class the following semester. All of them would be seniors in my department's publishing studies sequence, the most difficult sequence to get into (due to the number of seats available). Thus, the sequence has the highest standards for students—standards that, in my experience teaching in this sequence, the students surpass on a weekly basis. They are the best of the best. On the one hand, I admit feeling guilty about throwing them into such a massive project, and one that I would see professional benefit from. On the other hand, students in this sequence crave real-life and practical publishing experiences, and this project was unlike any they would work on in their other publishing classes. Most students wanted something "digital" in this sequence, and many waited a semester to take this class with me because it dealt specifically with digital topics. This class opportunity was the perfect solution to my metadata problems, and I vowed from the beginning to credit the students' data-mining work, either through acknowledgements or co-authorship, as the case warranted.[4]

Falling Action: Teaching Metadata to Make the Journal Sustainable

To collect this data—in what turned out to be over 800 webtexts from *Kairos*'s then fifteen years of publication—I created a syllabus for my senior-level publishing class that included a ten-week sequenced assignment of mining the metadata, which I discuss in more detail below, and a reading list on metadata, open access and digital publishing, and nontraditional scholarship. Some of these readings included Baca's (2008) *Introduction to Metadata*, Fitzpatrick's (2010) *Planned Obsolescence*, Borgman's (2007) *Scholarship in the Digital Age*, and Willinsky's (2009) *Access Principle*; I purposefully used the open access versions of these texts when they were available. Based on those readings, we discussed issues such as these:

- What is scholarship, and why is peer review important?
- What role does peer review play in your professors' lives?
- What does open access mean?
- How does being open access impact the sustainability of digital scholarship?
- What are these "webtexts" we're working with?
- What is metadata, and why is it important to digital publishing and to webtexts in particular?

The students were eager to discuss these topics in detail since most of the concepts were brand-new to them, and all directly related to their major. For instance, the students had no idea what tenure, or the tenure track, was, even though these concepts pervade their university lives through their professors.[5] Tenure relates directly to the ideologies and processes of scholarly publishing, and so to be better editors and publishers, these publishing studies students would need to know as much about this form of scholarly communication as they could. We had long discussions—in relation to reading the peer-review sections of Fitzpatrick's (2010) book supplemented by my personal experiences and research regarding the use of digital and open access, peer-reviewed scholarship in applying for tenure[6]—about why professors have to research, what the outcomes of that research look like in different humanities fields, where and how it gets published, who reviews it, what editorial reviewers get paid, and what getting a peer-reviewed article published in a scholarly journal means in relation to their teaching effectiveness and tenure. All of this information was crucial for students to know so they could better understand why an author or an editor might face certain institutional and disciplinary challenges when choosing to publish in an open access journal, never mind in a medium—such as webtexts—that differs from traditional forms of scholarly communication.

Open Access

The first major lesson of the class centered on understanding the importance of open access. Students in the publishing sequence are trained primarily in print-based, literary and nonprofit (grant-funded and subscription-based) publishing, and they know how to edit, design, market, and distribute literary texts. But prior to this class, they hadn't considered what access they'd have to these texts, or to any of the scholarship professors require them to cite in their own papers, once they graduate. John Willinsky's (2009) book provided a great and easy-to-read (so said the students) introduction to the principles of open access. For instance, Willinsky bluntly says:

> What is clear at this point is that open access to re-
> search archives and journals has the potential to change
> the public presence of science and scholarship and
> increase the circulation of this particular form of knowl-
> edge. What is also clear is that the role that open access
> will play in the future of scholarly publishing depends
> on decisions that will be made over the [next] few years
> by researchers, editors, scholarly societies, publishers,
> and research-funding agencies.

> This is a book that lays out the case for open access and
> why it should be a part of that future. It demonstrates
> the vital and viable role it can play, from both the per-
> spective of a researcher working in the best-equipped
> lab at a leading research university and that of a history
> teacher struggling to find resources in an impoverished
> high school. (ix–x)

To drive these points home, and perhaps much to the chagrin of my university's library officials and information technology staff, the students and I had frank conversations about the purchase of propri-etary software for creating bibliographies when dozens of open-source versions existed, which students could learn now, for free, and con-tinue to use long after they graduate. We also discussed the difference between open access and open source, and the fact that some open-source programs, like Zotero, could capture and store open access and openly available documents on the Web. To clearly demonstrate the levels of access that students would have after they graduate, I asked them to look up the CV of their favorite professor, find an article he or she had written, and see whether they could access the full text of that article online without going through our library's website. In every case, the answer was no. Yet they were, or would be, that high school teacher (or nonprofit editor) Willinsky referred to.

To compound Willinsky's point, I relayed the news of the National Institute of Health's decision to require scholars receiving NIH grants to publish their results in a venue that is open to the public.[7] In read-ing Borgman's (2007) book on digital scholarship, with its particular emphasis on e-science, we had already discussed the salary and grant-funding disparities between the sciences and the humanities and the fact that the sciences usually build paying for open access publishing into their grants, so the NIH's decision wasn't that big a deal, whereas open access in the humanities could be a financial hurdle as well as an ideological one. As a counterpoint to the NIH example, I told them an anecdote that Brett Bobley (2010), Chief Information Officer for the NEH, shared at a conference once:

> I get a little Google alert whenever various things occur, and I saw a little article about the fact that [a big-name scholar has published an article]... And I click on it and what comes up? A pay wall. It's printed in some journal, and that means I'll never get to read it. Ever. And I work for the NEH! I fund this stuff! Scholars all the time say to me, "Hey, Brett, did you read that article I published?" I go, "Did you publish it open access?" No. I never read it. I can't afford journal subscriptions.

Bobley reminds academics that if scholarship is not published open access, neither the funders nor the general public will ever see it. Given this information paired with the class discussions about tenure and peer-reviewed scholarship, the students could easily see why open access was an important point along the publishing and information communication spectrum. And, although this publishing course was not a special topics class in open access scholarship, most of our discussions came back to this issue throughout the semester, including why and how we were to collect metadata for *Kairos*.

Metadata for Webtexts

The connection between information literacy and the production of the metadata was implicit in the class, but I hope to make that connection explicit for readers in this section. The point is that technical tasks, such as metadata creation, should not exist outside of the critical, rhetorical contexts in which they are being performed if a full sense of information literacy is to be expected. In this case, the critical and rhetorical *topoi* include digital scholarship, peer review, open access venues, copyright, and other issues within the scholarly communicative landscape.

To prepare for the metadata-mining project, we spent the first few weeks of class reading about open access, peer review, and the kinds of digital media scholarship that *Kairos* publishes. We read Baca's (2008) *Introduction to Metadata*, which put into larger context some of the instruction sets on mining metadata from *Kairos*, which I provided students on a weekly basis. Based on the great questions raised by

Baca's book, such as why metadata is important, I wrote lengthy contextual explanations into the instruction sets for students as a way to reinforce the scholarly and publishing importance of creating metadata for digital texts. Their first handout explained several reasons why we were collecting metadata from *Kairos* and what that data would be used for:

1. It will be used by *Kairos* editors to populate a database they are creating. This database, which will interact with Open Journal Systems (a scholarly publishing platform) to allow readers, editors, and authors to better search for useful digital media scholarship in the journal.

2. It will allow for more accurate citation practices of the digital media elements within *Kairos* webtexts.

3. It will make previously published webtexts more accessible for more users—both for scholars doing Web-based researchers [*sic*] and for users who are differently abled.

4. It will serve as a prototype for metadata in all future *Kairos* submissions, so that authors will begin to create their own metadata upon submission to the new database/system; thus making the gathering of metadata more sustainable in the future, based on your experiments and workflow recommendations.

5. It will be used by editors and researchers to discover new information (e.g., relationships, visualizations, search patterns, reading patterns, media-types, etc.) and to create new knowledge about digital media scholarship.

6. Once the metadata terms we are using have been conceptualized through your work and proven to be successful (or not), the metadata terms will be distributed to other digital media publications so as to become a standard for this kind of scholarly publication. (Ball 2011)

Because of the scope of this project, I knew it would be crucial to remind students that it was equivalent to an internship and would be a useful résumé line for them. (Although I wasn't expecting it, two students went on to get jobs where their primarily responsibilities were to work with metadata in digital publishing venues.) I translated to layperson's terms the 25 items that we would capture over the eight weeks of hands-on class time spent on this assignment: Authors, Designers, Creators, Author/Designer Affiliation, Academic Rank, Author/Designer (current) Emails, Webtext Title, Abstract, Publisher, Volume/Issue, Date Published, Section, Language, Peer-Reviewed Status, Peer-Reviewers, DOI, Rights, File Name, File Size, MimeType, Dublin Core Metadata Initiative (DCMI) Type, URI, Page Title, Alt Text, and Genre. These fields crossed three categories of data we wanted to collect: at the level of the webtext, at the micro-level of the media elements within a webtext, and contact information for authors. (There were thirty-five fields of metadata total, some referenced below and repeated across the webtext level and the media-element level, but I had to cut back based on what the students would be physically and emotionally able to accomplish during the term, so we ended up with nineteen. Space prevents me from detailing all of these fields.) I parsed the mining project into the assignments shown in Table 6.1, which I thought would create a workflow that made the most sense given the concepts, locations in the webtexts, and technologies students would need to find them.

Table 6.1
Metadata Elements Presented During the Semester

Week 1 [Feb 9]	Fields requiring Little Instruction
Week 2 [Feb 16]	Fields requiring Simple Lists (not MimeTypes) + DOI
Week 3 [Feb 23]	Rights + Affiliation, Rank, Email
Week 4 [March 2]	Abstract, Keywords + Notes [spring break]
Week 5 [March 16]	MediaID + FileName, FileSize, MimeType, DCMI Type, URI
Week 6 [March 23]	Page Title, Alt Text, Creator + [Webtext] DCMI Type, File Size, URI
Week 7 [March 30]	Genre [Webtext & Media tabs], Creator
Week 8 [April 6]	Update Rights & Affiliations fields

Every week, students would get another multipage handout describing in detail how to collect or create some grouping of this metadata. These handouts always included brief discussions about why fields as seemingly simple as Author, Title, Publisher, and Date might be difficult to find and might even be contested. For instance, the handout "Fields Requiring Little Instruction" included directions for finding authors, webtext titles, volume and issue, language, designers, and peer reviewers and was five single-spaced pages with four images—two each to demonstrate how to find designers and peer reviewers (information that is rarely included in webtexts). The description for finding authors alone included the following details (which probably won't make sense to readers, but did make sense to students since we'd spent a good deal of time looking at the journal before starting the project):

Authors:

1. To find the authors for a webtext, look at the Table of Contents (TOCs) for each issue of *Kairos* or on the "home" page for each individual webtext. To access the back issues, go to the *Kairos* home page (http://kairos.technorhetoric.net) and click on the tab at the top for "Issues." The TOC is on the main page of the journal, EXCEPT for the following issues: 7.3, 6.2, 5.2, 4.1, where the TOC for the "CoverWeb" section has to be accessed by clicking on the themes or the hyperlinked title to the CoverWeb.

2. Once you find the authors, copy them from the webtext and paste them into the Authors column in the Webtext tab of the Excel spreadsheet. Authors should be listed just like they appear in the webtext, including any middle initials, but NOT including any degrees or ranks (e.g., PhD, if it follows a name).

3. If there are multiple authors for a single webtext, they should be listed in the order they appear on the webtext, with commas separating each full name. BUT MAKE SURE TO DELETE the "and" which will usually be included in the TOC.

EXAMPLE:

Author listing in the TOC: Christopher Dean, Will Hochman, Carra Hood, and Robert McEachern

Author listing in the spreadsheet: Christopher Dean, Will Hochman, Carra Hood, Robert McEachern

Date of publication (another not-simple entry) would have been easier if the journal hadn't changed its publication schedule halfway through its history, or its name (a third entry that required choosing from multiple options) from *Kairos: A Journal for Teachers of Writing in Webbed Environments* to its current name in 2004.

In the schedule shown in Table 6.1, there was a definite split between the work completed before spring break and the work completed afterwards. After break, students had to move from browser-based mining to code-based and file-directory-based mining. That is, before spring break, they had been searching through the interfaces of the journal and webtexts to find the information they needed, using web browsers such as Firefox—technologies they were familiar with. After spring break, they had to use FTP programs and web-editing programs like Dreamweaver to download and search through the code, in some cases. The major hurdle here was not necessarily the difficulty level of teaching students what a DCMIType was and when a GIF is not a StillImage but a MovingImage.[8] The difficulty was that most of the students had never before made a webpage or put it on a server; they had to be taught how to search for, download, and install web-editing and publishing software on our lab computers and their laptops, then to complete intricate and extended searches in HTML code or file directories for the metadata information they needed. For instance, the most efficient and least technologically complicated way I could figure out how to mine for alt tags on all images was to have students search for the alt tag code in an entire issue of *Kairos*. For most of the students, this was their first introduction to HTML code, so the instructions on just this one part of the week's assignment were three and a half pages long, and that didn't include the definitions for terms such as *file directory, HTML tag,* and *SFTP program* (which had previously been covered). The instructions included definitions for nearly every step in setting up a site in Dreamweaver, including what Dreamweaver was and what open-source programs students could use if they didn't have Dreamweaver at home.

Each set of instructions also included Mac- and PC-compatible keyboard shortcuts or menu names. Most of each three-hour studio class had us working hands-on to start that week's mining assignment, troubleshooting the instructions when students inevitably ran into interface, architecture, or technology issues that didn't match every possible combination I could think of in advance. The instruction sets, initially created for a student with learning disabilities in the class, quickly became the reference for all students as we collaborated as a class on how to use and improve them. In and of themselves, they were a perfect example of how access for one can mean better access for all, a macrocosmic example of what alt tags do for each microcosm of a webtext. Finally, this course was a prime lesson in what Stuart Selber (2004) has termed the functional, critical, and rhetorical literacies inherent in being multiliterate in a digital age. Without the critical literacies of understanding digital scholarship, peer review, and open access publishing; without the functional literacies of tinkering with file directories in Dreamweaver, Firefox or Safari, and Filezilla; without the rhetorical literacies of applying typical units of analysis to webtexts (e.g., who is the audience, what is the text's purpose, in what context is it published, etc.), these students could not have *begun* to compete this project. But they did. And their data was, as much as could be expected, clean and excellent.

Denouement: The Pirates of Metadata Are Salvagers Extraordinaire!

This was a massive project—too big—which the students and I coped with in different ways. Students would come to class excited to tell me how they explained this metadata project to their history or biology major roommates. At the same time, they were exhausted by its menial orientation, not surprising given the cut-and-paste tasks at the heart of this project. The students completed the semester by producing an Excel spreadsheet for each of the journal's issues they were assigned to mine. On average, each spreadsheet contained 35,000 cells of data, and each student had at least two spreadsheets. My rough count is that students collected over a million cells of data. On its own, the data has the potential to shape the way scholars research and think about *Kairos* webtexts as representative of the history *and* future of design on the World Wide Web. This makes their work no small feat (the outcomes of which I discuss more below). The students coped by expressing how they felt week after week of mining metadata: Arrgh!!! It drove them crazy, but they also love-hated it. They started calling themselves the Pirates of Metadata and made their own logo and T-shirts, covered with metadata jokes only they would appreciate (see Figure 6.1). One of the jokes was a riff on our DOI schema—volume. issue.section.authorLastName-et-al—which was transformed into 5.11.kairos.arrgh-et-al for a tagline on the shirts (5.11 was for May 2011, when the class ended). They'd twisted the functional literacy of a DOI naming schema into a rhetorically appropriate parody—a

Figure 6.1
The Pirates of Metadata, Proudly Sporting their T-shirts

transfer that showcases, even in a minor and fun way, their critical-information literacy learning.

It was through the students' information literacy learning via this metadata project that they were able to make a significant contribution to digital publishing studies. And vice versa: because I reinforced weekly that the students were contributing to scholarship in digital publishing studies, they understood that their work had reach far beyond the classroom and were willing to push themselves harder to make that impact successful. To reach this outside-the-classroom audience, I asked students to write a report outlining their methods of data mining (particularly if they deviated from the instructions I provided) and include observations about their dataset and recommendations for stakeholders. Their audience was editors, librarians, information literacy scholars, and others who might implement a similar project with a scholarly multimedia journal in the future. Goals of the assignment included reflecting on what they learned from the metadata project in relation to the theoretical contexts of digital publishing studies and to summarize outcomes of that learning (via Findings, Discussion, and Recommendations sections) by providing succinct examples from their metadata sets. For instance, in the Findings section of the report, I suggested some kinds of data they might report on:[9]

- the kinds of genres they ended up using
- the number of media files they ended up with
- a short list of examples of how media files were named by the authors
- the sections their Volume.Issue covered
- the number of alt text or page titles (or not) used in their webtexts

This data was typical of those we spent more time discussing in class, as opposed to the more (but not exclusively) functional cut-and-paste fields such as Author, Volume.Issue, and URI. The question about which *sections* appeared in students' particular Volume.Issue, however, would elicit information critical to the historical changes in sections that *Kairos* has undergone (e.g., the first issues had a section called Pixelated Rhetorics, which morphed into *Kairos* Meet the Authors, which morphed into two different sections: Interviews and Praxis). Changes in sections sometimes indicated the peer-reviewed status (another metadata collection point) of webtexts, which has repercussions for authors' tenure and promotion. Although students wouldn't always know these larger issues that I, as editor, could easily interpret from the data, we discussed these issues in class, and if I suggested the impact factor of section changes, students could easily grasp its import to publishing studies as a whole. A quick overview of the students' outcomes and recommendations from this study shows the following import of seemingly functional topics such as *genre, media files, naming conventions,* and *alt text,* which the students and I have presented elsewhere (Ball et al., 2011):

- Web architecture has changed dramatically in fifteen years, with a noticeable shift between volumes 1–10 and 11–15. Journal architecture as a whole is messier than it should be (particularly in older issues), but individual webtexts have become more "deep" in their folder structures.
- File-naming conventions have become slightly more rhetorical (e.g., named according to rhetorical function, such as header. gif) and more technologically sustainable (e.g., fewer filenames in ALL CAPS or weird spaces).
- Genres and DCMITypes change dramatically as the journal grows.
- The number of webtexts published per issue has been halved.
- Accessibility elements such as alt text and page titles are missing from most early issues and are inconsistently used in later issues.

This is just a small sample of the observations students made in their reports about *Kairos* based on the metadata project. And a major observation that nearly all the students had was that mining metadata retroactively is costly and prone to human error. Some of the problems that students encountered in trying to mine metadata—such as finding accurate affiliations, ranks, and e-mail addresses for authors, particularly those in earlier issues—are already part of OJS or were already planned as part of the Kairos-OJS version. But the students came up with other recommendations or requirements that were incredibly insightful and that *Kairos* plans to implement in future iterations of our metadata-collection schema in OJS, such as:

- Webtexts need technology descriptions in abstracts that also describe the interactive designs of each piece.
- Accessible documentation (alt text, transcripts, reading instructions, etc.) should be a mandatory part of any webtext submission.
- A controlled vocabulary (if that's possible?) for webtext and media genres should be provided so that authors can tag their own elements from this set list.

Finally, students recommended that the labor of metadata be shifted to authors. This is not a surprising recommendation given the state of digital scholarly publishing at the moment. Calls for open access and collaboration are often accompanied by calls for crowdsourcing, which essentially means re-envisioning the labor structure of publishing. Students who were brand-new to digital publishing could, after only one semester of study, see this and agree that this discussion needs to take place. Their recommendations are important—and exciting, knowing that these students are the next generation of critically, rhetorically, and functionally literate editors of scholarly communication.

Acknowledgements

I owe thanks to Ryan Trauman for the idea of being able to remix and better cite media elements through metadata tagging. I also thank the editors and Isaac Gilman for great advice in shaping this chapter. Finally, the most thanks goes to the Pirates of Metadata: Sarah Chance, Lyndsey Eagle, Meghan Engel, David Gaudio, Susan Grogin, Melissa Hermann, Laura Patrick, Kira Plotts, Valerie Romack, Constance Ruholl, Kali Shevlin, Ameliah Tawlks, Amy Thomas, Kirsten Van De Veer, and Jessica Wosniak.

Notes

1. As of last count, the journal has over 45,000 unique hits a month, with readers in 180 countries (Eyman 2006).
2. *Kairos* advocates open-source software such as Cyberduck.
3. For more information about the Public Knowledge Project, see http://pkp.sfu.ca/history.
4. We have already co-authored a poster session on the outcomes of their mining workflow: see Ball et al. 2011.
5. Illinois State University is a second-tier school in the Normal tradition, well respected for its faculty teaching and its teacher-education programs, and the English department faculty typically teach two to three classes per semester, but the university still has strong research expectations, with peer-reviewed articles and scholarly books making up the bulk of what's expected prior to tenure.
6. See Ball 2009.
7. For more information, read the National Institutes of Health Public Access Policy Details at http://publicaccess.nih.gov/policy.htm.
8. There are twelve terms—or descriptors for "the nature or genre of the resource"—in the DCMI Type controlled vocabulary: Collection, Dataset, Event, Image, InteractiveResource, MovingImage, PhysicalObject, Service, Software, Sound, StillImage,

and Text (DCMI Usage Board 2012). *Kairos* uses only a subset of these Types (e.g., the journal doesn't publish PhysicalObjects, Events, or Services). All webtexts in *Kairos* are considered InteractiveResources under DCMI's definition, but not all GIFs are StillImages because animated GIFs *move*, which makes them MovingImages instead. In this case, information technology skills (e.g., knowing that .gif represents an image file) don't help a metadata miner understand the context in which that GIF is used. Instead, a student needs to understand the rhetorical context of the GIF by viewing it on the webpage in which it was published (e.g., what's the GIF *doing* and in what context) in order to evaluate its function within the webtext and thus tag it appropriately in the metadata.

9. One goal of this assignment was to teach students how to write business reports, a genre that publishing majors would need in their jobs. For the full assignment (and links to other assignments on the syllabus), see http://ceball.com/classes/354/spring11.

References

ACRL (Association of College and Research Libraries). 2000. *Information Literacy Competency Standards for Higher Education.* Chicago: ACRL, January 18. http://www.ala.org/acrl/standards/informationlit-eracycompetency.

Baca, Murtha, ed. 2008. *Introduction to Metadata,* 2nd ed. Los Angeles: Getty Research Institute.

Ball, Cheryl. E. 2009. "Tenure Letter." http://www.ceball.com/tenure/intro/tenure-letter.

———. 2011. "Metadata Project Description Sheets [English 354]." http://www.ceball.com/classes/354/spring11/wp-content/uploads/2011/02/spreadsheet-descriptions1.pdf.

———. 2011a. "Metadata Instruction Set: Fields Requiring Little Instruction." http://www.ceball.com/classes/354/spring11/wp-content/up-loads/2011/02/metadata-instructions-LITTLE.doc

Ball, Cheryl E., and The Pirates of Metadata. 2011. "Learning through Leading: Digital Media Scholarly Publishing." Poster presented at New Media Consortium conference, Madison, WI, July 19.

Bobley, Brett. 2010. "Opening Up the Ivory Tower? Access and Academic Publishing." Fora.tv. YouTube video. 2:56. From a discussion at the conference The Digital University, New York, NY, April 21, 2010. http://www.youtube.com/watch?v=7mRFRe4DxdM.

Borgman, Christine. 2007. *Scholarship in the Digital Age: Information, Infra-*

structure, and the Internet. Cambridge, MA: MIT Press.

DCMI Usage Board. 2012. "DCMI Metadata Terms." Dublin Core Metadata Initiative. June 14. http://dublincore.org/documents/2012/06/14/dcmi-terms.

Eyman, Douglas. 2006. "The Arrow and the Loom: A Decade of *Kairos*." *Kairos: A Journal of Rhetoric, Technology, and Pedagogy* 11, no. 1 (Fall). http://Kairos.technorhetoric.net/11.1/binder.html?topoi/eyman/index.html.

———. 2007. *Digital rhetoric: Ecologies and economies of digital circulation.* Dissertation. Michigan State University, Lansing, MI.

Fitzpatrick, Kathleen. 2010. *Planned Obsolescence: Publishing, Technology, and the Future of the Academy.* MediaCommons Press edition. http://mediacommons.futureofthebook.org/mcpress/plannedobsolescence.

Hitchcock, Steve, Leslie Carr, and Wendy Hall. 1996. "A Survey of STM Online Journals 1990–95: The Calm before the Storm." The Open Journal Project. Last updated February 14. http://journals.ecs.soton.ac.uk/survey/survey.html.

Selber, Stuart A. 2004. *Multiliteracies for a Digital Age.* Studies in Writing and Rhetoric. Carbondale: Southern Illinois University Press.

Willinsky, John. 2009. *The Access Principle: The Case for Open Access to Research and Scholarship.* Cambridge, MA: MIT Press.

Wysocki, Anne. 2002. "Bookling Monument." *Kairos: a Journal of Rhetoric, Technology and Pedagogy,* 7, 3 (Fall). http://kairos.technorhetoric.net/7.3/coverweb/wysocki/.

CHAPTER 7

The Poster Session as a Vehicle for Teaching the Scholarly Communication Process

Merinda Kaye Hensley
University of Illinois at Urban-Champaign

Introduction

Teaching librarians will agree that information literacy concepts are best taught when students are invested in the outcomes of their learning. Student engagement can be demonstrated in many ways: a lesson that is directly tied to a course assignment, a one-shot session that incorporates student-driven activity, or a one-on-one teachable moment at the reference desk. For the past decade, efforts to improve the undergraduate experience have been taking place through the development of new curricular experiences including first-year seminars, writing-intensive courses, undergraduate research, global and service learning, capstone projects, and much more. These programs are a game changer for information literacy efforts, impacting the traditional ways librarians interact with students through the classroom experience and on the reference desk.

The curriculum changes in academia all have one aspect in common: they create an environment where the undergraduate student moves from being a consumer to being a creator of knowledge. Undergraduate students are increasingly contributing to the academic conversation by writing papers for their courses that are archived in the institutional repository and presenting their research results at conferences. In what ways should the librarian's approach to information literacy instruction adopt scholarly communication issues when the undergraduate student becomes the author?

Let us first consider two terms that are common in a librarian's vocabulary: *information literacy* and *scholarly communication*:

> To be *information literate*, a person must be able to recognize when information is needed and have the ability to locate, evaluate, and use effectively the needed information. (ALA 1989)

> *Scholarly communication* is the system through which research and other scholarly writings are created, evaluated for quality, disseminated to the scholarly community, and preserved for future use. (ALA 2003)

Librarians are intensifying efforts to influence developments around scholarly communication issues, and this advocacy is finding its way into the classroom. Warren and Duckett (2010) challenge librarians to consider undergraduates as a prime audience for discussing the economics of the publishing cycle:

> A greater awareness of where information comes from and where it is accessible is important for not only developing the evaluative skills needed to find and make the best use of information, but also to understand the social nature of information and knowledge. Shaping this contextual understanding of information has allegedly always been an aspect of information literacy, but in practice it is frequently overshadowed by a skills-based approach that focuses on teaching students how to find, access, and evaluate information. (350)

Since 2007, the University of Illinois at Urbana-Champaign has been working with a one-of-a-kind undergraduate research program, the Ethnography of the University Initiative (EUI), to assist students with developing and presenting research posters and publishing them in the institutional repository, Illinois Digital Environment for Access to Learning and Scholarship (IDEALS).[1] Undergraduate research programs offer new opportunities for librarians to weave together their expertise in areas of student learning, information literacy, and scholarly communication. In fact, one could argue that the librarian's expertise is best positioned to lead support for the last phase of the research process—publication and dissemination of original undergraduate student work. This chapter will examine the role of the librarian in teaching the scholarly communication process, outline the relationship between a library and a formal undergraduate research program, detail how the poster session operates, and look ahead to how libraries can support expanding undergraduate research programs.

Creating High-Impact Learning Experiences throughout the Undergraduate Experience

Undergraduate research experiences continue to gain momentum across types of institution as well as by discipline. The Council on Undergraduate Research (CUR),[2] an organization that focuses on providing support through publications and outreach, defines undergraduate research as "an inquiry or investigation conducted by an undergraduate student that makes an original intellectual or creative contribution to the discipline" (CUR 2012a). Research universities, such as the University of Illinois, continue to emulate the progress of liberal arts and four-year private institutions in refining undergraduate education to provide discipline-oriented research programs, such as undergraduate research opportunities, that provide a strong foundation in inquiry-based learning (Boyer Commission 1998). Librarians' efforts to expand the reach of information literacy have not gone unnoticed by the academy. The Association of American Colleges and Universities (AAC&U) includes information literacy in its outline of high-impact learning experiences,[3] which includes formal undergraduate research. "The goal is to involve students with actively contested questions, empirical observation, cutting-edge technologies, and the sense of excitement that comes from working to answer important questions" (Kuh 2008, 10). These high-impact learning experiences also generate new opportunities and environments for teaching librarians to engage students beyond the one-shot instruction session.

Not to be confused with curriculum of the past (e.g., the standalone research paper assignment), undergraduate research programs invite students into faculty-led research by allowing them either to design a research project of their own or to be a partner within a faculty member's research agenda. Students are mentored throughout the research process, including doing background research, gathering and organizing data, and contributing to the resulting scholarly output. Students benefit from exposure to the rigors of academia under the tutelage of a disciplinary expert, and the faculty member is enriched by the unobstructed and neophyte view of the student. Most significant, though, is that students publish and disseminate the results of their research in myriad ways: by publishing in undergraduate student journals, presenting at campus symposia and national conferences, creating research posters, and depositing their research in institutional repositories. Liberal arts and research institutions have been able to provide undergraduate research opportunities in the sciences by allocating resources for faculty to individually mentor undergraduate students as part of their research agendas and the goals of their departments. The social sciences and humanities have followed the lead of the science disciplines in fostering scholarly engagement through experiential learning opportunities, including immersive fieldwork and experiments, and by exploring the growing field of digital humanities. The new curricular landscape provides experiential opportunities for the librarian to lead discussions that will assist students in understanding the publication process, intellectual property issues, and the significance of archiving collections of student research.

The Role of the Teaching Librarian

Today's undergraduate students are sharing exponentially more information than their predecessors, their extensive Web lives exposed through a social media deluge. We know very little, however, about their understanding of the authorship and publication process within academic digital scholarly production.[4] Students are making decisions early in their academic careers that will influence how they capture and release information for the rest of their lives. When students participate in undergraduate research, they face new decisions regarding copyright, data management, open access (OA), authors' rights, and the creation of metadata for preservation purposes. The students' relationship to scholarly communication transforms from that of consumer to that of producer when they submit their research to an institutional repository or student journal or present at a conference. Librarians have the expertise to play an educative role throughout the process of publication, dissemination, and preservation.

Faculty may understand the value librarians bring to the classroom in teaching students how to locate, evaluate, and use information, but our narrative is only beginning to emerge on issues relating to the creation and curation of undergraduate student work. While discussion in the literature on the partnership between libraries and undergraduate research programs is scarce, Stamatoplos (2009) identified a new paradigm:

> Though their needs can in many ways resemble those of faculty researchers, such students understandably might not always think like experienced scholars. The librarian becomes a critical ally in the research process and a welcome guide to a more sophisticated approach to scholarship. The librarian can make a significant contribution to what is an inquiry-based model of teaching and learning both at the campus level and throughout the research community. (240)

Working with students on scholarly communication issues as they pertain to undergraduate research strengthens the role of the librarian in the publishing and dissemination process, affirming Ogburn's (2011) compelling phrase, "Lifelong learning requires lifelong access" (515).

Ethnography of the University Initiative at the University of Illinois at Urbana-Champaign

Background

Celebrating its ten-year anniversary in 2013, the Ethnography of the University Initiative (EUI)[5] is a collaborative program that engages students in ethnographic research about the University of Illinois at Urbana-Champaign community, including but not limited to the students' experiences in the community. Although based at the University of Illinois at Urbana-Champaign, EUI has explored multiple academic perspectives through courses at other universities, including University of Illinois at Chicago, Illinois State University, Parkland College, Ithaca College, and Syracuse University. EUI is, at its heart, a multidisciplinary endeavor, and while the number of courses affiliated with the program varies by semester, examples include agricultural and consumer economics, anthropology, Asian American studies, curriculum and instruction, educational organization and leadership, educational policy studies, kinesiology, natural resources and environmental sciences, rhetoric and composition, speech communication, and studio art. Each semester, EUI recruits faculty who teach established courses through the EUI structure. Courses taught as part of EUI operate in coordination with Institutional Review Board training and approval and library partnerships with the Student Life and Culture Archival Program (SLC), the University Library, and the institutional repository, IDEALS. Unlike undergraduate research programs in the sciences, where students are individually assigned to a faculty member, EUI courses form learning communities that are mentored together by the teaching faculty, the students' peers, and campus partners. From a student's perspective, core disciplinary concepts are taught by looking through an ethnographic or archival lens in order to gather qualitative or historical data around issues that most often resonate with the student's Illinois experience (e.g., campus safety, socialization, students with physical and learning disabilities, use of campus space). Student work culminates in the Bi-Annual Student Research Conference comprised of panel presentations, research posters, and most recently, multimedia presentations.

The University Library has been involved with EUI from its inception, although this relationship has matured over time. Library efforts have included leading one-shot library instruction on searching skills, maintaining a bibliographic list of publications about the University of Illinois, and membership on the EUI Internal Advisory Board.[6] While there are several subject specialist librarians that serve EUI, there is one over-arching library liaison that coordinates efforts across the Library. The SLC serves as a museum of university activities, collecting and archiving documents and artifacts that shine light on "student involvement in fraternities, sororities, student government, religious associations, publications, social events, athletics, and other activities that contribute to the total student experience in higher education" (SLC 2012). Each semester, the SLC invites students to learn how an archive is different from a library and how archival materials are stored and organized, and to explore the plethora of primary source materials related to the lives of past University of Illinois students. When the experience of archival research is interconnected with searching the institutional repository, a living history is formed that tells a story about the university and its culture throughout time:

> Students often pass through universities with little knowledge of the histories, mandates, regulations, economies, or values that have structured university organization and practices. Even a brief foray in the archives helps students to see the university as an evolving institution and to appreciate the historical specificity of their own inquiries. (Hunter et al. 2008, 43)

An established collection in the institutional repository presents new opportunities for publishing undergraduate student research. Instead of repeatedly asking the same questions from semester to semester, faculty members are able to encourage students to build on previous students' work by searching IDEALS during the formulation of their research questions. To date, over 600 student projects have been archived in IDEALS. Examples include studies of language barriers for the international campus community; ethics of animal care at the College of Veterinary Medicine; examination of social cultures across campus; investigation of the campus controversy about the retirement of a campus mascot; the freshman experience in dorms, cafeterias, and PanHellenic life; and much more.[7]

EUI is an example of the type of undergraduate research program in the social sciences and humanities described in the Boyer report: "The focal point of the first year should be a small seminar taught by experienced faculty. The seminar should deal with topics that will stimulate and open intellectual horizons and allow opportunities for learning by inquiry in a collaborative environment" (Boyer Commission 1998, 28). The University Library is a facilitator of student learning by virtue of its instructional mission, archives, student collections, and service ethos. Incorporating a student research poster session elevates the library's commitment to information literacy and scholarly communication by fostering inquiry at the undergraduate level through the publication of original student work.

An Example of EUI Student Work

While the scope of EUI's projects are too diverse and numerous to share within this narrative, a recent example serves to demonstrate the library's essential role. Students in a fall 2010 course Kinesiology/ Sociology 249: Sport and Modern Society (instructor: Synthia Sydnor)[8] examined the educational evolution of female faculty and their role in the history of athletics and sports scholarship. Eight student groups were each asked to examine the contribution and impact of an assigned female professor to today's University of Illinois kinesiology department. The students combined archival and ethnographic research to chronicle the faculty members' activities. Specifically, the students researched faculty papers in the University Archives and conducted ethnographic research through interviews with current professors, as well as students and family members who could speak to the intellectual life of the assigned faculty member. Toward the end of the semester, the liaison librarian taught an in-class session on how to create an effective research poster from the primary source material and qualitative data collected. At the end of the semester, each group presented its research as a poster at the EUI Bi-Annual Student Research Conference.[9]

Benefits from the EUI program for students include the opportunity to collaborate with faculty in the research and discovery process, contribute to the dialogue of a community of scholars, and gain presentation experience at the student conference. Students learn to do primary source and archival research, they collect and manage qualitative and quantitative data, and sometimes their research is used to provide feedback to the university on student issues. Because EUI frequently tackles controversial and challenging topics, students who identify with specific communities (e.g., international students, LGBT students, students of color) lend a unique voice to strengthening undergraduate retention,[10] which simultaneously lays the groundwork to improve students' confidence in applying to graduate school. Faculty benefit from seminars that explore student intellectual property rights and the pedagogical practices around ethnographic and archival research (EUI 2012a). Perhaps most interesting, reciprocal learning provides faculty members with a fresh look at the academy through the experiences of their students. And finally, EUI presents a new avenue for re-envisioning information literacy instruction by teaching the life cycle of scholarly communication.

The Evolving Role of the Library: Research Posters

As we have seen, the University Library works with EUI during several phases of the research process. The primary library liaison works with EUI to provide general library and poster development instruction. The University Archives and the SLC Archival Program work with courses to teach primary sources and strategies for performing archival research. The coordinator of IDEALS works with the EUI co-directors and program coordinator to create metadata and manage uploads of student projects to the institutional repository. These relationships support the liaison librarian's goal of engaging students in discussions around intellectual property, research, and publication.

Bi-Annual Student Research Conference

In 2006, EUI's Bi-Annual Student Research Conference consisted of a series of student-led panels. Although student participation was voluntary, teaching faculty strongly encouraged or mandated attendance at the conference. Students must apply to participate in the conference, and while no student has ever been denied an opportunity to present his or her work, many more students supported their peers by being in the audience rather than choosing to present. Panels were grouped by topic, and students were given up to five minutes to present their semester-long research, oftentimes with presentation slides. After each student had a chance to present his or her work, the audience was encouraged to ask questions of the panelists. Although the campus community is customarily invited, the majority of the audience consisted of peers, friends, teaching faculty, EUI coordinators, and librarians. When asked why they chose not to present at the conference, students indicated hesitation to participate because of the mystery of what a student conference entailed. Anxiety about public speaking and the ambiguity over what questions might be asked as a panel presenter overpowered any desire to share their research. The liaison librarian identified a new opportunity: a poster session would address the students' concerns while expanding the content of the conference by including students who wouldn't have otherwise taken part in the event.

In the sciences, poster sessions have been common at conferences for many years, and more recently poster sessions have been gaining momentum across disciplines, including the social sciences and the humanities. Posters provide the opportunity to break down research into core elements: an abstract, detailed methodology, visual presentation of data, and discussion of results. They also allow for informal conversation between the researcher and his or her audience. The liaison librarian proposed the idea of a poster session to the coordinators of the EUI program as a way to further engage students in the conference process, as well as an opportunity to teach scholarly communication concepts. The poster session was piloted in spring 2007 and became a feature of the student conference the following fall semester.

Why is a poster session an effective addition to a student conference? Poster sessions can be framed as a first step into the world of research dissemination while challenging students to think about how they are going to clearly and succinctly convey ideas and conclusions from their research. First, students must determine how to present quantitative and qualitative research data in a visual manner that balances aesthetics and information. Second, the opportunity to present a poster appeals to the learning strategies of those who would rather interact on a personal basis than risk facing a group; the amateur researcher is exposed to discourse in a safer environment than at the front of a room full of faculty and peers. And finally, the poster session is an exercise in professional development, allowing students to hone skills that will prove beneficial in graduate school or a professional job.

From the liaison librarian's perspective, the benefits of working with students on creating research posters drives progress toward meeting Standard Five of the *Information Literacy Competency Standards for Higher Education:* "The information literate student understands many of the economic, legal, and social issues surrounding the use of information and accesses and uses information ethically and legally" (ACRL 2000). First, undergraduate students engaged in formal undergraduate research programs have the opportunity to create new information. As part of that creation, students as authors must consider the ethical and legal ramifications of archiving their work in the institutional repository. Second, librarians are best situated to lead a conversation about the publication process by highlighting topics such as copyright, intellectual property issues, OA, and the significance of archiving collections of student work. Ultimately, these elements are woven into an instruction session about how to design a research poster while considering issues focused on the larger scholarly communication process.

Organizing the Poster Session

At the beginning of each semester, the liaison librarian is introduced to the teaching faculty as part of a larger orientation session that discusses the Institutional Review Board and ethical research standards specific to the structure of EUI, including best practices for using course management software, use of technology by student researchers, and strategies for undertaking archival research. Since the structure of

EUI does not require classes to participate in the student conference at the end of the semester, the orientation provides the liaison librarian a chance to promote the poster session while teaching faculty are still planning the semester. Increasingly over the past five years, the library's participation in the orientation has made a visible impact; faculty are choosing to encourage student participation in the conference and have promoted the poster session to their students in a variety of ways: as a mandatory assignment, for extra credit, or as a professional development opportunity. However, as part of the EUI structure, faculty members are required to donate class time throughout the semester for guest speakers in order to facilitate ethnographic and archival research (e.g., Institutional Review Board, the EUI coordinator). With tight schedules and significant course content to be covered, not every course is able to extend an invitation to the library liaison to teach students during class time about developing a poster. Getting into the classroom to teach the students about the poster session is the single largest challenge for this library initiative.

Teaching Posters

The pedagogical strategy for EUI courses focuses on inquiry-based learning, a form of active learning that aligns well with presenting a research poster. Inquiry learning is not about how much knowledge transfer can happen over the course of the semester; rather, it emphasizes the processes around student-driven questions and making meaning from the resulting research and observations. First, posters provide the opportunity for students (as knowledge producers) to contextualize and explain what they have learned. Second, the poster session creates a learning environment in which there is distributed knowledge sharing among the attendees. Each presenter and attendee brings his or her experience and knowledge to the conversation, giving the presenter a broader perspective on the research and oftentimes leaving the presenter with new questions. Teaching students how to develop a research poster provides an entry to the classroom to forge deeper relationships with budding researchers and the teaching faculty (who may also have questions about scholarly communication issues but are hesitant to ask).

The lesson plan for teaching research poster design is threefold: instruction in how to develop and design a compelling research poster, instruction in how to work effectively with data visualization tools, and an overview of scholarly communication issues. The lesson plan is taught in a fifty-minute session but can be condensed to thirty minutes with support from the corresponding online guide.[11]

The liaison librarian begins the session by asking students if they have previously presented or attended a poster session. Frequently, no one in the room has presented a poster but one or two are willing to share their impressions of attending a poster session, usually the campus student research symposium held each spring. Next, during a slide show of past EUI posters, students are asked, "What elements do or do not work for this poster?" "Does the visualization of this data tell a story?" "What would you do differently?" The liaison librarian also brings a physical poster to the library instruction session so that students can begin to envision how their research will translate into a poster presentation.

There are three elements students are asked to consider before designing a poster:

1. What information should be covered verbally in a lightning talk (1–2 minutes)?
2. What information is best shared visually on the poster?
3. What information should be conveyed through a handout?

The three elements should complement one another. When selecting which content is appropriate for each element, the librarian encourages students to tell a story, constructing a narrative that brings their research alive for the audience. The lightning talk should bring context to the visual information presented in the poster. Handout information should include complex background information, possibly a written abstract, more detailed results, references cited, and links to online portfolios.

The next section of the lesson plan, best practices for poster design, is covered only briefly, relying upon the more detailed information in the online guide. The liaison librarian outlines poster specifications using Microsoft PowerPoint, and although there are myriad software programs that can be used to create a poster including the use of institutional templates, most students prefer to start with software with which they are already comfortable.

Parallel to the *Information Literacy Competency Standards*, the *ACRL Visual Literacy Competency Standards for Higher Education* provide a framework for teaching students about visual literacy.[12] In order to develop an effective research poster, students must be able to choose, evaluate, and create visual images that concisely convey the talking points of their research.[13] Students may use a combination of visual images or create graphic representations from their data. The librarian demonstrates examples from past EUI posters, including use of charts, tables, graphs, tag clouds, infographics, and photographs, in order to spark inspiration. Visualization of data is a complicated topic, and most students have not gathered all of their data, usually qualitative ethnographic interview data, by the time of the library instruction. While the visualization of ethnographic data can be challenging for an experienced researcher,[14] one of the goals of the EUI curriculum is to expose students to the many aspects of data management. Visualization techniques help to tell a story and break up text-heavy poster presentations. Given the limited time available for library instruction, students are directed to an open library workshop on data visualization.[15] Students can also make appointments with the subject specialist librarian who specializes in data visualization or with the liaison librarian for personalized assistance.

The University Library has allocated funds each semester as an investment in undergraduate research so that students can present a professionally printed poster at the student conference. Since the printing budget is limited, the first twenty-five students to send an e-mail to the liaison librarian with their tentative poster title are allocated free printing. Others who would like to present a poster may pay for printing on their own, or their department may choose to cover the cost. The e-mail establishes a working relationship between the student and the liaison librarian. Over the following weeks, the liaison librarian communicates with the entire group, highlighting best practices and reminding students of deadlines. Oftentimes, students will set up individual consultation time to talk through their poster development. The liaison librarian makes suggestions for content, visualization, and design and reviews each poster for mechanical details, including spelling and grammar. When the liaison librarian works with a student over the course of a semester, she can reinforce her role in the research process in ways that one-shot sessions and chance encounters do not.

For most undergraduate EUI students, this is their first experience from being an information consumer to being a knowledge producer. While EUI would like to see all the student posters archived, submissions are voluntary, and not all students initially understand the value of submitting their posters to the institutional repository. During the instruction session, the liaison librarian shows the EUI online community and briefly discusses the benefits for the students: contributing to a knowledge base about their university, providing future students a record of past research, influencing the generation of future research questions, a permanent URL that can be used on a résumé, and positive online presence in search engines.

Finally, information about the University Library Student Poster Award is briefly addressed, including the rubric that is used for selecting the award winners. Students are reminded that they need to show effective visual elements of their research, demonstrate use of library resources, and properly cite all of their sources (usually though a handout). Students are also shown how to cite their poster presentation on their résumé, further emphasizing the professional nature of the conference.

There are myriad advantages for the library in teaching students how to design a research poster. First, it gives the librarian a chance to advocate for the role that teaching librarians can play in the research, publication, and dissemination process. Second, the librarian can discuss scholarly communication issues in the context of faculty curriculum goals. Third, conversation can begin to focus on copyright concerns for the student as author, an increasingly essential understanding whether a student chooses a path in the public or private sector. Fourth, the library can promote use of the institutional repository to future researchers, professionals, and current faculty as an archive as well as a resource.

Poster Printing

As anyone who has ever had a poster professionally printed knows, it is very expensive, and this is especially true on a student's budget. Nevertheless, seeing a colorful, professionally printed research poster on an easel is rewarding, and it cements the experience of what it means to be an author and experienced researcher. The University Library does not currently offer large-format printing to students and faculty, so the library negotiated with a local printing company to secure a discounted rate based on bulk printing. The posters are uniform in size (40 inches high by 30 inches wide) and printed in color on lightweight (60#) paper. The library administration's allocated fund pays for twenty-five posters to be printed each semester. The library also invested in standing easels, cardboard backings, and small binder clips to secure each poster. Students are encouraged to keep their posters after the conference.

University Library Student Poster Award

Since the fall 2009 semester, two students have been recognized with an University Library Student Poster Award, oftentimes including an additional honorable mention. The two top awardees are given a $25 campus bookstore gift card,[16] funded by the University Library and EUI. The awards are selected by the liaison librarian and the SLC Librarian or a member of the University Library User Education Committee, with input from the EUI directors and coordinator. The liaison librarian collaborated with the committee to draft and approve a rubric for the award.

The rubric evaluates three main elements for the posters: visual literacy, demonstration of use of library resources, and proper attribution and citation formatting. Within the subcomponents of the rubric, each poster is rated on a three-point scale (3 = exceeds, 2 = meets, 1 = does not meet) for each element. Visual literacy is examined by considering, "How did the student communicate their research through the use of visuals? (e.g., graphs, charts, infographics, tag clouds, photography)." Librarians look for evidence of use of library resources by asking the question, "Did the student use the archives, electronic resources, books in the collection, etc.?" And finally, the librarians look for proper citation management by asking, "Did the student use a single, consistent citation style? Did the student properly cite sources including images?"

At the Conference

The EUI Bi-Annual Student Research Conference is typically scheduled two weeks before the end of the semester and runs for five hours into the evening. Students arrive dressed in business-casual attire, with handouts ready, and excited to see their posters and talk about their work. The posters are scheduled between panel sessions; during one of the poster sessions, the EUI supplies pizza and drinks for attendees. The poster sessions are scheduled for thirty-five minutes, but conversations are often in full force at the hour mark. One of the liaison librarian's favorite inquiries is, "If you could continue this research next semester, what new questions would you ask?"

The implementation of the poster session has led to unexpected outcomes. The close quarters of the posters often leads to serendipitous exchanges between presenters. During a past conference, two students from separate classes, placed next to each other, had carried out similar research on dorm life. Before the poster session even started, the students held an intense discussion about their findings, to the delight of other presenters and attendees. It was a spontaneous exchange of ideas and an example of how inquiry-based learning allows students to engage in reciprocal critical thinking. Anecdotally, several teaching faculty members have shared with the liaison librarian that the process of creating posters has led to improved final papers; students were asked challenging questions during the poster session, which oftentimes led their final conclusions in a more reflective direction.

The development of research posters demonstrates oral and written work and provides an opportunity for critique of student work, a valuable element in thoughtful and progressive undergraduate education. The Boyer report emphasizes, "Dissemination of results is an essential and integral part of the research process, which means that training in research cannot be considered complete without training in effective communication" (Boyer Commission 1998, 32).

Archiving Student Work

While capturing student knowledge contributes to the larger EUI mission of examining the university over time, publishing original student research in the institutional repository also initiates an opportunity for creators of knowledge to curate their own collection. Students are brought into the world of information organization by participating in the process of choosing what to preserve, considering issues related to intellectual property, and generating the metadata attached to their materials. In working with the faculty supervisor, the liaison librarian and the IDEALS coordinator to archive their work, students learn to systematically catalog not only their research but also their larger online lives.

Approximately 50 percent of EUI projects have been preserved in the institutional repository since 2005. As of mid-October 2012, projects from the EUI community have been downloaded 247,808 times (EUI 2012b). There are eleven defined collections, including Diversity on Campus/Equity and Access, Globalization and the University, Student Communities and Cultures, Technology and Student Life, and University Units and Institutional Transformation. The project that has been downloaded most frequently (20,846 times) is titled, *UIUC Women's Crew: Origins, History, and Progress*.[17]

As part of the EUI process, students are given the option of signing an agreement for submitting their work to the institutional repository (IDEALS 2006). This is usually a student's first experience in navigating authors' rights and OA, providing an ideal opportunity to talk with students about intellectual property rights. The IDEALS coordinator worked closely with the EUI coordinator to draft the agreement that must be signed in order to deposit student work in the institutional repository. There is a train-the-trainer program in place where the EUI coordinator, with advice from the IDEALS coordinator, works with teaching faculty to emphasize talking points regarding intellectual property issues that need to be clarified for students. "Asking students to consider if and how they want their own work to be shared and used by others shifts the nature of discussions from cautionary and reactive to reflective and proactive, and explicitly acknowledges that the students' work is valued enough to be shared if they choose" (Davis-Kahl 2012, 213).

A wide variety of student materials are preserved in IDEALS: research proposals, annotated bibliographies, robust course management pages that include anonymized student discussions, interview and survey instruments, data in all forms, research process essays, final papers, slide presentations, posters, and media projects including podcasts and video.

The EUI staff, in collaboration with the IDEALS coordinator, creates metadata for the entire collection. Subject headings are provided to conform within the EUI community, and students are given the opportunity to provide abstract and keywords. Due to the open nature of the IDEALS platform, all records are indexed by online search engines and therefore findable by anyone with an Internet connection. Item records include the research question, instrument, methodologies, analysis of data, and in some cases, the raw research data (Shreeves 2009). Students must de-identify any research subjects, which means they anonymize their data, before it can be included in IDEALS. The teaching faculty and the EUI coordinator are responsible for ensuring that this has happened, and it provides an opportunity to talk further about data management issues. Submissions are not peer-reviewed, and all student work is accepted into the archive, although some students choose to anonymize or embargo their submissions given the controversial nature of the topics covered in the EUI courses. All coursework affiliated with EUI is identified as such in the item description so as not to confuse undergraduate student work with peer-reviewed faculty publications.[18] And most important, students retain copyright over their work.

The value of preserving original undergraduate student research includes these advantages:

- Future students, at Illinois and beyond, are able to find research on the same or similar topics.
- Past student work can be a starting point for current research topics and provide background information.
- Students can see how different research methods are used across parallel topics.
- Students are better able to differentiate their work from previous projects (Shreeves 2009).

When the archived student work is combined with primary resources from the Student Life and Culture Archival Program and the University Archives, EUI students are able to paint a more colorful, complex, and thoughtful picture of the Illinois community experience.[19]

Looking Ahead to Support Expanding Undergraduate Research Programs

Not surprisingly, new ideas have emanated from the original poster session as conceived five years ago. One semester, two undergraduate rhetoric professors teamed together, required each student to design a poster, and held their own conference of virtual posters presented on a projection screen. The faculty members were able to see the value of data visualization and presenting student research even if the conference was unable to accommodate the entirety of both classes.

As part of the move to facilitate multimedia student projects, the EUI program recently secured campus grant money to purchase technology for creating video and podcast projects. In partnership with the Undergraduate Library, this development parallels a new University Library initiative to build a media commons. The media commons recently hired a coordinator and will be located in the Undergraduate Library, which will provide space, furniture, and technology in support of multimedia production. In-house technology will include new hardware, software, media-viewing stations, collaboration rooms, a green screen, mobile whiteboards and screens, huddle boards with cameras, and loanable technology. The multimedia projects are also being archived in the institutional repository.[20]

Another opportunity for the library comes with the implementation of a student research symposium for the spring semester through the campus rhetoric program. The liaison librarian has provided similar library instruction similar to that given to poster presenters at the EUI student research conference.[21] The next stage for this program is to partner with the IDEALS coordinator in order to archive the posters, and possibly video of the presentations.

The University of Illinois at Urbana-Champaign is seeing an increase in disciplinary student research conferences, and the liaison librarian has been invited to teach about posters in the applied health sciences and the mechanical engineering departments. And finally, the campus is preparing to centralize support for formal undergraduate research. An inaugural director for the new Office of Undergraduate Research has been recently appointed.

"Traditional" undergraduate research initiatives can be difficult to implement at large research universities; there simply are not enough faculty mentors to work with students one-on-one across disciplines. At Illinois, EUI is a model program that builds an undergraduate research experience into an interdisciplinary course structure of learning communities. It is reasonable to expect that research institutions will continue to find creative ways to implement undergraduate research programs. The instructional mission of the library must also expand to reflect undergraduate students' movement from being information consumers to being knowledge creators and curators.

Conclusion

Formal undergraduate research programs have potential to stimulate original thought and conversation between students and within their academic disciplines. As the directors of EUI remind us, "Universities have increasingly recognized the importance of engaging students in active learning, relating that learning to students' lived experiences, and helping them recognize that they are creators of knowledge rather than mere recipients of learned truths" (Hunter et al. 2008, 42).

The library supports the value of undergraduate authorship through information literacy and scholarly communication instruction efforts, archival and online collections, and its service commitment to publish, disseminate, and preserve original student work.

Undergraduate students are scholars-in-training, and their roles as authors will undoubtedly impact the questions that are being asked in scholarship. It may be the librarian's hope that this impact be felt in the overall scholarly communication process for it is future authors who will use their knowledge of the scholarly communication process to advocate for a more open system of information sharing. In order for those hopes to be realized, the responsibility lies with the teaching librarian to examine our praxis in the campus classroom in order to nurture students as authors.

There is a paradigmatic shift on the horizon in the way librarians think about our mission in the classroom. In collaborating with formal undergraduate research programs, teaching librarians can provide a learning environment that is ripe for working with scholarly communication issues in all forms.

Acknowledgments

The author would like to thank the Ethnography of the University Initiative for enthusiastically teaming with the University Library to offer the poster session as part of the Bi-Annual Student Research Conference. This chapter was originally conceived as a poster at the Annual American Library Association Meeting in Anaheim, California, on June 24, 2012. http://hdl.handle.net/2142/34762.

Notes

1. The IDEALS website is at https://www.ideals.illinois.edu.
2. The CUR website is at http://cur.org.
3. Kuh (2008) argues that ideally students would have access to one high-impact experience per year. High-impact learning experiences include first-year seminars and experiences, common intellectual experiences, learning communities, writing-intensive courses, collaborative assignments and projects, undergraduate research, diversity and global learning, service and community-based learning, internships, and capstone courses and projects.
4. This idea was explored in an unfunded Institute of Museum and Library Services (IMLS) grant.
5. The EUI website is at http://www.eui.illinois.edu.

6. Members of the Internal Advisory Board are listed at http://www. eui.illinois.edu/people/internal.

7. IDEALS has a community dedicated to EUI, which can be explored here: https://www.ideals.illinois.edu/handle/2142/755.

8. For a more complete description of the project, see http://ahs. illinois.edu/untoldstory.aspx.

9. As a result of the collaboration, the librarian was invited to be a member of an advisory board, "Untold Story" Provost's Gender Equity Grant.

10. The Council on Undergraduate Research states that undergraduate research programs increase retention (see CUR 2012b), and the directors of EUI also cite anecdotal evidence from conversations with students in which they have discussed retention and applications to graduate school.

11. The online guide, "Preparing a Research Poster for the EUI Student Conference," is at http://uiuc.libguides.com/poster.

12. According to the document's definition of visual literacy, "Visual literacy is a set of abilities that enables an individual to effectively find, interpret, evaluate, use, and create images and visual media. Visual literacy skills equip a learner to understand and analyze the contextual, cultural, ethical, aesthetic, intellectual, and technical components involved in the production and use of visual materials. A visually literate individual is both a critical consumer of visual media and a competent contributor to a body of shared knowledge and culture" (ACRL 2011).

13. To help students find and evaluate images, the librarian refers to student to an online guide, "Finding and Using Images," at http:// uiuc.libguides.com/images.

14. For some interesting ideas on visualization of data, see Lengler and Eppler 2007, Chapman 2009, and Friedman 2007.

15. For more information about the Savvy Researcher workshop series, visit http://illinois.edu/calendar/list/4068.

16. One semester, the poster award was given to a group. The librarian worried needlessly about how the students would split a $25 award—they decided to purchase snacks with the gift card and share them during class time.

17. To see a current statistics report, see "Top Downloads for Ethnography of the University Initiative," https://www.ideals.illinois.

edu/handle/2142/755/report.

18. This text is placed on every EUI submission in IDEALS: "Note: This is a student project from a course affiliated with the Ethnography of the University Initiative. EUI supports faculty development of courses in which students conduct original research on their university, and encourages students to think about colleges and universities in relation to their communities and within larger national and global contexts."

19. See "Student Research Projects" at http://www.eui.illinois.edu/student/multimedia/AnUntoldStoryVirtualExhibit.aspx.

20. See "Multimedia Projects —Ethnography of the University Initiative" at https://www.ideals.illinois.edu/handle/2142/30631.

21. Unfortunately, the University Library cannot afford to fund the printing of posters for the growing number of student poster sessions campus-wide and as part of the disciplines.

References

ACRL (Association of College and Research Libraries). 2000. *Information Literacy Competency Standards for Higher Education.* Chicago: ACRL, January 18. http://www.ala.org/acrl/standards/informationliteracycompetency.

———. 2011. *ACRL Visual Literacy Competency Standards for Higher Education.* Chicago: ACRL, October. http://www.ala.org/acrl/standards/visualliteracy.

ALA (American Library Association). 1989. "Presidential Committee on Information Literacy: Final Report." American Library Association. January 10. http://www.ala.org/acrl/publications/whitepapers/presidential.

———. 2003. "Principles and Strategies for the Reform of Scholarly Communication 1." American Library Association. June 24. http://www.ala.org/acrl/publications/whitepapers/principlesstrategies.

Boyer Commission on Educating Undergraduates in the Research University. 1998. Reinventing Undergraduate Education: A Blueprint for America's Research Universities. Stony Brook: State University of New York–Stony Brook. http://www.niu.edu/engagedlearning/research/pdfs/Boyer_Report.pdf.

Chapman, Cameron. 2009. "50 Great Examples of Data Visualization." Webdesigner Depot. June 1. http://www.webdesignerdepot.com/2009/06/50-great-examples-of-data-visualization.

CUR (Council on Undergraduate Research). 2012a. "About CUR." Accessed December 6. http://www.cur.org/about_cur.

———. 2012b. "Fact Sheet." Accessed December 6. http://www.cur.org/about_

cur/fact_sheet.

Davis-Kahl, Stephanie. 2012. "Engaging Undergraduates in Scholarly Communication: Outreach, Education and Advocacy." *College & Research Libraries News* 73, no. 4 (April): 212–222. http://crln.acrl.org/content/73/4/212.full.

EUI (Ethnography of the University Initiative). 2012a. "Quick Facts." Accessed December 7. http://www.eui.illinois.edu/about/facts.

———. 2012b. "Total Downloads." Accessed October 20. https://www.ideals.uiuc.edu/handle/2142/755.

Friedman, Vitaly. 2007. "Data Visualization: Modern Approaches." *Smashing Magazine*. August 2. http://www.smashingmagazine.com/2007/08/02/data-visualization-modern-approaches.

Hunter, Gina, Nancy Abelmann, Timothy Reese Cain, Tim McDonough, and Catherine Prendergast. 2008. "Interrogating the University, One Archival Entry at a Time." *Change: The Magazine of Higher Learning* 40, no. 5: 40–45.

IDEALS (Illinois Digital Environment for Access to Learning and Scholarship). 2006. "IDEALS Deposit Agreement: Non-Exclusive Distribution and Preservation License." April. https://services.ideals.illinois.edu/wiki/bin/view/IDEALS/DepositAgreement.

Kuh, George D. 2008. *High-Impact Educational Practices: What They Are, Who Has Access to Them, and Why They Matter.* Washington, DC: Association of American Colleges and Universities.

Lengler, Ralph, and Martin J. Eppler. 2007 "A Periodic Table of Visualization Methods," version 1.5. Visual-Literacy.org. http://www.visual-literacy.org/periodic_table/periodic_table.html.

Ogburn, Joyce L. 2011. "Lifelong Learning Requires Lifelong Access: Reflections on the ACRL Plan for Excellence." *College & Research Libraries News* 72, no. 9 (October): 514–515.

Shreeves, Sarah L. 2009. "Student Research on the University and in the Institutional Repository." Digital Library Federation Spring Forum. Raleigh, NC May 5, 2009. https://www.ideals.uiuc.edu/handle/2142/13054.

SLC (Student Life and Culture Archival Program). 2012. Homepage. Accessed December 6. http://archives.library.illinois.edu/slc.

Stamatoplos, Anthony. 2009. "The Role of Academic Libraries in Mentored Undergraduate Research: A Model of Engagement in the Academic Community." *College and Research Libraries* 70, no. 3 (May): 235–249.

Warren, Scott, and Kim Duckett. 2010. "Why Does Google Scholar Sometimes Ask for Money? Engaging Science Students in Scholarly Communication and the Economics of Information." *Journal of Library Administration* 50, no. 4: 349–372.

CHAPTER 8

Sparking Creativity

[The Sparky Awards and Mind Mashup at the University of Florida]

Margeaux Johnson
University of Florida

Matthew Daley
University of Florida

Introduction

In 2009, the University of Florida (UF) Libraries began participating in Open Access Week events. Most of the event plans were directed as outreach to university faculty, medical researchers, and our own library faculty and staff in all departments. Librarians designed and developed a weeklong array of programs targeted toward these populations to raise awareness, start conversations, and garner support for open access (OA) initiatives. However, initial planning left one of the most vital groups of stakeholders out of the conversation—future researchers. As Davis-Kahl (2012) points out, "The open access movement has typically engaged graduate students and faculty in discussions and advocacy around changing the scholarly communication landscape" (212). This focus on faculty and graduate students leaves behind an important change agent—undergraduate students. What if, instead of focusing on the establishment, we took the time to educate undergraduates before they begin making decisions about their scholarly communication practices?

Recognizing that undergraduate students and their perspectives were missing from the academic dialogue surrounding scholarly communication and because of the shifting digital media landscape where our students live, we began to consider how to engage them in this topic, one that will no doubt become increasingly important as they pursue future paths as content creators, researchers, or simply members of our current online participatory culture.

The answer came in the form of a call from the Association of Research Libraries (ARL) Scholarly Publishing and Academic

Resources Coalition (SPARC) for the 2009 host-your-own Sparky Awards. "The Sparky Awards is a contest that recognizes the best new short videos on the value of sharing information, and aims to broaden the discussion of access to scholarly research by inviting students to express their views creatively" (McLennan 2009, 19). This contest inspired a tech-savvy group of librarians to create and host a local contest. We felt that the creative component and the prize element of the Sparky Awards @ UF would be an excellent opportunity to create interest and dialogue with the students and would meet our objectives of increasing student engagement in this topic.

A half-dozen library employees came together based on a shared interest in scholarly communication, open source software, and technology. The grassroots group represented professionals from various departments—IT, the Digital Library, the Humanities and Social Sciences Library, the Science and Engineering Library, and the Art Library. As we contemplated the idea of promoting a contest as an activity to engage student interest, the group decided that simply hosting and publicizing the Sparky Awards at the library was not enough; we were looking for active engagement in the topic, rather than passive participation in the form of lectures or talks. The team realized that the UF Libraries needed to provide a framework for undergraduates to understand open information sharing and access to media creation tools. This led to the development of a complementary program in the Information Commons—a Mind Mashup Workshop that focused on media creation.

As a means of framing our decision to develop the workshop and promote the contest, this chapter will first examine the gap in undergraduate engagement in scholarly communication issues and then detail the need to begin this conversation because of the current digital media culture. Finally, we will offer concrete details from the local Sparky Awards @ UF contest and Mind Mashup Workshop as models for undergraduate learning.

Open Access Outreach: Are We Leaving Out Undergrads?

"The student voice brings freshness and energy to this ongoing conversation, highlighting that the students are not only the stewards of new and social technologies, but also that they have the potential to reshape scholarly communication entirely—simply by holding fast to the sharing practices now a part of their daily lives" (McLennan 2009, 19). If McLennan's assertion is true, then why are methods for engaging undergraduate students with scholarly communication virtually nonexistent in the OA outreach literature?

With the exception of McLennan (2009) and Davis-Kahl (2012), very little has been published in terms of advocacy for integrating scholarly communication outreach toward undergraduates. One notable exception is Warren and Duckett's (2010) article about engaging science students with scholarly communications issues. Warren and Duckett outline discussion questions and teaching points that move students to a higher level of critical thinking than the traditional information literacy "skills-based approach that focuses on teaching students how to find, access, and evaluate information" (351). These questions are not relevant only to science, technology, engineering, and math (STEM) students; they can also be used to develop critical evaluations surrounding the social, political, and ethical implications of information production among undergraduates of all majors. It is important to begin these conversations with undergraduates because of the growing trends of media production and digital sharing.

"Undergraduates … have an important role to play as future graduate students, scholars, and as citizens, one that should catalyze librarians who serve this population to acknowledge and act on a shared educational imperative" (Davis-Kahl 2012, 212). Davis-Kahl goes on to argue that libraries' vision for undergraduate education should include engagement with scholarly communication issues. As participants in the current digital media landscape, undergraduates are content creators. This shift in the ability of who is able to create and distribute content is yet another reason to engage undergraduates in the discussion surrounding copyright, authors' rights, and scholarly communication in the Digital Age.

Current research-based approaches to OA examine faculty perspectives in the disciplines or provide strategic plans for OA change (Emmet et al. 2011; Renfro 2011). It is easy to find information about faculty attitudes or publishing preferences for OA in fields as diverse as engineering, business, and library science.[1] Strategic plans for OA action often omit student engagement and focus on faculty. This is true of national organizations, like ARL,[2] calls for action aimed at librarians in prestigious academic library journals,[3] and individual university plans.[4] Descriptions of Open Access Week involvement at major universities fail to identify undergraduate students as key stakeholders. For example, Cryer and Collins (2011) describe OA outreach events at Duke. In the introduction, they identify the major players they hope to engage as authors, funding agencies, publishers, and librarians. There is no mention of the public or students as a stakeholder group whom they hope to target, although later in the article they laudably identify global health students as a motivated group of professional students who are willing to engage in OA discussions.

The Digital Media Landscape: Exploring the Remix Territory of Digital Natives

Now that an argument for including undergraduates in the scholarly communication conversation is clearer, librarians need to understand the current culture of the digital native in order to develop a relevant curricular approach. To better understand the changing attitudes toward copyright and OA, it is worth exploring the recent evolution of the digital media landscape. Currently, there is a societal expectation that the access to digital goods, services, and information should be immediate and free, and this is precipitating changes in attitudes toward traditional copyright. It is common to share images via social networking sites like Facebook, Twitter, Flickr, Tumblr, and Pinterest without regard to photo credits. File sharing for copyrighted TV shows is rampant because watching the latest episode of a popular show is required for participation in the cultural conversation. Swapping music, games, and movies is a way of developing social bonds. It's less important to students who owns the material than what material is available when they need it and how it can be used for their purposes—a remix culture. Remix culture, a concept popularized by Lawrence Lessig,

> is a digital media practice and expression made by copying, editing and recombining pre-existing digital media. It describes a variety of sample-based and digitally manipulated music, video, text and mixed media.
>
> For Lessig, remix is not only a form of individual expression, it is a participatory mode of communication, one that marks a return to Jeffersonian ideals of democratic discourse. (Borschke 2011, 18)

A case in point: remixing permeates popular music and music video production—by both professionals and amateurs. Highly unlikely to disappear, this trend will, in fact, grow more complicated over time. From the 1989 releases of the Beastie Boys' *Paul's Boutique* and De La Soul's *3 Feet High and Rising*, through to the 1996 release of *Endtroducing* by DJ Shadow, a sixty-four minute album created purely of samples, remix culture is not entirely new; however, it has increased in popularity. The mantle of sampling and remix culture has been taken on by current artists like RJD2, Girl Talk, and Danger Mouse. When Danger Mouse released *The Grey Album*, a mashup of vocals from Jay-Z's *Black Album* with instrumentals from *The Beatles White Album*, he did not receive permission from EMI (the copyright holder to the Beatles' back catalog). This controversy led to Grey Tuesday,[5] where websites in support of copyright reform and the restructuring of the music industry postulated that as the *White Album* was released before federal copyright protection laws were implemented in 1972, that use of the album was fair use according to Section 107 of the copyright act.[6] While a number of cease-and-desist letters were sent out to participants (see Jensen 2004), no charges were brought.

The question is often whether or not the derivative work is accepted or challenged by the original copyright holder. Even though current copyright laws protect satire and derivative works that constitute a significantly new creative work, most sharing sites remove any works that are contested by a copyright holder without an opportunity for response from the remix creator. In 2007, Australian DJ Nick Bertke remixed chords and animations from Disney's *Alice in Wonderland* in his video "Alice" (Pogo 2007). As of 2012, the video has been viewed over nine million times. As reported in an NPR interview, shortly after the posting, "Bertke was contacted by Disney. But to his surprise, instead of a subpoena, the company offered him a job: a commissioned work, to be based on sounds from the Pixar movies" (NPR Staff 2012, para. 6). This is not the usual interaction that many Disney fans experience when they remix Disney content. In the current remix culture, what is accepted (even praised) and what is "scrubbed" from YouTube by copyright holders can be confusing for undergraduate students. Using examples of appropriation, remix, sampling, and derivative works in the classroom can help students understand the concepts of fair use, satire, and significant creative contributions.

According to Lessing, because of outdated copyright laws, "Our kids have been turned into criminals" (in Colbert 2009). Recent research indicates that almost half of adults "have bought, copied, or downloaded unauthorized music, TV shows or movies," while among young adults between 18 and 29 years old, "70% have acquired music or video files this way" (Karaganis 2011, 2).

Gregg Gillis of Girl Talk commented for Lessig's book *Remix*, and perfectly encapsulated the attitude of the current generation toward copyright, and even though he mentions music specifically, it can be applied to all media: "People are going to be forced—lawyers and... older politicians—to face this reality: that everyone is making this music and that most music is derived from previous ideas. And that almost all pop music is made from other people's source material. And that it's not a bad thing. It doesn't mean you can't make original content" (in Lessig 2008, 15). Permission is vital, legally, to move away from a "read only" attitude and toward a "read/write" culture, where the remixing and reimagining of others cultural works is legally tolerated, and even encouraged. Current outdated copyright laws make this an impossible goal.

Recent research by Wu et al. (2010) has shown four major trends in students' misunderstanding of copyright in relation to digital resources, including the beliefs that "digital resources should be shared," "downloaded digital resources are legitimately authorized and permitted," "all educational use is fair use," and "any downloading is permitted as long as you are paying tuition" (205–206).

If the attitudes described above are those which students believe in and are passionate about, then it is our duty as librarians to educate ourselves about these evolving attitudes and information needs to ensure that we continue to serve our students where they are now, rather than where they were a decade ago. It is crucial that we engage and educate them about Creative Commons, fair use, and authors' rights to have them work within the current legal parameters of sharing and remixing as much as possible.

Mind Mashup Workshop: Integrating Digital Remix Culture

In partnership with a local student organization, Florida Free Culture, librarians designed a Mind Mashup Workshop that would tap into the digital media landscape described above. It addressed remix culture and served to prepare undergraduate students for participation in the Sparky Awards, which are described in more detail in the following section. Librarians and undergraduate students collaborated to create sessions about Creative Commons, open source software, and "free culture" (Lessig's ideology). These sessions, held in the main library's Information Commons, promoted library space as a central information ground to learn more about scholarly communication concepts and develop multimedia projects.

The rich partnership formed between the libraries and the UF chapter of Students for Free Culture, known locally as Florida Free Culture, paved the way for the success of the Mind Mashup event. Florida Free Culture students were interested in shifting models of scholarly communication and invited Science and Technology librarians to present about open access, Creative Commons, and authors' rights at their regular meetings. These issues dovetailed with the group's mission "to advance cultural participation, especially in areas of new technology, and to promote intellectual property policy in the public interest" (Florida Free Culture 2012). The library was a natural fit for students with these goals since libraries promote informal education for cultural participation, provide technology resources for the public, and have clear stances on intellectual property that are in the public interest.

After a series of library presentations at Florida Free Culture meetings, the Florida Free Culture students approached librarians and offered to teach open source software that could be used to create Sparky Awards videos. The students identified Blender, Audacity, Inkscape, and Gimp as programs that would be particularly useful for student creation. After familiarizing themselves with the programs, librarians arranged for access to all these programs on Information Commons computers and worked with the students to develop an outline for the workshops. The agreed goal for the workshop was that by its end, students would understand the basics of Creative Commons, authors' rights, open access, and four open source software programs for media creation. At the workshop conclusion, they would be invited to share what they had learned by participating in the local Sparky Awards contest. This collaboration is described in detail as it relates to twenty-first century skills development in an article that argues librarian-student organization partnerships provide a high return on investment for library events (Johnson et al. 2011).

It must be emphasized that librarians did not steer the agenda for the Mind Mashup Workshop; rather, the Florida Free Culture club offered suggestions, and the librarians helped to fine-tune the details. All subjects were cotaught or peer-taught. It was a highly collaborative event where students took the initiative.

The two-hour workshop demonstrated not just how to use open source software, but also where to find Creative Commons–licensed works that can be adapted and modified. So, for example, in the Gimp portion of the workshop, the peer teacher demonstrated how to search Creative Commons and limit the search to works that students could modify, adapt, or build on. He explained which sites would yield the best results for visual images, specifically illustrations. Then he walked the participants through the process of downloading an image of an elephant and an image of a rocket. These images were imported into Gimp, and students were shown how to use the tools to crop, layer, color, and enhance the images. Finally he created a remixed image of the elephant's head in close-up holding the rocket in its trunk. He showed the students how to give attribution to the original images and how to save the new work. In planning the workshop, we realized that students would be able to follow along faster on their own laptops and that this approach would allow participants to bookmark information throughout the sessions. We made sure to include this information on all workshop promotion materials. Club members promoted the workshop by distributing flyers at the student union, posting an announcement on their blog, and discussing Mind Mashup in conjunction with a "Free your PC" (open source software distribution) event, where the UF Help Desk and IT Security team cleaned and secured laptops and installed open source software. The library promoted the event via library social media accounts (Facebook, Twitter, and a WordPress blog), posters within library buildings, and flyers at our reference desks. The planning and implementation of this event took less than a week. For more information, see Appendix 8.1: Mind Mashup Workshop Details.

Workshop Results

Even though there were only a few weeks to advertise the event, preparation for the workshop required minimal time. Return on investment was high, as approximately fifty students attended. The participants represented a wide range of disciplines and were enthusiastic about the topics. Students also commented on how helpful all the programs were for a variety of assignments. The LibGuide that librarians made in collaboration with Florida Free Culture students continues to be available as resource on open source software and finding media to remix.[7] Finally, the two-hour workshop inspired at least one entry for our local Sparky Awards contest. Positive outcomes of the workshop included solidifying the relationship between Florida Free Culture and the libraries, adding open source software to our public computers, and reaching a number of students across various disciplines.

Sparky Awards @ UF: Integrating an Undergraduate Contest into Open Access Week

Background: The Sparky Awards

Beginning in 2007, cosponsored by ACRL (Association of College and Research Libraries) and ARL, the Sparky Awards were an initiative of SPARC. This experimental awards program, which has since ceased, challenged participants to create short (maximum of two minutes) videos emphasizing the importance of open access.

The Sparky Awards were a great start to a different kind of conversation and an opportunity to promote library services—including the information commons or media services—and underscore that the library is a key part of everyone's learning experience. The library can be a place to edit video, browse media, work collaboratively, and learn about citations and copyright (McLennan 2009, 20).

Creators were asked to submit either an animation, a nonedited monologue (which could include interviews and dramatizations, but no additional external materials), or a remix video, which allowed students the opportunity to bring together legally obtained and authorized video files, music, and still images to develop an original video. Video creators retained all copyright permissions to their work, but in order to further expand the outreach of open access, the contest necessitated that all videos made for the awards be released under one of the six Creative Commons licenses.

UF librarians learned about the SPARC call to host a local Sparky Awards contest in the spring of 2009. The George A. Smathers Libraries at UF created an entry for the 2007 competition, and librarians were enthusiastic about getting involved again. An informal group of librarians, who were already involved in scholarly communication outreach on campus and who had also been working on integrating emerging technologies into library services, met to discuss the steps they would need to take to have a successful local contest. They developed a time line that served as a guide for the year-long effort, which included getting administrative support, determining campus partners, developing a marketing plan, recruiting judges, and organizing the culminating screening. Excited about the potential to involve undergraduates in the plans for the 2009 Open Access Week events, the grassroots group approached library administration with a clearly outlined plan for hosting a local contest. Our proposal provided an overview of the contest, clearly stated the purpose of the event, named campus partners, outlined the rules for submissions, and gave a budget and time line.

Promotion of Sparky Awards @ UF

Entry to the local Sparky contest was open to all UF students, and a team of tech-savvy librarians devised a number of ways to promote the submission of entries, which they clearly outlined and distributed library-wide. Print materials advertised the contest and the software available for media creation at the library. The graphically compelling flyers, bookmarks, posters, and postcards were distributed at circulation and reference desks, in classes, and in departmental buildings, with particular interest paid to communication venues in the School of Art and Art History. Subject liaison librarians and instruction librarians promoted participation by mentioning the Sparky Awards via Lib-Guides and during instruction sessions. The contest coordination team, formed out of a shared interest in free culture and open access, worked with UF librarians to ensure that announcements would be made throughout the fall semester, particularly to programs and departments that would have a particular interest in creativity, sharing resources, or open access. E-mail communications (see Appendix 8.2: Marketing Materials) served to inform colleagues about the contest and encourage them to announce it to their colleagues across campus.

Members of the team searched course catalog listings for media production classes and sent targeted e-mails to professors and teaching assistants in those departments. Advertisements in the library and on the library homepage notified students that the library would provide Flip video cameras for checkout and had video editing software available in the Information Commons. Commercials to advertise Flip video checkout (Daley 2010a, 2010b) appeared on branch library homepages and on technology LibGuides.

Furthermore, the team developed a website to promote the local contest and promoted the contest via social media sites, including the library's established Facebook and Twitter accounts. A Sparky Awards @ UF Facebook group served as a discussion board for students who were actively interested in creating videos for the contest. Librarians posted software tips and contest equipment availability reminders almost daily.

Local Contest Prizes and Judging

The library development officer secured funds from an anonymous donor that would provide for prizes. Because of the nature of the donation, cash prizes were not a possibility. The team decided that media creation tools would be an excellent prize and would motivate students to enter. The funds allowed for an iPod Touch for the winning entry and Flip video cameras for two runners-up. The library provided funds for refreshments for the local contest screening.

To bring additional attention to the competition, we were able to secure judges with both local and national reputations: Jim Liversidge, the curator of the Popular Culture Collections in the Department of Special and Area Studies Collections and a former local radio personality; Allison Bittiker, a local photographer and the assistant director for Programming and Events for the Florida Experimental Film and Video Art Festival; and Patrick Flanagan, the former Vice President for Florida Free Culture. This team of judges agreed to volunteer their time to rank the videos submitted for the local contest.

Local Contest Results

The competition received six entries from a variety of majors. We were happy to hear that they learned of the opportunity in four different ways: a poster in our main humanities library, through word of mouth from a friend, at the Mind Mashup Workshop hosted by Florida Free Culture, and in a local campus newspaper. This emphasized the importance of promoting the competition through standard advertising (posters and newspapers), but also through local outreach, as we targeted potentially interested parties through associated workshops.

While a rudimentary comprehension of information sharing existed in all the entries, they suffered from an inability to effectively translate their concepts to screen. The library provided software and tools, the Mind Mashup Workshop provided training, but overall we lacked a concrete synthesis of the two to help students develop their concept from page to screen. Greater revision, critique, and commentary on student ideas during their project development could have improved the quality of the videos. For example, nearly half of the entries used a box metaphor to represent information. We needed to encourage students to "think outside the box" and develop more creative submissions that would demonstrate a deeper understanding of the topic.

At a post-contest debriefing, the librarians involved in Sparky Awards @ UF brainstormed ways to improve the contest in future semesters. Interesting ideas included having an intense twenty-four hour film challenge for participants. This "library lock-in" challenge would start with a Mind Mashup-style workshop and conclude with a screening of a film created during the twenty-four hour challenge. Along the way, librarians and technical experts would provide feedback to nurture creative development of entries. A more traditional idea for improvement included a series of workshops to teach storyboarding and narrative development skills early on in the competition. Finally, the opportunity to embed the Sparky Awards as a credit-bearing assignment in a course was seen as an excellent way to cultivate better-quality submissions with a deeper understanding of scholarly communication. This approach was adopted the following year (2010) in the undergraduate honors course Discovering Research and Communicating Science. However, embedding is a limited approach that reaches out to only one course rather than the whole of the student body. Since 2009, we have not continued local involvement with the Sparky Awards or Mind Mashup Workshop because the direction of scholarly communication outreach at UF has changed, although future opportunities to explore OA outreach to undergraduates remain.

Conclusion

Engaging undergraduates in scholarly communication issues is crucial not only because they are the researchers of tomorrow, but also because the current generation's attitude toward copyright has changed. The cultural evolution of remixing, sampling, and sharing creative works precipitates the need for better understanding of author and creator rights. Digital media makes creation easy, and more students can participate than ever before. The Mind Mashup described in this chapter provided students with the tools and the copyright knowledge they needed to become informed creators of content. Furthermore, hosting a local Sparky Awards contest provided opportunities for students to interpret scholarly communication issues in a creative way and contribute their voices to the conversation. The coupling of these two events was a synergistic fusion of function and creative inspiration, which we would encourage other libraries to remix.

Mind Mashup Workshop Details
Workshop Description:

Members of the student group, Florida Free Culture, will hold a free workshop to demonstrate how to use open source software programs to remix images, music, and videos licensed under Creative Commons to create new content. Attendees are encouraged to bring their own laptop so they can bookmark and/or download these free resources and use them again.

Objectives:

By the end of this workshop students will:
- Understand the basics of Creative Commons, authors' rights, and open access
- Become aware of open source software that can be used in media creation
- Utilize media creation tools available in the UF Library Information Commons
- Explore Gimp, Audacity, Inkscape, and Blender to create a simple image, animation or sound clip

Materials:

- Presentation screen, presenter computer, and internet access
- Computer workstations or personal laptops for workshop participants
- CDs with open source software available for download
- Flyers for open access week
- Promotional materials—"I support Open Access" and "Creative Commons" buttons
- Refreshments (juice, cookies, and popcorn)

Workshop Outline: (Duration: 2 hours)

1. Introduction
   a. Invitation to participate in the local Sparky Awards contest at UF
   b. What is open access?
2. Creative Commons
3. Open Source Software Programs
   a. Gimp
   b. Blender
   c. Inkscape
   d. Audacity
4. Conclusion

APPENDIX 8.2

Marketing Materials

Postcard

Figure 8.1
The front of the Sparky Awards @ UF postcard gave contest information and the URL for the contest rules.

Figure 8.2
The reverse side of the Sparky Awards postcard provided a list of resources students could use to create videos at the UF Libraries Information Commons.

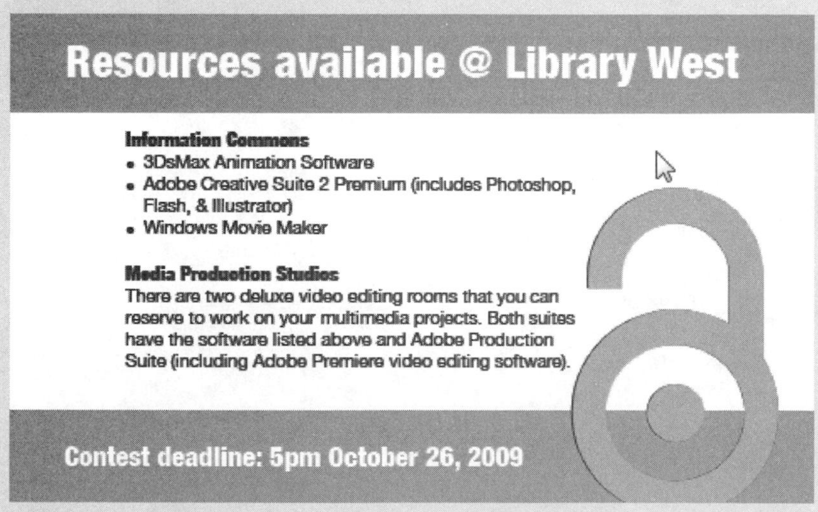

E-mail Message:

Dear Selectors & Instruction Librarians,

Please help us promote the UF Libraries Video Awards Contest this fall by spreading the word to all UF students! Here are a few ideas:

- Mention the Sparky Awards at your next instruction session. (Project the attached PowerPoint Slide on the screen as students enter or leave the classroom).
- We now have Flip video cameras that students can use to create their entries! Promote the contest in conjunction with our equipment loans & the software available in the Information Commons.
- Announce the contest to your departments, especially to programs/departments that care about creativity, sharing resources, or open access (Marketing, Art, Educational Technologies, English, Music, Visual Anthropology, etc).
- Include Sparky Award details on a LibGuide. (An image of the Sparky Logo is attached).
- Promote the contest by giving out flyers at reference desks, in classes, and in departments.

For more information on the Sparky Awards, please contact me. Thank you!

Notes

1. For more information about faculty attitudes or publishing preferences for OA in engineering, see Mischo and Schlembach 2011. For business, see Coonin 2011. For library science, see Johnson and Roderer 2008 and Xia, Wilhoite, and Myers 2011.
2. See Blixrud 2011.
3. See Renfro 2011.
4. See Rathe, Chaudhuri, and Highby 2010 and Emmett et al. 2011.
5. For more information, see EFF 2012.
6. For information on fair use, see US Copyright Office 2012.
7. The LibGuide is available at http://guides.uflib.ufl.edu/media.

References

Blixrud, Julia C. 2011. "Scholarly Communication and Public Policies: The Experience of the Association of Research Libraries." *Journal of Library Administration* 51, no. 5: 543–556. doi:10.1080/01930826.2 011.589326.

Borschke, Margie. 2011. "Rethinking the Rhetoric of Remix." *Media International Australia,* no. 141 (November): 17–25.

Colbert, Stephen. 2009. "Lawrence Lessig" (interview). *The Colbert Report.* January 8. http://www.colbertnation.com/the-colbert-report-videos/215454/january-08-2009/lawrence-lessig.

Coonin, Bryna. 2011. "Open Access Publishing in Business Research: The Authors' Perspective." *Journal of Business & Finance Librarianship* 16, no. 3: 193–212. doi:10.1080/08963568.2011.581606.

Cryer, Emma, and Maria Collins. 2011. "Incorporating Open Access into Libraries." *Serials Review* 37, no. 2 (June): 103–107. doi:10.1016/j.serrev.2011.03.002.

Daley, Matthew. 2010a. "Flip Video Commercial #1." YouTube video. UF Libraries. Uploaded January 26. http://www.youtube.com/watch?v=AQOYM0_IkLk.

Daley, Matthew. 2010b. "Flip Video Commercial #2." YouTube video. UF Libraries. Uploaded January 26. http://www.youtube.com/watch?v=0 UKgxpatcH0&feature=relmfu

Davis-Kahl, Stephanie. 2012. "Engaging Undergraduates in Scholarly Communication: Outreach, Education and Advocacy." *College & Research Libraries News* 73, no. 4 (April): 212–222.

EFF (Electronic Frontier Foundation). 2012. "Grey Tuesday: A Quick Overview of the Legal Terrain." Electronic Frontier Foundation. Accessed June 29. https://w2.eff.org/IP/grey_tuesday.php.

Emmett, Ada, John Stratton, A. T. Peterson, Jennifer Church-Duran, and Lorraine J. Haricombe. 2011. "Toward Open Access: It Takes a 'Village.'" *Journal of Library Administration* 51, no. 5–6: 557–579. doi:1 0.1080/01930826.2011.589345.

Florida Free Culture. 2012 "Florida Free Culture." University of Florida. Accessed June 29http://uf.freeculture.org.

Jensen, J. Christopher. 2004. "Re: The Grey Album and Misappropriation of Capital Records, Inc.'s Sound Recordings." February 24. http://www. chillingeffects.org/fairuse/notice.cgi?NoticeID=1132.

Johnson, Margeaux, Melissa J. Clapp, Stacey R. Ewing, and Amy Buhler. 2011. "Building a Participatory Culture: Collaborating with Student Organizations for Twenty-First Century Library Instruction." *Collaborative Librarianship* 3, no. 1: 2–15.

Johnson, Margeaux, and Nancy Roderer. 2008. "ASIS&T Scholarly Communication Survey: Open Access Authors." *Bulletin of the American Society for Information Science and Technology* 35, no. 1 (October/ November): 8–11.

Karaganis, Joe. 2011. "Copyright Infringement and Enforcement in the US: A Research Note." Columbia University, The American Assembly. November. http://piracy.ssrc.org/wp-content/uploads/2011/11/AA-Research-Note-Infringement-and-Enforcement-November-2011.pdf.

Lessig, Lawrence. 2008. *Remix: Making Art and Commerce Thrive in the Hybrid Economy.* London: Bloomsbury. http://www.scribd.com/ doc/47089238/Remix.

McLennan, Jennifer. 2009. "A Different Kind of Conversation: The Sparky Awards and Fresh Views on Change in Scholarly Communication." *Research Library Issues: A Quarterly Report from ARL, CNI, and SPARC (RLI),* no. 264: 19–21. http://publications.arl.org/rli264/20.

Mischo, William H., and Mary C. Schlembach. 2011. "Open Access Issues and Engineering Faculty Attitudes and Practices." *Journal of Library Administration* 51, no. 5–6: 432–454. doi:10.1080/01930826.2011. 589349.

NPR Staff. 2012. "Pogo: Harnessing the Innate Rhythm of Pop Culture." National Public Radio. May 6. http://www.npr. org/2012/05/06/150981484/pogo-harnessing-the-innate-rhythm-of-pop-culture.

Pogo [Nick Bertke]. 2007. "Alice (Disney Remix)." YouTube video. Uploaded July 18. http://www.youtube.com/watch?v=pAwR6w2TgxY.

Rathe, Bette, Jayati Chaudhuri, and Wendy Highby. 2010. "Open Access Advocacy: Think Globally, Act Locally." *Collaborative Librarianship* 2, no. 3: 162–168.

Renfro, Patricia. 2011. "Open Access within Reach: An Agenda for Action." *Journal of Library Administration* 51, no. 5–6: 464–475. doi:10.1080 /01930826.2011.589351.

US Copyright Office. 20112 "Fair Use." Accessed June 29. http://www.copyright.gov/fls/fl102.html.

Warren, Scott, and Kim Duckett. 2010. "Why Does Google Scholar Sometimes Ask for Money? Engaging Science Students in Scholarly Communication and the Economics of Information." *Journal of Library Administration* 50, no. 4: 349–372. doi:10.1080/01930821003667021.

Wu, Huan-Chueh, Chien Chou, Hao-Ren Ke, and Mei-Hung Wang. 2010. "College Students' Misunderstandings about Copyright Laws for Digital Library Resources." *Electronic Library* 28, no. 2: 197–209. doi:10.1108/02640471011033576.

Xia, Jingfeng, Sara Kay Wilhoite, and Rebekah Lynette Myers. 2011. "A 'Librarian-LIS Faculty' Divide in Open Access Practice." *Journal of Documentation* 67, no. 5: 791–805. doi:10.1108/00220411111164673.

CHAPTER 9

Communicating with Future Scholars

[Lesson Plans to Engage Undergraduate Science Students with
Open Access Issues in a Semester-Long Course]

Margeaux Johnson
University of Florida

Amy G. Buhler
University of Florida

Sara Russell Gonzalez
University of Florida

Introduction

In the three-credit information literacy course Discovering Research and Communicating Science (IDH 3931) at the University of Florida (UF), undergraduate science, technology, engineering, and mathematics (STEM) students explore the information landscape of scientific research and engage in complex issues surrounding research ethics, information use, and communication in STEM fields. Scholarly communication is a central theme woven throughout the course, and each semester the course devotes two weeks to exploring open access (OA) issues.

Lesson plans, learning objectives, lecture outlines, and projects synthesized over several semesters of teaching this course will be presented in this chapter as a way to scaffold undergraduate students' understanding of scholarly communication in the sciences. Pedagogically our approach is learner-centered and reflects Anderson and Krathwohl's (2001) revision of Bloom's Taxonomy. In the course, students move from lower-order thinking skills (understanding and identifying scholarly communication issues) to higher-order thinking skills (creating a multimedia project that expresses their evaluation of OA). Approaching learning about OA issues from a discussion-based, learner-centered model allows students, who are the scientists of the future, to create their own understanding of scholarly communication

163

and adopt attitudes that can enable them to make intelligent decisions about publishing throughout their careers.

Conceptually, the design of this course takes on a three-tiered approach (Figure 9.1) that is grounded in the Revised Bloom's Taxonomy (Anderson and Krathwohl 2001). *Foundation* lesson plans relate to lower-order thinking skills like recognizing, identifying, and understanding. *Framework* lesson plans utilize mid- to high-level thinking skills such as evaluating, appraising, comparing, and synthesizing the concepts that were previously introduced in the Foundation sessions. The ultimate products are assignments that challenge students to create and write, which constitute the *Building* tier. These correspond to higher-order thinking skills in the Revised Bloom's Taxonomy.

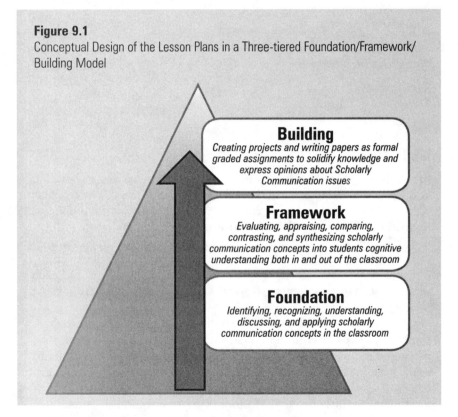

Figure 9.1
Conceptual Design of the Lesson Plans in a Three-tiered Foundation/Framework/Building Model

Building
Creating projects and writing papers as formal graded assignments to solidify knowledge and express opinions about Scholarly Communication issues

Framework
Evaluating, appraising, comparing, contrasting, and synthesizing scholarly communication concepts into students cognitive understanding both in and out of the classroom

Foundation
Identifying, recognizing, understanding, discussing, and applying scholarly communication concepts in the classroom

In practice, instructors introduce Foundations via lectures, demonstrations, and hands-on activities with databases. Next, the learning responsibility is shifted to students as they develop a framework to understand OA through a more open-ended exploration of the concepts presented in class. They become involved in Open Access Week events, participate in an OA debate, and form groups to storyboard videos and begin work on a final multimedia project. To solidify their knowledge, students create multimedia projects or write formal essays that help to build their personal perspectives on OA.

Discovering Research and Communicating Science—An Undergraduate Honors Course

In 2006, Dr. Sara Gonzalez, a former geophysicist turned physical sciences librarian at the University of Florida Marston Science Library, designed, developed, and co-taught a three-credit course that allows undergraduate STEM students to discover and utilize the scientific literature as well as convey their scientific knowledge using different media. The overarching goal of the course was to provide students with the skills necessary not only to succeed, but also to thrive as academic professionals and researchers in the sciences. As noted by Johnson and Gonzalez 2011:

> STEM undergraduates require specific IL (Information Literacy) and career skills to succeed in graduate school and eventually grow into global researchers. To remain competitive, undergraduates need to find scientific research opportunities within their first years of college. Therefore, beginning researchers should be aware of processes for scientific communication, funding, and literature searching. (93–94)

With this mindset, Dr. Gonzalez proposed Discovering Research and Communicating Science (IDH 3931) as a fall semester course in the Honors Program. The Honors Program at UF has a commitment to offering challenging courses with small course sizes that allow for deeper interactions with professors. Faculty from any UF department, including the libraries, can apply to teach through the Honors Program. While adding innovative or experimental courses can be a challenge through other departments at UF, the Honors Program embraces creative, interdisciplinary, and nontraditional offerings. Information literacy courses taught by librarians have been included in Honors Program since the 1990s; however, this course was the first attempt at creating a subject-specific information literacy offering. Not only was the course popular, it became highly valued by the director of the Honors Program, who also happened to be a STEM PhD. By 2010 the course became a fixture in the Honors course catalog, with several science librarians team-teaching and refining the course syllabus during each subsequent semester the course was offered.

Each year at the beginning of the fall semester, a small class of approximately twenty Honors students commit to learning more about STEM research through exploration of library resources, scientific literature databases, and the academic publishing model. The course includes guest lecturers from a variety of disciplines to speak about their research projects, available research opportunities, and the skills they see as essential for new STEM graduate students. Weekly assignments introduce the students to scientific publication processes and writing styles. Furthermore, students engage in discussion of topics including citation studies, publication formats, conferences, and funding.

Learning objectives for the course can be broken into two categories: (1) information literacy skills objectives and (2) life and career skills objectives. Johnson and Gonzalez 2011 describe these objectives (outlined in Table 9.1), as well as the details of initiating a subject-specific information literacy course.

Table 9.1

Learning Objectives for IDH 3931, as Applied to Information Literacy Skills and Life and Career Skills

Information Literacy Skills	Life and Career Skills
Students enrolled in IDH 3931 will be able to: • Access scientific information (online, in print, and in specialized museum collections) • Select appropriate databases to search scientific literature • Evaluate information and select relevant resources • Analyze information resources to effectively communicate science • Use information tools to pursue individual research goals • Understand the importance of research ethics, avoiding plagiarism, academic integrity, and citation styles	Students enrolled in IDH 3931 will: • Seek undergraduate research opportunities • Understand scientific communication processes: journal literature, societies, and conferences • Develop written communication skills (including abstract writing, proposal writing, curriculum vitae and bio sketch preparation, and manuscript preparation) • Understand the scientific funding process • Recognize the importance of open access publication models • Develop technology skills (including LaTeX, HTML, XML, and web design) • Develop presentation and oral communication skills • Understand the skills needed to apply for graduate or professional school in the sciences

While scholarly communication is not the only focus of this semester-long course, it does play a crucial role in the underlying basis for many of the topics. The intent in providing the lesson plans for various lectures, in-class activities, and assignments is to offer concrete sugges-tions for including scholarly communication issues throughout semester-long information literacy courses in various disciplines. While the ex-amples provided here are for a scientific information literacy course, the lesson plans and assignments could be adapted for other subject areas in the humanities, social sciences, arts, or health sciences. The lesson plans are uniquely geared toward developing a comprehension of scholarly communication over the course of a semester rather than through a one-shot workshop or a course-integrated information literacy session. The sample lesson plans represent the authors' synthesis and reflections on best practices for building this knowledge derived from our collective experiences over four iterations of planning and teaching the course.

Foundation: Identifying, Recognizing, Understanding, Discussing, and Applying Scholarly Communication Concepts in the Information Literacy Classroom
Presentations on Open Access Resources

IDH 3931 instructors laid the groundwork for students to begin un-derstanding and applying their knowledge of scholarly communication via presentations on publicly available resources like PubMed, arXiv, and the UF digital collections. As students are introduced to the rich variety of STEM databases, instructors discuss issues of access and availability. Instructors emphasize to which resources students will have consistent access outside of their affiliation with the university. Prices and restrictions on information are discussed hand-in-hand with social issues surrounding publicly funded research. Undergraduates are very aware of education costs and are in tune with social justice issues (Davis-Kahl 2012, 212). They are quick to make the connection be-tween public funding and the justice of public access. This is especially true in the case of medical literature, where inequalities of access to re-search may be a matter of life and death. For these resources, scholarly communication issues are interwoven with teaching the mechanics of access to the database. The emphasis in most cases is on the resource; however, students are slowly introduced to the vocabulary of scholarly communication, thus priming them for the more direct Foundation lectures on scholarly communication.

PubMed Lesson Plan
This lesson plan details a PubMed session for IDH 3931. Scholarly communication and OA are discussed in tandem with database fea-tures, search strategies, and resource access tips. While the focus may

be on navigating PubMed to locate and access resources, there is a continuing discussion of who has access to the medical literature, who pays for medical research, and how translational science influences medical practice. Students understand the concept of taking research "from bench to bedside," and they make the connection that access to research is a key step in facilitating the translational research process.

See Appendix 9.1: Foundation—Lesson Plan for Open Resources: The PubMed Database.

arXiv and Astrophysics Data Systems Lesson Plan

In the lesson plan for arXiv and Astrophysics Data Systems (ADS), students learn about subject repositories. Instructors for IDH 3931 discuss the "science of team science" and how discovery in physics and astrophysics requires data sharing to progress. An emphasis on the nature of funding from government institutions, the cost of equipment and instruments in the physical sciences, and the massive size of datasets in these fields underscores the need for OA.

See Appendix 9.2: Foundation—Lesson Plan for Open Resources: arXiv and Astrophysics Data Systems (ADS).

IR Submission

Once students begin to conceptualize the availability of free databases and freely accessible literature, as outlined in the lesson plans, they are given the opportunity to contribute their own work to the University of Florida Institutional Repository (IR@UF). This empowers students to begin sharing their scholarship and creates a pathway by which they can choose to continue contributing their own scholarship to the international conversation.

The introduction to institutional repositories activity builds off a previous poster presentation assignment, asking students to archive an electronic copy of their poster in the IR@UF (see Figure 9.2). The activity is voluntary; however, students are encouraged to create IR@UF accounts and self-submit their poster during class. The lecture focuses on the range of repositories for institutions and disciplines, the use of metadata for archiving information, the need to archive learning objects, and the content contained within the IR@UF. The concrete act of self-submittal reinforces the students' responsibility, as future scientific researchers, to make their findings publically available. The submitted posters also become a lasting record of products created in the course and help future students design their assignments. The students are typically engaged and enjoy the process of viewing previous students' submissions. This contributes to their own willingness to submit materials.

See Appendix 9.3: Foundation—Lesson Plan for Open Resources: University of Florida Digital Collections and the IR@UF.

Figure 9.2
The IR@UF has a self-submittal tool, pictured here. Student submission to the IR@UF provides an opportunity to discuss concepts like metadata, self-archiving of research, and access to learning objects.

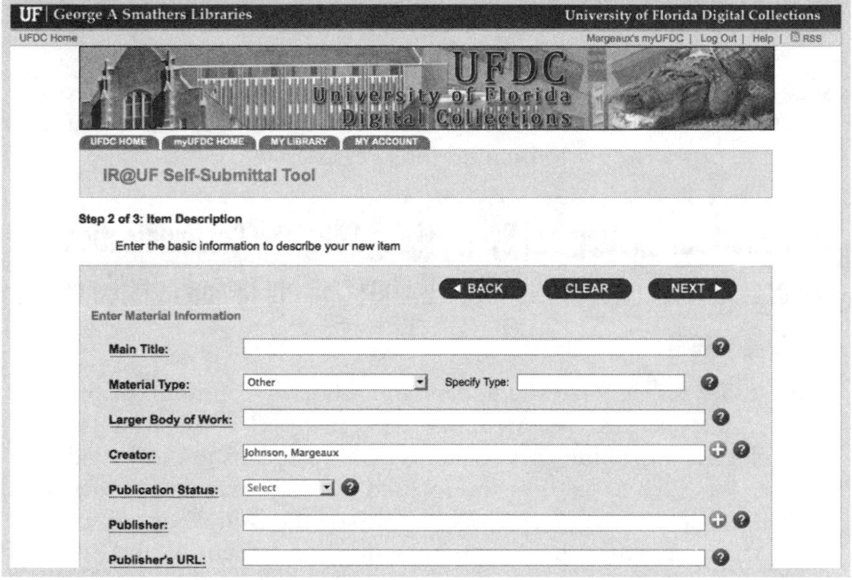

Lectures on Scholarly Communication

Also in the Foundation category of understanding and formulating a concept of scholarly communication issues are lectures on OA and scholarly communication in the sciences. The Scholarly Communication Librarian for UF addresses the class to provide an overview of the history and current challenges in scholarly communication, which focuses on the shift in scholarly communication models in the past decade. Perhaps one of the most compelling lectures of the whole course is a face-to-face discussion with a prominent scientific editor from UF. This lecture begins with a presentation about the scientist's own research, which lends credibility and prestige to his or her argument for involvement with OA publication. In recent semesters, Dr. Grant McFadden, the deputy editor for *PLoS Pathogens* and a well-respected microbiology and cell science professor, has engaged the students in a candid, in-depth conversation about his decision to be involved in OA publishing. In previous semesters, Dr. Tom Walker, a professor emeritus of entomology and a founding member of one of the earliest OA journals, *The Florida Entomologist* (which became OA in 1994), discussed the need for OA to push research in the sciences forward. Whereas students may view the Scholarly Communication Librarian's perspectives on OA as biased, the researchers' views are seen as an accurate weighing of pros and cons within their field. Students respond enthusiastically to the professors' presentations about their research and connect to the professors' insights on publication practices. Presenting multiple viewpoints ensures that students develop a holistic understanding of the issues.

See Appendix 9.4: Foundation—Lesson Plan for Lectures on Scholarly Communication: A Librarian's Perspective and Appendix 9.5: Foundation—Lesson Plan for Lectures on Scholarly Communication: The Open Access Journal Editor's Perspective.

Framework: Evaluating and Synthesizing Scholarly Communication Concepts into Students' Cognitive Understanding in and outside of the Classroom

After students recognize and understand scholarly communication issues in the sciences, they are ready for activities that encourage them to think critically about these issues. The lesson plans in the Foundation section, such as lectures and focused discussions, prime students to develop their own frameworks to evaluate the complexity of scholarly communication issues, compare multiple perspectives, and begin to develop a personal mental model of their roles as future researchers.

In the Framework section, IDH 3931 instructors provide the cognitive space for students to explore scholarly communication. The approach to learning is less didactic and more open-ended, with many possible outcomes or paths to discovery. The emphasis for learning in the lesson plans is to have students develop their own context for understanding. Activities include attending events associated with Open Access Week in order to write personal reflections and participating in a class-wide OA debate.

See Appendix 9.6: Framework—Lesson Plan for Open Access Week Activity.

The OA debate gives students the opportunity to perform the role of one of three stakeholders in the scholarly communication landscape—researchers, librarians, and publishers. This activity spans two class sessions and can be mediated by a guest judge (usually a librarian or a researcher). One class session is devoted to students collecting information about their assigned perspectives, synthesizing their arguments, and negotiating with their teammates regarding how they will present their perspective. The day of the debate itself is charged with energy as students advocate for their position. Past classes have yielded "winners" from multiple sides—yes, even the publishers have won. However, the crux of this activity is not the competition, but the thoughtful compilation of each team's position. Multiple perspectives presented by peers aid students as they continue on their journey toward solidifying a personal opinion. In keeping with the Framework approach, the information is developed internally by students rather than externally by experts.

See Appendix 9.7: Framework—Lesson Plan for Debate on Open Access: New Publishing Models.

Building: Creating Projects and Writing Papers as Formal Graded Assignments to Solidify Knowledge and Express Opinions about Scholarly Communication Issues

In the Foundation section, experts introduce students to the basic concepts related to scholarly communication. Following the introduction, students explore these concepts and formulate their own understandings through the lesson plans presented in the Framework section. The culmination of student engagement with OA issues is a formalized assignment that allows students to solidify and express their knowledge. Assignment outlines are presented in this Building section.

As a formal evaluation of their knowledge, students choose to either create an OA multimedia project or produce an OA paper. These assignments assess that students understand OA as a complex change in the publication system and ensure that students have cognitively developed a personalized perspective on scholarly communication in the sciences. The choice between the paper and the project allows for various learning styles. The paper is designed for students who prefer individual, written, analytical approaches to formalizing knowledge. The multimedia project is designed for students who prefer a team-based, visual, creative approach to formalizing knowledge. Both assignments carry the same weight in the overall course grade and both take a similar amount of time and effort for each individual student to produce. Furthermore, both assignments address the same three learning objectives. Students will be able to:

- synthesize the various arguments surrounding OA studied in class
- develop and express a personal opinion on OA and scholarly communication issues
- understand why scholarly communication models in the sciences have changed and how they relate to the student's future role as a scientific researcher

The multimedia project challenges students to work in teams and develop a short video. Their process must include synthesizing a perspective on the scholarly communication issues presented in class, developing a concept, storyboarding their shots, properly crediting the multimedia used, and sharing the final video online. The open-ended nature of this assignment has resulted in creative interpretations of the assignment. In the past students have developed narrative stories, conducted news-style interviews with experts, and created animations.

See Appendix 9.8: Building—Scholarly Communication Assignment: Open Access Multimedia Project.

The OA paper has concretely defined sections and is designed for students who prefer a more linear approach to learning. The paper must include the following sections:

- an introduction to OA concepts
- the history of the OA movement
- detailed analysis of the movement from the perspective of various stakeholders, including:
  — researchers
  — librarians
  — publishers
  — scholarly societies
  — the public
- a personal synthesis and understanding of OA
- a conclusion
- citations in APA format

The paper submissions are of very high quality. Whereas some students may deviate from a clear message in multimedia project, the structure of the paper lends itself comprehensive coverage of the topic.

See Appendix 9.9: Building—Scholarly Communication Assignment: Open Access Paper.

Conclusion

A discussion of the social, ethical, and legal implications of research is germane to the preparation of undergraduate students to become information-literate professionals. In particular, STEM students, who are future STEM researchers, need to form a clear understanding of scholarly communication issues to participate in the current scientific research landscape. It is essential to provide pathways for these students to develop their own perspectives on scientific communication processes.

Based on our experiences teaching multiple semesters of our course, we suggest a three-tiered scaffolding approach to integrating scholarly communication into semester-long courses—Foundation, Framework, and Building. In the first phase (Foundation), instructors introduce concepts underlying OA first in the context of database instruction, then via formalized lectures. This provides students with the scaffolding they need to explore the issues. In the second tier

(Framework), class time allows for discussion, reflection, and debate as students develop their own perspectives. Finally, in the culminating tier (Building), instructors design opportunities for students to formalize and share knowledge related to scholarly communication.

In our courses, we observed an increased awareness of open access to information from the beginning to the end of the semester. To assess this, we used a variety of formative assessment models, including engaging students with discussion questions in class activities. We also sought formative assessment through quizzes and reflective writing assignments. Prior to these lectures, students could not differentiate between free and subscription-based resources, and the majority of students were not familiar with the concept of OA. Many of the students in the course were pre-med, and recognizing the disparities in access to health information was particularly eye-opening. It was exciting as instructors to see the students, as future researchers, become passionate about the benefits and challenges of OA.

OA is a difficult and complex topic to understand, especially as an undergraduate student new to scholarly communication. Yet, as the students listened to the various speakers and worked in teams to prepare for the debate, we noticed their level of comprehension and awareness grow. From early exercises of submitting a previous assignment to the university institutional repository to sharing their culminating multimedia project on the open Web, students were given the opportunity to practice sharing their scholarship. Many previous students have kept in touch with us and have relayed successes in obtaining research positions, publishing papers, and being admitted to professional and graduate programs. We believe that the knowledge they have obtained about OA and scholarly communication will be invaluable as they interact with their lab mates, advisors, and future students as they progress in their STEM field.

The lesson plans and assignments in this chapter suggest one path to scaffolding scholarly communication for undergraduates in a credit-bearing information literacy course. It is our hope that these plans can be adapted, modified, and reinvented to meet multiple contexts while successfully following the model of Foundation, Framework, and Building that has succeeded in the Discovering Research and Communicating Science course.

Foundation—Lesson Plan for Open Resources: The PubMed Database

Class Title: Open Resources: The PubMed Database

Time Frame: 50 minutes

Format: Hands-on in a computer classroom

Class Overview: This session introduces students to PubMed, the premier free database in biomedical literature. Students use multiple types of search tools and techniques (e.g., keyword, nesting search terms, MeSH, etc.), accessing full-text articles from the database (e.g., PubMed Central) and manipulating results using tools such as Clipboard and My NCBI. Students learn that PubMed is free, but not all the articles are freely accessible, and students discuss issues of equality of access to health-related research.

Facilities Requirements, Materials, and Supplies
- Computer lab/classroom
- Handout (print or electronic)

Learning Objectives

Students will:
1. Understand what types of information are contained in PubMed.
2. Identify appropriate search terms using the MeSH database.
3. Use PubMed tools like Search History to perform a multiterm search in the database.
4. Recognize the importance of OA to medical literature for health professionals working in rural, international, or underfunded institutions.

Outline of Session:
1. Scholarly communication in the health sciences (class discussion):
   a. Funding for medical research
   b. Access to health science research
      i. Common databases
      ii. Consumer health information
   c. Translational science
      i. Bench to bedside
      ii. Bedside to bench
   d. NIH open access policy

2. Overview of PubMed (lecture):
   a. Types of materials indexed by PubMed
   b. NLM and PubMed

3. Hands-on searching:
   a. Phrase searching
   b. Order of terms/nesting
   c. Author searching
   d. Using limits
   e. Using search history
   f. MeSH database
   g. Displaying your results
   h. Accessing a journal article from the results list
   i. Exporting a record to citation management software like RefWorks

4. Conclusion:
   a. Discussion of what was learned. This discussion may be continued online through discussion board in the course management system.

Assessment: Assessment of comprehension for this session is incorporated into a broader quiz covering various databases. The quiz requires students to utilize PubMed to answer one or two reference questions. In addition, students will ask questions and engage in a discussion about the issues raised in class. If this is an appropriate database for a student's subject area, the student will use PubMed to find articles for other assignments in this course.

Foundation—Lesson Plan for Open Resources: arXiv and Astrophysics Data Systems (ADS)

Class Title: Open Resources: arXiv and Astrophysics Data Systems (ADS)

Time Frame: 50 minutes

Format: Hands-on in a computer classroom

Class Overview: This lesson introduces the arXiv and ADS databases, two open resources essential for disciplines in mathematics and the physical sciences. Students practice locating journal articles and pre-prints, explore the differences between the two databases, and learn how to search and retrieve astronomy literature using astronomical object IDs, positional coordinates, and keywords. Furthermore, students discuss the cost of physical science experiments and equipment, the size of datasets, and the need for large research collaborations in these fields, as well as how open sharing of information moves discovery forward.

Facilities Requirements, Materials, and Supplies
- Computer lab/classroom
- Handouts providing database URLs, descriptions, and search hints

Learning Objectives

Students will:
1. Recognize the different types of literature contained within ADS and arXiv.
2. Use multiple search commands, including Boolean logic, astronomical data, and keywords to locate information.
3. Differentiate literature contained within arXiv, an e-print repository, from ADS.
4. Understand the shift in scholarly communication in physical sciences that led to the development of subject repositories like arXiv.

Outline of Session:
1. Review of types of scientific literature and the peer-review process (class discussion):
   a. How do physical scientists and mathematicians communicate?
   b. How does research in the physical sciences differ from biological sciences and engineering?

    c. Who funds physical science research? What are the costs of labs and equipment in physical science?

    d. Size of datasets in physical science. How do you analyze terabytes? Why is team science so important?

2. Introduction to arXiv:
   a. Search by date and keyword

3. Introduction to ADS:
   a. Search by keyword
   b. Author and institution searching
   c. Search by astronomical ID
   d. Sorting records
   e. Retrieving records and outputting bibliographic information

4. Conclusion:
   a. Discussion of what was learned. This can be moved to the discussion boards in an online course management system if class time does not permit.

Assessment: Assessment of comprehension for this session is incorporated into a broader quiz covering various databases. The quiz requires students to utilize ADS and arXiv to answer one or two reference questions. In addition, students will ask questions and engage in a discussion about the issues raised in class. If this is an appropriate database for a student's subject area, he or she they will use ADS to find articles for other assignments in the course.

Foundation—Lesson Plan for Open Resources: University of Florida Digital Collections and the IR@UF

Class Title: Open Resources: University of Florida Digital Collections and the IR@UF

Time Frame: 50 minutes

Format: Hands-on in a computer classroom

Class Overview: In this session, students explore the science resources available through the University of Florida's Digital Collections (UFDC). Furthermore, students submit digital copies of their posters to the Institutional Repository (IR@UF) and learn about self-archiving as the "green road" in open access.

Facilities Requirements, Materials, and Supplies

- Computer lab/classroom
- Students must bring digital copy of their previous poster assignment.

Learning Objectives

Students will:
1. Explore the variety of science resources available in the UF Digital Collections, including the Herbarium Collections, Food and Agricultural Sciences materials, and Wetlands research
2. Discuss self-archiving of research as the green road to OA
3. Contribute a digital copy of their work to the IR@UF

Outline of Session:
1. The UF Digital Collections (UFDC):
   a. Open exploration of collections at UFDC—explore, then show and tell
      i. "In your research teams, search the UF Digital collections for an interesting object, research paper, video, or presentation."
      ii. "Share what you found with the class."
      iii. Emphasize the diversity and scope of research at UF and the diversity of the collections
   b. Searching digital collections
      i. Search tips, tricks, and drawbacks
   c. Science-specific collections
      i. Herbarium collections
      ii. Agricultural collections

       iii. Wetlands research

       iv. Discuss lack of physical, chemical, and mathematical sciences collections

       v. Discuss scope of Florida-based collections

2. Class discussion of repositories:

   a. Why create subject-based repositories or collections? What do you encourage by collecting in a subject-based collection?

   b. Why create institution-based repositories?

   c. Green road OA

   d. Authors' rights

   e. Guidelines for gray literature (conference presentations, posters, proposals)

   f. Guidelines for course materials

3. The Institutional Repository at UF (IR@UF):

   a. Introduction to searching the IR@UF

   b. Self-submission of student assignment

       i. Upload

       ii. Create basic metadata

       iii. Add abstract and subject-specific metadata

       iv. Save link for CV, bio sketch, and future assignments

4. Conclusion:

   a. Discuss what sharing your scholarship means. Why and how should we retain authors' rights?

Assessment: Assessment of comprehension for this session is incorporated into a broader quiz covering various databases. The quiz requires students to utilize UFDC to answer one or two reference questions. In addition, students will ask questions and engage in a discussion about self-archiving of materials in repositories.

APPENDIX 9.4

Foundation—Lesson Plan for Lectures on Scholarly Communication: A Librarian's Perspective

Class Title: Scholarly Communication: A Librarian's Perspective

Time Frame: 50 minutes

Format: Lecture/discussion

Class Overview: This session presents students with an introduction to OA and the role it plays in scholarly communication. This includes a brief history of the OA movement, the main characteristics of an OA publication, various OA initiatives, and how researchers can participate in OA.

Facilities Requirements, Materials, and Supplies
- Classroom with a computer podium and LCD projector is ideal to allow for visual presentation of concepts.
- Notepads or whiteboards
- Markers

Learning Objectives

Students will:
1. Define OA
2. Paraphrase the differences between OA and conventional publishing
3. Recognize ways to participate in OA as a researcher
4. Identify local initiatives in OA

Outline of Session:
1. Overview of scholarly communication
2. Differences between OA and conventional publishing models
   a. In teams, students draw the publication process on large notepads or whiteboards.
3. The definition of OA:
   a. How does OA change the traditional publication process?
   b. Have students revise their research publication model
4. Class discussion:
   a. Why is OA important?
   b. How does it change the impact of research?
   c. Who does it benefit? Who does it hurt?
   d. Who pays for OA? How is this different than traditional publication?
5. What *public access* means

6. International and national statements and mandates regarding OA
7. Ways to participate in OA:
   a. Self-archiving in a repository
   b. Publishing in an OA journal or monograph
   c. Hybrid models
8. Local OA initiatives:
   a. IR@UF, UF Open Access Publishing Fund, and policy
   b. Open Access Week

Assessment: Student comprehension is determined through students' interaction with the speaker and questions throughout the session. In addition, discussion of the presentation can occur asynchronously via discussion board, e-mail, etc. Information learned from this session is incorporated into the open access paper or multimedia project.

Foundation—Lesson Plan for Lectures on Scholarly Communication: The Open Access Journal Editor's Perspective

Class Title: Lectures on Scholarly Communication: The Open Access Journal Editor's Perspective

Time Frame: 50 minutes

Format: Lecture

Class Overview: This session exposes students to the OA publishing model and the interworking of an OA publication from an academic researcher and editor's perspective. **Facilities Requirements, Materials, and Supplies**

- Classroom with computer podium and LCD projector is ideal to allow for visual presentation of concepts.

Learning Objectives

Students will:
1. Understand OA from a scientific researcher's perspective
2. Describe how OA is impacting the publishing world

Outline of Session:
1. Editor's personal background as an academic researcher
2. Overview of OA
3. Facts about the OA model:
   a. OA is not a business model; it is a property of publication.
   b. Ability to pay plays no role in editorial process.
   c. Ensures stable model of global dissemination
   d. Fully OA or hybrid models of publishing thriving
   e. OA embodies the concept of peer review.
   f. Catalysts for change
4. Growth of OA publications
5. History of the editor's OA journal
6. Editor's role in the OA journal (how he or she became involved)
7. Fundamental shifts in OA publishing, including:
   a. Static document to living resource
   b. Journal level to article level
   c. Prepublication review and postpublication review
   d. Readers/authors decide value and impact.
   e. Community takes back the content.
   f. Knowledge is shared globally with all who choose to benefit.

Assessment: Information learned from this session is incorporated into the open access paper or multimedia project. Student engagement during discussion and informed questions during the presentation help to gauge student comprehension.

APPENDIX 9.6

Framework—Lesson Plan for Open Access Week Activity

Class Title: Open Access Week

Time Frame: Dependent on local OA events. In 2011, there were a variety of events held on October 26 from 1:00 to 3:30.

Format: Exploration of event and exploratory essay

Class Overview: Instead of a traditional in-class activity, one class period is cancelled and students are asked to attend Open Access Week events in late October. They discuss perspectives through roundtables, attend poster presentations, or go to a lecture. Then they write a brief reflection paper to demonstrate their developing understanding of scholarly communication and relate it to concepts learned in class.

Facilities Requirements, Materials, and Supplies: N/A

Learning Objectives

Students will:
1. Participate in Open Access Week, which is a miniconference environment
2. Synthesize ideas from presentations, roundtables, and poster sessions
3. Create a review of Open Access Week as an initial formal product that demonstrates evaluation of the issues surrounding OA

Outline of Session:
Attend the University of Florida Open Access Week events and write up a one-page review answering the following three questions:
1. What is open access, and how does it change scholarship in the sciences?
2. For you personally, what was the most interesting aspect of Open Access Week?
3. What are the implications of OA publications for international access, peer review, graduate research, and authors' rights?

Assessment: This activity is assessed through students' essay responses to the above questions. The development of this knowledge base contributes to the open access debate and the open access project or paper. This brief paper allows the instructor to assess if individual students need more understanding before they move forward to the higher-level evaluation needed for the culminating projects.

Framework—Lesson Plan for Debate on Open Access: New Publishing Models

Class Title: Debate on Open Access—New Publishing Models

Time Frame: Two class periods: 50 minutes for in-class preparation and 50 minutes for the actual debate. These should be held on separate days to allow teams time to formulate their argument and locate supporting evidence.

Format: Team-based learning activity

Class Overview: The class, divided into three groups, debates the merits of open access publishing from the perspectives of the three stakeholders: researchers, libraries, and publishers (corporate and society/nonprofit). This classroom exercise is designed to help students prepare for their graded OA paper or project.

Facilities Requirements, Materials, and Supplies
- Open space with access to tables or group meeting areas is ideal for this activity.
- Access to laptop, tablet, or mobile device for evidence gathering
- Access to notes from previous course sessions
- Handout detailing the guidelines for the debate
- General debate-judging rubric

Learning Objectives

Students will:
1. Define the issues surrounding OA from their assigned perspective
2. Explain how the OA publishing model impacts their assigned stakeholder
3. Evaluate the issues surrounding OA that impact stakeholders from all areas

Outline of Session:
1. Three- to five-minute opening statement from each team with respect to:
   a. Team's role—which perspective it represents
   b. Current state of participation in OA
   c. Concerns with current models or concerns with changing the current model
2. Moderators (instructors) ask follow-up questions that may include:

    a. Should the current peer-review system be modified?
    b. Which stakeholder should bear the publication costs?
    c. What actions should stakeholders at this institution take to participate in OA?
    d. Are the commercial publishers making unreasonable profits from their journals?
    e. What variation of the OA model seems the most financially viable?

3. Three minutes per team to address posed questions
4. Three-minute rebuttal per team
5. Three- to five-minute closing statement from each team with respect to:
    a. Summary of its position
    b. Recommendation for the scholarly publishing community

Assessment: Instructors assess this exercise through a general debate-judging rubric, many of which can be easily accessed online. Further, the knowledge gained by the students for this exercise is incorporated into the open access paper or multimedia project.

Building–Scholarly Communication Assignment: Open Access Multimedia Project

Assignment Title: Open Access Multimedia Project

Assignment Overview: The OA multimedia project gives students a chance to create a short film that embodies their perspectives on open access. Working in teams, students develop a message, storyboard how to express that opinion, and share a two-minute video that explains open access. This video should synthesize presentations, lectures, and readings from class to express a personal opinion on the issues surrounding scholarly communication in the sciences.

Learning Objectives

Students will:
1. Synthesize the various arguments surrounding OA studied in class
2. Develop and express a personal opinion on OA and scholarly communication issues
3. Understand why scholarly communication models in the sciences have changed and how they relate to their future role as a scientific researcher

Assignment Instructions:
1. Select a partner to develop a multimedia project detailing the team's personal views on OA from the perspectives of a student and future scientific researcher.
2. As a team, brainstorm ways to synthesize the OA and scholarly communication issues that have been presented in class. Decide together on what message to convey.
3. Storyboard a concept and plan the details of the project. For library resources and free media editing software, see the library guides at:
   a. www.uflib.ufl.edu/sparkyawards/resources.html
   b. http://guides.uflib.ufl.edu/media
4. Create a two-minute video and upload the project to a video-sharing site such as YouTube, Blip, or Vimeo.
5. Submit a document to the course website that includes:
   a. A title, a list of the group members and actors, and a link to the video
   b. The storyboard and a succinct overview of the team's perspective
   c. Credits for any media used to make the film

Grading Rubric

This assignment is 20 percent (or 20 points) of the overall course grade.

- Worked collaboratively with team member to develop a shared perspective [**1 point**]
- Message addressed the explicit theme of personal perspective on OA as a student and future scientific researcher [**4 points**]
- Video utilized multimedia, including at least two of the following: images, video, audio, music, text, or animation [**2 points**]
- Final submission included title, group, actors, link to video, storyboard, brief overview, and credits [**9 points**]
- Video was uploaded to a video-sharing site [**1 point**]
- Creativity of idea and concept [**2 points**]
- Technical skill [**1 point**]

APPENDIX 9.9

Building–Scholarly Communication Assignment: Open Access Paper

Assignment Title: Open Access Paper

Assignment Overview: Scholarly communication in the sciences is rapidly changing. New publication models such as the OA model have become the standard for publication in many scientific fields. It is essential to have an understanding of the arguments for and against this shift in scholarly communication. This individual assignment, in conjunction with in-class lectures and the in-class OA debate, will lay the foundations for understanding editor perspectives, researcher perspectives, economic arguments, and public access movements.

Learning Objectives

Students will:
1. Synthesize the various arguments surrounding OA studied in class
2. Develop and express a personal opinion on OA and scholarly communication issues
3. Understand why scholarly communication models in the sciences have changed and how they relate to future roles as a scientific researcher

Assignment Instructions

Open Access Paper:
1. Write an eight- to ten-page paper detailing the issues and perspectives surrounding OA. The paper should include:
   a. An introduction to OA concepts
   b. The history of the OA movement
   c. Detailed analysis of the movement from the perspective of various stakeholders including:
      i. Researchers
      ii. Librarians
      iii. Publishers
      iv. Scholarly societies
      v. The public
   d. A personal synthesis and understanding of OA
   e. A conclusion
   f. Citations in APA format
2. Submit your paper online to the course site.

Grading Rubric

This assignment is 20 percent (or 20 points) of the overall course grade.

- Paper included all required sections: introduction, history, analysis of multiple perspectives, conclusion, and citations [5 **Points**]
- Synthesis of personal perspective was insightful and demonstrated understanding of the issues [5 **Points**]
- Stakeholder perspectives (publishers, researchers, librarians, scholarly societies, and the public) were included in the viewpoints [**2.5 Points**]
- Paper is well written (uses academic language, is free of spelling and grammatical errors, is in the appropriate style, and demonstrates understanding of the issue) [**2.5 Points**]
- Citations are in APA format [**2.5 Points**]
- eight to ten pages [2.5 Points]

References

Anderson, Lorin W., and David R. Krathwohl. 2001. *A Taxonomy for Learning, Teaching, and Assessing: A Revision of Bloom's Taxonomy of Educational Objectives.* New York: Longman.

Davis-Kahl, Stephanie. 2012. "Engaging Undergraduates in Scholarly Communication: Outreach, Education and Advocacy." *College & Research Libraries News* 73, no. 4 (April): 212–222. http://crln.acrl.org/content/73/4/212.full.

Johnson, Margeaux, and Sara Gonzalez. 2011. "Creating a Credit IL Course for Science Students." In *Best Practices for Credit-Bearing Information Literacy Courses,* edited by Christopher V. Hollister, 93–108. Washington DC: Association of College & Research Libraries.

CHAPTER 10

Scholarship & Advocacy at the UVa Scholars Lab: An Interview with Bethany Nowviskie, Ph.D. and Eric Johnson

Stephanie Davis-Kahl
Illinois Wesleyan University

> *Editors' Note: In our own research for this volume, we came across the Scholars' Lab[1] at University of Virginia (UVA) and were struck by how its service offerings find a balance between scholarly communication and information literacy. Bethany Nowviskie, PhD, Director, Digital Research and Scholarship, and Eric Johnson, MA, MLIS, Head, Outreach and Public Services, agreed to speak with us about their work and how the scope of what they do at the Scholars' Lab enacts the connections between infrastructure, creation of scholarship, and the ethos of openness.*

Stephanie Davis-Kahl (SDK): Bethany and Eric, thank you so much for speaking with me today. To start us off, can you tell me how the Scholars' Lab was created? Who were the main players and main drivers behind it?

Bethany Nowviskie (BN): The Scholars' Lab was founded in 2006 as a partnership between the University of Virginia library system and campus Information Technology Services [ITS]. Three centers combined to bring together their staffing and services into one location: EText, the Electronic Text Center at UVa, which was one of the earliest digital humanities centers for the creation and analysis of electronic texts; GeoStat, a center for geospatial and statistical data analysis; and UVa Research Computing Support, a high-performance computing center that also manages site licenses for software across the university and trains users on statistical and mathematical software packages.

SDK: So there's definitely an educational element. Bringing the three groups together was not only about infrastructure, it's also about education.

BN: Yes, I think that's fair to say. All three of the centers had a mission to work within their subject domains to do training and to help people think through new possibilities for digital research and scholarship.

SDK: What areas of expertise and knowledge are key for the lab and the many services you provide?

Eric Johnson (EJ): We have a model in place that incorporates a couple of different approaches. One is a walk-in service area for students and faculty who are looking for help with software and hardware particular to the Scholars' Lab. We have students staffing a desk to help users at that level, and we have a group of staff members—software developers and GIS specialists—who help out with longer-term project work. They do consultations with faculty, graduate students, or undergraduates who are working on projects and need help.

Our Research and Development [R&D] team is a group of humanists who work in the digital realm doing software development support and long-term infrastructure and tool building for humanities work. Everybody here ends up with a different background in the humanities. Several of us have masters' degrees, a couple of us have PhDs. We have an ABD in history, two doctorates in English, two masters' in history, and a statistical analyst who has a degree in Physiology.

We have two consultants—one of them is the aforementioned statistical analyst—that are connected through our ITS department who support the statistical software and analysis work. The requisite background for our staff is one of well-roundedness and intellectual curiosity more than anything else, but we do have specialists in certain areas that we know are high need: for instance, in the areas of statistical analysis and GIS. The R&D team is trained pretty broadly in a number of software languages. We don't typically look for people with specific programming skill sets, but instead we look for a shared approach and the ability to pick up on the necessary languages depending on the nature of the project.

SDK: Eric, can you tell me about how you came to the Scholars' Lab?

EJ: Before I came here, I worked in both university libraries and museum libraries.[2] I'd come out of the library world but had an ongoing interest in the applications of information and technology in the humanities writ large. I did a lot of public services work, and then they posted this marvelous position, which is a great balance between the need to support public services work and the scholarly undertaking in the Scholars' Lab. I do outreach to faculty and students who may be working on digital scholarship and talk about how we can plug into their work as they're going along. I'm involved in a kind of a crossroad of traditional library public services work with cutting-edge, forward-facing creation of digital humanities scholarship. It's really a wonderful blend.

BN: Eric came to us, I think, because the Scholars' Lab has developed a profile as a major North American digital humanities center. A lot of people don't realize that we're administratively embedded within a library because we function so much like our peers, which are independent, faculty-run digital humanities centers. We got to know Eric first through hosting regional digital humanities conferences like THATCamp [The Humanities and Technology Camp] and in developing partnerships with other regional universities and cultural heritage institutions like Monticello.

SDK: What's the interaction like with the other librarians in the library?

EJ: It's good; it's been kind of a fun conversation because a lot of the librarians are interested in figuring out how to plug into the digital world. Some are traditionally trained subject librarians, and others are newer librarians, but across all the libraries on campus, the librarians are keenly interested in being part of the conversation around "digital" and what that will mean in terms of scholarship. In terms of scholarly communication issues, there's a big push for people to learn more about copyright and publishing. It's certainly recognized by the administration as an area that librarians should focus on. From our perspective, being embedded in the library provides us a good avenue for both outreach and keeping strong ties to the scholarly culture of a university because the library still very much represents that culture for a lot of people. It's been really beneficial in both directions.

BN: The library at UVa has invested in digital humanities from the outset. In fact, digital humanities in the United States got its start in UVa Library. We've fostered the creation of the Institute for Advanced Technology in the Humanities [IATH], which is still housed here in Alderman Library, and the EText Center and Geostat Center were created around the same time. Through them, the library could be pursuing creation of its own digital collections and thinking about how its content played into the faculty-driven projects that were happening out of IATH. As the Scholars' Lab has taken shape, it has come to incorporate both of those functions in some ways. Being administratively part of the library allows us to provide access for scholars to library content for use in their interpretive projects and a path for talking with institutional IT about how to get those projects hosted and supported. It also continues to help the library serve as an intellectual crossroads for the university community. The library belongs to everybody, so it's the perfect place to put an interdisciplinary unit like the Scholars' Lab.

SDK: How do you assess and evaluate the work that you do, especially since you're bringing together so many different people and projects?

BN: Assessment happens in different ways in different areas of the Scholars' Lab. Part of the assessment process in the Scholars' Lab R&D involves carefully choosing which faculty projects we partner with. It's part of our mission to collaborate with faculty and grad students on projects since our focus is on training and education and bringing certain areas of our staff expertise into play. We try to foster meaningful collaboration with scholars as they're creating their work. We are careful as we are making choices about which projects to partner on, and careful also to think about the impact that a project will have in any number of domains. One domain may be the subject area of the content and the audience for the project; the other could be a technical assessment that lets us know whether we're expending our software development resources effectively. For instance, we want to work on projects that contribute something unique to the world but that also build on strong foundations and hold some promise of sustainability. It's hard to quantify that kind of assessment.

I honestly think that the ability to choose our collaborations carefully and to say no to some opportunities is one reason that we're widely perceived to be successful. When I first took this position, I did not come in having a library background. Instead, I had worked as a grad student, postdoc, and Media Studies faculty member on digital humanities projects. There, I learned to ask hard questions about the intellectual contribution that any given project might make to its discipline and to the digital humanities community. The questions that I often got asked when we created the Scholars' Lab were, "What is your intake process for faculty projects?" "Is there an annual call, and do you promise to do a certain number per year?" and "Who chooses them?" People are often surprised to learn that we would foster some relationships and not foster others, but it's been a good thing for the university community. Our partnerships are genuine collaborations.

Scholars own their projects to a much greater extent than they would have with another model—they understand them top to bottom. They may not be able to code every piece of them, but at least they have a grasp on all of the pieces that go into making a project, and they're able to edit and produce their own content. This is particularly important to us when we work with graduate students because they are expected to defend dissertations and go away. We try to get their projects on a footing where they can easily be migrated to another university or to private hosting and also to cultivate in them an understanding of what it takes to run these projects. This wasn't always the case with library digital services before.

We also seek out a collaborator first, if we can see that there's something that a project provides to our larger portfolio or to the local community that's really needed. It gives us the ability to choose the projects that are going to be pursued. Where it's appropriate for the scholarship, we drive people toward common stable platforms, which allows us to focus our expensive and specialized resources on projects that will matter more.

SDK: It sounds like you start out with evaluation, using your mission and your resources as the primary filter, and the connections are made in order to further the scholarship in progress or that's just beginning. There's also the long-term view and ensuring the project can travel with the researcher.

BN: That's very true. And we try to stay a half step ahead. For example, several years ago, our digital humanities experts and software developers and librarians could see a spatial turn happening in various academic disciplines, and we could see a kind of conjunction ahead of advanced technologies in the geospatial realm, before our local community. The changing research questions that we were beginning to hear graduate students ask really inspired us. We were able to gear up, write some grants to create software, and host an institute on the spatial humanities that put us just slightly ahead of that curve. I think if we were being purely responsive to what people were asking us for at the time, we wouldn't have been able and ready to collaborate when scholars finally came to us asking for the service. As part of this process, we created a tool set using Omeka, called Neatline,[3] which is an application for geotemporal storytelling with archival collections. It's basically a tool for annotating maps and collections of documents or artifacts and putting those together in a kind of visual narrative both on a spatial and a temporal axis. Now we're ready for the projects that scholars are bringing us!

SDK: What are some of the challenges that you all face at the Scholars' Lab?

EJ: I'd say, of course, it's always a challenge, but a good one, to try to keep abreast of where scholarship seems to be headed. As Bethany mentioned, the spatial humanities emphasis here really came out of keeping our collective ear to the ground about what seems to be coming next—that will be an eternal question. Designing our services to meet evolving needs is always going to be something that we're working on and keeping ahead of as well.

BN: Funding streams for the work that we do are a concern. We are very unique as a digital humanities center not to have a lot of staff on soft money. The model at most DH centers that function outside of a library is to fund their software developers on grant money. We have not done that and intend not to, so when we bring grants in, the funds go towards the extra things for which we might not otherwise have had funding. Supplemental travel, extra equipment, and so forth. The spatial humanities work I mentioned earlier is a good example—we were funded by the National Endowment for the Humanities and later by Library of Congress to begin our investigations into this area. We had a grant from NEH to fund the Institute for Enabling Geospatial Scholarship, which we call the Spatial Humanities Institute. It was a two-year program that brought in around eighty scholars, software developers, and librarians from UVa and from outside the university for training, and it served as a catalyst for conversations about how the next generation of humanities inquiry could and should be using spatial tools and methods.

One thing that we haven't talked about yet is our strong focus on graduate students at the Scholars' Lab and the two graduate fellowship programs that we run. One is a graduate fellowship in digital humanities that is funded internally by the library and targeted at ABD grad students. It follows a traditional fellowship model: students work as solo scholars on a digital project related to their dissertation, and they have a year's worth of funding and assistance from the Scholars' Lab to realize their plans. The Mellon Foundation currently funds the other program through a project in the library called the Scholarly Communication Institute [SCI]. This year, SCI is focused on graduate education reform. The Scholars' Lab's graduate programs are a case study for SCI through what's we call the Praxis Program. It's a fellowship for six graduate students at a time. They come in as a team to learn soft skills, such as collaboration and project management, while they are learning some hard technical skills (like programming). Together, this translates into an ability to plan, design, execute, communicate, and manage a digital humanities project from scratch. Teaching time comes from our R&D group, which is also devoted to other kinds of scholarly project work and to developing infrastructure for our local digital content. A big challenge for us is finding ongoing funding streams to support the kind of work we do, especially when so much of it is geared toward fellowship money for graduate students and staffing time to spend on preparing them to be successful.

SDK: Since digital humanities has such deep roots at UVa, how does that translate into the undergraduate curriculum? Do you typically see undergraduates coming to you for help in the digital humanities?

BN: There's a real emphasis at UVa on undergraduates as researchers. There are a number of digital humanities projects in which faculty involve their students. Some of these projects are in the digital social sciences, so students take on a variety of roles: researchers, content providers, database contributors, and data analysts. There's also a lot of support and training, especially in GIS, coming from the Scholars' Lab for undergraduate classes at UVa. Every year our two GIS specialists run a standing workshop series during which they cover everything from basic to advanced kinds of spatial analysis. They also proactively work with faculty in the planning stages of their courses to create opportunities to teach sections that are GIS-focused.

EJ: Our staff may end up doing consultation work with undergraduates who come in with questions based on their course projects. There's a lot of one-on-one face-to-face training and assistance. Undergraduates are heavy users of our physical lab space as well. We have an array of high-end desktop computers with scanners that students can use. The Scholars' Lab also has a beautiful, sunlit, open room that they use to study. So we're playing the long game by mentoring undergraduates as future members of the Scholars' Lab community. Our speaker series is another outreach avenue. Anyone is welcome to come, and it's most heavily attended by faculty and graduate students, but undergraduates do pop in for that as well. The course focus is probably the major way we reach undergraduates.

SDK: Can you tell me a little bit more about the Scholars' Lab community and how you're building it?

EJ: It's something we're very conscious of, and it permeates a lot of what we do. The graduate fellowships are at the heart of the community because we certainly coalesce around assisting them and being energized by them. The kind of questions they have and the scholarly directions that they're interested in taking inform our services. We have an annual speaker series where we invite scholars from both off campus and on campus to come and share their work and outlook. We do a lot of outreach to various departments, as well as broadly to people who have expressed interest in being aware of our work and activities. This is a good opportunity for the kind of cross-pollinating conversation that I think is so vital to the digital humanities and to libraries generally.

There are so few opportunities for people to actually talk to folks from outside their disciplines in an environment that is so intentionally congenial as what we try to do here. Our speaker series is one way that we do that, and the workshop series that Bethany mentioned is another. We also have a specialist series every semester. We've done workshops on programming or on particular software packages, including some of the statistical packages. We're planning on doing some related to the Neatline software coming up in the spring. The workshops are a more hands-on opportunity for people to be a part of this community, and we are very intentional about finding out what areas people are interested in. We're very intentional about connecting individuals and/ or groups to help that cross-pollination.

SDK: How do you get people to think about sharing their projects, sharing the data that they've gathered through their projects? How does the Scholars' Lab contribute to the open data movement?

BN: The lab is filled with open access advocates, so in part, it's through our everyday practice. There is not a piece of code that we write that we don't put into an open repository. For those of us who publish, we do not publish in closed-access venues. We choose to publish our work in open access journals. We're able to do that in a way that many tenure-track faculty aren't because we're not trying to get over the hurdle of tenure. We have the ability to model attitudes toward sharing and also toward incremental publications that are harder to do in the humanities but are of great interest to emerging scholars. For instance, we provide humanities scholars with a model for making their practices mirror more closely practices of the free and open source software movement. We've also tried to be good stewards of all of the data that we are helping people to collect and share. For example, when we started the Scholars' Lab, all of the GIS information that the Geostat Center had collected over its fifteen-year existence was stored on physical media, so we had a conglomeration of closed media like CDs, DVDs, hard drives, etc. The only way to access the information was through a password-protected directory on a work-station in the lab. So a major project for the Scholars' Lab in its first few years was making all of that information open and shareable. We not only moved data from the closed physical media, but we also created infrastructure and a discovery interface through which faculty and researchers could search and share the data, and re-use it as web services. Open sharing is firmly within our ethos. We all try to pro-vide a model of openness that can be emulated in our practices at the Scholars' Lab.

With junior faculty and with graduate students, I see increasingly dif-ferent attitudes towards these issues. There are some who will want to play the game as it is written, and there are some who want to change the game. We're trying to enable the game changers.

EJ: The library is also engaged in this larger conversation around scholarly communication and what it means for libraries in an open access environment to support such a thing because the traditional model is not as open. Our question is, "What is the best way for the library to support open access?" Do we make ourselves advocates, or do we make ourselves supporters of other people who may be leading that charge?

SDK: So how are you involved in Libra [UVA's institutional reposi-tory]?

BN: Libra is run by a different group. The technical infrastructure is run by our online library environment department, and the related public services are managed by a new scholarly communication team, which is part of our humanities and social sciences services. But we do certainly talk to people about depositing their work in the repository, and we do a lot of counseling of graduate students who are thinking about new-form multimodal and digital dissertations, to think about how they can prepare their information to be archived. And we put our own work in there.

SDK: Do you think that the Scholars' Lab embodies this connection between scholarly communication and information literacy that we're trying to get people to see and work with more intentionally?

EJ: Writ large, we don't frame it that way, but I think it is the case that we are very much at the point of contact between the modes of production of scholarship, which are now increasingly digital. Not only production, but the communication of scholarship across all kinds of media and the information itself are in the digital realm. The increasingly easy-to-use tools allow people to do all kinds of unusual scholarship such as analysis of bodies of text or large masses of information with spatial humanities approaches. So from that we need to be able to figure out what this mass of information is and what we can do with it—that is very much where we pitch ourselves.

SDK: The community aspect of what you're trying to build also goes to the connection as well—for graduate students and undergraduates to understand that there is a community of scholars and that information sharing allows other people to use it and build on their work and others' work.

EJ: I think that is one of the big drivers of the idea of a community: a place where people are welcoming and where information is shared so that everybody benefits from it.

Notes

1. The UVA Scholars' Lab website is at http://www.scholarslab.org/.
2. Eric has an MA in U.S. history and an MLIS.
3. The Neatline website is at http://neatline.org.

CHAPTER 11

Modeling Academic Integrity for International Students

[Use of Strategic Scaffolding for Information Literacy, Scholarly Communication, and Cross-Cultural Learning]

Alex R. Hodges
American University

This chapter is a call to action and an overview of how several members of the American University (AU) library faculty and academic staff work together to foster international students' understanding of scholarly communication and information literacy. This collaboration is based on the foundation of cross-cultural communication. The AU Academics! Team provides educative opportunities for international students upon entry to the university and throughout their individual undergraduate and graduate degree programs. This collaborative effort from International Student and Scholar Services, the College Writing Program, the University Library, and the Academic Support Center, as well as academic departments, includes interactive sessions on information literacy and academic integrity at international student orientations. The academic integrity instructors work with teaching faculty to tie the content to disciplinary and programmatic learning objectives and additional course-integrated library instruction sessions, if requested by individual faculty. These instruction sessions may enhance what is learned through the initial international student–focused orientation.

Case Study Overview—The American University Environment

There is strong evidence in the literature that librarians currently provide information literacy instruction and outreach to international students (Hickok 2011; Hensley and Love 2011; Conteh-Morgan 2002; Peters 2010). However, evidence is not as strong that scholarly communication education is as well integrated for all students—not just for international students. Knievel (2008) discusses the opportunity to effect early adoption of open access practices via the University of Colorado's "Publish Not Perish" online tutorial, which has international impact (183). Jacobs and Berg (2011) and Elmborg (2006) remind librarians that one of our core missions is to reach out to the underserved, which from the perspective of the author of this chapter includes international student populations. Mullen (2011) describes how public services librarians can better use their platform of education and influence to impact greater adoption of open access materials as legitimate research resources. This education would incorporate learning about open access, fair use, and authors' rights issues. Often, librarians provide this side of scholarly communication education informally to our teaching faculty colleagues or to one another, and the information, if conveyed, may trickle down from teaching faculty to student. The AU information literacy plan (Hodges, Becher, and Reece 2012) is just one model for college and university educators to draw upon when developing instruction for international students. Admittedly, AU faculty and academic staff members also need to place more attention and time on scholarly communication education efforts.

The current AU environment for teaching international students about academic writing is politically charged because so much is at stake. International students are beholden to the federal regulations for their student visas, which stipulate that international students maintain responsible behavior. This behavior includes developing research ethics and academic integrity. Adjudication resulting in expulsion because of plagiarism results in revocation of a student visa. Thus, any irresponsible research and writing activity weighs heavily on an individual international student's ability to progress through American higher education. The culture of US higher education cannot groom or impact the careers of future scholars if they cannot remain in the country to complete their education. The global reach of US higher education cannot impact other cultures if Western-based grooming of scholarly communication practices cannot find its way back upon international students' return to their home cultures, where returned students might continue to work within academia or research. American educators are exporting Western standards of academic honor and scholarly impact via international students' learning, but first international students must be successful in their development of academic honor and information literacy. It is the American educator's responsibility to provide this foundational understanding, which librarians often teach in course-integrated information literacy instruction.

At AU, librarians have several inroads to teach international students information literacy and scholarly communication principles, but there are few opportunities to reach only internationals in course-integrated environments because international students are mostly enrolled alongside American students in mainstreamed, inclusive classrooms. Much of this instruction that targets international students must be done during orientations or at voluntary walk-in workshops.

The Academics! Team focuses on the concepts and consequences of academic integrity as it is contextualized within the system of Western scholarly communication. These sessions provide AU international students with an initial baseline understanding of scholarly expectations, research ethics, and campus support resources. Instructors aim to incorporate problem-based learning activities, such as manuscript contract negotiation, publication submission choice, and honor code violation adjudication. Lesson plans related to teaching these topics are integrated in the instructional strategies section of this chapter, and they incorporate scholarly communication education into information literacy instruction by offering librarians or other instructors techniques for how to teach international students about authors' rights, open access discovery, and academic integrity. Foremost, the lesson plans are tied directly to the Association of College and Research Libraries *Information Literacy Competency Standards for Higher Education* (ACRL 2000).

While the focus of these lesson plans and orientation sessions is on matriculated undergraduate and graduate students, the Academics! Team also aims to educate AU faculty and academic staff about the cross-cultural communication and scholarly communication dimensions that are involved in the support of multilingual writing and research. This kind of professional development outreach and support provides crucial scaffolding to instructors and support staff who need to understand the complicated dynamics of how cross-cultural communication success and distress affect the learning of both international and traditional students. The Academics! Team members lead sessions on writing and research at AU's annual Ann Ferren Conference on Teaching, Research and Learning. The team aims for attendees (inclusive of library and teaching faculty members and academic staff) to gain knowledge of practical teaching tips as well as to learn whom to contact across campus for further cross-cultural academic and pedagogical support in regard to working with international students. More specific team collaborations are discussed later in the chapter.

Additionally, the AU Library has provided lectures and discussions on issues related to scholarly communication and open access for the greater AU faculty to consider how these issues impact their research and teaching. The AU Library has invited speakers such as Julia Blixrud in 2009 and Heather Joseph in 2012, both from SPARC[1], and Stuart Shieber[2] from Harvard University's Office of Scholarly Communication and the Berkman Center for Internet and Society, to raise the profile and level of discussion of scholarly communication issues on campus. In 2011, AU librarians participated in the ACRL Scholarly Communication Road Show, which was hosted by the Washington Research Library Consortium. The road show helped raise AU librarians' consciousness to better integrate scholarly communication principles within information literacy instruction.

This ongoing work at AU builds upon and situates itself within the theoretical work contributed by applied linguists, academic librarians, and higher education professionals. This chapter calls for US academia—including the institution of this case study—to do more for our international students in terms of scholarly communication education. The AU approach is by no means perfected, and further assessment and retooling are critical as scholarly communication developments warrant. AU librarians have been fortunate to collaborate with AU's Center for Social Media (CSM) and Washington College of Law (WCL) to develop deeper understandings of scholarly communication issues across campus. Librarians have worked with colleagues from CSM and WCL to create campus-wide discussions and best practices for faculty ownership of intellectual property and use of multimedia under the fair use doctrine of copyright law. These activities have strengthened AU faculty's teaching of scholarly communication issues—especially as they relate to academic integrity and multimedia reuse in scholarship production—and it can be argued that this work strengthens all students' understanding of these issues as students create their own scholarly contributions. CSM and WCL members are a leading force—in tandem with the Association of Research Libraries (ARL)—in developing best practices and code for academic librarians' interpretation of fair use and copyright understanding. The AU Library endorses and adopts these best practices and code. This locally produced support provides excellent resources that librarians can use to build or retool their educative opportunities for campus constituencies (ARL, CSM, and WCL 2012; Aufderheide and Jaszi 2011). Subject liaison librarians benefit from understanding the work of CSM and WCL so that the best practices can be addressed in subject-specific library instruction. With the hope that the discussion reaches our students through classroom instruction, library instruction, and research experience, AU librarians have used the principles behind these resources to open discussions about scholarly communication among our library and teaching faculty.

At AU, which is a Carnegie-classified doctoral/research university, students from over 140 countries attend for a variety of time frames; some students may attend for a semester, others a year, while others attend for the duration of an undergraduate or graduate degree, or both. Much of the AU curriculum[3] is globally focused in nature. The AU School of International Service, with both undergraduate and graduate international studies degrees, comprises the largest school of its kind focused on international relations in the United States. The School of International Service is also AU's largest academic unit in terms of the enrollment of undergraduate and graduate students. The School of International Service and the Kogod School of Business enroll roughly the same number of international students and permanent residents. These schools hold the highest international student enrollment at AU.[4] This curriculum has many ties to other universities worldwide and draws students from schools all over the world (2012). Librarians and teaching faculty work with the International Student and Scholar Services office to ensure that students are acclimated to American (and mostly Western) higher education and research culture. Many students have studied English as a foreign language in their home countries. In general, but not always, their spoken and written English—the productive skills—are not as strong as their reading and listening abilities—the receptive skills. More often than not, international students need to take advantage of the university's academic support services in order to bolster their writing and academic skills. This need can, at times, cause anxiety, as the students are reluctant to ask for help, which in some cultures is a sign of weakness. Library outreach to international students through orientations and meet-and-greet events assuages this fear by developing social connections early in a degree program. Also, librarians explicitly must demonstrate their worth to international students in core instructional and reference work. American University has established a referral service for international students' academic support services among the Academics! Team members. For example, this service ensures that a when an international student is working in the Writing Center and the writing consultant notices the student needs to learn how to find better scholarly sources in databases, then the student is put in touch with either the subject specialist librarian or the librarian who manages international student outreach.

Cultural and Academic Issues Facing International Students

In order to understand any instructional outreach to international students, one must thoroughly understand basic issues of cross-cultural communication and theories of applied linguistics, or second language acquisition. Students' learning is impacted by societal norms and the influence of their first language's (L1) culture (Nunan 1999; Scollon, Scollon, and Jones 2012). There are several examples of cultural issues at play in the academic system: culturally appropriate power distance between classmates or between students and teachers; respect for authority that favors a top-down transference of knowledge directly from teacher to student; low context/direct culture (aka the

United States) that usually demands an egalitarian classroom environment where students have the assumed right to challenge their teachers' pedagogical methods and content knowledge. In addition, scholarly communication standards, such as use of citation, integration of evidence, and writing structure, differ across the world, and these differences are amplified by Western standards of academic integrity. Culturally, this main difference then affects international students' understandings of how scholarship is structured, cited, and disseminated. These are just a few of the cultural issues that affect classroom learning that librarians should be aware of when planning any information literacy session, but especially those integrating information on scholarly communication issues. In heterogeneous classrooms of second language (L2) learners, it is assumed that these cultural issues affect not only all classroom relationships but also eventual acculturation into the broader learning environment and target culture as well. If students—with help from their teacher's attention to cultural differences—can be made to feel comfortable in an open classroom so that they can take risks, respect one another to feel a sense of affiliation or camaraderie, and be scaffolded supportively to achieve course learning objectives, then the cultural issues that international students bring to the diverse classroom might not interfere with their ability to succeed in their target culture.

With this scaffolding in place at AU, international students have many chances to interact with AU librarians on campus and online. There are opportunities for interaction inside and outside of the classroom. American culture is low context, which means that the international student will experience sometimes-fleeting attention from many social or academic groups that may be targeting them. Even though Americans tend to be direct, social opportunities are not always expressed directly or expected to be taken seriously. This type of social hedging can be frustrating (or confusing) to international students. It can affect their in-class relationships with their American peers, especially when the international student comes from a culture where a social invitation is a formal communication that is meant to express friendship or membership. A failed connection to a social opportunity (whether academic in nature or not) might make an international student feel less like a member of the community, and this concept of fraternization or membership is a crucial component of a safe extended learning environment, where an international student should feel comfortable to express him- or herself, especially in academic work.

Instructional Strategies and Lesson Plans

During one-on-one interactions or referred appointments with international students, librarians also must be aware of an international student's well-being. Often, this observation is difficult to make because librarians traditionally do not get to build individual relationships with students over time. Librarians can make inroads with international students by better understanding the international student's point of view—especially in terms of the management of academic and cultural stress. Cultural stress—beyond language difference—involves students' levels of discomfort that are related to food, transportation, money, or friendship. Other issues—such as political turmoil or natural catastrophes—in the students' home countries also might affect their stress levels. These stresses appear during the student's cultural adaptation time, which occurs when entering an American university for the first time. Sometimes the stresses never fully go away, but students must learn coping strategies to work through stressors so the stressors don't negatively impact academic performance or personal well-being (Furnham 1993). The changes have the potential to lead to culture fatigue, which is extreme disorientation, discomfort, or shock one feels when immersed in a new culture or language. Initial arrival is a difficult time for international students in the new environment, and it can cause students to negatively compare the American target culture with their native culture. Librarians' awareness of international students' culture fatigue can help librarians determine with faculty when it is appropriate to integrate library-specific instruction into a course—too soon, and the students might not be able to incorporate the library lessons into their frame of reference; too late, and the students might have already developed their research habits.

This fatigue or depression can be confusing to professors, teachers, or librarians, especially when power distance differences are at play. In some high-context cultures, which use formal word choice and implicit, culture-specific communications that favor culture members, it is inappropriate for students to ask questions of, or even contact, the instructor (Hall 1976). This high power distance leads some Western teachers to interpret that the student might be lazy or uninterested in learning. However, it is important to recognize that the student may be feeling uncomfortable with the new responsibility to initiate communication with the professor. This distance—when combined with all of the other changes—complicates the connection between the teacher and student (Scollon, Scollon, and Jones 2012, 52–59). Librarians can help reduce this distance by deliberately integrating their educative opportunities throughout the academic careers of international students: planned orientations at entry, consistent outreach, course-integrated library instruction, office hours, walk-in classes, and for graduate students specifically, high-level support for manuscript preparation or discussions on negotiation of authors' rights.

One major example of how librarians can help international students is with the concept of "code switching" between formal, academic language and informal, colloquial language. Librarians provide instruction on how to find and use resources that can explain academic vocabulary or jargon. AU's librarians also provide instruction on how to write literature reviews and how to identify structural components of scholarly literature that are required for manuscripts in specific disciplines. AU students are instructed to use these manuscript examples as models for their own research and manuscript production. The concept of code switching is important for scholarly communication because international students need to adopt the ability to use academic register, or formal language, and discipline-specific structure in academic writing, presentations, and the classroom.

Another important consideration of code switching is how students relate to themselves or others as scholars. Student-to-student communication is a low power distance. Student-to-faculty member is a high power distance. However, language can be more informal in social situations in which the power distance is low, such as during a one-on-one consultation or during a small workshop. Any educator can explain informally concepts about culture and language that the international student might fear asking about in a classroom setting, especially if the classroom is not an ideal place to take risks to seek information. Librarians particularly can help internationals feel at ease in individual appointments, and if the student is at ease, librarians can make headway in informing the student about specific scholarly communication or information literacy principles that have not yet been mastered in the formal classroom setting. At the same time, librarians can provide empathy as a means for students to know that we care about and understand the issues they are facing by checking for understanding in subtle, nondirect ways, such as using student response systems or requesting anonymous feedback. This feedback helps librarians know that learning is occurring.

As educators, librarians can respond to the challenges of cultural issues by creating community-building opportunities inside and outside of our classroom. This approach can be implemented by conducting information literacy sessions that incorporate group work. In group work, active learning among all student group members is key. Role-playing or role reversal activities can also facilitate active, collaborative learning. If each student has an assigned role, then there is an expectation of contribution that ties to the greater whole or the learning objective. The more interaction among members, the more the international student becomes or feels part of the group. Sharing visual evidence or documentaries that showcase a scenario helps students to conceptualize that maybe they are not that much different in their basic needs from other acculturated students or vice versa. In Lesson Plan A (see Appendix 11.1), the instructor shows students contracts for signing away rights to a manuscript. The students must discuss the differences between the contracts and the manuscripts, which also helps students understand the principles of manuscript submission and then eventual online discovery by other scholars per Lesson Plan B (see Appendix 11.1). This simulation of verbal debate or negotiating activity can help international students develop or activate higher-order critical-thinking skills in bridging information gap or synthesis-related tasks. These types of activities are examples of informational interaction, and they foster a constructivist, collaborative effort to construct knowledge in context of the participants' functional experiences. AU librarians created these activities so that they could be used with upper-level undergraduate or entry-level graduate students in order to address scholarly communication and information literacy imperatives that had been neglected or underemphasized in course-integrated library instruction throughout and across the AU curriculum. The intensive requirements of AU's undergraduate capstone paper and the process for writing graduate theses and dissertations, as well as the changing landscape of publishing and intellectual property, necessitated their creation.

Discussion and understanding of these cross-cultural communication impediments is especially imperative when we must attend to internationals' understanding of our academic culture, of which the principles of scholarly communication are particularly complicated. We cannot teach progressive publishing practices without the baseline understanding of academic integrity expectations. We cannot reach our international students if we do not respect their potentially very different cultural viewpoints.

Educational Support Services for International Students

The following describes a shifting English for Academic Purposes (EAP) campus climate for international students at AU and how an academic writing curriculum provides authentic language support for AU international students. A major focus of AU education and outreach is on academic integrity and scholarly communication, both grounded in information literacy instruction efforts.

AU closed its long-running English Language Institute (ELI) in the early 2000s. It was one of the first ELIs in the United States. At this time, an approach to teaching international students from both an English grammar–focused and content-based curriculum changed to one that is now almost singularly focused on content-based instruction for its matriculated nonnative speakers (NNSs). The former ELI curriculum aimed to expand AU international students' language skills beyond successful use of grammar in academic writing. Academic writing is essential to understanding scholarly communication issues because it is the foundation of the students' communication skills in academic work, which fosters eventual global impact and lifelong learning. The students' development of spoken and written language and the ability to produce cogent writing and articulation are helped by learning how to use and integrate source texts, which back up their logic. These texts are found through library-based research and discovery. The international students, just like any other students, must learn to fit research and their newfound knowledge within their current and building worldview. This building worldview impacts their intellectual development and builds upon what they already know—their personal schema (Leki and Carson 1997). This strategy is very much situated in the communicative language teaching approach, which aims to incorporate content-focused learning for practical purposes. In this case, the purpose is academic learning and acculturation to Western standards of scholarly communication.

In 2003, a new campus-wide organizational structure was implemented to provide support for international students at AU. ELI instructors and staff previously provided much of the academic integrity support with assistance from librarians to integrate library instruction in the EAP writing courses. Three academic professional staff positions were created across campus in order to fill the void of the support provided previously by ELI staff: an international student writing coordinator in the department of literature (which houses the university's central writing center), an international student advisor in the office of International Student and Scholar Services, and an academic counselor for international students in the Academic Support Center in the university's campus life division, which houses a writing lab to support students with exceptional needs (inclusive of international students). This "triangle of support" works as an informal team with the library's instruction coordinator and the university's academic affairs office to teach and enforce scholarly communication standards and the university's academic integrity code.

At AU, the College Writing Program administers AU's undergraduate composition requirement for all matriculated students as well as a writing and cross-cultural communication course for international students, "Literature (LIT) 160: The Culture of Higher Education in the United States." The international student writing coordinator developed the LIT 160 curriculum in consultation with librarians and hired its instructors, as well as provided support for other graduate and undergraduate writing courses geared for international students. Each College Writing section has an assigned librarian who works with the writing instructor to integrate baseline information literacy instruction. The instruction coordinator provides targeted library instruction and personal appointments for the international students.

In addition to librarian-focused attention for international students, the international student writing coordinator spends time advising international students about their writing in one-on-one workshops to enhance not only grammar and structure but also the ability to create logical and well-supported arguments. She also trains graduate composition students who plan to teach writing, as well as her faculty colleagues, about cross-cultural issues and pedagogy that can better support international students' efforts in English language campus classrooms. Her challenge is teaching the average American professor to look at the diversity of international students with a different lens. For instance, she might recommend to her colleagues that they must come to understand the indirect rhetoric of some East Asian cultures. In the case of many Japanese students' writing, she suggests that faculty flip to the student's conclusion if the introductory paragraphs do not concisely make an argument. This generalization can be problematic, too, because it supports the argument that contrastive rhetoric is reductive. Making this assumption about all of East Asian student writing is dangerous, and it is noted that the stereotype—though easy to explain—is not always true (Connor 2003). Connor (2003) also writes that contrastive rhetoric can lead to the further marginalization of gender- and race-related issues in an educational setting. This possible marginalization clearly does not aid the development of authentic, multiple voice possibilities in oral or expository argumentation. Librarians teaching about scholarly communication might take the same advice as they are leading an in-class activity or reviewing an assessment.

As educators of the international student population, librarians should allow space for students to develop their voice—especially as instructional situations encourage active learning and collaboration. Teaching librarians are responsible for ensuring that their planned learning activities help international students make sense of the material with which they are engaging. Usage of the word *voice* relates to agency as a means of articulation, argumentation, or critical thinking, whether in written or spoken form.

Librarians' jargon-laden communication may be steeped in academic and library-specific language; thus, we should create educational opportunities that support international students' development of voice and understanding of how it relates to scholarly communication practices. Such activities can give students authentic "practice with the wide range of registers that they will encounter when they undertake university work" (Biber et al. 2002, 42). One example activity could involve a deeper understanding of plagiarism via role-playing. Role-playing allows students to read, problem-solve, and discuss cases of plagiarism within the context of adjudicating the violation. Consequently, students come to understand the issues of plagiarism from both sides: plagiarist and adjudicator. The activity engages students by involving them directly in determining if a possible incident of plagiarism or misuse of fair use requires a sanction, such as a chance to rewrite a paper or revise an assignment, or complete course failure, academic suspension, or expulsion.

Students regularly invoke copyright and fair use as they aim to integrate derived text and multimedia into their own work. Classroom or orientation assignments and their related library-specific activities may encourage students to state and argue their opinion. Librarians, faculty, and academic staff members have a chance to collaborate to design and deliver these activities. The aim of the activity addressed in Lesson Plan C (see Appendix 11.1) creates a dialogic exercise that increases "critical awareness about voice in the sense [that] self-representation can help learners maintain control over the personal and cultural identity they are projecting in their writing" or presentations (Ivanic and Camps 2001, 31). When students work together, they project and negotiate multiple authentic voices that show there is usually more than one way to draw a conclusion. Creating educative opportunities that allow such plurality of expression enable NNSs to showcase their authentic voices while learning the Western writing or publication standard.

While encouraging active learning and development of voice is extraordinarily important, librarians still need to focus on making sure that student collaboration in group work is on target with the learning objectives. As educators, librarians must provide direction, correction, and intensive feedback in order to underscore why anything taught in information literacy instruction is important. Also, student voices and their conclusions or contributions to class discussion may need correction or further discussion. Corrective feedback (CF), whether written or oral, is the way in which an educator provides the proper scaffolding to help the students stay on target or realign their line of thinking. In terms of CF strategies, Ferris (1997) explains that students care greatly about their teacher's feedback, but may sometimes "ignore or avoid the suggestions" (330). Ensuring that feedback is understood and melded into everyday teaching is time-consuming. Librarians, who may not have a role in summative feedback (the provision of grades), should ensure that this feedback makes it to the students whenever possible. A librarian may provide an overview of common errors that have been noticed, and the instructor of record might share this explanation of the errors to the students. Likewise, librarians play a role in correcting form, usage, and content understanding and can do so in conjunction with their teaching partners. Sheen (2007) argues "that focused linguistic CF is more effective when it incorporates both provision of the correct form and metalinguistic explanation" (278). In fact, this "explanation" can be reinforced during any in-person or electronic encounter, and librarians can seamlessly integrate linguistic advice when discussing or seeking student understanding of content. CF is a hallmark assessment technique of the lesson plans introduced in this chapter. Each lesson plan notes that the librarian should check for understanding via whole-group discussion or group report-back time. When a misunderstanding occurs—whether it be linguistic or content-based—the teaching librarian should provide a correction so that the whole group understands the correct information. This concept is especially important when working with international students because CF acts as a scaffold and corrects misunderstandings that may occur during active learning exercises, when new learning is taking place through discussion and oral language.

Conclusion: Next Steps

This chapter presents a number of different ways that librarians at American University have integrated scholarly communication and information literacy into international students' educational experiences. Even though we are working towards more connections between scholarly communication and information literacy, we acknowledge the difficulties in addressing scholarly communication issues with international students as adequately as we would like. The irony is that the issues have global impact and repercussions—especially as we export our notions of academic integrity and scholarly communication when international students return to their countries of origin as well as when our students go abroad for further education or work (Waters 2008). As public services librarians and educators, we need to do more to reiterate Mullen's (2011) viewpoint that we create the time and space for scholarly communication discussion in information literacy instruction.

In the future, further analysis could be done to track the integration of these scholarly communication instructional goals and the audiences they reach. There may be students who are not being referred to the Academics! Team by their assigned professors. Further research, in terms of additional interviews or a campus climate survey, could uncover how AU faculty members perceive the need for additional and more pervasive scholarly communication support for AU's nonnative English-speaking students.

Finally, the remaining issue this chapter raises is how to determine if there is *enough* support for international students, especially those at the graduate level, who may need higher-touch services and instructional outreach. While the student life component (social, cultural, and legal support) seems to be well developed at some institutions (Hickok 2011; Hensley and Love 2011), it is worth arguing that additional academic support could be beneficial more broadly throughout

American higher education for these students, especially those who do not progress through lengthy, tiered undergraduate academic programming. Many students may take credit courses for academic purposes, and then they may progress to a degree program. All the while, they are learning from scholars to possibly become scholars. This progression helps the students learn in time and build from a foundation.

Yet Atkinson and Ramanathan (1995) argue that many international students who have not had the foundational academic writing support will still struggle in their content-based courses, and in turn, whatever foundation they have been afforded affects their ability to take part in the scholarly communication process in their own right. Any librarian who teaches a one-off class or a workshop without prior knowledge of the attendees' abilities may be unable to meet his or her information literacy or scholarly communication learning objectives as well as to scaffold instruction appropriately in class or beyond class in programmatic learning objectives. At that point, addressing scholarly communication education and advocacy may become beyond the scope of possibility for international students until the larger academic community more widely embraces open access scholarship. In order to help other academics (international students included) embrace the principles of scholarly communication, librarians must seize the opportunity to work with their library and university administrators to create a culture similar to American University's, which integrates elements from SPARC, ARL, and the ACRL Scholarly Communication Toolkit.[5]

By using the recommendations for active, communication- and problem-based learning activities discussed in this chapter and those emphasized in the integrated lesson plans, librarians can be intentionally supportive and empathetic toward the cultural and academic struggles of international students as they deepen their understanding of scholarly communication and become information-literate by US higher education standards.

Acknowledgements

The author would like to thank his American University International Student and Scholar Services (ISSS) colleagues for their support and inclusion of the University Library in order to better reach American University's international student population. Additional gratitude goes to his immediate academic integrity and scholarly communication ISSS collaborators, Angela Dadak, Shari Pattillo, and Jawee Perla. The author performed initial second language acquisition and cross-cultural communication research for this chapter while he was enrolled in American University's TESOL program.

Lesson Plans

Lesson Plan A: Teaching Author Rights

Prep Time: 1–2 hours | Activity Time: 1 hour

Overview and Purpose	Information Literacy Standards Addressed
The instructor will teach international graduate students about authors' rights for theses and dissertations. Coverage will include discussion of author contracts for manuscripts and institutional repositories. The purpose of this instruction is to ensure that international graduate students understand the variety of options they may have as they venture into academic publishing.	**Standard Five** The information literate student understands many of the economic, legal, and social issues surrounding the use of information and accesses and uses information ethically and legally. **Performance Indicator 1** The information literate student understands many of the ethical, legal and socio-economic issues surrounding information and information technology. **Outcome B** Identifies and discusses issues related to free vs. fee-based access to information **Outcome D** Demonstrates an understanding of intellectual property, copyright, and fair use of copyrighted material

	Teacher's Role	Student's Role	Materials Needed
Objectives	Teach students to arrange for their rights as authors through contract acceptance and negotiation.	Learn how and where to place works to benefit their personal scholarly research and impact goals.	• Traditional journal article and initial contract • Open access journal article and initial contract • UMI thesis or dissertation and contract • Work deposited in institutional repository and contract
Instructions	Provide examples of different scholarly works and contracts from an institutional repository, an open access journal, a traditional journal, and a UMI thesis or dissertation.	Review the various works and contracts. Note fine print for third-party options. Note copyright; ability to post copies online and revise works postpublication.	
Activity and Assessment	Compare and discuss the differences in the contracts and publication types. Check for understanding via whole-group discussion.	Critically read contract language and ask for clarification of language. Work in groups, when possible, for better cross-understanding.	

Lesson Plans

Lesson Plan B: Teaching Open Access

Prep Time: 1–2 hours | Activity Time: 1 hour

Overview and Purpose	Information Literacy Standards Addressed
The instructor will teach international students about the differences between open access and subscription publications. Instruction will cover both how to search for the two categories and why one might consider publishing his or her own work in either venue. Another purpose of this instruction is to ensure that international graduate students, in particular, understand how to make decisions about choosing publication venues in their disciplines. Discussion should include impact metrics as well as the reality of academic tenure pressure, but also the benefit of a wider reach that open access distribution provides. Additionally, the economics of the publishing industry should be discussed.	**Standard Five** The information literate student understands many of the economic, legal, and social issues surrounding the use of information and accesses and uses information ethically and legally. **Performance Indicator 1** The information literate student understands many of the ethical, legal and socio-economic issues surrounding information and information technology. **Outcome B** Identifies and discusses issues related to free vs. fee-based access to information **Outcome D** Demonstrates an understanding of intellectual property, copyright, and fair use of copyrighted material

	Teacher's Role	Student's Role	Materials Needed
Objectives	Teach students to arrange how to find open access resources as well as understand open access venues for depositing work.	Learn how to search open access repositories. Explore open access methods of manuscript submission.	• Access to the Directory of Open Access Journals • Access to an institutional repository • Projection to demonstrate search and Google Scholar • ACRL Scholarly Communication Kit http://www. scholcomm.acrl. ala.org
Instructions	Provide search examples in order for students to access an institutional repository and an open access journal.	Search Google Scholar and access proprietary and open access scholarship. Observe authority and potential for impact.	
Activity and Assessment	Compare and discuss the economic and format differences in the publication venues. Teach citation impact. Check for understanding via whole-group discussion.	Critically compare different venues. Try to access fee-based and free works. Work in groups for better cross-understanding. Report back.	

Lesson Plans

Lesson Plan C: Teaching Academic Integrity and Fair Use

Prep Time: 2–3 hours | Activity Time: 1–1.5 hours

Overview and Purpose	Information Literacy Standards Addressed
The instructor will teach international graduate students about academic integrity via authentic scenarios and violation adjudication. Coverage will include discussion of authorial errors related to inappropriate collaboration, incorrect documentation, and cheating. The purpose of this instruction is to ensure that international graduate students understand the serious repercussions of academic integrity violation and how the errors correspond to misunderstanding scholarly communication practices and purpose (especially related to copyright, citation and fair use). It is recommended that instructors use a student response system (clickers) for this activity so that students are more willing to contribute their individual or group's thinking about what constitutes plagiarism. Rich discussion can ensue, and it is the responsibility of the instructor to provide verbal and visual corrections so that the students all have the same baseline understanding. Student visas can be at stake. Clarity is imperative.	**Standard Five** The information literate student understands many of the economic, legal, and social issues surrounding the use of information and accesses and uses information ethically and legally. **Performance Indicator 2** The information literate student understands many of the ethical, legal and socio-economic issues surrounding information and information technology. **Outcome F** Demonstrates an understanding of what constitutes plagiarism and does not represent work attributable to others as his/her own **Performance Indicator 3** The information literate student acknowledges the use of information sources in communicating the product or performance. **Outcome A** Selects an appropriate documentation style and uses it consistently to cite sources **Outcome B** Posts permission granted notices, as needed, for copyrighted material

	Teacher's Role	Student's Role	Materials Needed
Objectives	Teach students to adhere to academic integrity code.	Learn how to reason what is plagiarism and what constitutes fair use of multimedia.	• Student response system (clickers) • Institutional academic integrity code • Past campus academic integrity violation scenarios • Knowledge of institutional adjudication system for academic integrity violations • ARL, CSM, and WCL 2012 • Aufderheide and Jaszi 2011
Instructions	Provide examples of violations from an institutional history. Cover adjudication measures for violations. Discuss interventions and campus support.	Review the various violations. Understand role and responsibility as scholar. View campus support structure as means to avoid violations.	
Activity and Assessment	Provide support to group discussions and corrective feedback to group adjudication discussions. Manage clickers.	In groups, determine violations and adjudicate them. Use clickers to participate in whole-group discussion.	

Notes

1. See "What Is SPARC?" at http://www.arl.org/sparc/about/index. shtml.
2. See "Stuart Shieber" at http://cyber.law.harvard.edu/people/ sshieber.
3. The American University-wide curriculum aims to engage the campus with the world and the world with the campus. See more on global impact here: http://www.american.edu/discoverau/ global-impact.cfm.
4. See the American University *Academic Data Reference Book* (Table 11: International and Permanent Resident Students by Primary Major) at http://www.american.edu/provost/oira/upload/ ADRB-2011-12.pdf.
5. See ACRL's Scholarly Communication Toolkit at http://schol-comm.acrl.ala.org.

References

ACRL (Association of College and Research Libraries). 2000. *Information Literacy Competency Standards for Higher Education.* Chicago: ACRL, January 18. http://www.ala.org/acrl/standards/informationlit-eracycompetency.

ARL (Association of Research Libraries), CSM (Center for Social Media), and WCL (Washington College of Law) Program on Information Justice and Intellectual Property. 2012. *Code of Best Practices in Fair Use for Academic and Research Libraries.* January. http://www.arl.org/ bm~doc/code-of-best-practices-fair-use.pdf.

Atkinson, Dwight, and Vai Ramanathan. 1995. "Cultures of Writing: An Ethnographic Comparison of L1 and L2 University Writing/Language Programs." *TESOL Quarterly* 29, no. 3 (Autumn): 539–568. doi:10.2307/3588074.

Aufderheide, Patricia, and Peter Jaszi. 2011. *Reclaiming Fair Use: How to Put Balance Back in Copyright.* Chicago: University of Chicago Press.

Biber, Douglas, Susan Conrad, Randi Reppen, Pat Byrd, and Marie Helt. 2002. "Speaking and Writing in the University: A Multidimensional Comparison." *TESOL Quarterly* 36, no. 1 (Spring): 9–48. doi:10.2307/3588359.

Connor, Ulla. 2003. "Changing Currents in Contrastive Rhetoric: Implications for Teaching and Research." In *Exploring the Dynamics of Second Language Writing*, edited by Barbara Kroll, 218–241. New York: Cambridge University Press.

Conteh-Morgan, Miriam. 2002. "Connecting the Dots: Limited English

Proficiency, Second Language Learning Theories, and Information Literacy Instruction." *The Journal of Academic Librarianship* 28, no. 4 (July–August): 191–196. doi:10.1016/S0099-1333(02)00282-3.

Elmborg, James. 2006. "Critical Information Literacy: Implications for Instructional Practice." *The Journal of Academic Librarianship*, 32, no. 2 (March): 192–199. doi:10.1016/j.acalib.2005.12.004.

Ferris, Dana R. 1997. "The Influence of Teacher Commentary on Student Revision." *TESOL Quarterly* 31, no. 2 (Summer): 315–339. doi:10.2307/3588049.

Furnham, Adrian. 1993. "Communicating in Foreign Lands: The Cause, Consequences and Cures of Culture Shock." *Language, Culture and Curriculum* 6, no. 1: 91–109. doi:10.1080/07908319309525140.

Hall, Edward T. 1976. *Beyond Culture.* Garden City, NY: Anchor Press.

Hensley, Merinda Kaye, and Emily Love. 2011. "A Multifaceted Model of Outreach and Instruction for International Students." In *International Students and Academic Libraries: Initiatives for Success,* edited by Pamela A. Jackson and Patrick Sullivan, 115–134. Chicago: Association of College and Research Libraries.

Hickok, John. 2011. "Knowing Their Background First: Understanding Prior Library Experiences of International Students." In *International Students and Academic Libraries: Initiatives for Success,* edited by Pamela A. Jackson and Patrick Sullivan, 1–17. Chicago: Association of College and Research Libraries.

Hodges, Alex R., Melissa L. Becher, and Gwendolyn J. Reece. 2012. "Information Literacy Plan." American University Library. Accessed September 10. http://www.american.edu/library/instruction/information_literacy.cfm.

Ivanic, Rosalind, and David Camps. 2001. "I Am How I Sound: Voice as Self-Representation in L2 Writing." *Journal of Second Language Writing* 10, no. 1–2 (February–May): 3–33. doi:10.1016/S1060-3743(01)00034-0.

Jacobs, Heidi. L. M., and Salinda Berg. 2011. "Reconnecting Information Literacy Policy with the Core Values of Librarianship." *Library Trends* 60, no. 2 (Fall): 383–394. doi:10.1353/lib.2011.0043.

Knievel, Jennifer E. 2008. "Instruction to Faculty and Graduate Students: A Tutorial to Teach Publication Strategies." *portal: Libraries and the Academy* 8, no. 2 (April): 175–186. doi:10.1353/pla.2008.0020.

Leki, Ilona, and Joan Carson. 1997. "'Completely Different Worlds': EAP and the Writing Experiences of ESL Students in University Courses." *TESOL Quarterly* 31, no. 1 (Spring): 39–69. doi:10.2307/3587974.

Mullen, Laura Bowering. 2011. "Open Access and Academic Library Public Services: Roles for Reference and Instruction." In *Open Access to STM Information: Trends, Models and Strategies for Libraries,* edited by Anthi Katsirikou. IFlA Publications, no. 153. Berlin/Munich: De Gruyter Saur.

Nunan, David. 1999. *Second Language Teaching and Learning*. Boston: Heinle & Heinle.

Peters, Diane E. 2010. *International Students and Academic Libraries: A Survey of Issues and Annotated Bibliography*. Lanham, MD: Scarecrow Press.

School of International Service. 2012. "Abroad at AU: Partners." American University. Accessed September 10. http://www.american.edu/abroad-atau/partners.cfm.

Scollon, Ron, Suzanne Wong Scollon, and Rodney H. Jones. 2012. *Intercultural Communication: A Discourse Approach*. Malden, MA: Blackwell Publishers.

Sheen, Younghee. 2007. "The Effect of Focused Written Corrective Feedback and Language Aptitude on ESL Learners' Acquisition of Articles." *TESOL Quarterly* 41, no. 2 (June): 255–283. doi:10.1002/j.1545-7249.2007.tb00059.x.

Waters, Donald. 2008. "Open Access Publishing and the Emerging Infrastructure for 21st Century Scholarship." *Journal of Electronic Publishing* 11, no. 1 (Winter). doi:10.3998/3336451.0011.106.

CHAPTER 12

At the Nexus of Scholarly Communication and Information Literacy

[Promoting Graduate Student Publishing Success]

Marianne A. Buehler
University of Nevada, Las Vegas

Anne E. Zald
University of Nevada, Las Vegas

Introduction

Graduate students embarking upon a new phase in their educational careers may not realize the range of expectations, particularly the cocurricular or extracurricular expectation to participate in the scholarly communication process. Unforeseen faculty expectations may include a requirement to publish or copublish an article in order to pass a graduate course or to engage in grant-funded research that will result in conference presentations or publications. Learning about the publication process provides a key transitional experience between the independent intellectual endeavor of conducting research for course assignments and the social dynamics of being a professional researcher or scholar, interacting with a complex human system that encompasses significant variations of protocol. The initiate author must learn to decode and conform to the varied requirements of specific journals, using critical analysis and attention to detail. These lessons come to light and are made personal for the novice author as she transitions from being primarily a consumer to being a creator of published materials.

A widespread assumption is that faculty members mentor graduate students through the transition, however, research on graduate education indicates that the practice of mentorship varies widely. Librarians who are seeking hooks for information literacy connections with graduate programs are advised to look closely, yet discreetly, into the cultural dynamics of their liaison departments, as well as to gain familiarity with their department's resource requirements. Understanding the extent to which publication by graduate students is encouraged and supported through mentorship in specific departments or programs is vitally important for planning and implementing services around both information literacy and scholarly communication. Librarians who facilitate professional exchange between faculty and graduate students around the publication process can contribute developmentally to a key transformative experience whereby a graduate student begins initiation into the mores and intellectual habits of his or her discipline.

Faculty-Graduate Student Publishing and Mentoring Relationships

A 2005–2006 study, conducted by the Center for Innovation and Research in Graduate Education (CIRGE), surveyed recent University of Washington, Seattle, PhD social science graduates to inquire about the application of their education in their ensuing careers (Nerad et al. 2007). A particular policy recommendation outcome, based on graduate student responses, called for a PhD education paradigm shift focused on universities that "need to pay more attention to connecting research training with teaching, writing, and publishing" and bring it forth "from the margins to the center of PhD education" (6). Of the social science PhDs, 63 percent held either tenure-track or tenured positions, and in the study rated a few aspects of their current positions as "very important," including writing and publishing. Survey respondents "often viewed their programs as failing to train them well in research design and writing and publishing" (22). The study's recommendations reaffirmed the value of writing and publishing in the social sciences as a fundamental academic competency. PhD programs might consider whether they are preparing students for creating and collaborating in real-world applications of research across diverse disciplines and engaging with global colleagues (Nerad et al. 2007). Ann Austin's (2002) work offers a view into the experiences of those graduate students seeking an academic career. Through a review of prior quantitative studies combined with interviews of graduate students about their educational experiences, she identifies significant gaps in the socialization of graduate students for academic careers:

> Particularly noteworthy and a cause for concern is the lack of systematic professional development opportunities, minimal feedback and mentoring from faculty, and few opportunities for guided reflection. Although some students had faculty mentors who guided them carefully through the process, most did not. (104)

Students explore research areas and demonstrate their knowledge by writing, and most graduate students are acquainted with coursework writing. Adapting to a more challenging writing style for a different purpose is less familiar terrain. For example, aligning a manuscript to the specific requirements of an academic journal may be daunting. Graduate students' professional identities are in constant development within their respective disciplinary cultures, and whether they choose to focus on a nonacademic research career or to pursue the academic track, they will be required to write for publication (Salas 2009). The studies by Nerad et al. (2007) and Austin (2002) highlight a gap that librarians can fill by facilitating mentorship between faculty and graduate students around publishing endeavors.

Most graduate students experience a substantial amount of contact with faculty members and consider the relationship an important facet of their educational experience. Mutual support between faculty and students and their wide-ranging mentoring relationships may encompass a "nurturing process in which a more skilled or experienced person, serving as a role model, teaches, sponsors, encourages, counsels and befriends a less skilled or less experienced person" (Anderson and Shannon 1995, 29). Faculty mentoring of graduate students is a "significant aspect that fosters student success" (Lechuga 2011, 757).

As evidence of good faculty mentorship practice, Lechuga's 2011 qualitative study examined tenured and tenure-track Latino faculty in STEM fields (science, technology, engineering, mathematics) centered on an instructor's professional work life and motivational aspects of mentoring students. The study found that working relationships between graduate students as employees and faculty as employers contributed to academic socialization and had mutual advantages for both groups. The study also identified characteristics of graduate students that faculty deemed vital for the faculty member's work. As an employer, one biology professor stated that he considered the most important ability for a graduate student employee is to be able to work and publish independently. Other faculty consistently concurred that with quality graduate students, they could write papers and formulate new proposal ideas with increased productivity.

As agents of academic socialization, faculty in the study furnished their students with professional development prospects. One mechanical engineering professor provided his graduate students with presenting and publishing opportunities, using research monies to send students to conferences. Through these opportunities, graduate students accelerated the intellectual productivity of his lab. Another engineering study respondent asked his and other graduate students to review his journal manuscripts and encouraged them to be active in the scientific community by volunteering scholarly services in professional societies (Lechuga 2011). Though the employer-employee lab context for mentorship is discipline-specific and more common in the STEM fields, we can accept the general premise that students who have the capacity to navigate the scholarly communication publishing process set themselves up for opportunities and academic success. Librarians need to complement, not intervene, where there are productive mentor-protégé relationships among faculty and students.

Information Literacy, Scholarly Communication, and the Graduate Student

Our literature documents the myriad challenges of providing library instruction for graduate students as well as the benefits of adopting multiple instructional strategies (Sadler and Given 2007; Williams 2000). Strategies that complement curricular integration for graduate students have been addressed in the literature and include topical workshops and tutorials (Rempel and Davidson 2008; Knievel 2008). Further studies of graduate student information behavior document the informality of their research practices and the infrequency of graduate student use of library services (Barton et al. 2002; Bright et al. 2006; Kayongo and Helm 2010; Simon 1995), signaling an opportunity for our services. Librarians have addressed these challenges by adapting disciplinary instructional strategies to integrate information literacy concepts, including those related to scholarly communication issues, into graduate study (Donaldson 2004; Brown 1999; Jacobs, Rosenfeld, and Haber 2003; Newby 2011).

However, there are distinctions in patterns of graduate education, particularly for those on the academic track, which make curricular integration of information literacy less systematic and therefore only one of several strategies that a library may pursue to engage graduate students in this learning domain. Significant learning experiences for graduate students, such as the thesis or dissertation, and initial forays into the world of publishing occur primarily outside the classroom and curricular structures.

In redefining the liaison librarian role, Karen Williams (2009) challenges us to move "from a collection-centered model to an engagement-centered one" (3). Conceptualizing graduate student education as a process of role transformation (Fleming-May and Yuro 2009) provides the engagement-centered library strategies for interaction with graduate programs, faculty, and students (Austin 2002; Nerad 2004). Information literacy learning outcomes for graduate-level education have not been clearly articulated. Examples from professional practice and the library literature assume that performance indicators from, or similar to those of, the Association of College and Research Libraries (ACRL) *Information Literacy Competency Standards for*

Higher Education (ACRL 2000) can simply be applied at higher levels of sophistication (UMUC Library 2012; Murry, McKee, and Hammons 1997). Because significant graduate-level learning occurs outside the classroom during the research and writing process itself, librarians have often found teachable moments by making connections to the challenging, integrative tasks of writing research proposals and literature reviews, writing and placing articles in journals, and the thesis or dissertation itself (Libutti and Kopala 1995; Onwuegbuzie 1997). To have an impact on graduate education, librarians need alternatives to the curricular integration strategy that has been so powerful for undergraduate information literacy efforts.

Scholarly communication provides a framework for an engagement-centered approach to information literacy programming for graduate students. The publication process can be identified as an information literacy "threshold concept" with particular immediacy for graduate students. As discussed by Townsend, Brunetti, and Hofer (2011), threshold concepts are transformative, integrative, irreversible, troublesome, and bounded:

> Threshold concepts are *like* learning objectives in that they can provide a focus for curriculum design and may prove to be a tool with which to measure student learning. However, threshold concepts *differ* from learning objectives in that they are gateways for student understanding that, once traversed, transform the student's perspective. (855)

The process of getting published as an information literacy threshold concept for graduate students, as an alternative to defining standards and learning outcomes, provides a significant strategy for the engagement-centered librarian because, as Meyer and Land (2011) point out in their article, "Stop the Conveyor Belt, I Want to Get Off," "The threshold model ... relies on disciplinary expertise rather than 'managerial' theoretical templates" (as cited in Townsend, Brunetti, and Hofer 2011, 855).[1]

For graduate student authors entering into the hurly-burly of publishing, these concepts become immediate questions and practical learning challenges due to their personal engagement in the publishing process. The unevenness of faculty mentoring in this arena, documented in literature discussed earlier, provides opportunities for engagement-centered liaison librarians to build information literacy programming.

Additionally, librarians committed to information literacy instruction have an opportunity to direct students, especially those in STEM disciplines, to the rapidly expanding selection of resources that push at the once-rigid boundaries of scholarly publishing venues for locating and interpreting educative materials. Scientists and scholars are embracing social media such as blogs, Twitter, open notebooks, and repositories such as Databib and *Open*DOAR as interactive and collaborative community spaces "to watch the process of scholarly knowledge construction as it happens" (Deitering and Gronemyer 2011, 494). The erudite discussions can lead graduate students to be more attentive to what is being said about the intellectual content they discover. Students' ability to participate in these dynamic scholarly conversations provides "an excellent way for students to find out about the texts, to understand the context, and to find consensus and controversy" (Deitering and Gronemyer 2011, 498–499). Graduate students have opportunities to embrace these social networking and social awareness tools, such as coauthorship networks, to enhance the scholarly communication process that fits their discipline.

Key to enacting engagement-centered librarianship as it pertains to information literacy and scholarly communication for graduate students is the knowledge and expertise that librarians can bring to framing all these concepts within the context of their development as scholars and within their disciplines' publishing practices. The next section will explore how librarians at the University of Nevada, Las Vegas, collaborate with faculty and administrators to build a program around these key issues for graduate students.

The UNLV Scholarly Communication Seminar

The University of Nevada, Las Vegas (UNLV) Libraries hosts several graduate seminars focusing on significant elements of scholarly communication that can be tied back to the ACRL Information Literacy Standard Five:[2] using RefWorks (an online citation management tool) and addressing copyright, plagiarism, and scholarly communication issues. We also offer a session about how to effectively design assignments to incorporate research-based learning in the classroom. For the past two years, the Sustainability Librarian/Institutional Repository (IR) Administrator has drawn upon her background in scholarly communication and various publishing models to offer seminars on the process of engaging best practices to successfully publish a journal article. Academic faculty and librarians have been invited to participate in the seminars to add diverse disciplinary perspectives and real-world examples to the workshop content. Several invitees have enthusiastically lent their scholarship perspectives and publishing experiences. A team synergy exists among the various professionals who contribute their skill sets and time to the workshop, including: the libraries' liaison to the Graduate College, who focuses on logistics; subject liaisons from the library, who participate as panelists to share their experiences as authors; technical writers; the IR Administrator, who is responsible for the content and presentation; and invited academic faculty.

Academic librarians with scholarly communication skill sets have offered their expertise as leaders in utilizing new tools and services, such as institutional repositories, open access publishing, social media tools, educating for understanding authors' rights, and copyright services. There are multiple models for incorporating scholarly communication expertise in academic libraries. Some libraries consolidate these responsibilities in a single position, other libraries ask liaisons to have a baseline of knowledge, and still other libraries practice a blend of these models. Whatever scholarly communication staffing model is adopted, liaison librarians can leverage their teaching expertise into the scholarly communication domain. Whether that involves building their own knowledge through attending an ACRL one-day institute or partnering with the library's scholarly communication expert, there is clearly room for librarians to take initiative on behalf of graduate student professional development in the area of publishing, open access, copyright, and authors' rights as social systems, not merely technological systems.

The majority of students who attend the open seminar use the online signup form provided by the Consortium for Faculty Professional Opportunities (CFPO),[3] an efficient method of previewing the number of students and their department affiliations. Students from STEM and social sciences predominate, although the humanities, education, hotel administration, and the allied health fields are also represented in the registration. Participants in the three seminars represented the following disciplines: 36 STEM (45 percent), 21 social sciences (26 percent), 8 education (10 percent), 7 nursing/health (8 percent), 4 humanities (5 percent), and 3 hotel (3 percent). Graduate students may apply their scholarly communication seminar attendance to workshops/modules required to receive a UNLV Graduate Research Certificate. Seminar advertising channels indicate that students registered for the Research Certificate Program through UNLV Today (daily faculty/staff e-newsletter), the UNLV graduate e-mail distribution list, the libraries' website, Facebook, and Twitter accounts, faculty and associate deans, and word-of-mouth.

Scholarship of Writing

The seminar emphasizes that scholarly writing can be challenging and rewarding. Attendees learn where to find publishing opportunities, the essentials of making an article stand out, academic writing styles, manuscript components, the article submission and peer-review editorial process, options and tools for retaining key copyrights, and the importance of open access to research. Graduate students are made aware of the variety of factors that may influence why some scholarly articles get published or not. Editorial board members' and reviewers' expressed opinions can sway editorial conclusions. Decision factors may also include the significance, innovative perspective, relevance, or timeliness of a topic to a journal's audience. Manuscripts should contain elements of new and useful information that contribute to the body of published literature. The quality of a paper's presentation and its adherence to guidelines play a role in it being published. Acceptance rates, given the supply and demand for specific topics, may also be affected, particularly if there is a manuscript backlog (Overholser 2011). The library workshop highlights these details for graduate students, empowering them to take a more informed role in the publication process.

The outlined elements described below represent the most recent iteration of the seminar that has evolved over the preceding six years of incorporating new resources and responding to participant feedback. While there is a plethora of scholarly communication substance to consider presenting in one and one half hours, part of the instruction time is expended soliciting faculty and student questions and sharing publishing anecdotes. Students possess a broad range of scholarly communication knowledge, hence the seminar's ultimate goal is to completely describe and disclose the value of the erudite landscape. Presentation materials are archived in the UNLV Libraries Scholarly Communication LibGuide,[4] and a detailed outline is provided to the students as a takeaway.

Seminar Evaluations and Comments

At the conclusion of the seminar, participants complete an evaluation, the results of which are used to ensure continuous improvement of seminar content. Taking the next step of reporting seminar evaluation results to the library instruction coordinator or scholarly communications officer (if extant) will document the extent of library programs. Since the publication of the *Value of Academic Libraries: A Comprehensive Research Review and Report* (Oakleaf 2010), academic library administrators are exploring strategies to document not only collection growth and program activity, but also library impact on institutional goals. Institutional goals for graduate education may include degree completion by graduate students, the rate of publication by graduate students prior to completion, or postgraduate employment. While direct causation between seminar participation and any of these outcomes cannot be proved, libraries are increasingly gathering and analyzing a variety of data to identify patterns of activity and impact. As illustrated in Table 12.1, evaluations of the publishing seminar have been consistently positive.

Table 12.1
Seminar Evaluation Totals

The following activities contributed to my learning in this workshop:	Strongly Agree	Agree	Neutral	Disagree	Strongly Disagree	
Do you feel the seminar content added worthwhile information to your knowledge about the writing aspects of a journal article?	11	8	1			Engineering Sept 2012
	15	9	8	1		Multidisciplinary Sept 2012
	11	6	3			Multidisciplinary Nov 2012
Do you feel the seminar content added worthwhile information to your knowledge of publishing an article?	13	5	1			Engineering Sept 2012
	15	15	3			Multidisciplinary Sept 2012
	12	6	2			Multidisciplinary Nov 2012
Given what you heard/learned today about the benefits of retaining author rights, would you consider providing open access to your article(s)?	5	11	2	1		Engineering Sept 2012
	10	14	8			Multidisciplinary Sept 2012
	12	7	1			Multidisciplinary Nov 2012
Discussion facilitated exchange of expertise among participants.	12	6	1			Engineering Sept 2012
	13	10	10			Multidisciplinary Sept 2012
	12	5	3			Multidisciplinary Nov 2012

Comments from the evaluation forms provide evidence of the seminar's impact:

What aspects of the workshop were the most valuable for you?
"Practical information about the culture and protocols, understanding of Open Access, presenter and others in audience were good sources of information, retaining copyrights, issues discussed during Q&A."

"The most valuable information was the handout and going over the general process."

What aspects of the workshop were the least valuable for you?
"I only went to the workshop to learn more about publishing so the writing section was a refresher for me."

Describe one thing that you learned that you expect to use or to share with others:
Frequent comments in response to this prompt include: "The importance of Open Access," "Information about joining a listserv," "Impact factors," "The publishing review process."

Is there anything else you want to tell us?
"I walked away from the workshop feeling my time was well spent."

"This is a great topic that would benefit almost all graduate students and many undergraduate students. Perhaps discipline-specific workshops can be offered."

One recent significant enhancement to the seminar based on attendee feedback was the insertion of "authorship order" information. Graduate students need to be advised to address this potentially sensitive topic carefully but forthrightly with their faculty coauthors toward the beginning of the coauthorship process. This issue was raised by a seminar attendee and subsequently rated a comment on the workshop evaluation:

One piece of information of which I found most helpful, although the whole workshop was valuable, was to establish who will be first and second author on the publication and what is expected. Although this tip is a very obvious one, I believe people tend to forget this very important detail.

This is an essential topic for the seminar, as students may choose not to voice an opinion if they feel dissent or misinterpret faculty author order choices. Within the faculty-student collaborative relationship is the typically unspoken but omnipresent power imbalance. This may be especially true in situations where graduate student publishing expertise and competence are minimal and the faculty member is relied upon for guidance (Morisano et al. 2009). An authorship and authorship order discussion will optimally begin at the initiation of a research project. On behalf of authors in all disciplines, four primary models used for listing authors were identified by the American Political Science Association Working Group on Collaboration: "1) alphabetical order, 2) reverse alphabetical order, 3) non-alphabetic order, and 4) connected by *with* rather than *and*, denoting clearly unequal contributions" (Lake 2010, 43).

Listing authors by relative contribution is the norm in the hard sciences, which include physics, chemistry, biology, medicine, and engineering. The senior author who may be a principal investigator or a faculty advisor is listed last, an esteemed position comparable to first author status. This "relative-contribution/senior-author model" (Lake 2009, 43) is also employed in the social and physical sciences. A discipline's convention for article author order will play a role in the faculty's decision of who is listed in what sequence. Political science's dominant surname order leans towards listing authors alphabetically, as does economics, communications, sociology, and anthropology (Lake 2009). Authorship order may evolve over a project's time line to better reflect actual contributions from the researchers (APA Science Student Council 2006).

Another change prompted by positive feedback from administrators, faculty, and students to the multidisciplinary offerings of this seminar is the development of discipline-specific framing for the publishing seminar content. Programming directed to graduate students has received additional emphasis for the library due to the relocation and reconfiguration of the Lied Library's Graduate Student Commons. The new commons was collaboratively designed between the Graduate Professional Student Association and the libraries. The commons' more prominent physical location has prompted increased interaction between these two organizations. Liaison librarian–led workshops hosted in the new commons space are planned on topics such as the scholarly communication seminar, copyright for graduate students, organizing a writing circle, and personal information management. The institutional repository, Digital Scholarship@UNLV, is also gaining momentum, with greater graduate student and faculty knowledge resulting in higher numbers of item deposits. In fact, seminar evaluation data shows graduate students' responsiveness to open access, with no fewer than 70 percent of seminar participants willing to consider retaining author rights and open access to their publications (see Table 12.1).

The library offerings of this seminar have received support from multiple departments and colleges. The faculty panels have included participants from diverse departments such as English and business. The associate dean of engineering has routinely supported the graduate seminar by promoting it to the college's engineering faculty and students. In one particularly interesting development, UNLV's College of Engineering recently hired an engineer part-time for her technical writing skills to assist faculty in their grant proposals and support student publication writing skills. The outreach initially leveraged by the engineering collaboration has flourished into a disciplinary subset of the full seminar, "Engaging in Best Practices to Successfully Publish a Journal Article: For Engineers." The first discipline-specific seminar was offered in Fall 2012 to engineering students. A scholarly communication team (engineering faculty; a technical writer who is also an engineer; the engineering liaison; head of educational initiatives; and the sustainability liaison/IR administrator, who has a substantial background in scholarly communication) planned and presented the seminar to support them in their publishing endeavors.

Initially presented solo by the sustainability liaison/IR administrator for a multidisciplinary audience, the graduate seminar is additionally offered by discipline experts (academic and library faculty) in partnership with the IR administrator to a discipline-specific audience. The variety of perspectives and experiences that have contributed to the development of the seminar provides a well-rounded and holistic view of what students can expect during the publication process as well as the necessary tools for publishing success.

Serious undergraduate researchers and their advisors have also expressed strong interest in attending the seminar. Welcoming the undergraduates has the potential to encourage their aspirations to become graduate students and empower them on their scholarly paths. Both undergraduate and graduate students have a need to understand the difference between research discovery and access. They have a right to know how intellectual content is packaged and distributed, the technologies and tools used for discovery and access, and the bottom line of fundamental economic factors (Warren and Duckett 2010). When students are given "a broader context for how peer-reviewed, scholarly, and research articles are shaped by social and economic forces" (Warren and Duckett 2010, 354) in an instructional setting, scholars-in-training can make informed decisions regarding their own work and influence others. When it is impressed upon students that access to higher education scholarly works may be more difficult after they graduate, their attitudes about procurable research may inform their own more "open" publishing habits.

Conclusion

Information literacy can be understood on multiple levels, that is, as a knowledge/competency domain and as an educational process expressive of the library's educational mission. The strategies and structures used to build information literacy into curricula and student learning experiences are as important a focus as the content itself. Workshops on publishing and scholarly communication provide a meaningful context to engage graduate students with integrative information literacy concepts. Discipline-specific seminar offerings on publishing and scholarly communication provide liaison librarians a cocurricular mechanism for relationship building that is crucial to twenty-first century library services. Since research and publication are topics at the core of faculty identity, librarians are advised to propose library instruction in a manner that emphasizes the complementary expertise that various partners can bring to this venture on behalf of graduate students. A by-product of student learning is that academic faculty gain knowledge of open access publishing tools, as well as librarians' expertise with copyright, licensing, and open access.

The Seminar

Engaging in Best Practices to Successfully Publish a Journal Article

What follows is an expanded outline of the seminar content.

I.   **Opportunities for publishing—where are they?**
     This portion of the seminar introduces locating potential publishing venues that are typically useful: e-mail discussion lists in a particular subject area or more general fields of interest, publisher e-mails and websites, and professional organizations, e.g., IEEE, Nature, ACM, APA, MLA. Faculty or librarians may suggest specific journals and also direct students to two comprehensive publishing directories, Cabell's Directory of Publishing Opportunities and Ulrich's, which are both subscription-based and delineate manuscript specifications, the submission process, and other journal-related data.

II. **Research each potential journal on your list before submission.**
     A.   **Who is the audience of the particular journal to which you are submitting?**
          - Every journal has a topical and type-of-article focus. Graduate students are advised to conduct thorough research before submitting to a journal.
          - Submit a query letter e-mail to journal editors. Submit a few query letters to appropriate journals at one time. When the seminar is attended by graduate students from multiple disciplines, they are advised of significant variations of practice related to query letters. For example, authors in the humanities do not submit a query letter, but instead e-mail a cover letter and a concise statement of journal "fit" along with the manuscript.

     B.   **Required template**
          Some journals require authors to use a preformatted template. Association for Computing Machinery (ACM) example: http://oldwww.acm.org/crossroads/submit/.

     C.   **Impact factors: primarily in the sciences**
          Article Half Life, Eigenfactor, h-index, Altmetrics, etc.

     D.   **Author name and affiliation should always be consistent on all publications.**
          Carefully consider your author's professional name that ideally will be used in all published material. Subsequent articles should use the exact name with or without initials for consistency in indexing and discovery purposes.

III. **Writing your article—we write because we want people to read our research.**
The purpose or function of an article is to be original, while also highlighting/citing significant research results or expressing theoretical conclusions. There are different types of articles that may affect their journal placement:

- **Article (full paper)**—definitive accounts of significant studies/experiments.
- **Humanities article**—historical or literary evidence in a theoretical framework.
- **Review article**—summarizes the progress in a particular area or topic during a preceding period.
- **Case study**—a qualitative exploration of descriptive research.

What will make your work different and stand out?
An article that is publishable typically incorporates some unique ideas "while remaining well-integrated with the established literature" (Overholser 2011, 116). Highly rated papers discuss essential issues, and the conclusions seem to contain valued materials in a particular field. The following points are emphasized for seminar attendees:

- Review the literature that has already been written on your proposed topic. Are there gaps in the literature? Is the literature out of date? Scholarly content research tools may include a web-scale discovery tool, such as Summon, individual research databases, or Google Scholar to locate appropriate intellectual content.
- Choose a topic of interest that meets the criteria or focus of the targeted journal. Research potential journals!
- Citations: Cite resources, chase citations, consider using seminal works where appropriate for a baseline or comparisons.
- Ensure your work will make some type of original contribution: originality of thought or angle is always a plus. Write to be cited!
- How/why is your paper different from other articles on the same or similar topic?

IV. **Major Paper Components**
    A.   **Title**
        The title of an article reflects the paper's content and is useful for research indexing. It is best to use effective keywords that are specific, spell out all words using no abbreviations/acronyms.

- Attracts a potential audience by the use of topical

words of interest to the reader—catchy titles are a plus (adds interest if appropriate).
- Aids in online retrieval and keyword indexing.
- Use enough words to get your title across, but not lengthy.
- Usually a title and abstract are confirmed after the writing is complete.

B. **Abstract**
Clarify your paper's goal by creating a one-paragraph abstract: ~80–250 words.
- Problem/purpose of research.
- Indicate theoretical or experimental plan used.
- Summarize principal findings.
- Point out major conclusions.

C. **Standard outline organization or empirical** (observations/experiments)
Article paper—may vary by publication and parallels the scientific method.
- Introduction—1 to 2 paragraphs may include previous findings.
- Literature review.
- Experimental details and hypotheses.
- Results—summarize data collected and statistical treatment.
- Discussion—interpret and compare results; be objective.
- Conclusions—place interpretation into context of original problem.
- Summary and further research—future opportunities for study.
- Acknowledgements: support and financing from people and organizations.
- Other material dependent on publication.

D. **Technical writing is different from prose.**
It is precise and unambiguous.
- Basic outline for humanities—theoretical framework to support conclusions: study of the human condition, using methods that are primarily analytical, critical, or speculative.
- Use gender-neutral language—choose terms that do not reinforce outdated sex roles.

E. **Scholarly communication, copyright, and open access**
The second part of the presentation, condensed and more intense because of the obscure concepts, builds upon the initial seminar outline and introduces:

- **Author order in a multiple-author article:** Discuss at outset, typically determined by faculty depending on who is doing the most research and writing. Initial decisions may evolve to reflect actual contributions.
- **Peer-review process and writing tips:** 1) Submit article to a journal editor, one journal at a time. 2) Editor establishes and maintains journal standards by selecting competent referees. E-mails article to 2–3 reviewers or referees to evaluate article. 3) Editor determines the summary review decision based on reviewers' evaluations and journal focus guidelines. 4) Editor may accept article with suggested changes or decline acceptance. 5) Article rejected? Submit to other journals, one at a time.
- **What reviewers look for when an article is submitted:** Is the article technically correct? Does it fit the mission of the journal? Does the article make a contribution to the field? Is it timely, classic information, or "old hat"? How well is the article written? Does it fill a gap in the literature? Copyright ownership, retaining copyright to one's intellectual content, the nature of publishing agreements, author addendums, Creative Commons licensing and, open access to research, as well as a brief tour of UNLV's institutional repository, Digital Scholarship@UNLV (http://digitalscholarship.unlv.edu/) are essential elements to be acquainted with in the current and future scholarly communication milieu. University mandated e-theses/dissertations are a prime visual example to show graduate students how their research is showcased in an open access scholarly venue.

This seminar outline was created by Marianne A. Buehler for: "Engaging in Best Practices to Successfully Publish a Journal Article," last updated September 2012. It is licensed under the Creative Commons Attribution-NonCommercial-ShareAlike 3.0 Unported License: http://creativecommons.org/licenses/by-nc-sa/3.0/.

Notes

1. The Meyer and Land (2007) article, "Stop the Conveyor Belt, I Want to Get Off," can be found at http://www.timeshighereducation.co.uk/story.asp?sectioncode=26&storycode=90288.
2. ACRL Information Literacy Competency Standard Five: "The information literate student understands many of the economic, legal, and social issues surrounding the use of information and accesses and uses information ethically and legally." (ACRL 2000).
3. The Consortium for Faculty Professional Opportunities is a committee comprised of administrators from multiple campus entities, established to sustain professional development programming after the budgetary elimination of the Teaching and Learning Center in 2010.
4. The UNLV Libraries Scholarly Communication LibGuide can be found at http://guides.library.unlv.edu/scholarlycommunication.

References

ACRL (Association of College and Research Libraries). 2000. *Information Literacy Competency Standards for Higher Education.* Chicago: ACRL, January 18. http://www.ala.org/acrl/standards/informationliteracycompetency.

Anderson, Eugene M., and Anne Lucasse Shannon. 1995. "Toward a Conceptualization of Mentoring." In *Issues in Mentoring,* edited by Trevor Kerry and Ann Shelton Mayes, 25–34. London: The Open University, Routledge.

APA Science Student Council. 2006. "A Graduate Student's Guide to Determining Authorship Credit and Authorship Order." http://www.apa.org/science/leadership/students/authorship-paper.pdf.

Austin, Ann E. 2002. "Preparing the Next Generation of Faculty: Graduate School as Socialization to the Academic Career." *Journal of Higher Education* 73, no. 1 (January/February): 94–122.

Barton, Hope, Jim Cheng, Leo Clougherty, John Forys, Toby Lyles, Dorothy Marie Persson, Christine Walters, and Carlette Washington-Hoagland. 2002. "Identifying the Resource and Service Needs of Graduate and Professional Students." *portal: Libraries and the Academy* 2, no. 1 (January): 125–143.

Bright, Alice, Joan Stein, Carole George, Erika C. Linke, Terry Hurlbert, and Gloriana St Clair. 2006. "Scholarly Use of Information: Graduate Students' Information Seeking Behaviour." *Information Research* 11, no. 4 (July): paper 272. http://informationr.net/ir/11-4/paper272.html.

Brown, Cecelia M. 1999. "Information Literacy of Physical Science Graduate Students in the Information Age." *College and Research Libraries* 60, no. 5 (September 1): 426–438.

Deitering, Anne-Marie, and Kate Gronemyer. 2011. "Beyond Peer-Reviewed Articles: Using Blogs to Enrich Students' Understanding of Scholarly Work." *portal: Libraries and the Academy* 11, no. 1 (January): 489–503. http://muse.jhu.edu/journals/portal_libraries_and_the_academy/v011/11.1.deitering.html.

Donaldson, Christy A. 2004. "Information Literacy and the McKinsey Model: The McKinsey Strategic Problem-Solving Model Adapted to Teach Information Literacy to Graduate Business Students." *Library Philosophy and Practice* 6, no. 2 (Spring): 1–9. http://digitalcommons.unl.edu/libphilprac/19/.

Fleming-May, Rachel, and Lisa Yuro. 2009. "From Student to Scholar: The Academic Library and Social Sciences PhD Students' Transformation." *portal: Libraries and the Academy* 9, no. 2 (April): 199–221.

Jacobs, Susan Kaplan, Peri Rosenfeld, and Judith Haber. 2003. "Information Literacy as the Foundation for Evidence-Based Practice in Graduate Nursing Education: A Curriculum-Integrated Approach." *Journal of Professional Nursing* 19, no. 5 (September): 320–328.

Kayongo, Jessica, and Clarence Helm. 2010. "Graduate Students and the Library: A Survey of Research Practices and Library Use at the University of Notre Dame." *Reference and User Services Quarterly* 49, no. 4: 341–349.

Knievel, Jennifer E. 2008. "Instruction to Faculty and Graduate Students: A Tutorial to Teach Publication Strategies." *portal: Libraries and the Academy* 8, no. 2 (April): 175–186.

Lake, David A. 2010. "Who's on First? Listing Authors by Relative Contribution Trumps the Alphabet." *PS: Political Science and Politics* 43, no. 1 (January): 43–47.

Lechuga, Vicente M. 2011. "Faculty-Graduate Student Mentoring Relationships: Mentors' Perceived Roles and Responsibilities." *Higher Education* 62, no. 6 (December): 757–771.

Libutti, Patricia, and Mary Kopala. 1995. "The Doctoral Student, the Dissertation, and the Library: A Review of the Literature." *Reference Librarian* 22, no. 48: 5–25.

Meyer, Jan, and Ray Land. "Stop the Conveyor Belt, I Want to Get Off." *Times Higher Education*. August 17, 2007. http://www.timeshighereducation.co.uk/story.asp?sectioncode=26&storycode=90288.

Morisano, Dominique, Thomas F. Babor, Erin L. Winstanley, and Neo Morojele. 2009. "Getting Started: Publication Issues for Graduate Students, Postdoctoral Fellows, and Other Novice Addiction Scientists." In *Publishing Addiction Science: A Guide for the Perplexed,* 2nd ed., edited by Thomas F. Babor, Kerstin Stenius, Susan Saava, and Jean O'Reilly, 50–69. London: International Society of Addiction Journal Editors.

Murry, John W., Jr., Elizabeth Chadbourn McKee, and James O. Hammons. 1997. "Faculty and Librarian Collaboration: The Road to Information Literacy for Graduate Students." *Journal on Excellence in College Teaching* 8, no. 2: 107–121.

Nerad, Maresi. 2004. "The PhD in the US: Criticisms, Facts, and Remedies." *Higher Education Policy* 17, no. 2 (June): 183–199.

Nerad, Maresi, Elizabeth Rudd, Emory Morrison, and Joseph Picciano. 2007. *Social Science PhDs—Five+ Years Out: A National Survey of PhDs in Six Fields—Highlights Report.* CIRGE Report 2007-01. Seattle, WA: CIRGE. http://depts.washington.edu/cirgeweb/c/publications/142.

Newby, Jill. 2011. "Entering Unfamiliar Territory: Building an Information Literacy Course for Graduate Students in Interdisciplinary Areas." *Reference and User Services Quarterly* 50, no. 3: 224–229.

Oakleaf, Megan. 2010. *Value of Academic Libraries: A Comprehensive Research Review and Report.* Chicago: Association of College and Research Libraries, September. http://www.ala.org/acrl/sites/ala.org. acrl/files/content/issues/value/val_report.pdf.

Onwuegbuzie, Anthony J. 1997. "Writing a Research Proposal: The Role of Library Anxiety, Statistics Anxiety, and Composition Anxiety." *Library and Information Science Research* 19, no. 1: 5–33.

Overholser, James C. 2011. "Reading, Writing, and Reviewing: Recommendations for Scholarly Manuscripts at the Graduate and Professional Level." *Journal of Contemporary Psychotherapy* 41, no. 2 (June): 115–122.

Rempel, Hannah Gascho, and Jeanne Davidson. 2008. "Providing Information Literacy Instruction to Graduate Students through Literature Review." *Issues in Science and Technology Librarianship,* no. 53 (Winter–Spring). www.istl.org/08-winter/refereed2.html.

Sadler, Elizabeth (Bess), and Lisa M. Given. 2007. "Affordance Theory: A Framework for Graduate Students' Information Behavior." *Journal of Documentation* 63, no. 1: 115–141.

Salas, Alexandra. 2009. "Graduate Preparedness Strategies for Graduate Writing." *Hispanic Outlook in Higher Education* 19 (April 6): 28–29.

Simon, Charlotte Ellen. 1995. "Information Retrieval Techniques: The Differences in Cognitive Strategies and Search Behaviors among Graduate Students in an Academic Library." PhD diss., Wayne State University.

Townsend, Lori, Korey Brunetti, and Amy R. Hofer. 2011. "Threshold Concepts and Information Literacy." *portal: Libraries & the Academy* 11, no. 3 (July): 853–869.

UMUC (University of Maryland University College) Library. 2012. "UMUC Information Literacy FAQ for Faculty." Accessed June 29. http://www.umuc.edu/library/libhow/informationliteracy.cfm.

Warren, Scott, and Kim Duckett. 2010. "Why Does Google Scholar Sometimes Ask for Money? Engaging Science Students in Scholarly Communication and the Economics of Information." *Journal of Library Adminis-*

tration 50, no. 4: 349–372.

Williams, Helene C. 2000. "User Education for Graduate Students: Never a Given, and Not Always Received." In *Teaching the New Library to Today's Users: Reaching International, Minority, Senior Citizens, Gay/Lesbian, First-Generation, At-Risk, Graduate and Returning Students, and Distance Learners,* edited by Trudi E. Jacobson and Helene C. Williams, 145–172. New York: Neal-Schuman.

Williams, Karen. 2009. "A Framework for Articulating New Library Roles." *Research Library Issues: A Bimonthly Report from ARL, CNI, and SPARC,* no. 265 (August): 3–8.

CHAPTER 13

Scholarly Communication in the Dentistry Classroom

Abigail Goben
University of Illinois at Chicago

Introduction

After formal classification in the mid-90s, the concept of evidence-based practice has become widespread throughout medical education. When the College of Dentistry at the University of Illinois at Chicago (UIC) launched a new curriculum based on small-group learning in the fall of 2011, a liaison librarian was embedded in the classroom to assist in educating students in information literacy as it related to evidence-based dentistry (EBD). Scholarly communication concerns, including the scholarly research process, access to literature, open access, copyright, etc., were integral components of the information literacy and subject material being taught, which provided an opportunity to introduce these subjects within the context of the curriculum and with ready applicability to the students. The embedded librarian taught four sessions with dentistry faculty, exploring information resources, the EBD process, and community information. In the fall of 2012, the curriculum developed is being repeated and expanded with plans for formal evaluation. In addition to working with the traditional dental students, the liaison librarian also participated with the curriculum for international dentists who are gaining two-year certification, whose knowledge of scholarly resources, processes, and access issues varies widely depending on country of origin. The role of the liaison librarian within the international dentistry program continues to develop and become more formalized. Primary successes to date include increased awareness demonstrated by students of aspects of scholarly communication insofar as these aspects relate to their current educational and clinical needs, and opportunities for expanded discussions with faculty regarding current scholarly communication trends and challenges. Some barriers exist to successful replication of this format, with the greatest being the time dedicated by the liaison librarian. However, this is countered by the many opportunities that exist to expand the discussion to developing understanding of scholarly communication issues and opportunities, to improve student and faculty research, and to promote the library and the liaison librarian as an authority on these subjects when questions arise.

Background

Dentists differ from other medical and nursing students in that following their graduation, they are often unaffiliated with a medical institution. Though they may participate in a group practice, the burden of accessing scholarly literature to maintain current awareness of trends and new research often falls to the sole practitioner. On their own, dentists are far less likely to fund purchasing access to full-text databases and multiple journals, or even to be able to regularly purchase articles through interlibrary loan. A physician, in comparison, is often affiliated with a hospital that provides access to databases such as UpToDate or DynaMed, whose focus is getting current research trends to working professionals. Professional dental organizations, such as the American Dental Association, allow members access to a few select journals and provide some assistance in accessing literature, but this help comes with a fee. Thus, practicing dentists face barriers to accessing full-text literature in medicine, which could inhibit their ability to find the best research to support patient care.

This burden is particularly onerous in relation to the adoption of evidence-based practice (EBD). Defined in 1996, EBD is the idea that treatment decisions should be based on a combination of the practitioner's expertise, the best research studies available at the time of treatment, and the patient's medical history and preference (Sackett et. al 1996). Though initially defined for use by medical doctors, evidence-based practice rapidly expanded to other areas of medical practice, such as dentistry and nursing. Along with their clinical and medical training, dental students must begin the practice of EBD so that they may be confident practitioners once they have graduated. Dentists must be able to identify sources of research studies, evaluate the studies for accuracy as well as relevancy to their patients, find or suggest alternative treatments, and identify the outcome that they are seeking from their literature search. In addition, these treatments must be evaluated specifically for the patient and explained so that the patient is able to provide informed consent when participating in the treatment (ADA 2012).

Teaching EBD provides an opportunity to bring information literacy and scholarly communication to the forefront of dental education, supporting students' curricular and continuing-education needs. When information literacy instruction is integrated into the EBD curriculum, it is provided just as the students are developing and then demonstrating their ability to find information in the classroom and clinical settings. Teaching and collaborating directly with the subject faculty allows the instruction to be tailored so that students find more immediate relevancy and application and observe their clinical faculty's use of information. With repeated emphasis throughout EBD assignments and during clinical experience, information literacy is reinforced. Further, EBD instruction includes discussions on the professional responsibilities of the clinician to stay informed and current on research while seeking the best possible treatment for the patient. Within these discussions, access to information for both the clinician and the patient arises, lending a wealth of opportunities to discuss scholarly communication. As students continue to develop their understanding of resources and determining what access to resources exists within the university, they also are reminded of what access they may lose upon graduation. When scholarly communication is introduced in context of the resources regularly used in their own research and student dentists are asked to consider their own future professional interests and patient needs, they deepen and expand their understanding of the process by which scholarly literature is developed and disseminated.

In the practice of EBD, dentists must identify patient characteristics, interventions or treatments, comparisons to other treatments, and the desired outcome. This method is referred to as the PICO process and is designed to help practitioners quickly create a searchable clinical question at chairside (Huang, Lin, and Demner-Fushman 2006). The dentist may then take this question to scholarly resources in order to identify relevant literature. When searching, the dentist must also evaluate the authority of the literature that he or she has identified. This is taught as a hierarchy, with an editorial as the lowest level of evidence, progressing through individual cases or case studies up to clinical trials, and peaking with the systematic review, which is a comprehensive and unbiased critical review of all studies and literature on a specific topic (ADA 2012). Figure 13.1 displays the hierarchy traditionally used to teach evidence-based practice.

Figure 13.1

The Evidence-based Pyramid (with less authoritative literature at the bottom, progressing up to the "best" literature with the systematic review at the peak)

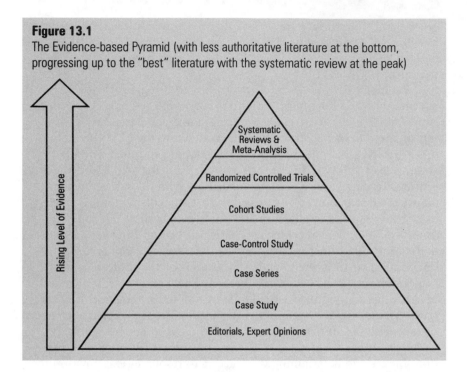

Practitioners must also be able to identify different types of studies, both by structure (case, cohort, controlled, randomized controlled, double-blind randomized controlled) and category (diagnosis, etiology, therapy, prognosis).

Librarian Liaison Embedding

In the fall of 2011, the UIC College of Dentistry transitioned traditional dentistry students from a lecture-based curriculum to one based on small-group and case-based learning. During creation of the new learning objectives, faculty identified that students would have greater need to locate and evaluate information for themselves, rather than receiving it from instructors. Students had two identified information needs: finding basic medical and dental information to answer questions that came up during their small-group learning sessions and identifying appropriate resources to provide evidence-based answers to clinical-style questions. Though the majority of the first-year dental curriculum continues to be focused on general medicine, during the subsequent three years, students would advance to assisting with or performing supervised dentistry in clinics at the school, where they would be answering clinical questions. Students would also engage in research in collaboration with faculty and be expected to write several research papers as they proceeded through the curriculum. To promote success in these areas, faculty wanted to ensure the foundational information skills were progressively developed during the first year. The solution was to embed a dentistry liaison librarian as part of the professional development section of the curriculum, which includes EBD, ethics, health disparity, community awareness, and business skills. The liaison librarian was embedded specifically in a course that met in five sessions over the fall semester in order to cover aspects of information literacy, EBD, and the PICO process. The course takes ten weeks, with each session offered to half of the first-year class at a time, creating a structure that allows for more interaction between faculty and students and provides opportunity for smaller group work within the sessions. During the semester, students also have reading assignments and are assigned to complete an online tutorial provided by the library (UIC 2012). Questions from these sessions are included on periodic exams administered separately from the class.

Class-by-Class Inclusion

As no single class was specifically focused on aspects of scholarly communication, a brief description of the material covered in each class was provided with relevant elements highlighted. For purposes of this chapter, the elements are those identified by Duke's Scholarly Communication Librarian Kevin Smith (2011): publishing, copyright, open access, and research.

The first session focused specifically on finding resources for small-group questions and EBD. During this session, the liaison librarian led the instruction and activities, with the dental faculty offering supporting information as it related to future assignments. For the small-group questions, students were directed primarily to textbooks and other general medical resources, both assigned texts and other resources provided by the library. While these introductory materials would see them through the majority of the cases presented to their small groups, first-year students also have research opportunities and begin to prepare for evidence-based clinical care that starts in the second year. To develop their research skills, the library liaison had students use the PubMed database via the publicly accessible interface. The database was chosen for breadth and depth of content, but also because students would continue to have access to PubMed following graduation, and it would be part of their lifelong learning as practicing dentists.

As part of being introduced to PubMed and accessing journal articles, the dental students discussed how they currently find full-text articles as part of their searching strategies. At UIC, PubMed is prox-

ied through Serials Solutions to allow examination of all library resources. Before this was demonstrated, however, the librarian reviewed
the total number of records and how many were available as full text
through PubMed Central, a free full-text archive of biomedical literature provided by the National Institutes of Health via the National Library of Medicine. At present, PubMed contains more than 21 million
citations of biomedical literature, with 2.4 million available as full text
in PubMed Central (NCBI 2012). This presentation included discussion of the NIH Public Access Policy, which requires that researchers
receiving funding from the National Institutes of Health submit final
peer-reviewed manuscripts upon acceptance for publication, with an
embargo of no more than one year allowed before the article becomes
freely available (NIH 2012). To provide context, students were asked
to consider how they would access full-text articles after graduation
and how members of the public might gain access to this research
literature. Open access, institutional and disciplinary repositories, and
finding access to federally funded research were explained as part of
the toolkit that students would take forward to find information. The
opportunity was also taken to demonstrate the costs of access to literature without library resources (approximately $30 per article), though
students were encouraged to contact the liaison librarian and use interlibrary loan while they were pursuing articles during their education.

Building on this foundational knowledge, the second class session
introduced EBD and the process of using it, as well as using the PICO
model to develop a structured question when working with a patient
or starting to approach a research project. One of the advantages
of introducing EBD early in the four years of dental school is that
students who may not be interested in research see more immediate
application of research literature to their daily practice. In this session,
the dental faculty led the instruction with assistance from the liaison
librarian. Dental students were introduced to the history of EBD and,
using a case example, went through the basic five steps of formulating
a question, identifying articles and other resources, critically appraising the evidence, applying the evidence, and re-evaluating the application of evidence.

Examining the EBD process required that students review the research process insofar as it leads to publication. Here the liaison librarian had the opportunity to discuss with the students not only at what
stages research could be published but also what elements of copyright
researchers are usually asked to relinquish, what access they personally may have following publication, and what access other professionals may have. The liaison librarian and faculty also discussed the
tenure process for the academic researcher, using their own careers as
examples, in order to provide students context for where the literature

was being generated. To conclude the session, students participated in an active learning exercise, creating sample PICO questions in groups and describing their intended research process using PubMed or other information resources. The exercise provided reinforcement of the process reviewed in class and the importance of searching the literature. It also gave students the opportunity to review material from the first session and to identify any remaining questions.

The third session was a focused discussion on health disparities, led by the associate dean of Prevention and Public Health Services. Although not one of the instructors for this session, the liaison librarian attended it to be able to include the examples and discussions in future sessions.

The fourth session, led by the dentistry faculty with the assistance of the liaison librarian, returned to the EBD process that had been defined during the second session. Having developed questions and scenarios where they would need to use scholarly literature, students learned the levels of evidence. This refreshed the conversation on the publishing process from the second session and introduced the institutional review board process. Students also were introduced to different kinds of studies in the four therapy areas of etiology, diagnosis, therapy, and prognosis, as well as cohort trials, randomized controlled trial, double-blind controlled trials, systematic reviews, etc.

Next, students were tasked with bringing together the information-seeking skills and EBD concepts as presented in class, readings, and the online tutorial for an in-class group project. Presented with a case scenario, groups had to develop a PICO model to define their question, identify what kind of study they thought would be useful, use PubMed to identify relevant literature, evaluate the level of evidence in the literature they found, and report to the class. Faculty and other students provided feedback for each group, and there was further discussion about the research process.

The fifth session focused on community information. As part of their education, dental students intern at safety-net clinics throughout the Chicago region and with national and international partners. In this session, led by the liaison librarian following an interactive presentation by dental faculty, students discussed where they, as consumers, find information about services available within their community and statistics about their own community. This provided an opportunity to reprise the discussion from the first session about accessing information, the cost of that access, and how the NIH Public Access Policy is providing federally funded research for those without academic affiliation.

In class, students were put into pairs and given a regional safety-net clinic to use as their community base. For each community, students identified available strengths, such as number of dentist offices, specialty dentists, water fluoridation, and grocery stores; potential barriers, such as lack of public transportation, parking costs, and liquor stores; features of the safety-net clinic; and local, state, and federal information data and requirements. Students then gathered again as a group to review the material collected, discuss barriers to information gathering, and identify their roles in providing public health information to patients. Pursuant to the last topic, consumer-focused health resources were discussed as ways to provide information to patients. Students identified potential needs from the websites of professional dentists providing public health information such as multiple languages, elementary reading level, and the possibility that commercial consumer health websites might contain bias. Students were also exposed to statistics captured on the city, state, and national levels, with open access to this data being pointed out as a benefit.

Outcomes

Because the inclusion of the liaison librarian is in its second year, formal evaluation is currently in development by the librarian and lead dentistry faculty member. The two faculty members have reviewed learning objectives for each session and are developing a combination of multiple-choice quizzes and survey questions. Incoming students will be given a quiz at the beginning of the semester to evaluate their information-seeking skills and EBD awareness; the quiz questions will then be used as a basis for test questions for evaluations that occur throughout the semester. The same instrument will be used again at the end of the semester to determine the effectiveness of the series of instructional sessions and to set benchmarks for the identified learning outcomes. The liaison librarian is developing questions related to information seeking and scholarly communication within the EBD process.

International Students

The international dentistry program at UIC accepts practicing dentists licensed in another country into a rigorous two-year program to become licensed in the United States. These practitioners come from a wide variety of educational backgrounds and as such have a broad range of abilities in locating scholarly literature, understanding of the publishing process, and knowledge of copyright. During the orientation and initial summer semester, the liaison librarian has met twice with the incoming class to discuss library resources and accessing scholarly literature through PubMed, which is a new resource for about half of the class. Following this session, the liaison librarian has introduced scholarly communication through one-on-one consultations with the international students who are undertaking research. In the fall of 2012, the liaison librarian will be more formally embedded into the EBD portion of the international student curriculum and will have an opportunity to review these subjects in more depth with the class as a whole.

Opportunities

While formal outcomes have not yet been established, informal appraisal indicates that students and faculty are becoming more aware of aspects of scholarly communication and see the liaison librarian as a resource for this information. With the discussions started in the classroom, the liaison librarian has been able to expand conversations about understanding current legislation surrounding open access, finding publishing opportunities, using other library resources such as the institutional repository, learning more about retaining copyright, and obtaining sponsorship from the library open access fund to produce open access articles.

There are a number of opportunities to further the inclusion of scholarly communication topics in the classroom. Newly introduced faculty development seminars will be an opportunity to review open access challenges and opportunities and use of open textbook materials. The liaison librarian will include rebranded library e-scholarship services on the dentistry research guide in fall of 2012.

Potential Barriers to Anticipate

There are inevitably some challenges that librarians wishing to take on this form of embedded librarianship and information literacy education will face. A faculty member in the department or discipline who is willing to share classroom time or a curriculum director who is willing to find time to ensure the students are working with the librarian is a must. The liaison librarian needs to coordinate closely with the discipline faculty to create a progressive syllabus that can lead students through different information literacy skills within discipline-specific content, especially as it may relate to scholarly communication issues and trends. Both the liaison librarian and the discipline faculty member must also be prepared to discuss publishing standards for that discipline, including open access mandates, institutional review board requirements, and study design and execution.

Perhaps the most obvious barrier is the time release needed from other responsibilities so that the librarian can prepare for class, teach, meet with students, and provide informal and formal feedback. In this instance, approximately thirty-five hours was spent in class with the students over the course of the semester, with additional time needed for preparing materials and meeting with disciplinary faculty. This time requirement would make it more difficult for the library to scale embedded librarianship to multiple departments.

Conclusion

Despite the potential challenges of obtaining faculty collaboration, working with a new curriculum format, and finding the required time, the inclusion of the library liaison in the EBD coursework proved successful enough to repeat and expand upon in the following academic year. As the students advance through the new curriculum, the department faculty and liaison librarian will be looking at the students' research pursuits and papers to evaluate whether improvement has occurred in their information literacy and scholarly communication skills. Further evaluation of the program is under development, with quiz and survey questions as well as assignment modification under consideration.

While many liaison librarians have the opportunity to provide targeted instruction, a model where the librarian is present throughout the entire semester is rarer. These repeated instructional opportunities allow for a broader discussion of scholarly communications as applied to student interests and research. It also provides the opportunity for the librarian to establish the library as a resource to assist students as they examine and evaluate literature for inclusion in their own work and identify concerns about copyright, access, and the research process. By demonstrating equal footing with the disciplinary faculty in the classroom, the librarian can become a research partner for both students and faculty. The time required for this model is significant; however, by offering it specifically to graduate students in a professional program, students who are more likely to have research needs and run into the barriers within scholarly communication can be reached early in their careers as researchers or academics. Successful faculty-librarian collaboration and instruction can improve emerging awareness of scholarly communication issues while engaging a more informed student and faculty body and facilitate future engagement in the research process.

References

ADA (American Dental Association). 2012. "About EBD." ADA Center for Evidence-Based Dentistry. Accessed June 25. http://ebd.ada.org/about.aspx.

Huang, Xiaoli, Jimmy Lin, and Dina Demner-Fushman. 2006. "Evaluation of

PICO as a Knowledge Representation for Clinical Questions." In *Bio-medical and Health Informatics: From Foundations to Applications to Policy: AMIA 2006 Annual Symposium Proceedings*, edited by David W. Bates, John H. Holmes, and Gilad J. Kuperman, 359–363. Bethesda, MD: American Medical Informatics Association.

NCBI (National Center for Biotechnology Information). 2012. "PubMed Central." US National Library of Medicine, National Institutes of Health. Accessed June 25. http://www.ncbi.nlm.nih.gov/pmc.

NIH (National Institutes of Health). 2012. "National Institutes of Health Public Access." Accessed June 25. http://publicaccess.nih.gov.

Sackett, David L., William M. C. Rosenberg, J. A. Muir Gray, R. Brian Haynes, and W. Scott Richardson. 1996. "Evidence-Based Medicine: What It Is and What It Isn't." *BMJ* 312, no. 7023 (January 13): 71–72.

Smith, Kevin. 2011. "What Does Scholarly Communications Mean to You?" *Scholarly Communications @ Duke* (blog). August 12. http://blogs. library.duke.edu/scholcomm/2011/08/12/what-does-scholarly-communications-mean-to-you.

UIC (University of Illinois at Chicago) Library of the Health Sciences. 2012. "Evidence-Based Practice in the Health Sciences: Tutorials." Accessed June 25. http://ebp.lib.uic.edu.

CHAPTER 14

Scholarly Communication in the Field

[Assessing the Scholarly Communication Needs of Cooperative]
[Extension Faculty and Staff   ]

Christine Fruin
University of Florida

Introduction

The trend at most university libraries has been to dedicate significant funding, time, and human resources to the promotion of scholarly communication through on-campus service and outreach. Like many campuses across the country, the University of Florida (UF) has identified scholarly communication as a strategic initiative. Through the leadership and initiative of the new Scholarly Communications Librarian and subject liaisons, scholarly communication is promoted on campus through individual consultations, workshops, and general outreach. Issues promoted to faculty, campus administration, and students include maintenance and promotion of an institutional repository, establishment of an open access publishing fund, promotion and use of a state-supported open journal system, and support of UF's faculty senate in its campaign for a campus-wide open access mandate. Important scholarly communication issues for UF's teaching faculty and researchers are copyright, open access, and citation management, as well as the impact of these issues upon their own research and publishing. During the 2011 UF College of Agricultural and Life Sciences (CALS) Teaching Symposium, the library identified a new community for engagement around scholarly communication issues: faculty researchers from the Institute of Food and Agricultural Sciences (IFAS) and cooperative extension offices. This group indicated a high need for education and training on copyright and open access and the impact of these issues on their own scholarship, as well as on the public education and outreach activities conducted by the extension offices.

While the Scholarly Communications Librarian and other librarians routinely respond to scholarly communication questions from and provide regular outreach and instruction on scholarly communication topics to on-campus teaching faculty and support staff, presently there is no mechanism to deliver this type of training and information to UF researchers who primarily work off-campus in the state of Florida's sixty-seven county extension offices and thirteen Research and Education Centers (RECs). To determine how to best address this need, the Scholarly Communications Librarian, with the assistance of one of the agricultural librarians, successfully applied for internal grant funding. The Scholarly Communication and Cooperative Extension grant proposed to assess the scholarly communication needs of faculty and staff working in the extension offices and to plan for the library's delivery of educational services. In this chapter, the author will review the challenges inherent in delivering library services to cooperative extension offices and describe why scholarly communication training should be part of those services. The author will then discuss the survey developed to assess the scholarly communication needs of UF faculty and staff and how the results of that survey may be used to plan and implement a scholarly communication program for the UF/IFAS cooperative extension offices.

Challenges in Providing Library Services to Extension Offices

In 1914, Congress enacted the Smith-Lever Act of 1914,[1] which established a partnership between land-grant universities and the US Department of Agriculture. According to the Smith-Lever Act, the purposes of extension were the development of practical applications of research knowledge and the delivery of instruction and demonstrations of existing or improved practices and technologies in agriculture. In fulfilling this purpose, cooperative extension offices shared a function with libraries: providing the public with access to information (Rozum and Brewer 1997, 161).

The information needs of UF extension faculty vary from those of their on-campus teaching faculty counterparts. Not only do extension faculty need access to information for purposes of their own research, but they also "need to be informed consumers of the information stored and disseminated by research libraries and serve as mediators between the research information and the ultimate consumers of that information, e.g., the farmers in the field" (Tancheva, Cook, and Raskin 2005). As academic libraries work with extension offices, it has proven to be a challenge to deliver the information resources as well as the instruction and consultation in locating and evaluating information. One of the challenges has been access to information resources. Extension offices typically lack space or funds to house physical information resources locally. Further, the offices may be hundreds of miles from the UF campus and its libraries. Thus, extension personnel had to rely upon document delivery through interlibrary loan and library courier. However, technological developments have allowed for greater access to literature and other information through electronic databases. UF subject liaisons also utilize content management tools such as Springshare's LibGuides, RefWorks, library blogs, and course management systems such as Sakai to organize content and links to subject specific resources. Technologies such as live chat and videoconferencing for the delivery of instruction also help UF librarians stay connected with extension office staff and faculty researchers.

However, access to resources is not always fast and trouble-free. Connection speeds may vary among offices, and connection to IP-authenticated databases by proxy server or VPN can sometimes be confusing and require dedicated technical support from either UF library or IT staff to address connections issues by these distant users (McKimmie 2003, 30). Another challenge posed by the logistics of serving distant offices has been the delivery of consultation and instruction. The distance between extension offices and the UF libraries often precludes extension agents from participating in instruction opportunities offered on campus, and librarians, with budget cuts and juggling multiple responsibilities, rarely have time or opportunity to provide instruction on-site at extension offices.

A final challenge in the effective delivery of information and services to extension offices has been the lack of expertise of librarians who specialize in extension as part of their liaison assignment. In a 2005 USAIN survey of ARL member land-grant institutions about collaboration among libraries and cooperative extension, no data was found to support the dedication of a professional librarian to outreach and service to extension offices. Rather, the majority of survey respondents indicated that reference questions from extension personnel were handled "in the same manner" as reference questions received in the libraries (Hutchinson et al. 2005). Recognizing the need for supporting this key community, UF in 2005 hired its first Outreach Librarian for Agricultural Sciences, whose duties are to plan, coordinate, and deliver library services to IFAS's off-campus users, who are primarily those working within extension. The result of creating this position was an increase in not only awareness but also usage of library resources by extension personnel (Davis 2007). Further, with the hiring of the Scholarly Communications Librarian, a natural teamwork opportunity arose to provide well-rounded instruction in library resources and scholarly communication to those working in extension.

Scholarly Communication and Extension

Library services such as interlibrary loan, instruction, and access to resources are clearly needed by those working in cooperative extension, and libraries have responded by dedicating professional staff to serving extension offices and crafting communication channels and information portals to serve those needs. At the same time, academic libraries increasingly have become the primary coordinator and resource for scholarly communication efforts and outreach, including publishing support, copyright education, and open access advocacy. Scholarly communication was identified by the Association of College and Research Libraries (ACRL) Research Planning and Review Committee as a top trend in academic libraries in both 2010 and 2012 and is also represented in the most recent "ACRL Plan for Excellence" (ACRL 2011; ACRL Research Planning and Review Committee 2010, 2012). Academic librarians have led the effort to educate faculty and students about authors' rights and open access publishing options and to recruit content for institutional repositories. More recently, some academic libraries have become involved in publishing endeavors by creating and hosting open journal systems and vocally advocating for publishing reform (Mullins et al. 2012).

However, scholarly communication outreach efforts have largely been limited to those teaching and researching on campus. There is little evidence that scholarly communication outreach has been a priority for those working outside the main campus. At UF, faculty and researchers working in extension have indicated that those conducting research and community education through their cooperative extension offices also need these same services and information. As educators who provide education in the community rather than the classroom and more often via digital means, extension staff have questions about the application of fair use to their endeavors. As researchers engaged in publishing and collaboration with other researchers, extension staff also have questions about different publishing models, including open access; how to read and negotiate publisher agreements; and how to maximize their influence and impact within their fields of research. If academic libraries are providing this information and instruction to on-campus constituents, they similarly should be providing this as part of outreach to extension offices.

The libraries at UF, through the work of the Scholarly Communications Librarian with the assistance of the libraries' Scholarly Communications Working Group[2] and library liaisons, regularly provide on-campus faculty and researchers with scholarly communication training and resources. However, there was no mechanism to deliver this type of training and information to UF researchers in the field.

Further, a search of the literature and informal conversations with a few scholarly communication librarians at other land-grant institutions revealed that delivery of scholarly communication instruction to those working in extension had not been studied or implemented as a service. As a means of addressing this need expressed by faculty and researchers at the 2011 teaching symposium, the Scholarly Communications Librarian and an agricultural sciences librarian ("grant team") applied for and received internal grant funding to create and distribute a survey to those working in the sixty-seven cooperative extension offices and thirteen RECs across the state of Florida. A survey was developed cooperatively with the content expertise of the grant team and the methodological expertise of UF's Collaborative Assessment and Program Evaluation Services (CAPES). The grant team, with assistance from CAPES, analyzed the survey results and then devised a pilot program for delivery of scholarly communication training and resources to select extension offices.

Assessing Scholarly Communication Needs of UF Extension

The UF/IFAS extension offices employ persons in varying capacities, including clerical workers, extension agents who provide community education, and doctorally trained faculty who conduct scientific research in the field. The grant team decided to target the assessment instrument toward those working in the extension offices who were most likely engaged in scholarly research and education. To help identify who should receive the survey, the grant team established the following required criteria:

- Primary job is not clerical or office support.
- Delivers, produces, or supervises the delivery or production of community education materials and/or programming.
- Job title includes the term *agent*.
- Conducts research in the field.
- Holds faculty rank at the University of Florida.
- Serves as director of extension office or regional center.

See Appendix 14.1: County Extension Survey.

A student assistant hired by the grant team reviewed the websites for IFAS and each of the county and regional extension offices and compiled a contact list of 580 individuals meeting the respondent criteria. The survey link was sent to persons on the contact list, and 149 persons (25.7 percent) representing 47 of the county offices and 10 of the RECs replied. The survey was designed to solicit feedback on several defined areas: the demographics of the respondents, the demographics of the populations served by the respondents' cooperative extension office, the research habits of the respondents, and the respondents' attitudes and knowledge about specific scholarly communication issues. The questions related to the respondents' demographics provided us with an overview of the level of formal education those working in cooperative extension have achieved, as well as a sense of how many years they have spent teaching in higher education or working in the extension environment. The questions about the service population's demographics were tailored toward informing us about the respondents' perceptions of their constituents as opposed to numerical data. We were curious to see if there was any correlation between respondents' perceptions of the education or literacy level of the population and their concern with scholarly communication issues. Questions about the respondents' research habits informed us about their use of technology as a means of conducting and organizing research. Finally, the questions about scholarly communication issues measured their knowledge and understanding of copyright law, including their rights as authors, fair use of copyrighted materials, and understanding of the open access model of publishing.

Survey Results

Preliminarily, the survey polled respondents on the location of their office, their primary job responsibilities, and their perceptions of the populations served by their office. The majority of the respondents held a master's degree (51.6 percent) as their highest degree, with 35.5 percent holding a doctorate. Most respondents indicated that their service populations were a mix of rural and urban communities (49.6 percent), while the remaining respondents served more rural clients (34.1 percent) than urban (16.1 percent). The respondents perceived their service populations as mixed in their educational background. More than half of the extension offices with representatives responding to the survey indicated that they served about an equal mix of persons with and without college degrees (52.5 percent), while 40.0 percent of the offices served clients who mostly did not have a college degree, and only 7.5 percent served clients that mostly had college degrees. This resulted in most of the clients being literate (79.5 percent had more than 75 percent literacy; 16.4 percent had 50–75 percent literacy; and only 4.1 percent had less than 50 percent literacy at their site).

The grant team designed the remainder of the survey, which can be viewed in its entirety at the conclusion of this chapter, to assess the knowledge level and training needs of extension personnel in three primary areas: scholarly publishing experiences; copyright literacy; and research habits, including use of various technologies for conducting and organizing research. In the area of scholarly publishing experiences, the grant team endeavored to determine not only the frequency with which those working in cooperative extension publish scholarly articles, but also their understanding of their rights as authors and how that understanding impacted their interactions with publishers. With regard to published articles in peer-reviewed journals, 42.3 percent reported publishing in such journals. Of those who had published in a peer-reviewed journal, 56.8 percent had read and signed a publication agreement, and only 1.4 percent had attempted to negotiate or change the transfer-of-copyright provision. Most of the respondents were also not knowledgeable about open access. Only 2.5 percent were very knowledgeable and advocated for open access; 21.7 percent were familiar with the concept; 25.8 percent had heard of it but were uncertain how it applied to them; and 50.0 percent had not heard of it. Consistent with their knowledge about open access, only 10.6 percent had consulted or published in an open access publication.

To assess copyright literacy, the grant team primarily inquired into respondents' knowledge about fair use. Figure 14.1 shows that the county extension employees clearly lack knowledge about copyright. For example, 63.2 percent were uncertain about what rights they retain when publishing their work, and only 30.6 percent understood their rights as an author. In addition, 77.5 percent did not feel confident doing a fair use evaluation. That same percentage also indicated that they wanted to utilize a resource such as a guide or workshop to learn more about copyright issues, including their rights as authors and fair use.

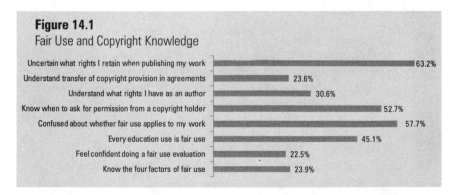

Figure 14.1
Fair Use and Copyright Knowledge

Uncertain what rights I retain when publishing my work	63.2%
Understand transfer of copyright provision in agreements	23.6%
Understand what rights I have as an author	30.6%
Know when to ask for permission from a copyright holder	52.7%
Confused about whether fair use applies to my work	57.7%
Every education use is fair use	45.1%
Feel confident doing a fair use evaluation	22.5%
Know the four factors of fair use	23.9%

When asked how often respondents were required by their work to use copyrighted works or to cite copyrighted works, 30.9 percent replied "Frequently," 31.7 percent replied "Sometimes," and 37.4 percent replied "Rarely" or "Never." In addition, about a third (32.5 percent) had sought permission from a copyright holder to use portions of a copyrighted work. The respondents' best description of their attitudes with respect to using copyrighted works is seen in Table 14.1. The majority of the respondents always include citations and use only that quantity of a work that would qualify as fair use.

Table 14.1
Respondents' Use and Citation of Copyrighted Works

	Research	Teaching
I use materials freely and without seeking permission or including citation to the original source because my use is for educational purposes	5.4%	11.0%
I use materials freely and without concern of copyright status or getting permission because I always include a citation	16.2%	21.1%
I always include a citation and use only that quantity of a work that would qualify as fair use	55.9%	48.6%
I never use more than 10 percent of any work	5.4%	7.3%
I never use copyrighted works in my research and only use my own words or materials found in the public domain	17.1%	11.9%

Survey results showed that respondents used different sources for information when conducting research (Figure 14.2). The two most widely used sources were EDIS[3] and the Internet. About two-thirds of county extension agents responding to the survey use journals or their colleagues as resources, while less than half use the library or library catalog, professional societies, and subject databases.

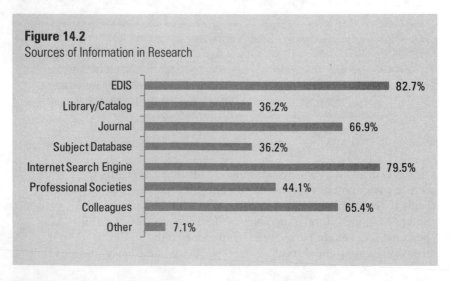

Figure 14.2
Sources of Information in Research

EDIS — 82.7%
Library/Catalog — 36.2%
Journal — 66.9%
Subject Database — 36.2%
Internet Search Engine — 79.5%
Professional Societies — 44.1%
Colleagues — 65.4%
Other — 7.1%

None of the tools commonly used to organize research and citations were widely used by the respondents (Figure 14.3). More than half reported that they did not use any organizational tool, and 21.7 percent still use paper files.

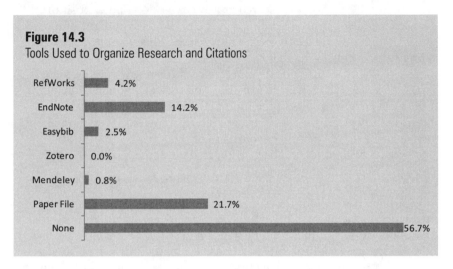

Figure 14.3
Tools Used to Organize Research and Citations

The question on the technology used in research and teaching showed that almost everyone uses PowerPoint. Every other technology was used by less than half of the respondents. The most widely used tools after PowerPoint were videoconferencing, social media, and Go-ToMeeting. Although the listed technologies or software applications were not reported to be widely used, survey respondents did indicate an interest in learning about the technologies available and how they can be used in research and outreach.

Discussion

The survey results clearly showed that the county extension employees are not ready to use the full range of technologies available, nor do they clearly understand the issues related to copyright, fair use, and open access. Their level of knowledge and understanding did not differ much from what is typically encountered by the Scholarly Communications Librarian and the subject librarians when providing consultation and education to teaching faculty found on-campus. While those engaged in research and teaching on-campus author and produce educational works for consumption by colleagues and enrolled students respectively, those working in extension are translating their research into works more suited for the general public as well as for distribution in community education endeavors. Regardless of whether the provider of learning materials is a faculty member on-campus or a researcher working in a remote extension office, the understanding of the application of fair use is just as important, and the survey indicates that those in extension are confused about its application. Use of open access for publication of research done in extension and deposit of research into the institutional repository, particularly in light of the mission of land-grant universities to provide public education, are of particular importance for those working in extension. The survey results show that respondents possess very little knowledge of these issues; however, the interest in learning more is high enough to mandate inclusion of open access in the training regime. Further, it was also clear that the survey respondents are interested in learning more about these issues to make more effective use of scholarly communication and the associated tools. The greatest challenge, then, is how to best reach those working in extension.

In order to address the knowledge gap and the expressed interest in learning more about the issues addressed in the survey, the grant team devised an in-person, half-day training program to be conducted as a pilot project at the county extension office and the REC that had the highest participation rate in the survey. Invitations were sent via e-mail to those persons working in the two facilities that had the highest numbers of survey respondents. Flyers advertising the workshop were also sent to the two facilities. The grant team will travel to each of the two locations and present the workshop to those in attendance. UF's videoconferencing service, Polycom, will also be offered as an option for participating in the workshop if face-to-face attendance is not possible. The workshop will be primarily lecture style with accompanying slides and live demonstrations of relevant websites and electronic resources.

The workshop program will begin with a brief overview of the Smathers Libraries' minigrant program and the background and purpose of the Scholarly Communication and Cooperative Extension grant. This overview will be followed by a one-hour presentation by the Scholarly Communications Librarian on copyright and fair use. Attendees will receive tips on how to read and negotiate typical publication agreements, including how to locate and use author's addendums such as the SPARC Author Addendum. Further, specific examples of print, nonprint, and digital or online resources are used to demonstrate the application of fair use to the education and research work of those working in extension. After time for a break and for questions and answers on the copyright and fair use presentation, the agriculture librarian will provide a hands-on demonstration of the use of EndNote Web for citation management and required IFAS faculty publication reporting. Attendees will learn how to create their account and how to search and export citations not only from licensed databases but also from the electronic repository of documents maintained by UF/IFAS. The last hour of the workshop will cover open access as a publishing model. Attendees will be introduced to the concept and importance of open access and will be shown how they, in their role as authors and researchers, can participate in open access. Specifically, local open access opportunities will be covered, including the University of Florida Open Access Publishing Fund and the University of Florida Institutional Repository.

Feedback will be solicited from workshop attendees on the usefulness and relevance of the content covered during the workshop as well as the effectiveness of the live and in-person delivery method. The grant team will review the workshop feedback in conjunction with the survey results to determine how future training of those working in the extension offices should be conducted and what content should be covered. The grant team hopes that the feedback will help to further tailor the content to the specific needs of the extension and possibly identify needs not previously identified through the survey instrument. Should the live and in-person method of training prove ineffective or poorly attended, the grant team may apply for additional grant funding through the Smathers Libraries minigrant program to cover costs of producing a high-quality interactive training video that can be accessed at the convenience of extension faculty and staff. The grant team is also contemplating experimenting with videoconferencing or software such as Blackboard Collaborate as a means of conducting training at more remote cooperative extension offices.

Conclusion

The faculty and staff of the IFAS cooperative extension offices and RECs are actively engaged in outreach, research, and teaching in the course of their assignments and responsibilities as faculty and agents within the extension program at UF. These activities suggest the importance of understanding how to effectively communicate to their constituents and their colleagues through various scholarly media. The survey conducted by the grant team demonstrates that extension employees are not ready to use the full range of technologies available, nor do they clearly understand the issues related to fair use, open access, and their own rights as authors. However, it is equally clear that they are interested in learning more about these issues to make more effective use of scholarly communication and the associated tools. As such is the case, the grant team will endeavor to develop an education and training program to inform those working in extension about these issues. Utilizing in-person and online training as well as specialized resources and guides on scholarly communication, the grant team hopes to determine what are the most effective methods for delivering scholarly communication services to those teaching and researching in the field. With available technologies and a commitment to teaching and outreach to extension personnel, there will be many opportunities to create a thought-provoking and interactive program around scholarly communication.

APPENDIX 14.1

County Extension Survey

1. Name

2. E-mail Address

3. In what IFAS Extension Office or Center are you located? [Respondents could choose from a drop-down list of all the county offices and RECs in Florida.]

4. What is the primary agricultural focus of the Extension Office or Center where you are located?

5. Do you hold a position in a CALS department at the University of Florida?

6. If you hold an appointment in a UF academic department, please specify the department.

7. What is your highest degree of education?

8. What is your current job title? [The most common titles within IFAS were listed, with an option to manually enter a job title.]

9. Please indicate the number of years of work [0–3, 3–5, 5–10, 10–15, 15–20, 21 or more] experience in:

   a. Higher Education
   b. Extension Services
   c. Teaching

10. The communities served by your Extension Office or Center are:
    a. Mostly rural
    b. Mostly urban
    c. A mix of rural and urban

11. The education level of the people receiving services from your Extension Office or Center is:
    a. Most have college degrees
    b. Most do not have college degrees
    c. About an even mixture of those with and without college degrees

12. The literacy level of the people receiving services from your Extension Office or Center is:
    a. 75% or more are literate
    b. 50–74% are literate
    c. 25–49% are literate
    d. Less than 25% are literate

13. When interacting with people in the communities served by your Extension Office or Center, communication is primarily:
    a. In person (e.g. walk-ins, live demonstrations)
    b. By telephone
    c. Online (e.g. e-mail, webinar)

14. How often does the staff, including researchers, of the Extension Office or Center meet?
    a. Never
    b. Weekly
    c. Monthly
    d. Quarterly
    e. Annually

15. How often does the Extension Office or Center staff meet with other staff of the Regional Center?
    a. Never
    b. Monthly
    c. Quarterly
    d. Annually

16. What sources do you use for information when conducting research? (Check all that apply.)
    a. EDIS
    b. Library/Library Catalog
    c. Journal
    d. Subject Database
    e. Internet Search Engine (e.g. Google)
    f. Professional Societies
    g. Colleagues

17. What tool do you use to organize your research and citations?
    a. RefWorks
    b. EndNote or EndNote Web
    c. EasyBib
    d. Zotero
    e. Mendeley
    f. Paper file
    g. None

18. What forms of technology do you use when doing research/ teaching? (Check all that apply)
    a. PowerPoint
    b. Blackboard Collaborate (formerly Elluminate)
    c. GoToMeeting
    d. Video Conferencing (e.g. Skype)
    e. Social Media (e.g. Facebook, Google+, Twitter)

    f. YouTube

    g. Dropbox

19. Are you interested in learning about these technologies and how they can be used in your research and outreach?

    a. PowerPoint

    b. Blackboard Collaborate (formerly Elluminate)

    c. GoToMeeting

    d. Video Conferencing (e.g. Skype)

    e. Social Media (e.g. Facebook, Google+, Twitter)

    f. YouTube

    g. Dropbox

20. How often does your work require you to use copyrighted works or to cite to copyrighted works?

    a. Frequently

    b. Sometimes

    c. Rarely

    d. Never

21. Have you ever sought permission from a copyright holder to use portions of a copyrighted work? (If yes, please describe the situation and how you went about requesting permission.)

22. Has your research been published in a peer-reviewed journal?

23. If you have published in a peer-reviewed journal, did you read and sign a publication agreement?

24. If you have published in a peer-reviewed journal, did you attempt to negotiate or change the transfer of copyright provision in the publisher's agreement?

    a. Yes, but the terms were not changed.

    b. Yes, and the terms were changed.

    c. No

25. Who have you sought opinion/consultation from about fair use or other copyright matters arising from your own copyrighted works or using the copyrighted works of others? (Check all that apply.)

    a. I have not sought opinion/consultation.

    b. Librarian

    c. Colleague

    d. Copyright workshop

    e. Lawyer

    f. Copyright Clearance Center

26. Indicate your level of agreement (Strongly Agree, Agree, Disagree, Strongly Disagree) with the following statements:

a. I know the four factors of Fair Use.

b. I feel confident doing a Fair Use evaluation.

c. I believe that every educational use is Fair Use.

d. I am often confused about whether Fair Use applies to my research and teaching.

e. I know when I have to ask for permission from a copyright holder.

f. I understand what rights I have as an author of my original work.

g. I understand the transfer of copyright provision found in most publisher agreements.

h. I am uncertain what rights I retain when publishing my work.

27. Which statement best describes your attitude about using copyrighted materials in your research and writing?

a. I use materials freely and without seeking permission or including citation to the original source because my use is for educational purposes.

b. I use materials freely and without concern of copyright status or getting permission because I always include a citation.

c. I always include citation and use only that quantity of a work that would qualify as fair use.

d. I never use more than 10 percent of any work.

e. I never use copyrighted works in my research and only use my own words or materials found in the public domain.

28. Which statement best describes your attitude about using copyrighted materials in your teaching?

a. I use materials freely and without seeking permission or including citation to the original source because my use is for educational purposes.

b. I use materials freely and without concern of copyright status or getting permission because I always include a citation.

c. I always include citation and use only that quantity of a work that would qualify as fair use.

d. I never use more than 10 percent of any work.

e. I never use copyrighted works in my teaching and only use my own words or materials found in the public domain.

29. Would you utilize a resource such as a guide or workshop to learn more about copyright issues including your rights as an author and fair use?

30. Have you used a work licensed through Creative Commons?

a. Yes

b. No, but I have heard of Creative Commons.

c. No, and I have never heard of Creative Commons.

31. Have you licensed any of your own works through Creative Commons?

    a. Yes

    b. No, and I am not interested.

    c. No, but I would like to learn how to use Creative Commons.

32. Which of the following statements best describes your understanding of open access?

    a. I am very knowledgeable about it and a vocal advocate of open access.

    b. I am familiar with the basic concept of open access.

    c. I have heard of open access but am uncertain about how it applies to me.

    d. I have never heard of open access.

33. Have you ever consulted or published in an open access publication?

34. Which of the following items are in the public domain? (Check all that apply)

    a. Works of the federal government

    b. Any material found on the Internet

    c. Any work that is no longer in print

    d. Works published before Jan. 1, 1923

Notes

1. 7 U.S.C. §341 et seq.
2. The UF Libraries Scholarly Communications Working Group is charged with working with the Scholarly Communications Librarian in a team effort to coordinate activities and develop instructional materials in support of scholarly communications, scholarly publication reform, intellectual property issues, and open access activities and programs provided by the Smathers Libraries at the University of Florida. The working group, while it also has the responsibility to foster such professional development among library faculty and staff, is comprised of members with the following attributes: knowledge of open access trends and development; knowledge of scholarly publishing and new models for scholarly communication; understanding of the issues involved in open access and ability to explain its importance and justify increased participation with it; willingness to become familiar with scholarly communications policy issues; understanding of faculty concerns regarding open access publishing; willingness to share information and communicate effectively with each other; and strong positive relationships with teaching faculty.
3. EDIS, or the Electronic Data Information Source of UF/IFAS Extension (http://edis.ifas.ufl.edu), is a comprehensive, single-source repository of all current UF/IFAS numbered peer-reviewed publications.

References

ACRL (Association of College and Research Libraries). 2011. "ACRL Plan for Excellence." April. http://www.ala.org/acrl/aboutacrl/strategicplan/stratplan.

ACRL Research Planning and Review Committee. 2010. "2010 Top Ten Trends in Academic Libraries: A Review of the Current Literature." *College and Research Libraries News* 71, no. 6 (June): 286–292. http://crln.acrl.org/content/71/6/286.full.

ACRL Research Planning and Review Committee. 2012. "2012 Top Ten Trends in Academic Libraries: A Review of the Trends and Issues Affecting Academic Libraries in Higher Education." *College and Research Libraries News* 73, no. 6 (June): 311–320. http://crln.acrl.org/content/73/6/311.full.

Davis, Valrie. 2007. "Challenges of Connecting Off-Campus Agricultural Science Users with Library Services." *Journal of Agricultural and Food Information* 8, no. 2: 39–47.

Hutchinson, Barbara, Amy Paster, Randy Heatley, Lyla Houglum, and Pat Wilson. 2005. "Cooperation among Libraries, Cooperative Extension, and Agricultural Experiment Stations in Land-Grant Universities: The Results of a 2004–2005 Survey." United States Agricultural Information Network. June 10. http://usain.org/library_extensioncollab/CollaborationReportFinal6-05.pdf.

McKimmie, Tim. 2003. "Reaching Out: Land Grant Library Services to Cooperative Extension Offices, Experiment Stations, and Agriculture Science Centers." *Journal of Agricultural and Food Information* 4, no. 3: 29–32.

Mullins, James L., Catherine Murray-Rust, Joyce L. Ogburn, Raym Crow, October Ivins, Allyson Mower, Daureen Nesdill, Mark Newton, Julie Speer, and Charles Watkinson. 2012. *Library Publishing Services: Strategies for Success.* Final research report. West Lafayette, IN: Purdue University Press E-books, March. http://docs.lib.purdue.edu/purduepress_ebooks/24.

Rozum, Betty, and Kevin Brewer. 1997. "Identifying, Developing and Marketing Library Services to Cooperative Extension Personnel." *Reference and User Services Quarterly* 37, no. 2: 161–169.

Tancheva, Kornelia, Michael Cook, and Howard Raskin. 2005. "Serving the Public: The Academic Library and Cooperative Extension." *Journal of Extension* 43, no. 3 (June). http://www.joe.org/joe/2005june/iw3.php.

CHAPTER 15

Teaching Our Faculty

[Developing Copyright and Scholarly Communication Outreach Programs]

Jennifer Duncan
Utah State University

Susanne K. Clement
Utah State University

Betty Rozum
Utah State University

University faculty members rarely like to hear what they are doing is wrong, let alone illegal. So woe to the librarian who presumes to bear the bad news that, in fact, these selfsame faculty members are flagrantly violating copyright law; this messenger should probably expect to receive an earful about the way things should be as opposed to how they are. Even if faculty members completely agree with the arguments in favor of broader and more open access to published research, it often falls upon librarians to explain the intricacies of Title 17 of the US Code (US Copyright Office 2011), or copyright law, and how publisher contracts and institutional licenses can further limit what faculty members generally expect should be fair educational use.

In fall 2009, the director of our Natural Resources Library presented a copyright awareness program to the faculty of the Utah State University (USU) College of Natural Resources at their annual fall retreat. The college's dean had specifically requested this program, and the librarian was prepared primarily to discuss issues with an author's posting a PDF of his or her own research articles on publicly accessible departmental or personal websites. (In the process of recruiting faculty members to deposit their published research in our newly minted institutional repository, the library had become aware that there were some researchers who maintained PDFs of their published research on the open Web.) This was to be an opportunity to educate faculty members about securing specific rights of their own published works.

Surprisingly, many researchers were actually aware of this problem, and most seemed to understand the related issues. What really raised their hackles, however, was discovering that the manner in which they distributed material to their students was likely a flagrant violation of copyright law. Most did not realize that, in many cases, redistributing published articles via mass e-mail to a class or by posting PDFs to an openly accessible course website intended primarily for students could clearly infringe the right of the copyright holder (in most cases, the publisher rather than the author).

In truth, most faculty members are so busy with research, grant writing, and teaching that few have time to even think about the continually changing landscape of copyright law. Although faculty are prolific producers and users of copyrighted works, they are often more concerned with ensuring that their articles are published than the terms of publication and how they can use the articles in their future teaching and research. However, once we started a conversation with faculty members about some of these issues, we discovered they were very interested in having the university provide them with the resources to establish a broad overview of the unforeseen ways copyright might be affecting their teaching and research. Unfortunately, many universities, have no copyright attorney on staff or unit devoted to copyright issues; this was certainly the case at USU.[1] What is the role of the librarian in helping faculty when they clearly need, and even want, to understand copyright, but the university has not made available the appropriate resources?

Inception of the USU Copyright Committee

At USU, recognizing the need for this type of education and knowing there was no funding in the foreseeable future for additional staff to devote to copyright, the library dean decided to take action. In the summer of 2009, the Merrill-Cazier Library administration formed the USU Copyright Committee, bringing together people from across the campus, each of whom had specialized expertise or interest in copyright issues. By building on and organizing the specialized knowledge of each of the various committee members, the library hoped to create a central resource for the entire university, rather than having expertise siloed in individual units across campus. The library dean charged the committee to:

- Develop an overall understanding of copyright, including expertise in areas such as digital collections, institutional repositories, electronic reserves, authors' rights, fair use, the TEACH Act,[2] and learning management systems;
- Develop and implement an outreach program to provide

training and increase awareness of copyright issues of interest to the USU library staff and the campus community;

- Serve as an advisory group for the library and USU community as new copyright questions arise; and
- Develop, document, and maintain library copyright policies.

This chapter will describe the process through which this group developed a basic understanding of copyright as it relates to higher education, as well as the outreach programs it established in response to the committee charge.

Committee Structure

Over time, the composition of the committee has evolved, but the group includes both library and nonlibrary representatives. Committee members from the library represent electronic reserves, interlibrary loan, the institutional repository, the digital library, collection management and licensing, distance education library services, and library administration. Other members include representatives from the Faculty Assistance Center for Teaching (FACT, which facilitates our course management system and streaming media services), the Regional Campus and Distance Education academic unit (RCDE), the USU Bookstore, central Information Technology (representatives specializing in security, take-down notices, and student labs), the USU Press, the Technology Commercialization Office, and the student government.

The University Counsel's office serves in an advisory role to the group. The library dean met with University Counsel to discuss the work and plans of the Copyright Committee and to determine how the university's legal office would like to be involved. At that time, USU did not have an attorney with intellectual property background, so our counsel was pleased to have a group take the initiative to develop a centralized resource for the campus. Our counsel was willing to review documents as needed but was happy to let the Copyright Committee compile documents and provide educational resources to the campus.

The committee, meeting monthly for the first year, had as its first tasks introductions and group education. Because each person was immersed in his or her own responsibilities, most committee members were unaware of the day-to-day impact of copyright restrictions outside of individual units. How were we to build more overall and expert knowledge? In order to develop a deep bench of copyright expertise, the library dean committed to funding specialized training for the group as well as for individuals. Group training was administered through a series of licensed webinars, in which the group participated together.[3] Individual training was provided by the University of Maryland University College (UMUC) Center for Intellectual Property, which offers a certification program in order to help professionals begin developing comprehensive background knowledge of copyright law and its current application in higher education. The objective of certification is not to gain the expertise of a copyright lawyer but rather to gain exposure to a wide range of topics in order to become a campus (and professional) leader for matters related to copyright. Because our committee did not initially include anyone who was an intellectual property attorney—and because many university counsel offices do not, in fact, necessarily have expertise in this area—the Copyright Committee decided that having a new committee member obtain the UMUC copyright certification on an annual basis would greatly enhance the expertise and authority of the group. By the end of 2012, USU will have sent three committee members through the certification program.

Developing Campus Outreach Initiatives

The group understood that it was imperative to gain the support of the university administration if we were to be successful in reaching out to colleges and departments on-campus and gaining traction as recognized experts. Our initial attempts at outreach came not through the Copyright Committee itself or even through the library. Instead, the committee sought the endorsement of top-level academic administrators, who we thought might be able to get the attention of the faculty. With support from the provost, the library's dean brought the question of copyright education to the attention of the other deans at the weekly Dean's Council meeting. This brief presentation led to financial contributions from the deans to purchase for the campus a three-part, commercially produced webinar series (Academic Impressions 2010c, 2010d, 2010e) on copyright issues related to teaching and research. Promoted as an opportunity sponsored by the deans (in fact, academic deans hosted and introduced the presentations for the committee, illustrating the high-level support for this initiative), this series of events validated the authority of the Copyright Committee and gave it much-needed exposure in its efforts to reach faculty members.

The committee felt that one of the primary ways in which we could meet our charge to provide campus outreach in training and increase awareness of copyright issues was to create a website that, although it was a more passive form of education, would incorporate the group's collective expertise on matters related to copyright. We did not want a simple one-page link from the library website. Rather, our goal was to build a robust destination site for the campus community that would be linked from the university's website. The Copyright Committee chair asked the group to submit ideas regarding the information that should be included on the site. Subsequently, she convened a small subcommittee that organized and outlined the site, returning to the experts to have them write the actual content. Simultaneously, she worked with the library's graphic designer so that the page would be consistent in look and feel with the university website while maintaining a distinct design presence in order to promote our new Copyright@USU brand. The resulting site[4] incorporates the Copyright Committee's collective insights, presenting information for multiple audiences (users versus creators of copyrighted information; faculty versus students) and is also organized by subject.

The Copyright@USU website was to be instrumental in providing our subject librarians with an orientation to copyright issues as well as in assisting them with outreach to their liaison departments. We have encouraged our subject librarians to familiarize themselves with some basic copyright issues and concepts through attendance at licensed webinars and other online educational opportunities. However, we certainly do not expect that they will become copyright experts—in fact, one of the functions of the Copyright Committee is having a place that the departmental liaisons can turn when members of their departments have thorny copyright questions.

In conjunction with the website, the group established an e-mail list that fields copyright questions for the campus.[5] An alias, which is broadly publicized across campus, sends the messages to everyone. In this way, anyone who feels that he or she has relevant information to answer the question can chime in on the discussion. Initially the committee members discuss the question among themselves, and then the committee chair responds to the person who sent the message. We have also created marketing materials, such as notepads, to promote the website and the e-mail alias.

Outreach Programs

With a formal structure, support from the campus administration, training, a comprehensive website, and a communication strategy, the committee was ready to implement its outreach program. Since 2004, the library has consistently provided outreach to our academic departments at their annual fall departmental retreats. Each year, the library dean determines an area of focus so the librarians can develop a consistent and well-thought-out message to deliver. Topics have varied throughout the years for what we call our road show series, but in 2010, there was no debate. We would use our road shows as an opportunity to focus on copyright. The Copyright Committee assigned a road show subcommittee, composed of representatives from the library (administration, digital initiatives, collection development, and reference) and the USU Press, which was tasked with developing a fifteen-minute presentation with a fifteen-minute question-and-answer period that could be delivered to the annual academic departmental retreats in late summer 2010. These retreats are full-day meetings in which academic departments gather to discuss their priorities and concerns, and it can be a real challenge to secure time for guest presentations. The group conceptualized two parallel programs and solicited feedback from the Library Advisory Council regarding which program would be most valuable to the research and teaching faculty. The Library Advisory Council is a committee composed of representatives from each of the university's colleges, the Graduate Student Senate, and the Associated Students of USU, and it is charged with providing the library with advice, feedback, and direction. That spring we presented two concepts: "Securing the Scholarly Record" (covering authors' rights) and "Fair Use in Teaching" (educating faculty about sharing course materials). The Library Advisory Council wanted both topics developed and suggested that departments should choose the presentation they wanted. The retreats are held in August, and the road show subcommittee had several months to prepare. The subcommittee continued to review and revise the presentations and delivered both to the subject librarians to orient them to the content and to obtain suggestions for improvement, including how to adjust the presentations for specific disciplines.

The Copyright Committee used relationships established by subject librarians with academic department heads to schedule time during the annual retreats. The committee felt we would have more luck securing a coveted place on these notoriously crowded agendas by making a connection through a librarian whom the department already knew as opposed to an unknown university committee chair. Subject librarians were assured that they were not expected to be experts on copyright and that a member of the Copyright Committee would be delivering the presentation. Subject librarians would accompany committee members to the departmental meetings and provide the introductions, while also briefly promoting relevant library collections and their own services.

We formed a group of eight Copyright Committee members who had sufficient expertise with the topics to present either road show and to field questions. Ideally, two members of the group attended each presentation to assist with the question-and-answer sessions since we anticipated receiving a wide variety of queries. Fourteen of the presentations were scheduled over three days, so we were not always able to send two Copyright Committee members along with the subject librarian.

"Securing the Scholarly Record"

Our presentation "Securing the Scholarly Record" focused on ensuring that authors understand and retain rights to their own intellectual property as they go through the publishing process (USU Copyright Committee 2010b). It also allowed the library to promote our institutional repository, which, at that time, was in its infancy. The presentation covered four broad areas: the elements of a publication contract, authors' rights and the SPARC addendum, open access, and Digital Commons (the USU institutional repository).

The presentation began by asking questions such as this: "You have just published an article in the journal *Nature* and, wanting your colleagues and students to read it, you post the publisher PDF on your personal website. Can you do that?" Most faculty members understood that posting a published article on a personal website was probably not permissible according to the contract they signed, but most also acknowledged that they rarely read their publishing agreements carefully and thus did not know exactly what was allowed. Most faculty refer to the document they sign with a publisher as a "copyright release form," when in actuality what is signed is a legally binding contract between the author and the publisher stipulating what authors may and may not do with their own written work.[6] Thus, it is extremely useful to know what such legal terms as *grant, warrant, exclusive,* and *indemnify* signify within contract law. Using the contract experience of the director of the USU Press, the majority of the presentation covered an overview and explanation of basic contract language authors might come across. We were careful to point out the differences between journal and book publishing and between academic and nonacademic publishing. Publishing contracts differ considerably from publisher to publisher, but regardless of how they are structured, all have sections in which the author grants rights to the publisher, the author warrants the work submitted, and the publisher promises to publish and distribute the work.

Briefly, the grant clause is the part of the contract in which the author grants and assigns to the publisher the right to copy and distribute his or her work and in which the author either grants, assigns, or transfers all copyrights to the publisher or allows the publisher to secure copyright in the author's name. In the warrant clause, the author affirms authorship as well as ownership of the work (as the two are not the same in contract law). In most instances of scholarly publishing, the author and the owner of the intellectual property in question are the same. There are cases, however, in which the author does not own his or her own intellectual property. For example, an author may have already signed over the copyright to another publisher (e.g., perhaps a chapter of a book has already been published as a journal article). Copyright becomes even more complex if research is federally funded or the author is a federal employee. The author must warrant that he or she has the right to transfer copyright. The warrant clause will also ask authors to warrant that they have obtained permissions to use others' work in their work, that they are not infringing on others' copyright, and that the author, not the publisher, is responsible for the content of the work. Further, in the indemnity clause, the author agrees that the publisher will not be held responsible for claims of copyright infringement by third parties and that the author is personally responsible for all the content.

Most publishing contracts—especially for journal publications—leave the author with few rights, though the author might retain the copyright in some instances, such as for works of fiction. The author may or may not retain the right to republication or to publish competitive or derivative works. Newer publishing contracts increasingly are including the right to deposit some version of the work in a local institutional repository, and a growing number of publishers allow the use of publishers' PDFs in institutional repositories.

Following the overview of key contract terminology, we encouraged authors to save copies of their contract, correspondence with the publishers and editors, and each of the versions of the manuscript submitted to editors and publishers, including preprints, the final edited and refereed copy, and the final proof. Based on the groans in the audience (which were not unexpected), most faculty members rarely retained this many records for each of their publications. As one prolific researcher stated, "That would require a filing cabinet all on its own!"

The next section of the presentation moved from reviewing publishing contracts to reviewing alternatives to traditional publishing. Rarely did we encounter faculty members who had tried to change their contracts to obtain more rights for themselves, and in only a couple of instances had a faculty author purchased the open access rights to his or her work. We talked about why it is important to retain more of the rights to one's own work—not only for personal reasons, but also for the fiscal benefit of your institution (e.g., library budgets). We also encouraged faculty to amend the traditional publishing contracts by attaching the SPARC Addendum (SPARC 2012). We covered the different types of Creative Commons licenses available for nonpublished works such as PowerPoint presentations, posters, syllabi, and other class material. The open access discussion covered several topics, including the Budapest Open Access Initiative and how to negotiate, purchase, and fund the open access rights. During the open access discussion, we purposely cited several nonlibrary research articles that reported the benefits to authors of publishing in open access journals, such as being cited sooner and more frequently.[7] We wanted to demonstrate that open access is important to researchers across disciplines and is not just a library issue.

The final part of the presentation featured the USU institutional repository (IR), Digital Commons. We briefly explained what an IR is and how to get work deposited in Digital Commons. As we had confirmed earlier in the presentations, few authors had saved older publishing contracts, and we introduced them to tools such as SHERPA-RoMEO[8] that can help determine which version of a work can be archived in an IR. At the time, USU's Digital Commons was still very new on our campus, and one result of this presentation was a sharp increase in interest in participation in Digital Commons. Digital Commons staff were inundated with vitas faculty wanted posted.[9] Also, we suspect the conversation laid the foundation for the adoption by the USU Faculty Senate of an open access and authors' rights policy in spring 2012 (USU 2012).

"Fair Use in Teaching: Or, How Not to Break the Law in Your Classroom"

In contrast to the focus on the potential hazards involved in *creating* copyrightable content in "Securing the Scholarly Record," the second road show presentation focused on *using* copyrighted materials, primarily in the classroom (USU Copyright Committee 2010a). Faculty members have a complex relationship with copyrighted materials—often wanting tight control when they author works but assuming liberal rights when using the intellectual property of others in a classroom. The goal of this presentation was threefold: first, overriding the key misconception that educational use equals fair use; second, informing faculty of their many options in using copyrightable works; and third, helping faculty members develop an appropriate sense of the risks involved.

The presentation opened with a short overview of copyright law, including a discussion of what is copyrightable, an explanation of the exclusive rights of copyright holders, and a summary of penalties for copyright infringement. Then we shifted sharply to address the question of fair use, introduced with one simple slide: "Just because it is for educational purposes does not make your use fair." Faculty tend to fixate on the first fair use factor, the nature of their use (educational), without realizing that it is imperative to weigh all four factors together. This confusion is understandable, and the idealist in all of us may wish that the first factor would govern all use at an educational institution. However, it falls to the realists to explain the law. The presentation moved forward to explain the four factors and how a delicate balance must be maintained. Since the time of the road show presentations at USU, there have been some significant developments that we would certainly have to address should we decide to repeat these presentations. The Association of Research Libraries has released its *Code of Best Practices in Fair Use for Academic and Research Libraries* (ARL, CSM, and WCL 2012), which has certainly provided solid explanations of community practices that are somewhat more liberal than those we described in 2010. In contrast, however, Judge Orinda Evans's district court decision in the Georgia State e-reserves case has drawn a "bright line" reading of fair use.[10] Neither of these documents was available at the time of our road show presentations.

The presentation's discussion of how to conduct a reasonable fair use analysis focused on an explanation of all four factors addressed in Title 17: the purpose and character of the use, the nature of the work, the amount of the work used, and the market effect a use might have on a work. Technically, none of the factors outweighs the others, although historically factor four seems to generate the most concern. The key message for faculty who undertake a good faith analysis is to decide whether or not a use is truly a fair use (and document their analysis), which will protect both them and their institution against claims of copyright infringement. The presentation encouraged faculty to maintain records of their own analyses, showing a tool developed at the University of Minnesota for this purpose (University of Minnesota 2010).

Because the purpose of the presentation was to discuss when fair use was and was not appropriate, we also took the time to explain the codified classroom exemptions such as Section 110(1),[11] which explicitly permits displays and performances (of video, for example) in a face-to-face teaching setting. Realizing the complexities of the TEACH Act, as well as the limitations on our time, this presentation did not cover Section 110(2).[12] Instead, we saved that for a separate presentation specifically prepared for and delivered to our Regional Campus and Distance Education faculty.

Naturally, faculty members were not sure of what to do about uses not covered by fair use or a statutory exemption. We mentioned services such as the library's electronic reserves or the USU Bookstore's academic publishing division (course packs), but the preferred way to disseminate content to students is through course websites and learning management systems. Mentioning permissions often generated looks of annoyance. However, what faculty (sadly) seemed not to realize was that the library had often prepaid for their use in the form of site licenses. Thus, we simply encouraged faculty to provide links to licensed content rather than downloading copies. In a teaching environment, showing faculty how to provide authenticated links makes much more sense, as securing permission to download and post copies is not generally a part of their workflow. Explaining the nature of vendor contracts not only served the purpose of showing faculty how to provide legal links to licensed materials, it also afforded the library the opportunity to remind faculty of the integral role we play in providing content for research and teaching, showing them the scope of our electronic collections. Finally, talking about vendor contracts gave us the opportunity to remind faculty of the general terms of our campus site license agreements (including prohibitions of such activities as downloading entire journals, posting electronic copies to websites and e-mail discussion lists, sharing access credentials with friends or colleagues not affiliated with our institution, redistributing licensed content, making commercial or noneducational use of licensed resources, or using technologies to facilitate access to these resources outside of the university network). While perhaps somewhat unrelated to copyright law per se, these contractual restrictions do govern the terms of our use of the electronic collections specifically and work in tandem with copyright law. The road show seemed an excellent time to illustrate this relationship.

Just as we took the opportunity to remind faculty of resources that the library had already licensed for their use, we also (as in the presentation "Securing the Scholarly Record," described above) tried to make sure that faculty were aware of the world of freely available open access resources, including materials in the public domain, designated open access collections (focusing on our own Digital Commons), Creative Commons material, and other OpenCourseWare resources.

In wrapping up the presentation, we attempted to get faculty members to think about decisions relating to using copyrighted materials in terms of risk—and their own comfort level with risk taking. Having provided them with a broad outline of the requirements of the law as well as the potential damages, we illustrated our risk-taking model with a traffic light where "go" represents no to low risk; "caution," only moderate risk (provided guidelines are followed); and "stop," high risk (see Figure 15.1). Ultimately, the library is not the copyright police; however, librarians have taken it upon ourselves to inform our user community of both their rights and their responsibilities. It is up to the individual to behave in a legal and ethical manner.

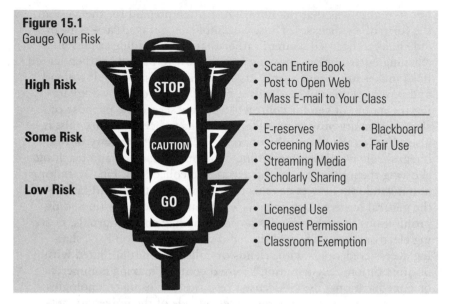

Figure 15.1
Gauge Your Risk

High Risk
- Scan Entire Book
- Post to Open Web
- Mass E-mail to Your Class

Some Risk
- E-reserves   • Blackboard
- Screening Movies • Fair Use
- Streaming Media
- Scholarly Sharing

Low Risk
- Licensed Use
- Request Permission
- Classroom Exemption

Road Show Results

The subject librarians were very successful in securing a place on the agendas for departmental retreats. The team presented the road shows to twenty-three of forty-four different academic departments, with two departments having us visit twice to meet with those who had been unable to attend the retreat. We were pleased that we reached nearly half of the departments on campus. Ten of the presentations were "Fair Use in Teaching," six were "Securing the Scholarly Record," and six included both topics.

The presentations were an enormous success. During our visits, we advertised our website, which was not quite public yet, as well as our new e-mail address, and received many follow-up questions as a result of the talks. We stated up front that the fair use presentation would focus on face-to-face instruction, but it was clear from the questions we received that there was a need for educating our campus about the TEACH Act and copyright in an online environment, which we later developed as a separate presentation. In addition to questions about teaching in an online environment, we had several questions about electronic reserves, use of media in the classroom, open access, and the consequences of copyright violation.

Conclusions

There are several factors that have contributed to the success of the Copyright Committee. First, it had immediate support and funding from the top university administrators. The library dean secured the support for the committee and its work from the provost and the other deans. Second, it included representatives from across the campus. Though the committee structurally resides within the library, copyright is not just a library issue. The committee, using as a mantra the title of the popular book *Crowdsourcing: Why the Power of the Crowd Is Driving the Future of Business* (Howe 2008), includes campus-wide expertise and perspective that have greatly facilitated what it does and given it additional credibility the campus-wide expertise and perspective have greatly facilitated what the committee does and given it additional credibility as a trusted source on issues related to copyright (although coordinating a large group is time-consuming). Recognizing the need for dedicated staff to focus on issues related to copyright, the library in the summer of 2012 hired its first copyright librarian.

Going forward, the Copyright Committee has several challenges. First and foremost, how can we maintain the cohesiveness of a campus committee while maintaining our current level of campus exposure? We know from the responses to the road shows that faculty want additional information and resources on copyright, especially as it relates to teaching in the online environment. Though our website has a section for students on copyright, the committee has not yet targeted students for specific copyright presentations. Libraries connect with students all the time through library instruction programs (information literacy), but beyond talking about copyright in conjunction with plagiarism, information literacy in practice is more about familiarizing students with library resources than informing them about issues relating to intellectual property—their own and that of others.[13] Moreover, how do we ensure that our communications are positive without coming across as though we are the information police? The committee is still working on developing a plan that will address this conundrum.

We also face the challenge of keeping the committee up-to-date regarding copyright and our subject librarians aware of important issues. As we mentioned earlier, our subject librarians have connections to the academic departments on campus and are a great frontline resource for disseminating information. Because we keep them informed of the basics of copyright issues, they are able to serve as one more connection to the Copyright Committee. It is, however, difficult to encourage busy librarians to take the time to attend training programs and keep up with the latest rulings. We take advantage of meetings to offer short briefings every now and then on important developments, such as the Georgia State case.[14]

More broadly, how do we want to balance our role of encouraging campus copyright compliance with that of advocating for expanding fair use and open access? This is perhaps our greatest challenge of all. There is substantial tension between attempting to ensure that the campus is educated about what is and is not acceptable vis-à-vis Title 17 versus advocating for open access solutions, expanding the public domain, and pushing the boundaries of fair use. The first half of that equation seems limiting and frightening, while the second half is liberating and exciting. How do we educate about the limits while promoting the possibilities?

In summary, the prospect of addressing copyright issues on campus can be daunting and overwhelming. However, doing so has also presented the library with unique opportunities. Librarians built partnerships with university administration and other units to advance copyright awareness. Through their understanding of publishing, authorship, and teaching, librarians have bridged an important communication gap between different campus constituencies, many of which are cognizant of only one side of the issue. Going forward, we have found that by engaging people from every area of the campus that is involved in copyright issues, we are able to pool our knowledge, share our experiences, and distribute the workload of educating the campus about this important issue.

Notes

1. In fall 2011, Utah State University hired its first dedicated intellectual property attorney, who became a member of the USU Copyright Committee right away.
2. Technology, Education, and Copyright Harmonization Act of 2002, 17 U.S.C § 110(2) (2002), http://www.copyright.gov/title17/92chap1.html#110.
3. We specifically participated in "Applying the Fair Use Doctrine" and "Copyright Considerations for e-Reserves" (Academic Impressions 2010a, 2010b). Online education can be obtained from several other organizations and companies, including Center for Intellectual Property, Association of Research Libraries, American Library Association, and Copyright Clearance Center, to mention just a few.
4. The Copyright@USU website is at http://www.usu.edu/copyrightatusu.
5. The address of the copyright questions e-mail list is copyright@usu.edu.
6. Until the author signs a contract with a publisher, copyright law provides the author—the original copyright holder—with several

exclusive rights: the right to copy, distribute, reproduce, display, and perform. Unless the copyright holder transfers all or some of these rights to the publisher, the publisher would be in copyright violation for distributing the work.

7. We specifically referenced four articles: Norris, Oppenheim, and Rowland 2008; Davis et al. 2008; Eysenbach 2006; and Hajjem, Harnad, and Gingras 2005.

8. SHERPA/RoMEO is at http://www.sherpa.ac.uk/romeo.

9. After faculty submit their vita, IR staff and liaison librarians will investigate copyright status and obtain permission to post final PDFs whenever possible. If permission is not obtained, links will be provided to the publishers' websites. (Thus, if the viewer's institution subscribes to the journal, access should be immediate.) If the author provides the final post–peer-reviewed manuscript version, it too will be uploaded.

10. Cambridge University Press et al. v. Patton et al., (N.D., Ga. 2012), http://docs.justia.com/cases/federal/district-courts/georgia/gandce/1:2008cv01425/150651/423.

11. 17 U.S.C § 110(1), http://www.copyright.gov/title17/92chap1.html#110.

12. Technology, Education, and Copyright Harmonization Act of 2002, 17 U.S.C § 110(2) (2002), http://www.copyright.gov/title17/92chap1.html#110.

13. Specifically, Standard 5 of the ACRL *Information Literacy Competency Standards* (ACRL 2000) says, "The information literate student understands many of the economic, legal, and social issues surrounding the use of information and accesses and uses information ethically and legally." A core outcome of this standard is that students should demonstrate "an understanding of intellectual property, copyright, and fair use of copyrighted material."

14. Cambridge University Press et al. v. Patton et al.

References

Academic Impressions. 2010a. "Applying the Fair Use Doctrine." Webcast recorded October 5. Session 1 in *Libraries and Copyright: Fair Use and e-Reserves* by Academic Impressions.

————. 2010b. "Copyright Considerations for e-Reserves." Webcast recorded October 12. Session 2 in *Libraries and Copyright: Fair Use and e-Reserves* by Academic Impressions.

————. 2010c. "Copyright for Classroom Teaching." Webcast recorded April 12. Session 1 in *Copyright Essentials for Faculty* by Academic Impressions.

————. 2010d. "Copyright Regulation outside the Classroom." Webcast recorded April 14. Session 2 in *Copyright Essentials for Faculty* by Academic Impressions.

————. 2010e. "Faculty Rights under Copyright Law." Webcast recorded April 16. Session 3 in *Copyright Essentials for Faculty* by Academic Impressions.

ACRL (Association of College and Research Libraries). 2000. *Information Literacy Competency Standards for Higher Education.* Chicago: ACRL, January 18. http://www.ala.org/acrl/standards/informationliteracycompetency.

ARL (Association of Research Libraries), CSM (Center for Social Media), and WCL (Washington College of Law) Program on Information Justice and Intellectual Property. 2012. *Code of Best Practices in Fair Use for Academic and Research Libraries.* January. http://www.arl.org/bm~doc/code-of-best-practices-fair-use.pdf.

Davis, Phillip M., Bruce V. Lewenstein, Daniel H. Simon, James G. Booth, and Matthew J. L. Connolly. 2008. "Open Access Publishing, Article Downloads, and Citations: Randomised Controlled Trial." *BMJ* 337 (July 31): a568. doi:10.1136/bmj.a568.

Eysenbach, Gunther. 2006. "Citation Advantage of Open Access Articles." *PLoS Biology* 4, no. 5 (May): e157. doi:10.1371/journal.pbio.0040157.

Hajjem, Chawki, Stevan Harnad, and Yves Gingras. 2005. "Ten-Year Cross-Disciplinary Comparison of the Growth of Open Access and How It Increases Research Citation Impact." *IEEE Data Engineering Bulletin* 28, no. 4 (December): 39–47.

Howe, Jeff. 2008. *Crowdsourcing: Why the Power of the Crowd Is Driving the Future of Business.* New York: Crown Business.

Norris, Michael, Charles Oppenheim, and Fytton Rowland. 2008. "The Citation Advantage of Open-Access Articles." *Journal of the American Society for Information Science and Technology* 59, no. 12 (October): 1963–1972.

SPARC (Scholarly Publishing and Academic Resources Coalition). 2012. "Resources for Authors." Accessed December 17. http://www.arl.org/sparc/index.shtml.

University of Minnesota. 2010. "Thinking Through Fair Use." University of Minnesota University Libraries. https://www.lib.umn.edu/copyright/fairthoughts.

US Copyright Office. 2011. *Copyright Law of the United States and Related*

Laws Contained in Title 17 of the United States Code. Circular 92. Washington DC: US Copyright Office, December. http://www.copyright.gov/title17.

USU (Utah State University). 2012. "USU Policy 535: Open Access to Scholarly Articles." May 30. http://www.usu.edu/hr/files/uploads/535.pdf.

USU (Utah State University) Copyright Committee. 2010a. "Fair Use in Teaching: Or, How Not to Break the Law in Your Classroom." USU Merrill-Cazier Library. August. http://digitalcommons.usu.edu/lib_present/19.

———. 2010b. "Securing the Scholarly Record." USU Merrill-Cazier Library. August. http://digitalcommons.usu.edu/lib_present/20.

The Right to Research Coalition and Open Access Advocacy: An Interview with Nick Shockey

Stephanie Davis-Kahl
Illinois Wesleyan University

> *Editors' Note: In this interview, we wanted to get a sense
> of how information literacy and scholarly communication
> connections are enacted in the advocacy context. The Right
> to Research Coalition (R2RC), sponsored by the Scholarly
> Publishing and Academic Resources Coalition (SPARC),
> is a perfect case study. Nick Shockey, Director of R2RC,
> discusses the education and outreach work of the coalition
> and how librarians play an integral role in students' learning
> about their rights as creators.*

Stephanie Davis-Kahl (SDK): Nick, thanks so much for agreeing to be interviewed for our book. I'd like to begin with talking about librarians specifically. What particular strengths can librarians bring to the Right to Research Coalition [R2RC]?

Nick Shockey (NS): Librarians share a unique strength with students in that they both affect all areas of campus. Librarians serve as a resource for all departments and offices. Students obviously touch all parts of the campus as well, so that's a strength that librarians can use to their advantage when pushing for priorities such as OA [open access] policies. Librarians are also subject matter experts when it comes to OA. They're the ones who have to pay the bill for all these expensive journals, and most librarians have a good grasp on why journals have become so expensive. They have the understanding to explain the problems with a closed scholarly communication system and the opportunities of OA in a way that engages both faculty and students.

SDK: What about contacts with students, integration into curriculum?

NS: Absolutely. Whenever librarians interact with students in the class-room or in the library, those are great opportunities to bring up OA, especially when you're discussing the resources the library has to offer. It's a very natural time to bring up that this is what the library currently offers, but if academic publishing was structured to make research re-sults openly available, we'd be able to offer much more. These interac-tions are a good opportunity to get students to think about the choices they face when it comes to publishing their own work. The same goes for faculty as well. When librarians interact with faculty asking for help with research or for help in getting an article, those are all natural places to bring up OA. Unfortunately, when students and faculty are doing their research and come across an article they can't get access to, I think there's a natural inclination to think that is just the way it is. There's very little transparency for users to see why they can't get the articles they don't have access to—they just see a pay wall or pop-up asking them to pay thirty dollars per article. They don't see that there's a publisher making high margins on the other side and raising prices by five, six, seven percent every year, year in and year out. How could they? There's no mechanism in place to bring students' attention to the problem as they're encountering it. This is where I see librarians step-ping in to play an important role, to raise awareness about open access where students may not otherwise see the problem.

SDK: In your conversations with the steering committee and the mem-bers of R2RC, do you think that they're aware that librarians have this depth of knowledge and this specific perspective?

NS: Whenever we do outreach to our members, one of the things we always mention is that when you get back to your campus, if OA is something that interests you, you need to talk to your librarian. For all the reasons I just mentioned, librarians are the source for institu-tion-specific information: for example, how much your institution spends on journal resources or what your most expensive journal is. It's actually the first thing we tell students to do when they get back to campus: talk to the librarians. We strongly encourage students to make those connections, and it's certainly something that our Steer-ing Committee and Coordinating Committee members are aware of and tell their own individual members. We will continue working with the library community to encourage outreach to students and student leaders. Combining both of these efforts, we hope to make students and librarians partners in promoting OA on campus.

SDK: Shifting gears a little bit—how do you think your work as an advocate and as an educator represents what we're trying to do with this book, which is to build and foster connections between information literacy and scholarly communication and provide models for people to use in their own work? Do you see yourself at the intersection of these two areas?

NS: Yes. The Internet has made concepts like licensing and the implications of licensing choice on the ability to reuse content a crucial component of information literacy now more than ever, and there's significant overlap between OA and IL. We should educate students about licensing while they're still forming their own publishing habits, so when they're lead authors, they understand the benefits of licensing their work in a way that allows others the rights to redistribute, repurpose, remix, and reuse without ambiguity. Granting users those rights clearly and openly is crucial to allow them to use licensed materials. If they have to ask your permission explicitly, chances are many uses and reuses of your work won't occur.

I think that OA education also has a robust intersection with information literacy in the sense that it encourages students to start thinking about these issues from a content producer's point of view. So, when they become authors and publish their own articles, they've already begun to think about what it means to be a responsible steward of their work. They can see the connection between the pay walls they encounter during their research and the choices they make during publication.

SDK: For graduate students, that's definitely the case, and I think we're beginning to see that more with undergraduate students. Do you see that with the Right to Research Coalition with more undergraduates becoming involved?

NS: R2RC does skew towards graduate students, which is natural given their reliance on the academic literature. But undergraduates interact with academic literature as well, and our work with undergraduates will only increase. I believe open access is something that's very important to bring up as early as possible with students—they will likely have their first research experiences as undergraduates, and many of them will publish their first papers as undergraduates. It's crucial to expose students to OA early as they're still forming their publishing habits. There is a real risk that they might not import the same values they have for other information—that it should generally be open—to scholarship. They may have their first experiences with research and publication with a professor who is more conservative or not aware of OA, and that experience could inform the rest of their career. For this reason, I think it's every bit as important to engage undergraduates about open access as it is to engage graduate students, even it if takes a bit more effort since the undergrads may not be as naturally engaged with publishing as their graduate counterparts.

SDK: I think there's the consumer perspective as well. Our students are very aware of the costs of their education, and I'm sure you saw this at Trinity, too, where there would be people who had scholarships and grants and they were working a job on-campus and maybe a job off-campus. And with the downturn in the economy, students are even more aware of the costs associated with becoming a college graduate. We emphasize that students lose access to databases and information sources when they graduate and that OA is trying to change that model. The consumer approach seems to have resonance.

NS: Just to build on that briefly—raising awareness about the cost of journals is one of the most effective tools librarians have for getting students and faculty to take interest in OA as an issue. It's a great entry point to begin the broader conversation about OA since most students and many faculty members are unaware of how fantastically expensive some journals are. Most likely they don't realize the very dramatic increase in prices over the last twenty or thirty years doesn't just affect serials budgets, but also affects the library budget as a whole and the library's ability to acquire books or provide additional services. When students are frustrated that the library is not open longer, as was the case on Trinity's campus, you can draw a connection to the fact that, if you have to spend more and more on journal subscriptions, it cuts into how much you can provide in building hours or additional services. If you look at the ARL library data, monograph acquisition budgets are essentially flat over the past twenty-five years, whereas serials budgets have gone up over 400%.[1] So journal costs have a much broader impact than simply what resources are available on a given campus. As budgets have had to swell to keep pace with large journal price increases, that's money that can't go toward other library services or other parts of the university.

When talking about costs of publishing, I'm always sure to be clear that OA isn't without cost either, but there's strong evidence to show that a transition to an open scholarly publishing system would significantly reduce those costs. In an OA world, the economics of publishing would be much different. Publishers wouldn't hold the same unique position of power that they have in the current model at both ends of the market. Researchers have to publish in certain, high-impact journals to advance their careers, which means the owners of those journals have a strong grip on the production side of the market. On the consumer side, they own the content and can ask whatever price they want for access. I believe it is precisely this position that has allowed publishers to charge the prices libraries face today. While there are still costs in an OA world, publishers won't be in that uniquely powerful position over both authors and readers. With a move to an OA model, we could reasonably expect a drop in the cost of the overall scholarly publishing ecosystem, but again, that's not to say that there wouldn't be costs involved in an open system. There are real costs to be covered, but we can do it in a much more efficient way. I believe we can create a system that costs much less and allows access to all, rather than continuing to rely on this subscription model that's very expensive and doesn't do a particularly good job of leveraging the Internet to expand access to this information.

SDK: There's also the "research as a public good" argument, and the social justice angle to OA.

NS: That's one tool that librarians have to make sure they have in their toolkit when reaching out to students about OA—that is, to hammer home that OA is really and truly a social issue. It's not an issue that's confined to the library or to the academy; open access has a dramatic social impact. When you think about medical research, OA has the power to unlock and supercharge the process. Openness can, not only speed the development of new drugs and treatments, but also bring those new advancements into medical practice more quickly. The vast majority of doctors practice outside of an academic setting and may not be able to pay for access to medical research. The way we structure our scholarly publishing system makes it difficult for those doctors to access the results of the most recent medical research, even though we spend over $30 billion every year funding these studies. Medical research is only one example. OA can similarly accelerate research in clean energy, or computing, or the work that CERN [the European Organization for Nuclear Research] does in physics. Open access impacts such a wide, diverse set of issues because academic research is the foundation for so much of our modern technology. When academic research is slowed, so is the pace of innovation across a modern economy.

Another issue students often don't realize when they're using library resources is that students elsewhere don't have the same access that they do. Again, there's nothing there to show them the broken publishing system in place behind their library portal. There's nothing to make them realize that their peers in low- and middle-income countries may have access to very little, and that lack of access has a direct effect on their ability to get a world-class education and contribute to progress in their country. One of the great things about my job at the Right to Research Coalition is that we are a fully international organization that works with students in Europe, Africa, and around the world. It's been a real pleasure to work with students around the world and hear directly from them about the barriers that they face—and there are some very significant barriers. They often have to rely on their peers in other countries to pass them articles when they don't have access; it really inhibits their ability to get a complete, up-to-date education and become the world-class researchers they're capable of being. These students I've met from parts of Africa—we work predominantly with medical students there—are clamoring for a research-based education. They appreciate the importance of research-based training even when, interestingly enough, some of their professors don't feel its important to incorporate the journal literature. There is a burning desire to access these journals that they're locked out of simply because their institutions don't have the money to pay for subscriptions. Even Harvard can't afford access to everything it needs, so you can imagine the great challenges students face in less wealthy countries.

But open access isn't just important to students and researchers on university campuses. It also affects practicing doctors in these countries, and that has a very real impact. There are tragic cases of health professionals switching how they treat their patients based on abstracts—all they could get access to—and switching to less effective treatments, contributing to increased mortality rates. If they had been able to read the full text of the article, they would have likely realized that it didn't apply to their situation. It's important to realize that open access and the closed system it replaces do have a direct human impact.

Lastly, I think one of the cruelest ironies of a closed scholarly publishing system is that, when we're doing research on diseases like AIDS or malaria that have a disproportionate impact on the developing world, the breakthroughs we make are often published in journals that are so expensive that the practitioners, doctors, and policy-makers in the most affected countries can't get access to them. Even though the breakthroughs exist, doctors may have a much harder time translating that into improved outcomes and lives saved. Policy makers in those countries tasked with creating good public policy face the same problem—if they can't access the most up-to-date information, they can't make the best decisions for their country.

SDK: In the past three years, the international membership in R2RC has skyrocketed. Was this an explicit goal, or did this evolve over the development of the coalition?

NS: Going back to the beginning—we started in June 2009—we launched the Student Statement on the Right to Research after the Student Summit on OA. Gavin Baker, a previous Student Outreach Fellow at SPARC and my predecessor, led the development of the statement, laid the groundwork and worked with the six original signatories of the Student Statement. I worked closely with SPARC over my last couple of years at Trinity University, where I was an undergraduate, and was involved as a participant in the discussions leading up to the Student Statement. The Student Statement started as a petition calling on university leaders, governments, students, and researchers to do what they could to make research openly and freely available. When I came to SPARC in June of 2009, it was originally a temporary position to get the Student Statement off the ground, but we were able to generate so much interest so quickly that SPARC realized this was a new program area and a real opportunity to create change. SPARC saw the long-term importance of outreach to the student community to ensure they were educated about and engaged with this issue. SPARC has a large portfolio of initiatives to promote open access, and I think it's to SPARC's credit that it realized students are the next generation of researchers, professors, and policy makers upon whom the long-term success of the OA movement will rest.

Over the first year we transformed from a petition into the Right to Research Coalition. The early membership realized—and this was something that came out of the OA Summit here in [Washington] DC that summer after we launched—that we needed a membership organization to foster connections and continue engagement. We didn't want to have organizations sign the statement with the best of intentions but then lose momentum over time and drift away. Over the next year, we worked on putting infrastructure in place, culminating with the launch of our current website, which went live in the summer of 2010. It was also that summer when we began to make a concerted effort to expand internationally. In our first year, we felt we'd established a good foothold in North America, not only in the US, but in Canada as well. One of the most interesting things about OA and why it's such a powerful issue is that it affects students similarly no matter where they are in the world and no matter what they're studying. It's the only issue I can think of that has this unique ability to bring students together. As a priority, it makes just as much sense for the International Federation of Medical Students' Associations as it does for the Caltech Graduate Students Council, the European Federation of Psychology Students' Associations, or the Medical Students' Association of Kenya. The issue of access to research affects them all in similar ways. Even more importantly, the solutions to the problem are the same no matter where you are or what you are studying. That's why we pushed to make the R2RC international as early as we did. We wanted to bring all students along at the same pace and not have to build localized momentum in one area like North America but leave students out in other parts of the world. We took some time in the beginning and focused a lot on our coalition-building efforts, and that investment paid off quickly. Today, over half of our members are based outside of North America, predominantly in Europe but also in Africa, the Middle East, and South America, and that's expanding every day. We now have sixty-two member organizations that represent approximately seven million students. Our members represent just over one hundred countries around the world.

SDK: One of the challenges on a college or university campus is that students are an ever-changing population. How does the coalition deal with that?

NS: That is definitely one of the most significant challenges we face and something we've struggled with. On one hand, the turnover is a tremendous opportunity because every year we have new students to work with, we have new students to educate. But it's also one of our greatest challenges because to keep our members active, we have to maintain relationships over annual leadership transitions and keep our organizations engaged. Our members need to be willing to dedi-cate time to R2RC even though they are full-time students and also have roles within their home student organization. There are certainly cases where we've had an active member drift away when the students within that organization who drove their work graduated. We're in the process of creating a new structure for the coalition that we think will be a good solution to hedge against this problem of turnover. We have created, as of now, two coordinating committees that are geographical-ly based: one for North America and one for Africa, Europe, and the Middle East. Once fully up and running, all of our member organiza-tions will have two liaisons to those committees—one primary liaison that's someone on the board of that organization, and an alternate liaison which is preferably a future leader that can learn about the is-sue and the R2RC then transition to a primary role at the appropriate time. This structure should guard against loss of engagement when our students inevitably graduate, and it will also help facilitate knowledge transfer within our member organizations to ensure expertise isn't lost. We'll see how it plays out—the idea is actually something I picked up during my time at Trinity. On particularly important university committees, like the University Curriculum Council, they would ap-point two student leaders so their two-year terms would overlap. One student member would always have experience with the committee, rather than having to start from scratch every year.

SDK: So after people graduate, after they leave their student organizations and the Right to Research Coalition, how do you stay connected with them? Do you have an infrastructure to do that?

NS: At the moment, we do not. Being a young organization, we don't have too many R2RC alumni just yet. It's on our radar and something that came up at our first General Assembly this past July in Budapest. It's certainly something that we will want to take advantage of in the future. As the students we work with move on, they will become practitioners, professors, and researchers, which likely means they will become members of scholarly and professional societies. As members, they can influence those societies to become more progressive on issues like OA or Open Educational Resources (OER). If they're faculty, they could become new champions for institutional OA policies or authors of open textbooks. I think they will be a rich resource a few years down the road and something we'll definitely want to leverage.

SDK: How did your time at Trinity help you get to this point? Did you always want to work for a nonprofit? How did working with the library and the faculty help you be successful now?

NS: Trinity played a central role in starting me down this path. The faculty nurtured my interest in OA and OER. Our University Librarian, Diane Graves, and my mentor at Trinity, Erwin Cook, who was the chair of our classics department at the time, were supportive of my efforts every step of the way—from approaching university administrators to helping think through how to engage the professors on campus. Diane was on the SPARC Steering Committee when I was becoming interested, so I was extraordinarily lucky to have an expert like her around. I don't know if I would have become so involved if I didn't have her support and expertise; she's the one that connected me with SPARC and their initial efforts to engage students. She is directly responsible for my interest and for my coming to work for SPARC. So obviously, I feel librarians have an important role to play in cultivating an interest in OA within their students.

SDK: And it sounds like your student leadership experience also had a very formative role in preparing you to work with different kinds of people: not only your peers, but also people who were in authority roles and in roles that could mentor you and help guide you along the way.

NS: Oh, absolutely. Before I was involved in promoting OA, I was involved in trying to get Trinity to adopt an open courseware (OCW) program similar to what MIT has done. In support of those efforts, I talked to a sizable proportion of the student groups on-campus to raise awareness and ask them to sign a petition urging the administration to establish an open courseware program. That sort of coalition building, even though it was just a petition, was certainly helpful in getting experience in what I'd later be doing with the R2RC. As part of this effort to promote OCW at Trinity, I ran for and was elected to our Association of Student Representatives (ASR) so I could leverage our student government to push this OCW idea forward. In that role I was able to make ASR the second student government in the US to call on Congress to pass the Federal Research Public Access Act (the first was the University of Florida, led by Gavin Baker). Through those efforts, I made connections with Trinity's administration; I became comfortable working with university leadership—building relationships and trying to sell them on ideas—and that experience has been phenomenally useful and would have been regardless of the field I ultimately entered.

SDK: So you've been doing this for about five years all told, from your time at Trinity up until now, is that correct? So how have you seen OA advocacy change and grow over that five years?

NS: It's incredible—I feel like I happened to come along at the perfect time. OA, as a term, turned ten years old this year with the tenth anniversary of the Budapest Open Access Initiative—so I came in at about the halfway point. The change has been remarkable. When I first became involved in 2007, the NIH Public Access Policy was just about to become law. It was great to dive in right as that happened and see firsthand the remarkable job SPARC and Heather Joseph, SPARC's Executive Director, did to support the policy's passage. With that as a starting point, the progress has been dramatic. For example, we will soon have to revise our Student Statement on the Right to Research because it lists the total number of OA journals at just over 4,000, which was accurate when the statement was drafted; however, there are now well over 8,500. The number of OA journals has more than doubled. The number of institutional and funder OA policies has increased significantly as well. Harvard passed its institutional OA policy, the first here in the US, right before I graduated from Trinity, and it has served as a model for others around the world. Trinity was actually the first primarily liberal arts college in the US to pass an institutional OA policy, and it was great to be part of those efforts while I was a student. I'll always remember driving home for the holidays during my first year at SPARC when Diane called to tell me Trinity's Faculty Senate had officially passed the OA policy.

The past year has seen open access take on an even higher profile. This year alone we've seen three or four articles in the *Economist*, OA has been in the *New York Times* on a number of occasions, it's been in a lot of other leading publications, including the *Guardian*. Two R2RC members, the American Medical Student Association and the National Association of Graduate-Professional Students, published an op-ed in the *Washington Post* this summer. 2012 has seen OA transition into a mainstream issue. When I first started, OA was a conversation primarily between librarians and publishers. Now it's becoming an issue for the public at large, and we've seen the interest continue to build. In Congress, we've been pushing the Federal Research Public Access Act (FRPAA) which would require all publicly funded research be made freely available within 6 months of publication. It had over thirty co-sponsors in the House and was completely bipartisan. There has been significant interest from the White House as well. In the first year of President Obama's administration, the Office of Science and Technology Policy issued a request for public comment on opening access to publicly funded research and then issued another request the following year. In 2012, the White House We the People petition for OA reached its goal of 25,000 signatures in only two weeks[2]. There has been a great deal of interest from the executive and legislative branches, both of which hold the power to unlock all federally funded research. It's been exciting to hear friends and colleagues outside of the OA community become increasingly aware of the issue. I feel we are at the brink of switching the default open, making public-access policies a common practice among research funders. Hopefully we'll continue to see an even faster shift in that direction. I believe we're at the inflection point in the curve toward openness, and there couldn't be a better time for students and librarians to work together to drive a conversation about OA on their campus.

Finally, I see the student role in promoting open access as that of a catalyst. Institutional OA policies are ultimately decided by a university's faculty. These aren't top-down changes or ones the students vote on. A lot of work must be done to change attitudes and correct misconceptions in order to secure faculty support for an OA policy. It's not something students can pass. It's not something librarians can pass alone. What students and librarians are well positioned to do is to help raise awareness of OA and to identify and recruit opinion leaders and champions for OA. After you find these individuals, you can leverage them by holding events or writing op-eds in the campus newspaper to raise awareness and build support for the issue. That's how the momentum for these policies and changes in attitude take hold. Students and librarians are uniquely positioned to foster those conversations, to drive those events, and to bring the rest of the campus community together to have the discussions that result in an OA policy.

From my experience, when students become active advocates for OA, it makes faculty take notice, even to the point of reevaluating their own opinions. Students have a significant role to play in initiating a wider discussion about OA on campus, which can often be one of the more difficult parts of passing a policy. As we've seen on numerous campuses, students can provide the impetus to start the conversation or reinvigorate it. Having an open community discussion helps to create and identify champions as well as communicate the benefits of open access, including the citation advantage correlated with making an article openly available or how rich institutional repositories help raise the profile of an institution as a research center. Processes will differ from institution to institution, but this was my experience at Trinity, and I imagine it would hold true elsewhere. Again, somebody has to be behind the scenes, driving these conversations, putting on the events, and creating the initial momentum. Librarians have a critical role to play in nurturing students' interests in OA and making the case for OA to faculty.

Notes

1. ARL. 2006. Monograph and serial expenditures in ARL libraries, 1986–2011. http://www.arl.org/bm~doc/t2_monser11.xls (accessed January 14, 2013).
2. The White House petition site, We the People, at https://petitions. whitehouse.gov, allows individuals to create and sign online petitions on issues of concern to them. When a petition meets the signature threshold, the administration reviews and responds to it. The petition to "require free access over the Internet to scientific journal articles arising from taxpayer-funded research," created May 13, 2012, had over 50,500 signatures in early January 2013 (https://petitions.whitehouse.gov/petition/require-free-access-over-internet-scientific-journal-articles-arising-taxpayer-funded-research/wDX82FLQ).

CHAPTER 17

ACRL's Scholarly Communications Roadshow

[Bellwether for a Changing Profession]

Joy Kirchner
University of British Columbia Library

Kara J. Malenfant
Association of College and Research Libraries

Introduction

At its heart, the ACRL Scholarly Communications Roadshow program highlights the need to redefine what it means to be a librarian in the twenty-first century. For over a decade, the Association of College and Research Libraries (ACRL) has been committed to its scholarly communication initiative as one of its highest strategic priorities. Professional development and continuing education for academic librarians are cornerstones of the initiative. The Roadshow's responsive curriculum has grown to support academic librarians as they stretch their professional muscles in new ways. Attuned to a changing community, Roadshow presenters continuously update the curriculum, and it has shifted focus from imparting a basic awareness of the dynamics in the current system of scholarly communication to facilitating participants' deeper understanding and engagement or commitment to changing the system.

More than meeting the community where it is, the Roadshow program challenges participants to assume ever more active roles in accelerating the transition to a more open system of scholarship. The Roadshow program has set goals to stimulate new thinking about the future of library services, to provide practical ideas on developing services, and to discuss emerging themes, such as the use of alternative metrics in reward systems and the intersections of scholarly communication and student learning.

Through the Roadshow, ACRL not only reached those who may not attend national conferences or work at large research universities,

Creative Commons Attribution-NonCommercial (CC BY-NC)
http://creativecommons.org/licenses/by-nc/3.0/

but also asserted that scholarly communication issues are central to the work of all academic librarians and all types of institutions. In this chapter, we describe how the program has evolved to support academic librarians as they assume new roles as contributors of knowledge creation, advocates of sustainable models of scholarship, and partners of faculty in both research and educational processes.

Background and Context

Within ACRL's current strategic plan, there are three primary goal areas of focus for 2011–2016: the value of academic libraries, student learning, and the research and scholarly environment. The goal for the research and scholarly environment strategic area is, "Librarians accelerate the transition to a more open system of scholarship." The specific objectives are:

1. Model new dissemination practices.
2. Enhance members' ability to address issues related to digital scholarship and data management.
3. Influence scholarly publishing policies and practices toward a more open system.
4. Create and promote new structures that reward and value open scholarship. (ACRL 2011)

This commitment to hastening a more open system of scholarship is not new. ACRL has long endeavored to reshape the system of scholarly communication, focusing on the areas of education, advocacy, coalition building, and research. Starting in January 2000, an ACRL task force on scholarly communication began discussing how ACRL might contribute to shaping the future of scholarly communication and stated that such discussion "requires envisioning what such a future might be like" (English et al. 2002, 4). In the task force's January 2002 report to the ACRL board, they had determined that the issues surrounding scholarly communication and publishing were of major import to ACRL members. The task force recommended that ACRL, as one of its highest strategic priorities, be actively engaged in working to reshape the current system of scholarly communication, with activities to include educational work, political advocacy, coalition building, and research. In describing the broad-based educational work, the task force identified a new role for ACRL:

> Given the complexity of these issues, and the importance of working on them in a sustained way over time, we believe there is a critical need for ACRL to mount ongoing programs to educate academic librarians about

> scholarly communication issues and for ACRL to create
> support mechanisms, programs, and publicity efforts
> to help make faculty researchers and higher educa-
> tion administrators more aware of the importance of
> these concerns. ACRL's broad membership base and its
> strong record in programming and continuing education
> puts the association in a unique position to be effective
> in these areas. (English et al. 2002, 6)

Based on the recommendations in the report, ACRL launched its scholarly communication initiative in spring 2002 as one of its highest strategic priorities. ACRL's new standing committee of the Board, the Scholarly Communications Committee, then focused on continuing education for academic librarians by developing a preconference for the ALA Annual 2004 in Orlando, Florida: Scholarly Communication 101: An Introduction to Scholarly Communication Issues and Strate-gies for Change. Presentations from this preconference included:

- Anatomy of a Crisis: Dysfunction in the Scholarly Communi-cations System (by Lee Van Orsdel)
- Copyright, Licensing, and Information Policy: Mine, Mine, and Well, Mine! (by Dwayne Buttler)
- Fostering a Competitive Market (by Ray English)
- Open Access (by Karen Williams)
- Scholarly Communication: Legislative and Political Advocacy (by James G. Neal)
- Scholarly Communication: Strategies for Change (by James G. Neal)

These presentation materials became the foundation of the ACRL Scholarly Communication Toolkit, which was launched in March 2005 to support advocacy efforts for academic and research libraries.

The path from this initial preconference to creating a sustained Roadshow workshop with a "101" basic level approach was not entirely linear, and next we will describe in the stages leading up to it. In addition to offering this very first preconference in 2004 aimed at a basic 101-level education, members of the Scholarly Communications Committee, together with staff, began exploring a new project with the Association of Research Libraries (ARL) to jointly promote the development of library-led outreach programs. The two organizations recognized a shared concern for supporting academic and research libraries in their growing efforts to develop campus outreach pro-grams. Through the ARL/ACRL Institute on Scholarly Communication (ISC), the organizations have sought to aid libraries in developing their outreach programs by offering websites with resources and plan-ning guides, topical webcasts, workshops, and an immersive learning experience. This signature two-and-a-half day event, first offered in

July 2006, prepares participants to become local experts within their libraries and provides a structure for developing a program plan for scholarly communication outreach that is customized for each participant's institution.

Many of the members of ACRL's Scholarly Communications Committee worked as faculty to design and deliver initial offerings of the immersive event for the ISC. In this capacity, they recognized the wide variance in background understanding and engagement in scholarly communications as a critical perspective for academic libraries and librarians. They saw a strong need to provide librarians with contextual understanding in order to help them take action and develop campus outreach programs. While many librarians understood that copyright, information economics, business models, open access, and other scholarly communications issues are important, they did not have enough background in these issues to begin taking action in their own library and campus settings.

Many academic librarians, therefore, continued to require a basic approach before being able to benefit from the more advanced work on program planning offered via the ISC. To help this segment of the community, ACRL committee members decided in 2008 to return to the "101" idea and develop a workshop specifically targeting librarians who were new to scholarly communications issues. It was felt that such a program could serve as a bridge course toward more advanced opportunities such as the ISC.

As one way to understand the varying levels of readiness within the community, we looked to an article by Joyce Ogburn (2008), which has served as a cornerstone text for the ISC. In it, she proposes a series of five stages through which libraries, by programmatic efforts, will advance:

1. *Awareness:* having basic knowledge of the issues
2. *Understanding:* higher order of knowledge, intelligence, and appreciation
3. *Ownership:* commitment and obligation
4. *Activism:* goal-directed, concerted, and purposeful action
5. *Transformation:* attainment of a profound alteration of assumptions, methods, and culture

Defining and applying these stages, she wrote, "can help establish and guide a program by setting direction and goals, tracking progress, identifying landmarks, and noting achievements...The stages reflect an evolution from local action to collaborative efforts with the goal of achieving widespread change" (Ogburn 2008, 45). These stages provide a useful theoretical framework against which to consider how ACRL's curriculum for the Roadshow has evolved to support a community in transition, as we'll describe next.

From Conference Workshop to Roadshow

The Roadshow curriculum was initially developed by members of the ACRL Scholarly Communications Committee in a proposal for a basic half-day workshop offered in person as part of the ACRL 14th National Conference, Push the Edge: Explore, Engage, Extend, in Seattle, Washington, March 12–15, 2009. Workshop leaders, known experts from the committee, developed the curriculum based on learning outcomes and speaker guidelines delineated in the proposal. Two members of the committee, Joy Kirchner (University of British Columbia) and Lee Van Orsdel (Grand Valley State), worked in consultation with staff liaison Kara Malenfant to lead and guide the development of the program in accordance with the committee's goals and in keeping with ACRL's commitment to continuing education in this area. They created a twofold vision for the workshop:

- Develop an ACRL educational offering that provides the library community with well-developed basic scholarly communications program.
- Use the workshop as an opportunity to broaden expertise in scholarly communications by seeking out new, but knowledgeable and engaged, librarians for whom this opportunity to present would be good national-level exposure. Partner these new librarians with seasoned Scholarly Communications Committee experts or faculty from the ISC.

The workshop was titled "Scholarly Communication 101" and was developed with the possibility of future offerings in mind. Two other presenters joined Kirchner and Van Orsdel in Seattle: Sarah Shreeves (University of Illinois at Urbana-Champaign and a faculty member with the ISC), and Molly Keener (Wake Forest University), a newcomer. The four presenters worked together to develop the following modules for the half-day workshop:

1. Introduction and economic issues
2. Open access and openness as a principle
3. Copyright and intellectual property
4. New modes and models of scholarly communication

While it was in development, the presenters discussed the upcoming workshop with the ACRL Scholarly Communications Committee at a January 2009 meeting. Then-ARL staff member Karla Strieb (née Hahn) commented that librarians at the workshop may eagerly approach the presenters and invite them to offer a reprise on their campuses. Sensing an opportunity to further ACRL's strategic goals[1] by taking the workshop out and extending its reach, Malenfant suggested the committee develop an ACRL-subsidized Roadshow program that institutions could apply to host. This plan was enthusiastically endorsed by the ACRL Scholarly Communications Committee and implemented quickly thereafter.

In early March 2009, ACRL announced that it would carry the costs to take the workshop, "Scholarly Communications 101: Starting with the Basics," on the road to five locations, chosen through a competitive process, in summer 2009. Promotion was queued up so that the Roadshow was advertised with flyers and announcements at the ACRL 14th National Conference in Seattle.

In preparing to take the workshop on the road, presenters adapted the curriculum based on what they had learned. Additional presenters were recruited from available ISC faculty: Kevin Smith (Duke University) and Terri Fishel (Macalaster College). When announced, the Roadshow was promoted in this way:

> Led by two expert presenters, this structured interactive overview of the scholarly communication system highlights individual or institutional strategic planning and action. Four modules focus on new methods of scholarly publishing and communication, copyright and intellectual property, economics and open access. As a result of the workshop, participants will understand scholarly communication as a system to manage the results of research and scholarly inquiry, enumerate new modes and models of scholarly communication and select and cite key principles, facts and messages relevant to current or nascent scholarly communication plans and programs at their institutions. "Scholarly Communication 101" is appropriate for those with new leadership assignments in scholarly communication as well as liaisons and others who are interested in the issues and need foundational understanding. (ALA 2009)

Mentoring New Presenters

In addition to developing programming that would educate librarians with new responsibilities for scholarly communication, the Roadshow has also served as a vehicle for directly mentoring newer librarians by expanding the presenter pool to bring in different areas of expertise within scholarly communication at large. To that end, a call went out to both faculty members of the ISC and the ACRL Scholarly Communications Committee asking for recommendations for new presenters. These calls resulted in recruiting a newer librarian, Keener, to be part of the group designing and delivering the workshop at ACRL National Conference 2009. Once the Roadshow was launched, more presenters were needed, resulting in a similar call to ISC and committee members to recruit an additional newer librarian, Molly Kleinman (University of Michigan). Members of the committee mentored Keener and Kleinman as appropriate in both developing the curriculum and in teaching.

As the Roadshow continued, the team of expert presenters was enlarged to accommodate an expanded program and replace those who discontinued their service to the program. A model for expanding the pool was discussed by the ACRL Scholarly Communications Committee, where it was decided that a formal selection process and mentorship program should be integrated into the Roadshow program, with specific funding earmarked for this purpose. ACRL sent out an announcement seeking expressions of interest from prospective presenters to all major scholarly communication lists in March 2011. This opportunity was also widely advertised at the ACRL 2011 conference, and a formal selection and interview process took place for two new presenters over a two-year period. Ada Emmet (University of Kansas) was selected in 2011, and Stephanie Davis-Kahl (Illinois Wesleyan University) was selected in 2012.

Program Revision in 2012

Constant revision and updates to the program have been a critical staple in the Roadshow curriculum development. Workshop presenters are active in developing the program because they are keenly aware of how quickly the scholarly communication arena is evolving. They collaborate frequently to reflect on the program deliverables, determine what improvements are necessary, and revise the program and handouts as new information emerges in this arena. They are attuned to the shifts they are observing in the community over time as library programs evolve through Ogburn's stages.

Recognizing this evolution relies on more than just a tacit sense; there is data to support the observation that libraries are becoming more engaged and taking on more activities related to scholarly communication education and outreach. Prior to each Roadshow, participants are asked to identify one person from each library to answer a series of questions—a census if you will. The purpose is to better understand the state of scholarly communication education and outreach efforts at the library level in the short term and the long term. The online questionnaire presents a checklist of some eighteen scholarly communication activities (e.g., outreach events for faculty on scholarly communication topics, an institutional repository, a fund to pay author fees for open access journal publishing, etc.) and asks the submitters to identify their library's current activities and its future plans. In nearly all cases, there has been an increase in the number of libraries offering these activities over the last four years. (For complete text of questions and data underlying the graph in Figure 17.1, see Appendix 17.1: Responses to Pre-Workshop Questionnaire on Library-Level Engagement.)

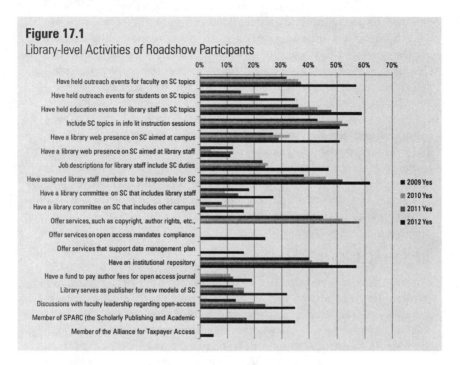

Figure 17.1
Library-level Activities of Roadshow Participants

Given this evidence that libraries felt a sense of ownership and were increasingly committing resources to implement education and outreach activities, it was felt that the community had largely moved beyond Ogburn's first stage of awareness of the issues and that it was time to shift the program offerings from a 101-level curriculum aimed at basic knowledge deliverables to a more advanced program. ACRL sought to marshal resources to do this work well and named Kirchner, who had been acting as coordinator of the presenter group, as ACRL visiting program officer to lead that change. After three years of revisions, in 2012 the Roadshow was substantially modified and renamed, "Scholarly Communications: From Understanding to Engagement."

This title dropped the 101 designation and the term *basics* to reflect the transition from the program's earlier goal of providing a base-level understanding of scholarly communication. As of 2012, the program is now a more robust professional development offering and has extended from a half-day to a full-day workshop. New learning objectives were crafted to better reflect new deliverables (see Appendix 17.2.).

The Roadshow is now aimed at those with administrative responsibilities or new leadership assignments in scholarly communication or digital publishing, as well as liaisons and any others who are seeking to advance their professional development in scholarly communication. Broad goals of the revised program are designed to stimulate new thinking about the role of scholarly communication in the future of library services, to provide practical ways for participants to develop service models for scholarly communication in their libraries, and to empower participants to help accelerate the transformation of the scholarly communication system.

As the program matured, ACRL introduced a cost-sharing model to align the program more closely with other ACRL professional development opportunities. (ACRL is committed to underwriting the bulk of the costs for delivering the Roadshow, and the cost for the five successful host institutions is $2,000. Separate from this competitive application process, ACRL will now offer the program at full cost to institutions wishing to license it.) The revised workshop was piloted at the ALA Midwinter Meeting 2012 and was one of the best-attended ACRL daylong offerings at an ALA Midwinter Meeting in several years. In evaluating this offering, a standard ACRL instrument was used to allow data to be collected in a way that would tie the data back to ACRL's key performance indicators for professional development programs.

Looking Back

The program was initially developed to help libraries that were just starting to consider how to develop campus outreach programs, with an aim of supporting Ogburn's first stage (awareness: having basic knowledge of the issues). However, it quickly evolved to assist participants in thinking through service models for their scholarly communication activities and rapidly began to incorporate a higher level of knowledge and appreciation of the more nuanced aspects of scholarly communication. For instance, while open access awareness and education was the chief discussion point in the first Roadshow, by 2012, presenters became aware that open access is largely well understood and that there was a need to shift that segment of the workshop to focus more on emergent areas and the politics of open access and openness in practice.

The presenters have been increasingly challenged with developing a curriculum to suit all library types. They have increasingly recognized, throughout the four years of the Roadshow, that scholarly communication is no longer the focus of just large, research-intensive institutions. Accordingly, the program evolved to broaden the discussion from a publishing and research perspective to encompassing more of a teaching and learning perspective. This redesign allows it to resonate more with librarians undertaking scholarly communication activities at institutions with a primary focus on undergraduate education. The curriculum also evolved to include more material designed to assist liaison librarians who are working with students and with faculty as teachers, not just researchers. The presenters further redesigned the material to be applicable to any size institution. To further understand how the Roadshow could better support liberal arts colleges, Kirchner recruited Davis-Kahl (prior to her selection as a new presenter) to help the committee gather information about scholarly communication activities, priorities, needs, and current programs at small liberal arts colleges as a way of guiding our future training efforts. This work is currently underway in summer 2012.

In addition to adjusting the curriculum to meet the needs of librarians at different types of institutions, the presenters have discussed how to address the differences within disciplines regarding scholarly communications. It seems very important, and still more aspirational than real, for the Roadshow to help librarians deal with the actual conditions and variance in attitudes regarding scholarly communication in art history, English, biology, or physics, for example. While presenters have declared themselves anxious to address disciplinary differences, the best method of doing so is unclear. They see disciplinary differences as an important aspect of the intersection between scholarly communication and information literacy, and it is a recurring theme during debriefing calls and retreats.

Emerging Themes in 2012

In 2012, the curriculum was reshaped to build in more engagement with participants on how their libraries could create value-added services in the system of scholarship. This included thinking beyond open access and institutional repositories to consider other mechanisms to enhance knowledge exchange and mobilization, new forms of both creation and dissemination of scholarship, and means for tracking those developments on our own campuses. The presenters more deliberately included case studies in the curriculum to both instigate discussion and showcase how other institutions created such value-added services as supports for the open exchange of scholarship, open education services, publishing services, and copyright services. Several emerging themes surfaced by 2012. These include e-science, data management, scholarly communication as it relates to student learning, and how emerging alternative metrics to evaluate scholarship may change faculty reward systems (e.g., promotion and tenure). While this chapter cannot explore each of these emerging themes in depth, we chose to focus on two that are relevant, given the subject of this book.

First, we look at the emerging theme of scholarly communication and student learning. The 2012 Roadshow program saw an increased interest in developing scholarly communication programs that focused on undergraduate publishing support as a result of the increased number of institutions placing strategic emphasis on undergraduate research. As a result, the Roadshow provided more emphasis on ways in which scholarly communication programming can support such institutional imperatives. The Roadshow presented case studies on how scholarly communication librarians or liaison librarians are working with faculty to provide avenues to give their undergraduate students publishing experience, typically through open access avenues. Examples include faculty who have created assignment-based models ranging from student article submissions to open access student journals to the launching of a student open access journal where students are assigned specific editorial roles as defined in such open access journal programs as Open Journal Systems. Other examples include student submission of exemplary undergraduate student work in institutional repositories. Still other faculty are providing their students with opportunities for publishing experience through other "open avenues," such as wikis or through submission to *Wikipedia*.[2]

Next we look at another emerging theme around the use of alternative metrics in rewarding and valuing open scholarship. The Roadshow has always addressed the role of promotion and tenure in the segments on the system of scholarly communication and as an influencing factor in the economics of traditional scholarly publishing. However, in the most recent cycle of Roadshows, there was increased interest in delving more deeply into exploring programmatic roles for libraries and librarians in promotion and tenure arenas. Through facilitated dialogue, presenters and participants explore a role for libraries in assisting promotion and tenure committees with the evaluation of newer forms of scholarship. As promotion and tenure committees are increasingly faced with evaluating newer forms of digital scholarship, libraries could potentially play a role in providing context and understanding of new models of scholarship and supporting alternative metrics (altmetrics) on their own campuses as a means of offering support for scholarship or promotion and tenure cases that are not well supported by traditional citation metrics. Discussion included how libraries can play a role in supporting or creating altmetrics to provide other avenues to demonstrate impact of an author's or creator's work beyond traditional avenues and how such models would be especially useful for those faculty seeking to demonstrate value for new models of scholarship. Presenters and participants have also discussed collections statistics, institutional repository statistics, and how libraries can utilize, support, or contribute to the growing number of emerging altmetric tools in development.[3]

Looking Forward

To a large degree, the Roadshow program focuses on transitions occurring in research, publishing, teaching, and learning practices brought about by new technologies. Those changes and the need to both respond and proactively shape a future that fully leverages the affordances inherent in new technologies, is at the heart of the Roadshow programming. The Roadshow curriculum is likely to evolve to capture more thinking about the following trends:

1. *Value-added library services and mechanisms to enhance knowledge exchange, translation, dissemination, and mobilization, especially to support open exchange of research and scholarship.* Linked to this discussion is the growing importance of the accessibility and reuse of research data as an important emergent and complex new arena in scholarly communication as libraries begin to develop service models in support of data management. The intersection of scholarly communication and data curation will need to be explored.

2. *The intersection of information literacy and scholarly communication.* ACRL has begun to explore this trend through this book and a forthcoming white paper. Likely the Roadshow program will evolve as these investigations continue.

3. *The growing value of "personal collections," open education models, and open research data.* How these *collections* contribute to scholarship and scholarly practice will likely be tracked in the Roadshow program.

4. *How actively institutions wish to support, preserve, and promote new forms of scholarship.* As colleges and universities are faced with the challenges of reviewing emerging forms of scholarship and scholarly communication for promotion and tenure considerations, they (perhaps with help from their libraries) will need to this issue. Key questions for future scholarly communication programming will likely include tracking and thinking through the following:
    *   How is the emerging landscape of scholarly communication and contribution shifting?
    *   How might promotion and tenure processes be adapted to support knowledge production, transmission, and preservation in an increasingly participatory culture?

- What approaches to promotion and tenure review are being adopted and used by leading institutions in light of the changing landscape of scholarly communication and contribution? Are there emerging best practices at the disciplinary level that might serve as a model for others?
- What metrics of scholarly communication and impact will be relevant for promotion and tenure committees in a shifting landscape of scholarly communication? How will this differ by discipline? What role can librarians play in providing altmetrics in support of new models of scholarship?
- What is the role of community engagement in emerging forms of scholarly communication?
- In what ways can libraries assist with supporting sustainable scholarship in both its emerging formats and traditional formats?

Conclusion

In its fourth year, and with the 2012 workshops completed, the Roadshow will have visited seventeen different states, the District of Columbia, one US territory, and one Canadian province. The twenty workshops offered over these four years will have reached 1,272 participants from 344 different colleges and universities. (For a breakdown, see Appendix 17.3.) Participants have given consistently high evaluations with comments such as these:

- "I liked how simple the presenters made a very complex subject appear…I hope that I can do the same in the future."
- "It helped me connect issues in a coherent way—the relationship between open movement, copyright, economics etc.— good to have a conceptual framework."
- "My epiphany moment was how much faculty plays a role and how, as a library, we can engage faculty in these discussions."
- "I came away with concrete ideas to take back to my campus. Many time [*sic*] at conferences or workshops I come away inspired but lacking in concrete solutions or initiatives. This time I was not only informed and inspired, but came away with ideas appropriate for my institution."
- "The two presenters were stunningly knowledgeable, but also very accessible and willing to field questions as they arose. Great information presented. I came back energized and fired up."

While it is clear that the Roadshow has been a catalyst for many participants to create or expand scholarly communication programs in their own libraries (Vandegrift and Colvin 2012), there have also been some positive unexpected outcomes. Presenters have heard that simply seeing the advertisement itself spurred some institutions to take scholarly communication more seriously. Some prospective hosts, whether selected or not, reported that the act of applying (and securing partners for their application) has been a springboard for beginning their own local scholarly communication educational programs. Several unsuccessful applicants, for instance, went ahead and launched their own local "Roadshow" workshops. We have encouraged this by adding Roadshow materials to the ACRL Scholarly Communication Toolkit [4] under a Creative Commons license. In extending the reach of the Roadshow this way, we hope that librarians will make use of these tools, including short videos, presentation templates, and handouts, to enhance their own knowledge or adapt them to offer related workshops on their own campuses.

From a library association perspective, the Roadshow has been an extraordinary opportunity to support members in a much-needed way. It has directly supported ACRL's strategic priorities, and the responsive curriculum is a model for how the association can meet the changing reality of our work as academic librarians. By subsidizing the Roadshow, ACRL has reached those who may not attend national conferences or work at large research universities. Through the Roadshow, ACRL intends to send a clear message that scholarly communication issues are central to the work of all academic librarians and all types of institutions. ACRL challenges all librarians to extend their curiosity and be more responsive to their community, finding appropriate insertion points where there is a need on their campus. Through the combination of excellent presenters and forward-thinking curriculum, ACRL is supporting members of our profession as they assume new roles as contributors of knowledge creation, advocates of sustainable models of scholarship, and partners of faculty in both the research and educational processes.

Acknowledgements

The authors wish to acknowledge the excellent work of members of the Roadshow presenter team who have undertaken the efforts described in this chapter with dedication and verve. They are Ada Emmett, Stephanie Davis-Kahl, Molly Keener, Joy Kirchner, Sarah Shreeves, Kevin Smith, Lee Van Orsdel, and past presenters Molly Kleinman and Terri Fishel.

Responses to Pre-Workshop Questionnaire on Library-Level Engagement

	2009 60 responses			2010 57 responses			2011 50 responses			2012 37 responses*		
	Yes	No	No, but planned in the next 12 months	Yes	No	No, but planned in the next 12 months	Yes	No	No, but planned in the next 12 months	Yes	No	No, but planned in the next 12 months
Have held outreach events for faculty on scholarly communication topics	32%	40%	28%	36%	36%	27%	37%	55%	8%	57%	30%	14%
Have held outreach events for students on scholarly communication topics	15%	73%	12%	25%	68%	7%	22%	76%	2%	35%	49%	16%
Have held education events for library staff on scholarly communication topics	36%	47%	17%	43%	46%	11%	48%	46%	6%	59%	32%	8%
Include scholarly communication topics in information literacy instruction sessions for students	43%	47%	10%	52%	44%	4%	54%	44%	2%	51%	35%	14%
Have a library web presence on scholarly communication topics aimed at campus community	27%	50%	23%	33%	43%	24%	29%	57%	14%	51%	32%	16%
Have a library web presence on scholarly communication topics aimed at library staff only	12%	78%	10%	4%	82%	15%	12%	86%	2%	11%	81%	8%
Job descriptions for library staff include scholarly communication duties	23%	68%	8%	25%	62%	13%	24%	70%	6%	47%	44%	8%
Have assigned library staff members to be responsible for scholarly communication activities	38%	50%	12%	46%	41%	13%	52%	44%	4%	62%	24%	14%
Have a library committee on scholarly communication that includes library staff only	18%	73%	8%	9%	89%	2%	14%	86%	0%	27%	68%	5%

	2009 60 responses			2010 57 responses			2011 50 responses			2012 37 responses*		
	Yes	No	No, but planned in the next 12 months	Yes	No	No, but planned in the next 12 months	Yes	No	No, but planned in the next 12 months	Yes	No	No, but planned in the next 12 months
Have a library committee on scholarly communication that includes other campus stakeholders (e.g., faculty, editors, university press, research office)	8%	82%	10%	20%	67%	13%	2%	90%	8%	16%	68%	16%
Offer services, such as copyright, author rights, and/or open access mandates compliance advising	45%	45%	10%	52%	34%	14%	58%	42%	0%	n/a	n/a	n/a
Offer services on open access mandates compliance or advising	n/a	n/a	n/a	n/a	n/a	n/a	n/a	n/a	n/a	24%	49%	27%
Offer services that support data management plan compliance or advising	n/a	n/a	n/a	n/a	n/a	n/a	n/a	n/a	n/a	16%	57%	27%
Have an institutional repository	40%	50%	10%	41%	46%	13%	47%	43%	10%	57%	32%	11%
Have a fund to pay author fees for open access journal publishing	0%	100%	0%	11%	87%	2%	12%	86%	2%	19%	70%	11%
Library serves as publisher for new models of scholarly communication (e-journals, etc.)	12%	88%	0%	16%	73%	11%	16%	72%	12%	32%	59%	8%
Discussions with faculty leadership regarding an open access resolution for my campus	13%	62%	25%	20%	53%	27%	24%	70%	6%	35%	51%	14%
Member of SPARC (the Scholarly Publishing and Academic Resources Coalition)	n/a	n/a	n/a	n/a	n/a	n/a	17%	83%	0%	35%	65%	0%
Member of the Alliance for Taxpayer Access	n/a	n/a	n/a	n/a	n/a	n/a	0%	100%	0%	5%	95%	0%

2012 Roadshow Learning Objectives

Overall Program Learning Objectives

Participants will:

- Enhance understanding of scholarly communication as a system to manage the results of research and scholarly inquiry.
- Increase their ability to examine, and initiate or support new models of scholarly communication (e.g., research and social interaction models such as blogs, new ways of peer review).
- Select and cite key principles, facts, and messages relevant to their own scholarly communication plans and programs (current or nascent).
- Identify concrete actions that they may take back to their institutions and in their positions to help accelerate the transformation of the scholarly communication system.

Module Learning Objectives

1. Scholarly Communication System Module
Participants will:

1.1 Understand that the scholarly communication systems is made up of many interlocking systems
1.2 Understand the basic, traditional iterations in the life cycle of scholarship
1.3 Identify how disruptions are changing the traditional system of scholarly communication

2. Economics Module
Participants will:

2.1 Understand some of the basic economic realities of the traditional scholarly publishing system

2.2 Recognize the connection between authors' copyright management practices and monopolistic pricing in the scholarly journal market

2.3 Consider and reflect on alternative models and funding sources for scholarly publishing

3. Copyright Module
Participants will:

3.1 Understand how copyright arises and identify types of material that are likely to be subject to copyright protection

3.2 Identify the likely copyright owners of academic works and have a reasonable awareness of the rights attendant on such protection

3.3 Be familiar with rights transfer and retention language commonly used in publishing contracts

4. Open and Openness Module
Participants will:

4.1 Understand the conceptual underpinnings of open movements

4.2 Understand what the open access and public-access movements are

4.3 Identify current events within the open- and public-access movements

4.4 Identify other open movements

5. Faculty and Student Engagement Module
Participants will:

5.1 Identify and examine current models and programming that support "openness"

5.2 Explore new models and tenure and promotion considerations

5.3 Explore models that you might consider piloting or experimenting with

5.4 Consider what next steps you might take

APPENDIX 17.3

Roadshow Hosts and Participants

Year	Host	Location	# Participants	# Institutions
2012	Atlanta University Center Robert W. Woodruff Library	Atlanta, GA	69	18
	Colorado State University	Pueblo, CO	27	13
	James Madison University	Harrisonburg, VA	49	18
	University of New Mexico	Albuquerque, NM	62	5
	University of Toronto	Toronto, ON	58	19
2011	City University of New York (23 colleges)	Brooklyn, NY	81	29
	Washington Research Libraries Consortium	Washington, DC	73	13
	University of Hawaii at Manoa	Honolulu, HI	51	8
	St. Thomas University	St. Paul, MN	45	10
	Academic Library Association of Ohio	Columbus, OH	95	38
2010	Auraria Library	Denver, CO	71	17
	Bryan College	Dayton, TN	33	12
	Florida State University	Tallahassee, FL	93	30
	Kansas State University	Manhattan, KS	60	27
	Lehigh Valley Association of Independent Colleges	Bethlehem, PA	43	18
2009	ACRL Louisiana Chapter	Baton Rouge, LA	81	21
	State University of New York	Buffalo, NY	79	22
	Texas Tech University	Lubbock, TX	46	4
	University of Puerto Rico at Mayagüez	Mayagüez, PR	67	4
	Washington University	St. Louis, MO	89	18
TOTAL			**1,272**	**344**

Notes

1. When the workshop was offered in March 2009, ACRL was operating under its previous strategic plan, "Charting Our Future: ACRL Strategic Plan 2020" (ACRL 2004). That plan contained forty strategic objectives, and in order to focus energies, in May 2009 the board identified six as strategic priorities for 2009–2013 (see ACRL 2009). Identifying the top priorities further supported ACRL's decision to invest in offering the workshop as a Roadshow because it directly addressed one of these six: "Enhance ACRL members' understanding of how scholars work and the systems, tools, and technology to support the evolving work of the creation, personal organization, aggregation, discovery, preservation, access and exchange of information in all formats."
2. Examples showcased include University of British Columbia's Dr. Jon Beasley Murray's undergraduate *Wikipedia* assignment for his Spanish literature class (Jbmurray 2009).
3. See Altmetrics at http://altmetrics.org/tools for a growing list of alternative metric tools in development.
4. The ACRL Scholarly Communication Toolkit is available at http://scholcomm.acrl.ala.org/.

References

ALA (American Library Association). 2009. "ACRL Offers Scholarly Communication 101 Road Show." News release. March 3. http://www.ala.org/news/news/pressreleases2009/march2009/acrlscroadshow.

ACRL (Association of College and Research Libraries). 2004. "Charting Our Future: ACRL Strategic Plan 2020." Approved June 26. Last updated May 13, 2009. http://www.ala.org/acrl/sites/ala.org.acrl/files/content/aboutacrl/strategicplan/ACRL-SP-5-09.pdf

ACRL (Association of College and Research Libraries). 2009. "Strategic Priorities: 2009–2013." Last updated May 18. http://www.ala.org/acrl/sites/ala.org.acrl/files/content/aboutacrl/strategicplan/priorities0913.pdf.

ACRL (Association of College and Research Libraries). 2011. "ACRL Plan for Excellence." April. http://www.ala.org/acrl/aboutacrl/strategicplan/stratplan.

Buttler, Dwayne. 2004. "Copyright, Licensing, and Information Policy: Mine, Mine, and Well, Mine!" Presentation at Scholarly Communication 101: An Introduction to Scholarly Communication Issues and Strategies for Change, preconference for the ALA Annual Meeting,

Orlando, FL, June.

English, Ray. 2004. "Fostering a Competitive Market." Presentation at Scholarly Communication 101: An Introduction to Scholarly Communication Issues and Strategies for Change, preconference for the ALA Annual Meeting, Orlando, FL, June.

English, Ray, Karyle Butcher, Deborah Dancik, James Neal, and Catherine Wojewodzki. 2002. *Report of the ACRL Scholarly Communications Task Force*. Chicago: ACRL, January. http://www.ala.org/acrl/sites/ala.org.acrl/files/content/issues/scholcomm/doc12.0.pdf.

Jbmurray. 2009. "User:Jbmurray/Madness." *Wikipedia* user page. Last updated May 1. http://en.wikipedia.org/wiki/User:Jbmurray/Madness#First_steps:_.22our.22_project_.

Neal, James G. 2004a. "Scholarly Communication: Legislative and Political Advocacy." Presentation at Scholarly Communication 101: An Introduction to Scholarly Communication Issues and Strategies for Change, preconference for the ALA Annual Meeting, Orlando, FL, June.

Neal, James G. 2004b. "Scholarly Communications: Strategies for Change." Presentation at Scholarly Communication 101: An Introduction to Scholarly Communication Issues and Strategies for Change, preconference for the ALA Annual Meeting, Orlando, FL, June.

Ogburn, Joyce L. 2008. "Defining and Achieving Success in the Movement to Change Scholarly Communication." *Library Resources and Technical Services* 52, no. 2 (April): 44–53.

Vandegrift, Micah, and Gloria Colvin. 2012. "Relational Communications: Developing Key Connections." *College and Research Libraries News* 73, no. 7 (July): 386–389. http://crln.acrl.org/content/73/7/386.full.

Van Orsdel, Lee. 2004. "Anatomy of a Crisis: Dysfunction in the Scholarly Communications System." Presentation at Scholarly Communication 101: An Introduction to Scholarly Communication Issues and Strategies for Change, preconference for the ALA Annual Meeting, Orlando, FL, June.

Williams, Karen. 2004. "Open Access." Presentation at Scholarly Communication 101: An Introduction to Scholarly Communication Issues and Strategies for Change, preconference for the ALA Annual Meeting, Orlando, FL, June.

Author Biographies

Juan Pablo Alperin is a doctoral student in the Stanford University School of Education as well as a researcher and systems developer with the Public Knowledge Project. He holds a Bachelor's degree in Computer Science and a Master's in Geography from the University of Waterloo, Canada. In the last five years, Juan has delivered workshops for journal editors all over Latin America, has been an invited speaker at numerous international conferences on scholarly publishing, and continues to work on the award-winning software Open Journal Systems (OJS). While at Stanford, Juan is focused on understanding the effects of open access in Latin America, with the belief that it serves as a model for bringing research to the public in other parts of the world.

Dr. Cheryl E. Ball is an Associate Professor of New Media Studies in the English Department at Illinois State University. Since 2006, Cheryl has been editor of the online, peer-reviewed, open access journal *Kairos: Rhetoric, Technology, and Pedagogy,* which exclusively publishes digital media scholarship and has readership in 180 countries. She has published articles in a range of rhetoric/composition, technical communication, and media studies journals including *Computers and Composition, C&C Online, Fibreculture, Convergence, Programmatic Perspectives,* and *Technical Communication Quarterly.* She has also published several textbooks about visual and multimodal rhetoric, including most recently *Visualizing Composition* with Kristin L. Arola (Bedford, 2010). Her books include *RAW: Reading and Writing New Media* (with Jim Kalmbach, Hampton Press, 2010) and *The New Work of Composing* (with Debra Journet and Ryan Trauman, http://ccdigitalpress.org/nwc), an open access, screen-based collection. Her online portfolio is at http://www.ceball.com/.

Stephanie Brenenson has focused on the areas of academic librarianship and information literacy for more than thirty years. In her prior position as Coordinator of Library Instruction at Florida International University (FIU), she played a key role in the development of FIU's Information Literacy Program. In her current position as Graduate Studies Librarian, she promotes and cultivates research skills and services to support graduate research and teaching. Outside of FIU, Stephanie serves as an adjunct professor for the University of South Florida, School of Information (1999-), teaching the core graduate reference course, and for University of Maryland University College, Graduate School of Management and Technology (2010-) teaching the mandatory information literacy course. Additionally, she has consulted on information literacy program development and classroom assessment. Stephanie completed ACRL's Information Literacy Immersion Program (2001) and Scholarly Communication Institute (2012). She earned her Master of Science in Library Science at Columbia University (NY) and Bachelor of Arts degree at SUNY Fredonia.

Marianne A. Buehler is currently the Urban Sustainability Librarian and manages the Digital Scholarship@UNLV institutional repository at the University of Nevada, Las Vegas. She received a Master of Arts in Information Resources and Library Science at the University of Arizona, and a Bachelor of Arts in English, from the University of Maine. Her applied research and publications are focused on scholarly communication, such as open access journal publishing, traditional/self-publishing, and copyright. She also engages in scholarly communication intersections within information literacy, social media applications, and in archival materials. Marianne's monograph, "Demystifying the Institutional Repository for Success" will be published in December 2012.

Amy G. Buhler is the Associate Chair of the University of Florida's Marston Science Library. Amy handles collection management, library instruction, literature search assistance, and faculty/staff consultations in the areas of Agricultural & Biological Engineering, Biomedical Engineering, Mechanical and Aerospace Engineering, and Nuclear and Radiological Engineering. Prior to her work at Marston, Amy was a medical librarian for six years at the University of Florida Health Science Center Libraries where she worked with the College of Dentistry as well as the Departments of Surgery and Neurosurgery. She holds a Master of Science in Library Science from the University of North Carolina at Chapel Hill and a Bachelor of Arts from the University of Florida. Her research interests include assessment of information seeking behaviors, library instruction, and the marketing and outreach of library services.

Gail Clement currently serves as head of Digital Services & Scholarly Communication at Texas A&M University, leading a team of five librarians engaged in digital collection development, online publishing, and open access advocacy. As a campus copyright specialist, she develops and delivers programming for students, staff, faculty and affiliated agency personnel to increase awareness about scholarly publishing issues, authors' rights, fair use, and open licensing. She serves as liaison to the University's Thesis Office, as faculty representative to the University's Honor Council, and as Library representative to the University's Research Data Taskforce. Gail holds a Bachelor of Arts in Geology from Carleton College, a Master of Science in Geology from the University of Oregon, and a Master of Arts in Library and Information Science from the University of South Florida. She has earned Certificates in Digital Library Development from Cornell and Berkeley and in Copyright Management from the University of Maryland's Center for Intellectual Property and the Special Libraries Association.

Susanne K. Clement is the Special Projects and Assessment Librarian at Utah State University. Prior to that she was the director of the Quinney Natural Resources Research Library, also at Utah State University. At the University of Kansas she was head of collection development for nearly five years. She has served on several ALCTS CMDS committees and presented at national and regional conferences, including: Conference on University Education in Natural Resources, ACRL, Charleston, NASIG and Utah Library Association. Among her recent publications include (with Jennifer Foy) "Collection Development in a Changing Environment: Policies and Organization for College and University Libraries," (CLIP Note #42) published by ACRL in 2010 and "From Collaborative Purchasing Towards Collaborative Discarding: The Evolution of the Shared Print Repository" in *Collection Management* 2012 (37:3/4).

Matthew Daley has a Master of Science in Library and Information Science from Florida State University and a Bachelor of Arts with Honors in Fine Arts from Newcastle University, England. His creative interests include naïve art and the exploration of narrative within found media. He has worked in a number of roles at the University Of Florida Libraries since 2002, but his current position is that of graphic designer/webmaster at the Health Science Center Libraries.

Stephanie Davis-Kahl, Co-Editor is the Scholarly Communications Librarian at Illinois Wesleyan University. She provides leadership for scholarly communication programs and services, including Digital Commons @ IWU (http://digitalcommons.iwu.edu). She works with students, faculty and staff to provide guidance on authors' rights, copyright, and open access. As Managing Faculty Co-Editor of the *Undergraduate Economic Review*, she works closely with students on the publishing process. She provides research consultation, collection development and instruction to four departments at IWU, supervises

Access Services, and is involved in faculty governance. She is active in the Association of College and Research Libraries, and her research interests include library publishing, undergraduate research and scholarly communication programs at liberal arts colleges. She earned her Bachelor of Arts in East Asian Studies from Oberlin College and her Master of Science in Library Science from the University of Illinois at Urbana-Champaign.

Kim Duckett is the Associate Head for Digital Technologies and Learning, Research and Information Services at North Carolina State University Libraries. Her work focuses on trends in teaching and learning, the intersections between learning technologies and libraries, and needs assessment for space planning. She has a long-standing interest in teaching students about scholarly communication issues and has co-authored and co-presented with Scott Warren on this topic. Additionally, she is the project lead for the "Peer Review in 5 Minutes" video, used at institutions around the world. She was named a *Library Journal* Mover and Shaker in 2009.

Jennifer Duncan has served as the Head of Collection Development in the Merrill-Cazier Library at Utah State University since 2009. Prior to holding that position, she worked in e-resource licensing and management since 1999. Jennifer received a certification in Copyright Management and Leadership from the University of Maryland University College (UMUC) and has served as a teaching assistant in the UMUC certification program.

Christine Fruin leads the University of Florida Libraries' outreach efforts to build a scholarly communications program in support of scholarly publication reform and open access activities at UF. This role includes educating the university community about open access resources and services, scholarly publication modes and reform, and copyright issues and their impact on scholarly inquiry and instruction. Fruin earned a Juris Doctorate from Southern Illinois University, a Master of Science in Library and Information Science from the University of Illinois and a bachelor's degree from Knox College. After graduating from law school, she practiced law for a year before joining Lexis Nexis as an editor. She worked for Lexis Nexis for several years and during that time returned to graduate school to earn her master's degree. She worked as an e-resources librarian for a major hospital, as a senior law librarian conducting intellectual property and business intelligence research for a large Chicago law firm before heading to the University of Illinois system to work as the director of collection and research services and scholarly communications officer for the Springfield campus's Brookens Library.

Julia Gelfand is the Applied Sciences & Engineering Librarian at the University of California, Irvine Libraries. She has followed scholarly communication issues since the early 1990s and is particularly interested in the implications for the sciences. She has written about and lectured widely on the intersections of library/author/publisher/vendor relationships, collection development, scholarly communication and information metrics and altmetrics and has been internationally recognized for her contributions to grey literature. She has taught graduate level courses in library and information science at several institutions. A graduate of Goucher College, she has a Master of Arts and Master of Science from Case Western Reserve University and is active in many professional organizations, including the Association of College & Research Libraries, American Library Association, American Association for the Advancement of Science, Society of Scholarly Publishing (SSP), International Federation of Library Associations.

Isaac Gilman has been a member of the Pacific University Library faculty since 2008, and is primarily responsible for managing the University's institutional repository, CommonKnowledge, and coordinating the Library's scholarly communication and publishing services. He has taught courses in research methods and scholarly journal publishing and is currently co-editor of the *Journal of Librarianship and Scholarly Communication*. He is a graduate of the School of Library, Archival, and Information Studies at the University of British Columbia.

Abigail Goben is an Assistant Information Services Librarian and Assistant Professor at the University of Illinois Chicago Health Sciences Library. Goben also holds an appointment as an Assistant Professor at the UIC College of Dentistry. Goben is a member of the American Library Association, Library and Information Technology Association, and the Library Society of the World. Goben is presently pursuing tenure at her institution through publication in open access journals and other open access opportunities. She blogs about the tenure process and other library related subjects at http://hedgehoglibrarian.com. Her research interests include data and digital curation for librarians and the use of early 21st century technologies for professional communication and collaboration.

Sara Russell Gonzalez was formerly the Physical Sciences Librarian at the Marston Science Library at the University of Florida. She holds a Bachelor of Science in Geophysics from the California Institute of Technology, a Doctor of Philosophy in Seismology from the University of California, Santa Cruz, and a Master of Science in Library and Information Science from Florida State University. Her research interests include science literacy education, the library's role in upholding academic integrity, and the changing nature of scientific communication. She may be contacted by e-mail at srgonzalez@gmail.com.

Merinda Kaye Hensley, Co-Editor, is the Instructional Services Librarian and Assistant Professor at the University of Illinois at Urbana-Champaign. She is also the Co-coordinator of the Scholarly Commons, a library unit that serves the emerging research and technology needs of scholars in data services, digital humanities, digitization, and scholarly communication. She teaches, coordinates and provides leadership for the Savvy Researcher, an open workshop series addressing advanced research and information management needs of graduate students and faculty (http://www.library.illinois.edu/learn/). Starting spring 2013, Merinda will teach LIS 590AE: Advanced Information Literacy and Instruction at Illinois. She is active in ACRL, serving as Member-at-Large (2010-2012) for the Instruction Section and is currently a member of ACRL's Student Learning and Information Literacy Committee. Merinda presents nationally and internationally on her research, incorporating scholarly communication into information literacy instruction and improving teaching skills of new librarians. She earned her Bachelor of Arts in Political Science from the University of Arizona and an Master of Science in Library Science from the University of Illinois at Urbana-Champaign.

Alex R. Hodges is Associate Director, Instruction & Curricular Services, and Associate Librarian, at American University in Washington, D.C. Since 2007, Alex has led the AU Library's efforts to integrate information literacy instruction throughout all facets of the AU curriculum. Alex also serves as the AU Library's liaison to the School of Education, Teaching & Health (SETH), where, as Affiliate Associate Professor, he also teaches courses on educational technology and children's literature. Alex's additional background in TESOL assists campus-wide efforts to teach international students about American standards of academic integrity and scholarly communication. He began working in academic and research libraries in 1998, and before joining the American University faculty in 2004, he worked within library systems at the University of Maryland, College Park, the University of Florida, and the National Gallery of Art.

Eric Johnson is a librarian working as the Head of Outreach & Public Services at the Scholars' Lab in the University of Virginia Library. He holds an MA in US History (George Mason University) and an MS in Library and Information Studies (Florida State) and has research interests in information sharing among creative people; citizen history;

user-generated content in libraries, archives, and museums (LAMs); museum and library history; hospitality theory as applied to LAMs; public service librarianship; and communities of practice. Before working at UVa, he worked in libraries at Thomas Jefferson's historic home, Monticello, and at the University of Richmond. He also serves on the board of directors of the Lewis & Clark Exploratory Center in Charlottesville, VA, and is a member of the Rivanna Master Naturalists.

Margeaux Johnson is a Science & Technology Librarian at the University of Florida, where she coordinates information literacy instruction for the sciences and integrates technology into library learning environments. Her research interests include 21st Century Skills, games-based learning, and New Media Literacies. She served as a Co-PI on the NSF ethics in education grant "Gaming Against Plagiarism" (http://blogs.uflib.ufl.edu/gap/) and was a member of the NIH VIVO Collaboration (http://vivoweb.org/).

Joy Kirchner is the Scholarly Communications Coordinator at University of British Columbia where she oversees the University's Scholarly Communications & Copyright office based in the Library. Her role involves coordinating the University's copyright education services, identifying recommended and sustainable service models to support scholarly communication activities on the campus and coordinating formalized discussion and education of these issues with faculty, students, research and publishing constituencies on the UBC campus. Joy has also been instrumental in establishing the Provost's campus wide Scholarly Communications Steering Committee and associated working groups where she sits as a key member of the Committee. Joy is also chair of the University's Copyright Advisory Committee and working groups. She is also a faculty member with the ARL/ACRL Institute for Scholarly Communication, she assists with the coordination and program development of ACRL's Scholarly Communications Road Show program, she is a Visiting Program Officer with ACRL in support of their scholarly communications programs, and she is a Fellow with ARL's Research Library Leadership Fellows executive program (RLLF). She holds a Bachelor of Arts and a Master of Library and Information Studies from the University of British Columbia.

Kara J. Malenfant is a senior staff member at the Association of College and Research Libraries, where she coordinates government relations advocacy and scholarly communication activities and is the lead staff member on the Value of Academic Libraries initiative. She provides consulting services on organizational development and use of ACRL's standards for libraries in higher education. Kara began her position at ACRL in fall of 2005, after working for six years at DePaul University Libraries in Chicago. Prior to her experience as a librarian, Kara worked in Washington for the Armenian Assembly of America and served as a Peace Corps volunteer in the first group posted to the Republic of Armenia. Kara holds a Doctor of Philosophy in Leadership and Change from Antioch University and a Master of Science in Library Science from the University of Illinois at Urbana-Champaign.

Bethany Nowviskie, Ph.D. is President of the international Association for Computers and the Humanities, Director of Digital Research and Scholarship for the University of Virginia Library system (a department which includes the Scholars' Lab), and Associate Director of the Scholarly Communication Institute, a Mellon-funded think tank for the transformation of the humanities in the digital age. She has been active in the digital humanities as a researcher, designer, teacher, and administrator since the mid-1990s. Among her notable projects are Temporal Modelling, the Ivanhoe Game, Juxta, NINES, Blacklight, #Alt-Academy, and Neatline. Nowviskie also chairs the Modern Language Association's committee on information technology and is a member of the boards of ADHO, centerNet, and MediaCommons.

Catherine Palmer is the Head of Education and Outreach at the University of California, Irvine Libraries, where she provides leadership for the Libraries' outreach and instruction programs and information literacy initiatives. Prior to that, she served as the English and Comparative Literature and Classics librarian and the Instructional Services Coordinator at UC Irvine. She has held previous librarian positions at Sinai Hospital in Detroit, Michigan and at the Alma College Library. She holds an Master of Arts in Library Science from the University of Michigan where she also received a Bachelor of Arts in History and English. Her current professional interests include assessment of library contributions to student learning, effective marketing of library services, and the alignments between scholarly communication and information literacy.

Betty Rozum has served as Associate Dean of Technical Services (Digital Initiatives, Materials Acquisitions, Collection Development, Cataloging, and Digital Library Services) at Utah State University since 2001, and is involved in copyright and scholarly communication issues, serving on the campus Copyright Committee, and the Institutional Repository Advisory Board. She serves as a subject librarian and is interested in using institutional repositories to promote faculty and student's research in new ways.

Nick Shockey is the director of student advocacy for the Scholarly Publishing and Academic Resources Coalition (SPARC) and founding director of the Right to Research Coalition (R2RC). Supported by SPARC, the R2RC is an international alliance of local, national, and international student organizations that advocate for researchers, universities, governments, and students themselves to adopt open scholarly publishing practices. Under Nick's direction, the R2RC has grown to represent just under 7 million students in more than 100 countries around the world and has facilitated student lobbying in hundreds of Congressional offices. Prior to joining SPARC, Nick was a student activist, working locally to make Trinity University the first small, liberal arts university in the United State to pass an institutional open access policy. He also worked nationally with SPARC in launching its student campaign. Nick was named a SPARC Innovator in 2007.

John Willinsky is Khosla Family Professor of Education at Stanford University and Professor (Limited Term) of Publishing Studies at Simon Fraser University, where he directs the Public Knowledge Project, which is dedicated to conducting research and developing software that extends the public and scholarly quality of academic publishing. His books include the *Empire of Words: the Reign of the OED* (Princeton, 1994), *Learning to Divide the World: Education at Empire's End* (Minnesota, 1998), *Technologies of Knowing* (Beacon, 2000), and *The Access Principle: The Case for Open Access to Research and Scholarship* (MIT Press, 2006).

Scott Warren is the Head of Collections as well as Bibliographer for the Sciences and Technology at the Syracuse University Library. Previously, he was the Associate Director of the Burlington Textiles Library and Engineering Services at the North Carolina State University Libraries. He began his career in 2001 as an NCSU Libraries Fellow. He holds a Master of Arts in Library and Information Studies from The University of Wisconsin-Madison and Bachelor of Science degrees in Physics, Mathematics, and Astronomy and a Bachelor of Science in History from The Pennsylvania State University. He has fathered several articles and presentations as well as two wonderful daughters. He has collaborated with Kim Duckett numerous times in the past and hopes to do so in the future as well.

Anne E. Zald is Head of Educational Initiatives, University Libraries, University of Nevada Las Vegas (UNLV). In that role she works with library and academic faculty to ensure that students are able to find, access, use, and critically evaluate information in all formats. To achieve this goal, Anne provides classroom instruction, professional development workshops, and collaborates with faculty to redesign assignments and courses. Anne also participates in the UNLV Faculty Institutes, campus collaborations that provide faculty professional development related to teaching and learning. Anne serves on the faculty for the Association of College and Research Libraries Immersion programs, providing professional development to academic librarians nationwide on teaching and managing library instruction programs.

DATE DUE

			PRINTED IN U.S.A.